MANAGING CULTURAL DIFFERENCES

Gulf Publishing Company
Book Division
Houston, London, Paris, Tokyo

Philip R. Harris
Robert T. Moran

MANAGING
CULTURAL
DIFFERENCES

Managing Cultural Differences

Library of Congress Cataloging in Publication Data

Harris, Phillip R   1926-

  Managing cultural differences.

  (Building blocks of human potential series)
  Bibliography: p.
  Includes index.
  1. International business enterprises—Management. 2. Ac-
  culturation. 3. Cross-cultural studies.
I. Moran, Robert T., 1938-   joint author. II. Title.
HD69.I7H355   658.1'8   79-50243

ISBN 0-87201-160-7

Building Blocks of Human Potential Series
Leonard Nadler, Series Editor

The Adult Learner: A Neglected Species, by Malcolm Knowles
The Adult Educator—A Handbook for Staff Development, by Harry
G. Miller and John R. Verduin
Managing Cultural Differences, by Philip R. Harris and Robert T. Moran
The Conference Book, by Leonard Nadler and Zeace Nadler
The Client—Consultant Handbook, by Chip R. Bell and Leonard Nadler
Human Resource Development: The European Approach, by H. Eric Frank
Leadership Development for Public Service, by Barry A. Passett
People, Evaluation, and Achievement, by George Nixon
The NOW Employee, by David Nadler
Handbook of Creative Learning Exercises, by Herbert Engel

Acknowledgments

We wish to express our gratitude and appreciation to the following colleagues, scholars, and friends who contributed to this volume:

Leonard Nadler, Ph.D., of George Washington University, Washington, D.C., for his encouragement of this undertaking and first editing of the manuscript

Walter Schratz, Ph.D., of the Westinghouse Electric Foundation for the opportunity to test these concepts initially with Westinghouse multinational managers in "cultural awareness workshops"

Albert G. Bergesen, regional commissioner, of the United States Customs Service, who fostered further refinement of this material through a series of "managing cultural differences workshops"

Professor H. Eric Frank of the University of Bath and *Dr. Wolfgang Fassbender* of Diebold Europe who made it possible to introduce the European edition of this book through "managing cultural differences" lectures

Professor J.A. Kennerley of the University of Strathclyde who encouraged a further testing of the book in Glasgow with middle and senior management, as well as to provide a critique of the case study, "American Abroad in Great Britain"

A.P. O'Reilly, Ph.D., of AnCo-The Industrial Training Authority, Ireland, for his critique of the case study, "American Business Negotiations in 'Eire'"

Dorothy Lipp Harris, Ph.D., associate dean, School of Business and Management, United States International University, San Diego, California, who sparked the whole project from its inception and collaborated in the action research on it

George W. Renwick, vice-president of Intercultural Network, Inc. for being a friend and colleague, and for reviewing and suggesting changes for various sections of the manuscript

V. Lynn Tyler of the Language and Research Center at Brigham Young University for sharing many materials, reviewing a large portion of the manuscript, and constant enthusiasm and support

Thomas C. Stevens, Ph.D., corporate director, Human Resources for J.I. Case, for taking a chance on me by providing opportunities for me to share these ideas with many international managers at J.I. Case in the U.S. and Europe

Robert McMahon, Ph.D., professor of world business at American Graduate School of International management and *Charles P. Pieper* of the Boston Consulting Group for reviewing early drafts of some chapters and urging that the material be made more applicable to the real world of the international manager

Janet Perlman for preparing the index

Elizabeth, Sarah, Molly, and *Rebecca Moran* for always being ready to involve their father in their creative world of play and for asking many questions about the world, whose puzzle they are struggling with

Many U.S. and foreign graduate students at American Graduate School of International Management for assisting in the critique of the culture specific materials

Several secretaries at American Graduate School of International Management for helping to type portions of the manuscript

Many colleagues and business clients for unknowingly helping by sharing ideas and materials, and for being sounding boards for some of the ideas

Dedication

To our wives, Dorothy L. Harris and Virgilia M. Moran, whom we met in the course of our professional careers on foreign soil and international assignments, and who taught us so much in marriage about managing cultural differences!

Foreword

The terms "international" and "cross-cultural" are frequently used interchangeably and therefore incorrectly. Almost any international experience must be cross-cultural, but it is also possible to have a cross-cultural experience without leaving one's own country. This is true in many parts of the world and is certainly true, especially now, of the United States.

The authors of this book share with us the vast experiences they have had in the international arena, with obvious implications for all cross-cultural experiences. In many of the cases and incidents that make this book significant, only a slight rewording is needed to make the material equally applicable to those who never leave home. Increased international mobility means that many of us are now receiving foreigners into our "home."

There has certainly been a need for a book like this, which has the required detail without being difficult to read. The authors have taken a most complicated aspect of individual and organizational behavior and put it in understandable terms without losing the essence of the important points in the field. This has not been an easy task.

The authors do not rely only on their own work but cite the important contributions of others in the field and present the work of others in a meaningful and significant manner.

The first part of the book is concerned with the manager, broadly defined. Material is presented that highlights how the role of the manager is constantly changing under the impact of increased international exchanges. The manager who knows only his or her own country is doomed to become obsolete. Most organizations can no longer afford to employ culturally myopic managers. The cosmopolitan manager is required—one who is an intercultural communicator and transmitter. There are new areas of competence, most of which are not yet adequately reflected in the course offerings of many of the academic institutions involved in teaching managers. There are isolated seminars and conferences, and this book provides the groundwork for the kinds of learning experiences that must be included in such offerings.

At one time, the only concern was with the manager going abroad. Although this is still a significant concern, it is now exacerbated by the flood of foreign managers into the United States. We were successful during the 1960s, termed the Decade of Development, and now there are many more countries that invest in the United States. These countries send over not only their money, but also their managers to make sure that performance and product meet the needs of the foreign corporation. This is a reversal of the twenty years following World War II when most of the flow was from the U.S. to other countries.

There is still that flow, though not nearly of the proportions experienced in the post WWII era. The numbers may be fewer but the stakes have become higher. It is now much more expensive to send a manager (and family) to another country. The increased sophistication in other countries makes it mandatory that there be some learning experience provided for the manager (and family) prior to leaving the U.S.

The authors provide us with vivid examples of what can go wrong, and how the mistakes can be predicted and avoided by appropriate training and education experiences. They provide general theory as well as specific examples and suggestions.

This is a book to be read through, and then returned to frequently as the reader finds the need for specific segments, exercises, and resources, to learn from the significant work of these authors.

Leonard Nadler
July 1979

Contents

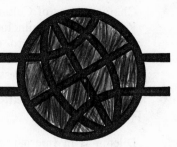

Unit 1
The Emerging Role
of the Multinational Manager

Unit 2
Cultural Impact
of International Management

Unit 3
Organizational Responsibilities
and Cultural Differences

Unit 4
Cultural Specifics for Management Effectiveness

1
The Manager
As a Cosmopolitan

Global Transformations

With the landing of man on the moon, the traditional images of the human species were ended. For millions of years, human beings thought they were earthbound. Now that such "perceptual blinders" have been torn asunder, we are challenged to look at our collective selves and our world in another way. Who and what are we? What are the upper limits of our potential? Is our real home as a race on this planet, or out there in the unexplored universe?

Our conception of reality changes as we create *new images* of our species, its place and purpose in existence. The revision of such images will probably be the greatest force for change in the century ahead. For as we project these new images of ourselves, our roles, our organizations, our world, we not only powerfully influence our own behavior, but also the responses of others to these different images. For example, when as inhabitants of the earth we envision our space and its society as a "global village," then perhaps as its citizens we might act differently toward our environment and toward our distant neighbors. When we think in terms of the whole "human family," then differences in that family are considered natural, unique, and precious. So too, as we develop a sense of "world culture," we grow beyond particular cultures, while cherishing and respecting our origins.

To grow beyond cultural limitations means to become truly cosmopolitan. The dictionary provides this interesting definition of that word: "belonging to the world; not limited to just one part of the political, social, commercial, or intellectual sphere; free from local, provincial, or national ideas, prejudices, or attachments." Literally, a cosmopolitan is one who functions effectively *anywhere* in the world. For a successful transition to the twenty-first century, which is the thesis of this book, we should all become more cosmopolitan human beings, especially if one is in a leadership position.

To understand the acceleration of human development consider human history in four principal stages: hunting stage, farming stage, industrial stage, and post-/superindustrial stage. The hunting stage, in which man's primary

1

concern was survival, lasted *millions* of years, over half of our species' existence. Gradually, an Agricultural Revolution transformed human life and society, and mankind devoted itself to domesticating animals and harvesting food. This farming stage lasted *thousands* of years before another turning point of human development emerged: the industrial stage. With the Industrial Revolution came shifts in population from the farm to the factory, from the country to the city. It was an era that saw marvelous scientific and technological breakthroughs, which accelerated human change. It was a period that lasted only a *few hundred* years. About the middle of the twentieth century, yet another profound transition occurred, the Cybercultural* Revolution. This post-/superindustrial stage, whose duration is measured in *decades*, has experienced more scientific and technological advances and a greater accumulation of knowledge than the millions of years that preceded it.

Such a rapid "compression" of our life and society means that we are the people of change and transition, caught in a pivotal position, challenged to create a new cyberculture to replace our traditional past. We are charged to expand our consciousness, our way of perceiving, thinking, and acting. Despite the progress of the human "mainstream," there are pockets of people still living as primitives in hidden jungles, just as there are groups in industrial societies. Unfortunately, there are persons in advanced technological civilizations who are past-oriented with the "mind-set" of the hunting, agricultural, or industrial stages of development. They have an archaic, culture-bound perspective of the human condition. But, as the homogenization of the human race takes place, the cosmopolitans will contribute to the creation of a new world order. Lewis Mumford reminded us in his work, *The Transformation of Man*, that we must form "new pictures" of human nature and the cosmos itself. The revolution underway in social roles and institutions, cultural premises and dominant values, attitudes and lifestyles foster further profound changes. One writer tried to express our unique position today as human beings by saying that we are between civilizations, and while we do not yet know what is to come, we have a sense of the new directions. William Irwin Thompson referred to us as the climatic generation of human cultural evolution. In 1975 Bruce Murray, the director of California Institute of Technology's Jet Propulsion Laboratory commented in his book, *Navigating the Future:*

Cyberculture is a term used to describe the society or culture of the emerging post-/industrial period of human development—sometimes referred to as the computer or technological age, or the knowledge society. It is derived from the word *cybernetics* (the science of control or communication in the animal and the machine). In other words, a culture dominated by cybernation, or the control of machines by computers that are programmed by human beings for a variety of tasks. Refer to Norbert Wiener's *Cybernetics*, (Cambridge, Mass.:The M.I.T. Press, 1961).

We are in the midst of the most rapid and significant period of change in man's history. We of this generation and the next two have the mixed privilege of playing leading roles in a central act of the human drama....I believe that mankind can overcome unprecedented challenges and, in doing so, evolve in culture and in consciousness into a greater species. We will be what we will be, what we make ourselves worthy of becoming.

Willis Harman of Stanford Research Institute maintained in his work, *An Incomplete Guide to the Future*, that the industrial-era paradigm is no longer viable for modern ideology or way to view our world. A *paradigm* is a conceptual model that influences our basic way of perceiving, valuing, thinking, and acting—a particular vision of reality.

Because of this situation, today's leaders must create new paradigms, more relevant organizational models, more appropriate management styles that are suitable for a superindustrial stage of development. Managers must be more innovative, as well as more cosmopolitan. They operate in a time of the world when a process of "planetization" is underway, and the traditional barriers that separated peoples—social, cultural, national, ethnic, economic, travel, or communication—are gradually crumbling. No longer can the leader permit differences in people to be obstacles to human relationships and interaction. Instead one must develop skills for dealing with diversity in individuals and groups.

Thus, cross-cultural education, training, and development become essential for those in management positions, if they are to operate effectively in a complex, world marketplace. Nowhere is this more evident than in the multinational corporation that acquires subsidiaries abroad, and sends its representatives as change agents in multicultural settings. In studying culture, whether within an organization or a nation, one analyzes the factors and influences that give a particular group of people identity and uniqueness. In the process, one should learn what those outside that group should know and understand in order to facilitate communication with these "others." This would be valuable for a consultant who needs to get insight into the organizational culture, a salesperson who goes from one part of a country to another geographical area (subculture), or a technician who is assigned to another nation. In all three instances, the persons require skills for dealing with cultural differences. For the professional or executive who must function in the international scene, increasingly more pluralistic or multicultural, intercultural awareness and skills are vital.

Changing Managers

The art and science of management, already in the midst of its own revolution, are relatively new products of this century. As management philosopher, Peter Drucker, has observed, all of the assumptions upon which management practice have been based for the last fifty years are obsolete. So managers are being challenged to change their assumptions about human nature, the work environment, and the practice of management itself. They are being forced to reconsider their image of their role, so as to alter their leadership styles and organizational culture in light of the new realities of the superindustrial age. Dr. John Platt, author of *The Next Step to Man*, underscores a number of crises that endanger society at this time. Among them he cites an administrative crisis in all forms of management—schools, business, government—primarily caused by lack of flexibility, speed, and knowledge to meet ongoing rapid changes.

The following eight concepts are essential to cross-cultural human resource development. They are explained in greater detail in the following chapters.

The Concept of the Cosmopolitan—learning to become a sensitive, innovative and participative leader, capable of operating comfortably in a global or pluralistic environment. This is a multinational, multicultural organization representative who can manage accelerating change and differences in his or her own life space. The cosmopolitan manager is open and flexible in approaching others, can cope with situations and people quite different from one's background, and is willing to alter personal attitudes and perceptions.

The Concept of Intercultural Communication—learning to become more aware of what is involved in one's image of self and role; of personal needs, values, standards, expectations; all of which are culturally conditioned. Such a person understands the impact of such factors on behavioral communication, and is willing to revise and expand such images as part of the process of growth. Furthermore, he or she is aware of such differences in others participating in human interaction, especially with persons from a foreign culture. As a manager, therefore, this individual would seek to get into the "world" of the receiver, and improve cross-cultural communication skills, both verbal and nonverbal. Not only does such a leader seek to learn appropriate foreign languages, but is cognizant that even when people speak the same language, cultural differences can alter communication symbols and meanings.

The Concept of Cultural Sensitivity—learning to integrate the characteristics of culture in general, with experiences in specific organizational, minority, or foreign cultures. Such a leader acquires knowledge about cultural influences on behavior; cultural patterns, themes, or universals; diversity of macrocultures and microcultures. As a cosmopolitan manager, this individual can translate such cultural awareness into effective relationships with those who are culturally different.

The Concept of Acculturation—learning to adjust and adapt to a specific culture, whether that be a subculture within one's own country or abroad. Such a person comprehends what is involved in self and group identity, and is alert to the impact of culture shock or differences upon one's sense of identity. Therefore, when operating in a strange culture or dealing with employees from different cultural backgrounds, this manager develops skills for adjusting and avoiding enthnocentrism.

The Concept of Cultural Management Influences—learning to appreciate the influences of cultural conditioning on the management of material and human resources. One's native culture affects the way a manager views every critical factor in the management process, from decision-making and problem-solving to supervision and appraisal. The cosmopolitan manager is aware that what is acceptable for leaders to do in one's culture, may be unacceptable and cause strife in another culture. Such an individual tries to adapt modern principles of administration to the indigenous circumstances, or educate the local populous to contemporary management practice and expectations.

The Concept of Effective Intercultural Performance—learning to apply cultural theory and insight to specific cross-cultural situations that affect people's performance on the job. The multinational manager must understand the peculiarities of a people that influence productivity at work. Such a leader makes provisions for foreign deployment, overseas adjustment and culture shock, reentry of expatriates, international report reading, changing organizational environment, and overcoming cultural handicaps and limitations.

The Concept of Changing International Business—learning to appreciate the interdependence of business practice throughout the world, as well as the subculture of the managerial group in all nations of similar ideology (e.g., capitalistic or communist nations). In the private sector, there is an emerging universal acceptance of some business technology—computers, management information systems, reporting procedures, accounting practices. Yet, the cosmopolitan manager is sophisticated enough to appreciate the effect of cultural differences on standard business practice, especially in terms of profits, organizational loyalty, and such common activities as reward/punishment of employees. The multinational or world corporation manager is also aware of acceptable, universal business principles and procedures.

The Concept of Emerging World Culture—learning to keep up with trends that break through traditional barriers between peoples of different cultures, to take care of human needs on a transnational basis, to develop new markets and services that contribute to a more polycultural society. Such a manager is alert to developments in the creation of an international culture, common to inhabitants of earth. He or she contributes to both personal and professional development opportunities in this regard for self and subordinates, as well as seizing every means for improving international business relations. The furtherance of world trade and commerce, the sharing of rich nations with less affluent countries, the cultural and commercial exchanges of the world's peoples—all foster human prosperity and development throughout the globe, and prepare us to function more effectively in the universe beyond this planet.

Such pregnant concepts are key ingredients in the competencies of the cosmopolitan. They also should be part of any program of cross-cultural education, training, and development. They certainly are the themes woven throughout this book. Although for convenience, our message is directed to the *manager*, it is equally applicable to any one in administration or professional life, such as teachers, attorneys, physicians, and others in helping relationships across cultures. This would include those in government military, religious, or foundation service. Managing cultural differences should be of equal concern to the membership of a city council or board of education, as it is to leaders in international trade associations. The import of this text is as valid for a member of a supranational scientific team of U.N. delegation as for those involved in transnational political or economic negotiations whether in the framework of NATO, OPEC, SEATO, WHO, or any other organization.

The following is an observation of the world corporation by Walter B. Wriston, chairman, First National City Corporation*:

The World Corporation—New Weight in an Old Balance

The development of the world corporation into a truly multinational organization has produced a group of managers of many nationalities whose perception of the needs and wants of the human race know no boundaries. They really believe in One World. They understand with great clarity that the payrolls and jobs furnished by the world corporation exceed profits by a factor of twenty to one. They know that there can be no truly profitable markets where poverty is the rule of life. They are a group that recognizes no distinction because of color or sex, since they understand with the clarity born of experience that talent is the commodity in shortest supply in the world. They are managers who are against the partitioning of the world, not only upon a political or theoretical basis, but on the pragmatic ground that the planet has become too small and that the fate of all people has become too interwoven one with the other to engage in the old nationalistic games that have so long diluted the talent, misused the resources, and dissipated the energy of mankind.

The international managers in the great world corporations are exposed daily to a bewildering variety of value systems and a steadily rising tempo of nationalism in many of the nation-states of the world. From

---

*From a speech given at the International Industrial Conference published in *Sloan Management Review*, Winter 1974.

this experience is emerging the perception that the relationship of the world corporation to the various governments around the world is worthy of reexamination.

The role of the world corporation as an agent of change may well be even more important than its demonstrated capacity to raise living standards. The pressure to develop the economy of the world into a real community must come, in part, from an increasing number of multinational firms which see the world as a whole. "Today's world economy . . . ," Peter Drucker has said, "owes almost nothing to political imagination. It is coming into being despite political fragmentation." The world corporation has become a new weight in an old balance and must play a constructive role in moving the world toward the freer exchange of both ideas and the means of production so that the people of the world may one day enjoy the fruits of a truly global society.

Global Leadership

Because organizations are changing in the way they operate domestically and internationally, the role of the manager is altered. It is more than a shift away from the traditional bureaucracy of the industrial age, or mere expansion into worldwide markets. There is a fundamental change in business perspectives toward a view of a world without borders, toward the creation of world corporations.

The public press and management literature are replete with generalizations and prognostications on these developments. A review of such thinking among corporate and government experts indicates that the emerging global corporations are the most dynamic agents of change in society today. Linked to global banking operations, they have budgets bigger than many nations, and foreign policies that affect world affairs as a whole. They function from continent to continent, slipping between the cracks of national jurisdictions. Superbly efficient organizations, they are themselves faced with the challenge of exercising corporate imperialism or social responsibility. Such enterprises move us toward a new economic order, but because they operate beyond the classic free market and competition with enormous international concentrations of wealth and resources, they require new forms of regulation and scrutiny.

Roy Ash, who headed a multinational corporation, predicts that in their ultimate form the new world corporations will require supranational chartering. Their markets and production centers already span the planet and eventually will include outer space. Their management will be transnational and mobile and without national identities—corporate citizens of the world.

Even unions, which survive in the supraindustrial age, will have to operate beyond national frontiers. Confronted with employers of multinational interests and influences, international worker solidarity is beginning to revive. Union leadership of the future will also have to become more cosmopolitan, be proceeding at an unusually slow pace and even the simplest decisions or commitments appear to take an inordinate amount of time. You begin to push a little harder and your frustrations mount as you begin to hear statements from the Japanese such as, "it will take a little more time" and "this is quite difficult." What should you do? What is happening to the negotiating process? How do the Japanese negotiate?

You are in Saudi Arabia attempting to finalize a contract with a group of Saudi businessmen. You are aware these people are inveterate negotiators, however, you find it difficult to maintain eye contact with your hosts during conversations. Further, their increasing physical proximity to you is becoming more uncomfortable. You also have noticed that a strong handgrip while shaking hands is not returned. When invited to a banquet, because you are left-handed, you use your left hand while eating. Your negotiations are not successfully concluded. What may have been the reason for this? What cultural aspects are evidenced in this interaction, which if known, could improve your communication with your Arab clients?

You are a black American manager of a group of Puerto Rican workers in a New York factory. You resent the constant use of Spanish among your subordinates because you only speak English. You suspect your employees use their language as a means of criticizing and mocking you—they are often laughing and you wonder what it is all about. In bicultural/bilingual areas with large Hispanic populations, why should supervisors have some knowledge of Spanish? Why do your subordinates feel more comfortable in their native language? How could your company facilitate their instruction in the English language? Or should it?

These examples suggest a few of the many ways that culture can influence an individual in communicating. In the past, many American businessmen were not overly concerned with the ways that culture influenced individual or organizational behavior. However, because of serious and costly errors, many managers, executives, and technicians working in multicultural environments are now asking themselves questions such as:

1. What do I have to know about the social and business customs of country X?
2. What skills do I need to be effective as a negotiator in country Y?
3. What prejudices and stereotypes do I have about the people in country Z?
4. How will these influence my interaction?

The study of organizational behavior in management schools, which in the past has been largely "culture bound," reflecting only the U.S. viewpoint, is now being considered from a variety of perspectives that take into account the cultural values and norms in the area being studied. This change in emphasis and orientation, although only a beginning, will result in more effective American negotiators and managers.

concerned about worldwide standards of workers, as well as issues of safety and health, especially for labor in developing countries.

The implications of these observations is that both management and labor will need cross-cultural competencies, a consciousness expressed in global concerns. As the late Milton Feldman, international consultant, reminded us, we must be aware of the ever growing interdependency and complexity of human society in which the contributions of all peoples are needed to sustain the delicate web of life. Therefore, both peoples and their cultures can no longer exist independent of one another, but meaningful intercultural interactions should be facilitated among the earth's inhabitants. Auerlio Peccei, director of Fiat and the Club of Rome maintains that the internationalization of society will be furthered powerfully by the global corporation. George Ball, former U.S. undersecretary of state, states that these great corporations that straddle the earth are able to utilize world resources with an efficiency dictated by the objective logic of profit. One might ask if their global leaders will have an equal concern for human welfare and ecological preservation. Perhaps the issue was put best by Barnett and Muller in their book, *Global Reach*:

> The global corporation is the first institution in human history dedicated to centralized planning on a world scale. Because its primary activity is to organize and to integrate economic activity around the world in such a way as to maximize global profit, it is an organic structure in which each part is expected to serve the whole. . . .The rise of such planetary enterprises is producing an organizational revolution as profound for modern man as the Industrial Revolution and the rise of the nation-state itself. . . .With their worldview, the managers of global corporations are seeking to put into practice a theory of human organization that will profoundly alter the nation-state system around which society has been organized for over four hundred years.

Thus, the reality to be faced by today's cosmopolitan manager is that the world of business must be treated as a single marketplace in which national boundaries serve as convenient demarcations of cultural, linguistic, and ethnic entities, but do not define business requirements or consumer trends. That is the view expressed by presidents of world trade corporations.

Cross-Cultural Studies

Knowledge about cultures, both general and specific, provides insights into the learned behaviors of groups. It helps the learner to gain awareness of what makes a people unique—their customs and traditions, their values and beliefs, attitudes and concepts, hierarchies and roles, time and space relations, and verbal and nonverbal communication processes. Such studies draw upon data from a variety of behavioral sciences, such as cultural anthropology, psychology, cross-cultural communication and linguistics. Information gained in these studies will enable managers to become more cosmopolitan, to cope more effectively abroad, to reduce stress and resolve conflict more readily in the international business arena. Such transcultural competency should be an integral aim of ordinary management or professional development anywhere in the world.

Writing in *Developing Human Resources*, Leonard Nadler suggests that the terms *training* be the focus of the job, while *education* be thought of with reference to the individual, and *development* be reserved for organizational concerns. Whether one is concerned with intercultural training, education, or development, employees need to learn about culture and cross-cultural communication if they are to work effectively with minorities within their own society or with foreigners encountered at home or abroad. For example, there has been a sudden increase in foreign investments in the United States—two million Americans now work within the borders of their own country for foreign employers. They had better have some cultural sensitivity in this regard, or their career development could be jeopardized. Management information specialists design computer programs, but how aware are they of their own cultural bias in this regard, how alert are they to the cultural needs of the users? Those engaged in the import-export trade, depending on their understanding and skill in cross-cultural relations, can advance or hamper their sales and exchanges. All along the U.S.-Mexican borders, twin plants are emerging that provide for a flow of goods and services between the two countries, but how knowledgeable are the participants of intercultural factors that influence their business? Whether one works in the exchange of people in the public or private sector, personnel require preparation to facilitate such cross-cultural transfers.

Too often employees in international business are fortunate if they receive some inservice training in foreign languages, or the technical aspects of world business and economics. Rarely, do they receive training, education, or development in cross-cultural matters. Yet many solid arguments can be put forth in this regard to minimize the waste of human and material resources in the world marketplace, and to capitalize on the human and material assets. Cross-cultural studies, for instance, can assist multinational managers to meet world competition, as well as cut costs in foreign deployment. Two major multinational corporations working in Iran in the late seventies reported respectively a premature return rate of 50% and 85% on American employees sent to that Middle Eastern nation. The estimated return cost for such personnel and their dependents ranged from $55,000 to $150,000 per family, and did not count replacement expenses. To cut down on such costly turnover, the price of establishing a program for transcultural effectiveness for overseas employees would be miniscule in comparison. In retrospect, one can wonder if Persian antipathy toward the presence of foreign corporations and their representatives might have been different if the aliens in their midst had been more sensitive to the strivings of the populace? Consider the significance of this report from *Time* (January 8, 1979):

> Not long ago, in an effort to overcome this insularity, one U.S. firm proposed a 30- to 50-hour orientation course for new employees of 100 American, European and Japanese companies. It would have included elementary Farsi, a brief history of Iran, and a cultural and sociological introduction to the country. Not a single company would agree to underwrite the cost, citing the uncertainties of Iran's economic and political situation. The results are painfully obvious. Says one U.S. economist: "Iranians want to know why Americans don't want to develop roots here. There's a lack of mutual trust."

Now that the gates of world commerce have been opened in the People's Republic of China, we may speculate on how prepared Western business people are to collaborate with this ancient people—products of a recent cultural revolution.

Compare the value of investment in human resource development for transnational operations versus the waste and damage caused, especially with host nationals, when disenchanted personnel are brought home ahead of schedule from international assignments.

Transcultural studies benefit employees because they:

1. Facilitate adjustment and productivity in a foreign country or at home with minority cultures.
2. Foster international good will and customer relations, as well as business and profits.
3. Increase human relations skills with foreigners, minorities or ethnic group representatives.
4. Offer better understanding of both domestic and international markets and reports related thereto.
5. Provide insight relative to organizational culture and personnel behavior.
6. Sensitize management to the needs of foreign nationals on assignment to corporate home culture.
7. Assist in reentry to one's native culture and organization upon return from abroad.
8. Help one to gain a better sense of self and cultural heritage for more effective intercultural interactions.

International relations, in general, are bound to be enhanced when management, sales, and technical personnel can manage cultural differences within the world marketplace.

Culture is fundamentally a group problem-solving tool for daily coping in a particular environment. It enables a unique group of people to grow in self-actualization, to create a distinctive world around them, to control their own destinies. Mankind alone among the planet's creatures seems to possess a sense of culture, so as to mold environment for our common good. Through genetic and cultural inheritance, *Homo Sapiens* occupies and utilizes a wider range of the earth than other species, and now probes the universe. Since human social and technological advancement are the legacy of all mankind, various peoples of diverse cultures should borrow from one another so that the exchange will promote a new level of human development.

This, then, is the rationale for this book, as well as for cross-cultural learning in general. Subsequent chapters will explore these issues and concerns in greater depth.

References

Barnett, R.J. and R.E. Muller, *Global Reach: The Power of the Multinational Corporation.* New York: Simon and Shuster, 1974.

Brown, L.R. *World Without Borders.* New York: Vintage Books/Random House, 1973. Center for the Study of Social Policy. *Changing Images of Man.* Menlo Park, Ca.: Stanford Research Institute, 1974.

Fabun, D. *The Dynamics of Change.* Englewood Cliffs, N.J.: Prentice-Hall, 1967.

Hall, E.T. *Beyond Culture.* Garden City, N.Y.: Anchor Press/Doubleday, 1976.

Harris, P.R. *Organizational Dynamics.* LaJolla, Ca.: Management & Organization Development Inc., 1973.

Murray, B. *Navigating the Future.* New York: Harper & Row, 1975.

Nadler, L. *Developing Human Resources.* Houston: Gulf Publishing Co., 1970.

Reischauer, E. *Toward the 21st Century: Education for a Changing World.* New York: Alfred A. Kopf, 1973.

Said, A.A. and L.R. Simmons, *Ethnicity in an International Context.* Edison, N.J.: Transaction Books, 1977.

Salk, J. *Man Unfolding.* New York: Harper & Row, 1972.

_____ *The Survival of the Wisest.* New York: Harper & Row, 1973.

Stavrianos, L.S. *The Promise of the Coming Dark Age.* San Francisco: W.H. Freeman and Company, 1976.

The Conference Board. *The Challenge to Leadership: Managing in a Changing World.* New York: Fress Press/Collier-Macmillan, 1973.

Weinshall, T.D., (ed.), *Culture and Management: Selected Readings.* New York: Penguin Books, 1977.

2
The Manager
As an Intercultural Communicator

The number of persons who leave their home cultures each year as representatives of their government agencies, multinational corporations, or as students, members of the military, and tourists, has continually increased. For example in 1979, among Americans* this number will exceed 14 million. At the same time the number of foreign nationals, who come to the United States, has also risen and in the same year will be over 18 million. As a result, interaction and communication among persons of different cultural backgrounds has come to be the norm rather than the exception. World travel by the masses only accelerates this phenomenon.

Participants in these intercultural experiences have learned that there are many problems when working or living in a foreign environment. Communication across cultural boundaries is difficult. Differences in customs, behavior, and values result in problems that can be only managed through effective cross-cultural communication and interaction. Persons of dissimilar backgrounds usually require a longer period of time than those of the same culture to become familiar with each other, to be willing to speak openly, to share sufficiently in common ideas, and to understand one another.

When people have misunderstandings or commit "errors" when working with persons from different cultures, they are often unaware of any problem. It is our hypothesis, that this is often the result of a lack of *cultural self-awareness*, which will be discussed in Chapter 4. Cross-cultural *faus pas*

---

*The word "American" is used throughout the text with the realization that it can also refer to persons of Latin America and Canada. A more appropriate term perhaps is "United States national," but this becomes cumbersome and so we use the word "American." A North American commonly includes U.S. and Canadian citizens, while South American normally refers to the Latin countries south of the U.S. border.

12

result when we fail to recognize that persons of other cultural backgrounds have different goals, customs, thought patterns, and values from our own. Condon and Yousef in their pioneer and popular book, *An Introduction to Intercultural Communication,* give excellent examples of a fictitious American, whose name is Richard and who makes unintentional, yet serious errors in three different countries:

> Meet Richard, a model American: friendly, easy-going, unpretentious, well-intentioned, practical. But poor Richard inevitably seems to run into problems when he is in other countries. The problems are especially annoying because they so often seem to arise when everything is going well and communication appears to be at its best.
>
> While visiting Egypt, Richard was invited to a spectacular dinner at the home of an Egyptian friend. And what a dinner it was! Clearly the host and hostess had gone out of their way to entertain him. Yet, as he was leaving their home he made a special effort to thank them for their spectacular dinner and sensed that something he said was wrong. Something about his sincere compliment was misunderstood.
>
> In Japan he had an even less pleasant experience, but he thought he had handled it well. A number of serious mistakes had occurred in a project he was supervising. While the fault did not lie with any one person, he was a supervisor and at least partly to blame. At a special meeting called to discuss the problem, poor Richard made an effort to explain in detail why he had done what he had done. He wanted to show that anybody in the same situation could have made the same mistake and to tacitly suggest that he should not be blamed unduly. He even went to the trouble of distributing materials which explained the situation rather clearly. And yet, even during his explanation, he sensed that something he was saying or doing was wrong.
>
> Even in England where he felt more at home, where he had no problems with language, this kind of misunderstanding occurred. He had been invited to take tea with one of his colleagues, a purely social, relaxed occasion. Tea was served along with sugar and cream. As he helped himself to some sugar and cream, he again sensed he had done something wrong.

Giving Richard and the persons he interacted with every benefit of intending well, we still have a misunderstanding which can be explained. Condon and Yousef continue:

> In *Egypt*, as in many cultures, the human relationship is valued so highly that it is not expressed in an objective but impersonal way. While Americans certainly value human relationships, they are more likely to speak of them in less personal, more objective terms. In this case, Richard's mistake might be that he chose to praise the food itself rather than the total evening, for which the food was simply the setting or excuse. For his host and hostess it was as if he had attended an art exhibit

and complimented the artist by saying, "What beautiful frames your pictures are in."

In *Japan*, the situation may be more complicated (or at least the typical Western image of Japan invites mysterious interpretations). For this example we can simply say that Japanese people value order and harmony among persons in a group, and that the organization itself—be it a family or a vast corporation—is more valued than the characteristics or idiosyncracies of any member. While this feeling is not alien to Americans—or to any society—Americans stress individuality as a value and are apt to assert individual differences when they seem justifiably in conflict with the goals or values of the group. In this case, Richard's mistake was in making great efforts to defend himself. Let the others assume that the errors were not intentional, but it is not right to defend yourself, even when your unstated intent is to assist the group by warning others of similar mistakes. A simple apology and acceptance of the blame would have been appropriate. (In contrast, for poor Richard to have merely apologized would have seemed to him to be subservient, unmanly. Nothing in his experience had prepared him for the Japanese reaction—in fact, he had been taught to despise such behavior.)

As for *England*, we might be tempted to look for some nonverbal indiscretion. While there are some very significant differences in language and language style, we expect fewer problems between Americans and Englishmen than between Americans and almost any other group. In this case, we might look beyond the gesture of taking sugar or cream to the values expressed in this gesture: for Americans, "Help yourself"; for the English counterpart, "Be my guest." American and English people equally enjoy entertaining and being entertained, but they differ somewhat in the value of the distinction. Typically, the ideal guest at an American party is one who "makes himself at home," even to the point of answering the door or fixing his own drink. For persons in many other societies, including at least this hypothetical English host, such guest behavior is presumptuous or rude. Poor Richard may object to this explanation, saying, "In other words, English people like to stand on ceremony." If so, he still does not understand. Another analogy may help Richard to appreciate the host's point of view: An American guest at an American party who would rearrange the furniture without being asked, suggest the dinner menu, and in other ways "make himself at home" also would seem to be presumptuous.

This synopsis of Richard, the insensitive businessman, can be found in many forms in the literature and the personnel files of multinational corporations and government agencies. These are replete with documentation of intercultural communication misunderstandings. Some are not serious, while others result in organizational and personal tragedies. The individuals affected include company presidents, ambassadors, expatriate technicians and managers, spouses, and tourists. Usually, the cause of the more serious problems is that interpersonal work or social relations with the host nationals have gone sour, not because of personality factors, but because of ineffective communications and a misreading of the verbal and nonverbal communication systems.

It is usually assumed by managers, educators, and writers that cultural differences are barriers and impede communication and interaction. In order to overcome these barriers one should understand the differences between one's own culture and another's. For example, in the United States we value promptness. We generally make use of schedules and evaluate each others behavior in these terms. In some countries, to arrive late is the norm rather than the exception and it has a different meaning depending on how late one is, the circumstances of the meeting, and how well you know the person.

It is an assumption of this volume that cultural differences, if well managed, are *resources*, not necessarily handicaps. This statement may appear to be somewhat idealistic and contrary to the experiences of many international sojourners. However, if these persons were better prepared, trained, and briefed for their assignment, the situation in another culture can be quite positive.

A beginning point in the training and preparation is to consider the manager as an *intercultural communicator*. But, the words "manager" and "management" are difficult to define. They do not have exact counterparts in many languages and do not have the same meaning in any language. In the past a manager was defined as someone who is responsible for the work of other people, but as stated in the first chapter, the assumptions upon which management practice has been based for the past fifty years are now obsolete. Drucker in his volume, *People and Performance: The Best of Peter Drucker on Management,* stated that a "manager can be defined only by that person's function and by the contribution he or she is expected to make . . . the one contribution a manager is uniquely expected to make is to give vision and ability to perform." Kast and Rosenzweig state that managers are "those who convert the disorganized resources of man, machines, material, money, time, and space into a useful and effective enterprise." To convert "disorganized resources . . . into a useful and effective enterprise" one must be an effective communicator. However, an effective communicator working with American nationals in the United States is not necessarily an effective communicator working with Japanese or Saudi Arabians in the United States, Japan, or Saudi Arabia. But what about communication—that magic word.

Cross-Cultural Communication as a People Process

The human being is a symbolic creature, as Leslie White reminded in his book, *The Science of Culture: A Study of Man and Civilization* (Farrar, Straus and Cudahy, 1949). With a power for abstraction, we possess both quantity and quality in our use of symbolic communication. Our developed brain permits us to put value or meaning to our diverse symbols which may differ by culture. Furthermore, human interaction is also characterized by a continuous updating of the meaning assigned to such symbols. Every journalist is aware, for instance, of the changed meanings given to words in a culture subject to rapid changes; word signs have been twisted as a means of exerting power or shock. All mankind is challenged to consider the fantastic new symbolizing faculties which emerging man is utilizing. In the past twenty-five years, we have expanded our capacities for symbolic communication beyond what was accomplished in the previous twenty-five hundred years. The human species is extending its communication capabilities beyond print to that of electronic technology; in the process our whole thought pattern is being transformed.

Every person is a versatile communicator. Language sets us apart from other creatures and seemingly is characteristic of the more developed brain. But humans have a wide range of communication skills that go beyond words to include gestures, signs, shapes, colors, sounds, smells, pictures and many other communications symbols. The diversity of human culture in this regard may be demonstrated in the "artist" who may communicate both thought and feeling in paintings, sculpture, music and dance. Through such media, the artist projects himself into people, things and surroundings. He projects his way of thinking, his temperament and personality, his joys and sorrows into the world around him or one he creates. But technological man has vastly expanded his media facility.

Every person operates within his or her own private world or perceptual field. This is what is referred to as life space, and it applies to individuals as well as to organizations and nations. Every individual communicates a unique perspective of the world and reality. Every culture reflects that group of people's view of the world. From time-to-time, a true professional must check out whether one's view of the world or that of an organization synchronizes with the collective reality. This is particularly essential when "objective reality" is subject to the phenomenon of accelerating change. Cultural groups may have distorted views of world reality, as did China during the period of the Maoist "Cultural Revolution."

Every person projects himself into human communication. We communicate our image of self including our system of needs, values and standards; our expectations, ideals, and perceptions of peoples, things, and situations. We project this collective image through body, bearing, appearance, tone of voice, choice of words, as well as through the content of the language in which we structure the message.

Every person is a medium or instrument of communication, not just a sender and receiver of messages. If a person is comfortable with himself, he is said to be congruent, and people usually respond positively. If he is uncomfortable with self, he is characterized as incongruent, and people will avoid him or respond negatively. The more aware the individual is of the forces at work within self which affect behavior, the more able we are to control his own life space.

Every generation perceives life differently. For example, the above concepts of behavioral communication can be applied to a generation of people. The people of each generation project a unique image of "their" world at a certain point in time. This image relflects a generation's system of needs, values, standards and ideals. The children of the "depression age" experienced life differently than today's children of affluence. As columnist Max Lerner pointed out (*Los Angeles Times*, February 1, 1970):

> All generations live in two worlds — an outer and an inner one. But each generation has its own inner universe — the subjective one, furnishing a window on the world through which it looks out at the outer universe. This inner world is formed early in the teens and twenties, perhaps thirties, and while it may continue to change in open-ended personalities, its basic frame remains much the same. My inner world was shaped by what happened in the 1920s, 30s and 40s; that of my son in the 1950s and 60s. We have different conditionings, hangups, life styles, and even vocabularies. Since the pace of social change which creates the gap is not slowing down, we shall have to learn with it, while making a creative leap of imagination to see the outer world through the inner window of the other generation.

If one expands upon Lerner's insight, related to adult and adolescent, the problem of communications between the generations and even cultures becomes more understandable. The supervisor of a young worker, for example, usually projects his generation's view of the world (past oriented) and finds it difficult to facilitate communication by coming into the reality of the younger employee (future oriented).

Communication is at the heart of all organizational operations and international relations. It is the most important tool we have for getting things done. It is the basis for understanding, for cooperation and for action. In fact, the very vitality and creativity of an organization or a nation depends upon the content and character of its communications. Yet, communication is both hero and villain. Not only is it the process which transfers information, meets people's needs, and gets things done, but far too often it is the process which distorts messages, develops frustration and renders people and organizations ineffective.

The Communication Process

Communication is a process of circular interaction which involves a sender, receiver and message. Man is a versatile communicator; he can communicate with nature, animals and other men. In human interaction, the sender or receiver may be a person or a group of people, such as those who make up an organization. The message conveys meaning through the medium or symbol used to send it (the *how*), as well as in its content (the *what*). Since humans are such intelligent, symbol-making creatures, the message may be relayed verbally, or nonverbally — words (oral or written), pictures, graphs, statistics, signs, gestures. The diversity of mankind's capacities to communicate range from smoke signals and the sound of drums to television and satellites. As a dynamic being, man is constantly inventing new and improved ways of communicating, such as the computer or videophone. However, regardless of the communication symbol, a sender and receiver are normally involved.

Both sender and receiver occupy a unique field of experience, different for each and every person. Essentially, it is a private world of perception through which all experience is filtered, organized and translated; it is what psychologists call the individual's life space. This consists of the person's *psychological environment* as it exists for him. Each and every person experiences life in a unique way and psychologically structures his own distinctive perceptual field. Among the factors that comprise one's field of experience are one's family, educational, cultural, religious and social background. The individual's perceptual field affects the way he receives and dispenses all new information. It influences both the content and the media used in communicating.

An individual's self-image, needs, values, expectations, goals, standards, cultural norms and perception have an effect on the way input is received and interpreted. Essentially, persons *selectively perceive* all new data, determining that which is relevant to, and consistent with, their own perceptual needs. Literally, two people can thus receive the same message and derive from it two entirely different meanings. They actually perceive the same object or information differently. Communication, then, is a complex process of linking up or sharing perceptual fields between sender and receiver. The effective communicator builds a bridge to the world of the receiver. When the sender is from one cultural group and the receiver from another, the human interaction is intercultural communication.

Once the sender conveys the message, the receiver analyzes the message in terms of his particular field of experience and pattern of ideas. Usually he decodes the message, interprets it for meaning and encodes or sends back a response. Thus, communication is a circular process of interaction.

The communicator, whether as an individual from a cultural group or as a member of an organization, transmits many kinds of behavior. First, he communicates the intended message on both a verbal and nonverbal level. We also communicate unintended behavior, or subconscious behavior, on both a verbal and nonverbal level. In other words, communication at any level involves a whole complex of projections. There is a "silent language" being used also in the process of human interaction. It includes such aspects as tone of voice and inflection of words, gestures and facial expressions. Some of these factors that affect the real meaning and content of messages are referred to as "body language," that is, the positioning of various parts of the sender's physique conveys meaning. The person himself is both a medium and a message of communication and the way in which we communicate is vastly influenced by our cultural conditioning.

Communication

Samovar and Porter in their book, *Intercultural Communication: A Reader*, define communication as "a dynamic process whereby human behavior, both verbal and nonverbal, is perceived and responded to."

For the manager working and communicating in a multicultural environment, we offer the following observations about the process of communication. These assumptions can also serve as practical guidelines for developing skills to become a more effective intercultural communicator.

1. *No matter how hard one tries, one cannot avoid communicating.* International managers may say they are restraining themselves and let the host nationals take the lead in negotiation situations in order to get a sense of what is happening. This may be an effective strategy. However, all behavior in human interaction has a message value and is communicating something to the persons present. While silent with words, body language is communicating. We communicate by our activity or our inactivity, by the color of our skin, as well as, the color of our clothes and by the gift we give or decide not to give. All behavior is communication because all behavior contains a message, whether intended or not.

2. *Communication does not necessarily mean understanding.* Even when two individuals agree that they are communicating or talking to each other it does not mean that they have understood each other. Understanding takes place when the two individuals have the same interpretation of the symbols being used in the communication process whether the symbols be words or gestures. The American manager who gives a gift of yellow flowers in France or white flowers in Japan has communicated something but probably not that which was intended. In France yellow flowers suggest infidelity and white flowers in Japan are given at funerals to indicate sympathy.

3. *Communication is irreversible.* One cannot take back one's communication. It can be explained, clarified, restated, but it cannot be wiped out although we may sometimes wish that it could. Once we have participated in a communication event, it is part of our experience and it influences present and future meanings. The American manager who has sharply disagreed with a Saudi Arabian in the presence of others has committed an "impoliteness" in the Arab world that is difficult to remedy.

4. *Communication occurs in a context.* One cannot ignore the context of communication which takes place at a certain time, in some place, using certain mediums. Such factors have message value and give meaning to the communicators. Communication by an American manager in England is within a context that affects the interaction in contrast to a domestic exchange. Also, a business conversation with a French manager in France during an evening meal may be very inappropriate.

5. *Communication is a dynamic process.* Communication is not static and passive, but rather it is a continuous and active process without beginning or end. A communicator is not simply a sender or a receiver of messages but can be both at the same time.

These statements briefly outline a number of important characteristics of intercultural communication. Some are obvious, others not, but all, if internalized and understood would result in more effective communication. Each of us has been socialized in a unique environment. However, important aspects of the environment are shared and these constitute a particular culture. Culture poses communication problems because there are so many variables not known to the communicators. As the cultural variables and differences increase, the number of communication misunderstandings increase. Those variables will be discussed in more detail in the remaining sections of this chapter.

Cultural Factors in Communication

Imagine yourself participating in the following cross-cultural situations that affect communication and understanding between two culturally different individuals. Then attempt to answer the questions posed before proceeding further:

> You are involved in a technical training program in Iran and one of your responsibilities is to rate persons under your supervision. You have socialized on several occasions and you and your family have spent some time with one of the Iranians you are supervising. The Iranian is an extremely friendly and hardworking individual, but had difficulty exercising the leadership expected of him. On the rating form you so indicated; and this was discussed with him by his supervisor. Subsequently, he came to you and asked how you could have said that about him because you were friends. You indicated that you also thought you were friends, but that you had an obligation to report deficiencies and areas to be improved upon to his supervisors. This statement was incomprehensible to the Iranian . . . . What cultural differences might cause misperceptions of performance appraisal and evaluation?

> You are negotiating a contract with a Japanese company and during the meetings there are times of silence on the part of the Japanese negotiating team. The negotiations, from your perspective as an American, appear to

According to Edward T. Hall in his book, *Beyond Culture*, the study of cultures and the consideration of ethnicities, is especially important for Americans because they are generally intolerant of differences and have a tendency to consider something different as inferior. Many of the foreign assistance programs by the superpowers generate antipathy among indigenous peoples because of the way they are treated by the representatives. Consider this Iranian businessman's commentary:

> More than anything, I believe, Iranians' public demonstrations of anger are an expression of deep anxiety about the conflicts brought about by Westernization.
>
> Rather than being supportive and understanding of the dilemma, almost all the foreigners I knew in Iran (chiefly Americans) were not only ignorant of their hosts' ways but downright insulting. I cannot count the number of times I saw Americans ridicule and humiliate their Iranian co-workers. They were "farkles"—something less than human; their ancient customs were "hokey-pokey." I even knew of a fellow who rode his motorcycle through a mosque. The anti-Western sentiment that today has Iranians in the streets hardly comes as a surprise.

This same problem is seen in the U.S. in the relations between blacks and whites. Some Americans see blacks as underdeveloped whites. In fact, American black culture, as every culture, is rich. It behooves us as the new cosmopolitan manager or student of management to understand other cultures and effectively work with them.

In the classical anthropological sense, culture refers to the cumulative deposit of knowledge, beliefs, values, religion, customs, and mores acquired by a group of people and passed on from generation to generation.

Cultures can be analyzed as high context or low context. This distinction was developed by Dr. Hall in his book, *Beyond Culture,* and is useful for the manager in looking for meaning in cross-cultural messages. A high context communication is one in which most of the information is either in the physical context or internalized in the person. A low context communication is one in which the majority of information is contained in the explicit code. The American culture is a low context culture, while the Japanese culture is extremely high. When a Japanese manager and an American manager work together, there are a great many possibilities for misunderstanding. The American is looking for meaning and understanding in *what is said*; the Japanese is looking for meaning and understanding in what is not said—in the silences and in the pauses between the silences. The American emphasis is on sending out or giving accurate messages (being articulate) whereas, the Japanese emphasis is on receiving messages that often do not have to be stated directly.

Levels of Culture and Human Interaction

Sharon Ruhly, modifying concepts presented by Hall in his now classic book, *The Silent Language*, provides a system for analyzing different levels of culture that are called the technical, formal, and informal. This is a useful scheme for understanding cultural content and the amount of emotion attached to the content.

The *technical* level of culture, using the analogy that culture is like an iceberg—part of it is seen but most is not—is in full view and the technical aspects of a culture are learned in a student-teacher relationship. An example of a technical aspect of the American culture is the alphabet. There is little emotion attached to the technical level and there are few intercultural misunderstandings at this level, as the reason for a disagreement is usually quite easy to determine. Managers operate at the technical levels of culture when discussing the tolerance points of certain metals; however, when two managers are interacting over a period of time, it is difficult to remain exclusively at the technical level.

Continuing with the analogy of the cultural iceberg, the *formal* level of culture is partially above and partially below sea level. We learn aspects of our culture at the formal level usually by trial and error. We may be aware of the rules for a particular behavior, such as, the rituals of marriage, but we do not know why. The emotion at the formal level of culture is high and violations result in negative feelings about the violator even though the violation is often unintentional. The fact that the violated rule is local, i.e., an aspect of one culture and not another and therefore does not apply to everyone, is difficult to admit. A visiting business representative who uses a social occasion in France to discuss business with a French executive is violating a rule at the formal level of that culture.

The *informal* level of culture lies below sea level and actions and responses are automatic and almost unconscious. The rules of a behavior activity are usually not known although we realize that something is wrong. Informal rules are learned through a process called modeling. One example is the role behavior for males and females that persons are expected to follow in some cultures. Another concerns the appropriate time for Jane Smith, the American manager in France to begin calling her colleague, "Denise" instead of "Mademoiselle Drancourt." Emotion is usually intense at the informal level when a rule is broken and the relationship between the persons involved is affected. Violations are interpreted personally and calling a person by his first name too soon could be interpreted as overly friendly and offensive.

Themes and Values in Intercultural Communication

Several years ago John Kouwenhoven wrote a series of essays entitled *The Beer Can by the Highway: or, What's American about America* seeking to discover common themes in American culture, especially its unique values.

Values in the U.S. organization include competition as a primary method for motivating members of a group, a stress on the individual as being the most important identity in our culture, and the form of activity related to "doing," "getting things done," or "it is better to do something than nothing." These values are a part of American culture and are not shared by all cultures. The concept of value has been studied by many social scientists, but Florence Kluckhohn and Frederick Strodtbeck in their classic study *Variations in Value Orientations* provide a definition: "a value is a conception, explicit or implicit, distinctive of an individual or characteristic of a group which influences the selection from available modes, means, and ends of actions." The reference to "explicit or implicit" indicates that many values that we hold may not be at a conscious level and it is these that cause the greatest difficulty in intercultural relations. This will be further discussed in Chapters 4 and 5. A framework to understand differences in values and the application to management situations will be provided in Chapter 6.

Variables in the Communication Process

Samovar and Porter identify eight variables in the communication process whose values are determined to some extent by culture. Each variable influences our perceptions, which in turn influence the meanings we attribute to behavior. The manager seeking to work effectively in a multicultural environment should be cognizant of these and seek to learn the cultural specifics for the country or area to be visited. (In Appendix A, a questionnaire to be used in preparation for an overseas assignment is included which reflects many of these perceptions.)

Attitudes are psychological states that predispose us to behave in certain ways. An undesirable attitude for managers working in a multicultural environment is ethnocentrism or self reference criterion. This is the tendency to judge others by using one's own personal or cultural standards. For example, instead of attempting to understand the Japanese within their own cultural context, an ethnocentric person tries to understand them as similar to or different from Americans. As managers, it is vital to refrain from constantly making comparisons between our way of life and that of others when abroad. Rather, we should seek to understand other people in the context of their unique historical, political, economic, social, and cultural backgrounds. In that way it is possible to become more effective interactors with them. Stereotypes are sets of attitudes in which we attribute qualities or characteristics to a person on the basis of the group to which that individual belongs. Many studies of comparative management facilitate the development of stereotypes in that "management" is discussed largely in terms of the management system in the United States, and thus becomes the basis of comparison with management practices in other countries. An underlying assumption usually is that the American management system is the norm and other systems are compared to the United States.

Social organization of cultures is also a variable that influences one's perceptions. Michael Flack has made a useful distinction for managers in describing two societal compositions: the *geographic* society, which is composed of members of a nation, tribe, or religious sect; and the *role* society, which is composed of members of a profession or the elite of a group. Managers are members of the same role society, i.e., the business environment, but they are often members of different geographic societies. At one level communication between managers from two different cultures should be relatively smooth. On another level, significant differences in values, approach, pace, priorities, and other factors may cause difficulties.

Thought patterns or forms of reasoning may differ from culture to culture. The Aristotelian mode of reasoning prevalent in the West is not shared by people in Asia. What is reasonable, logical, and self-evident to an American manager may be unreasonable, illogical, and not self-evident to an Asian manager. We may often sound just as illogical to them as they do to us.

Roles in a society and expectations of a culture concerning role behavior affect communication. When behavior is incomprehensible, it is very often because the rules concerning how a person in that position should act are unknown to us. The "meishi" or name card of the Japanese manager is important because it identifies his position in a company and therefore, the amount of respect that is appropriate. The length of time he has been in the company and his ability to make decisions are also known from his "meishi."

Language skill in a host country is acknowledged as important by international managers, but many believe that a competent interpreter is all that is necessary. Sapir and Whorf developed an hypothesis that states that language functions not simply as a method for reporting experiences, but also as a way of defining experiences for its speakers. Because culture and language are inseparably related, it is wise to rely heavily on competent interpreters to bridge cultural gaps.

Space is also a factor in the communication process. Americans believe that they own their bodies and they have a bubble around them that extends about two inches beyond their skin. If anyone breaks their bubble one must apologize and say "excuse me." The United States is a noncontact society. Other cultures, such as, the Latin Americans and Middle Easterners are contact societies and require relatively close physical proximity to others during a conversation. Between males, touching is very common and handshakes are frequent and last throughout a litany of greetings.

Time sense also impacts upon human interaction. Americans perceive time in lineal-spatial terms in the sense that there is a past, a present, and a future. We are oriented to the future and in the process of preparing for it we save, waste, make up, or spend time. Zen treats time as a limitless pool in which certain things happen and then pass. North Americans are often confused by the Latin time sense when they do business in South America. Subsequent chapters will develop this further.

Nonverbal communication also differs significantly across cultures and determines meanings. The left hand doesn't have any particular significance in the West, but in Moslem countries it is the "toilet hand" and should not be used for eating or giving or receiving gifts. The American OK nonverbal gesture is an obscene gesture in Brazil. Desmond Morris in his book *Manwatching* identifies many of the nonverbal gestures that have a meaning in one culture, but in another are either not understood, have no meaning, or, in some cases, have an obscene meaning. The well-trained and effective manager abroad endeavors to learn the body language of the culture where he or she is working.

The cosmopolitan manager, aware of the cultural dimension and seeking to improve performance, attempts to become a more professional communicator. That means understanding and applying the concepts and insights outlined in this chapter. It implies a continuing effort to enhance one's skills in intercultural interaction.

References

Cherry, C., *World Communication: Threat or Promise.* New York: Wiley-Interscience, 1971.

Condon, John C. and Yousef, Fathi. *An Introduction to Intercultural Communication.* Indianapolis: The Bobbs-Merrill Company, Inc., 1975.

Dance, Frank E. "The 'Concept' of Communication," *Journal of Communication.* Vol. 20, pp. 201-210, 1970.

Drucker, Peter F. *People and Performance: The Best of Peter Drucker on Management.* New York: Harper's College Press, 1977.

Flack, Michael J. "Communicable and Uncommunicable Aspects in Personal International Relations," *Journal of Communication.* Vol. 16, pp. 283-290, 1966.

Hall, Edward T. *Beyond Culture.* Garden City, New York: Anchor Press/ Doubleday, 1977.

Kluckhohn, Florence R. and Strodtbeck, Frederick L. *Variations in Value Orientations.* Evanston, Illinois: Row, Peterson and Company, 1961.

Kouwenhoven, John. *The Beer Can By The Highway: Essays on What's American About America.* New York: Doubleday, 1961.

Kroeber, A.L. and Kluckhohn, C. *Culture: A Critical Review of Concepts and Definitions.* Random House, Vintage Books: New York. (Originally published in 1952 as Vol. XLVII, No. 1 of the Papers of the Peabody Museum of American Archaeology and Ethnology, Harvard University.)

Morris, Desmond. *Manwatching: A Field Guide to Human Behavior*. London, England: Jonathan Cape, 1978.

Ruhly, Sharon. *Orientations to Intercultural Communication*. Chicago, Illinois: Science Research Associates, Inc., 1976.

Samovar, Larry A. and Porter, Richard E. *Intercultural Communication: A Reader*. Belmont, California: Wadsworth Publishing Company, Inc., 1976.

Smith, D.R. and L.K. Williamson, *Interpersonal Communication*. Dubuque, Iowa: Wm. C. Brown, 1977.

Smith, E.C. and Luce, L.B. (eds.) *Toward Internationalism: Readings in Cross-Cultural Communications*. Rowley, Massachusetts: Newbury House. Publishers, 1979.

3
The Manager
As an Agent of Change

Communication and Change

Communication is a prime dynamic that determines the kind and rate of change in society. Mass communication and its technology is one factor contributing to the acceleration in the rate of change. Communication involves the establishing of relationships, while change causes an altering of such relationships. Communication is an energy exchange, whereas change requires the shifting of energy priorities. Change challenges leadership to deal more effectively with differences, which occur when the status quo has been unfrozen because of new inventions, new insights, new attitudes, new people.

When a computer is introduced into a corporation, there is a change in role relationships. When a management information system is introduced into an office, the data available for decision-making affects relationships. When a local company moves beyond its borders into the international marketplace, there is not only a transformation of attitudes, but policies, procedures, and even structures may change. When minority people are brought into the workforce in greater numbers, there is an altering of relationships with the majority personnel. When women are promoted into a management made up largely of males, female relationships with male supervisors are subtly influenced. All such actions provoke change in organizational culture. So too, when managers, sales persons or technicians, as well as their families, are deployed overseas for a lengthy assignment, there is a profound transposition in their relationships to their "world" and the "foreigners" in it.

The paradox of change, as Benjamin Disraeli reminded us, is that it is inevitable and constant. Furthermore, it is an event and a process. It also forces

28

leaders to view it either as a problem or an opportunity. Today's managers operate in a world culture that has changed more rapidly and extensively than any other period in human history. To survive and develop, administrators need new skills to cope with change, as well as to build a new openness to it in their life-styles along with mechanisms for planned change in their systems.

This chapter views planned change in terms of three interactive cultures: (1) *cyberculture*—the urban, technological, superindustrial society that is emerging; (2) *organizational* culture—the base from which the cosmopolitan manager or professional operates; (3) *national* culture—the people and place in which one seeks to live and conduct business. Increasingly, that latter culture is different or foreign from the majority culture in which we were born and formed. The thesis here is that our behavior is influenced and we are changed by the impact of these three cultures upon us, especially as actors in leadership roles. But we need not passively react, for we have the means to temper or tamper with these interacting cultures. Specifically, modern management theory maintains that managers have a responsibility to be proactive agents of change. That is, they can initiate actions to correct obsolescence. Such innovative activity is not limited to one's corporation or agency, but extends into the community, wherever that may be. In a time when nation states seemingly falter, world corporations prosper. Skilled change agents are needed in this period in human development when politicians often feel impotent, as corporate executives exercise global influence.

Obviously, not all change is desirable. Critical choices have to be made about the overall wisdom of an alteration. Certainly, haphazard change is to be avoided. Because accelerating change is a reality of our world, change must be managed if it is not to cause disastrous dislocation in the life spaces of people and their organizations or societies. Perhaps the place to begin is for the reader to assess his or her attitudes toward change, as well as to consider *why* planned change is essential. It is a challenge to reeducate one's self and to reevaluate our psychological constructs—the way we read meaning into the events and experiences of our lives.

Human Factors in Change

Each of us has a set of highly organized constructs around which we organize our "private" worlds. We construct a mental system for putting order, as we perceive it, into our worlds. This intellectual synthesis of sense perceptions relates to our images of self, family, role, organization, nation, and universe. These constructs then become anchors or reference points for our mental functioning and well being. Our unique construct systems exert a pushing/pulling effect upon all other ideas and experiences we encounter. They assign meaning quickly and almost automatically to the multiple sensations and perceptions that bombard us daily.

Not only do individuals have such unique sets of constructs though which they filter experience, but groups, organizations, and even nations develop such mental frameworks through which they too interpret information coming from their environment. The intense interactions of various segments of their populations form construct sets that enable them to achieve collective goals. In this way a group, organizational, or national "style" or type of behavior emerges. Through communication in such groupings, people share themselves and their individual perceptions converge into a type of "consensus" of what makes sense to them in a particular environment and circumstance. Culture, then, transmits these common, shared sets of perceptions and relationships. But since human interaction is dynamic, pressures for change in such constructs build up in both individuals and institutions. For example, when a manager from Grand Rapids, Michigan, is transferred for three years to Riyadh, Saudi Arabia, that person is challenged to change many of his or her constructs about life and people. The same may be said for the corporate culture which that individual's company attempts to transplant from Midwest America to the Middle East. These forces for change can be avoided, resisted, or incorporated into the person's or the organization's perceptual field. If the latter happens, then change becomes a catalyst for a restructuring of constructs and an opportunity for growth. In other words, the employee and the company can adapt and develop.

New information, people, experiences, methods, policies, and technology threaten the present equilibrium. When the data is inconsistent with present constructs, some persons tend to resist. If the new input makes old constructs obsolete, but is of such a nature that it cannot be avoided, the resulting pressure or dissonance will usually energize the individual or the institution to change or modify the construct system. As the representatives of Western technology descend upon Saudi Arabia, many of whose leaders themselves are educated in the West, there is an obvious pressure in that ancient culture to moderate traditional views and norms that range from the role of women in business to the responsibility of leadership in the community. During the transition period from the customary to the revised constructs, a temporary confusion or disorganization may be evident until a renewed equilibrium or order is restored. A relative state of harmony or congruence then occurs until further changes set the process in motion again.

Human beings like to know what is expected of them and to anticipate the future. In attempting to predict what may happen to us, our culture provides a fund of knowledge and cues, so that we may act appropriately. Seemingly, when "everything nailed down is coming loose" and the old "truths" become questionable, we become uneasy. We are often upset because the factors and reference groups we used to count upon, especially in social situations, are either no longer relevant, or able to provide the former ego support. Many are thus beginning to wonder if the only "certainty" about the future is uncertainty and change. Even organizations are learning to function in a new state of ultrastability—beyond a static status with planned, continuous, cyclical change as its "normal" pattern.

Because people are usually disturbed by the unknown, it has been natural for people to fear change, and even to panic in times of unprecedented change. When that fear is so overwhelming as to paralyze individuals or institutions into inaction, then chaos may reign. Generally, we are comfortable with the status quo, but building change into life and work styles may soon become the norm rather than the exception. Organizations are already starting to reward innovation over conformity. Perhaps the point is best illustrated by Gail Sheehy in her best-seller, *Passages,* when she reminds us that our lives run in cycles that typically involve a pattern of continuous changes or developmental stages. Personal or career crises can be the mechanisms for constructive or destructive changes, depending on how we respond to the turning point. Was the sage right who observed that to live is to change, but to grow is to change often? Yet, that is a Western view of change—those in the East have a different perspective.

The fast pace of modern life, the demise of traditional values and supports intensify emotional stress and strain of change for human beings and their systems. Change can involve pain, whether it be the divorce of marital or business partners, the loss of job or loved one, a transfer within or outside one's country, the merger of two departments or two corporations. The cosmopolitan does not try to deny or minimize the negative impact of change upon people. Instead, such leaders attempt to help their personnel or their clients to plan for such change, to transform it, but at the very least to cope effectively with the challenge as a means for growth and improved quality of life.

Because culture provides conditioned control systems upon individuals and their institutions, the sensitive manager who operates abroad takes such powerful influences into consideration while attempting to introduce a new product or service, a new method or technology. In intercultural situations, we should be aware of the human factors involved with our proposed changes. Knowingly or unknowingly, we are agents of change in the life space of others with whom we relate. By exercising skill in planned change, we cannot only facilitate people's preparation and acceptance of change, but we may do it in such a way as to reduce stress and energy waste. Maximum two-way communication about the proposed change can create the necessary readiness for its eventual implementation. The pressure of sudden changes can be defused. While proposing innovations, leaders can endeavor to reduce the uncomfortable threat feelings of those involved. Thus, negative reactions like apathy or sabotage, protest or revolt can be minimized.

It is important for modern management to appreciate that for most of human history, the majority of the globe's inhabitants were raised in hierarchical societies where personal choice and progress were limited, and one's place was immutable. For generations people survived by remaining within their prescribed roles, adapting to the pattern of thought, belief, and action of their local cultural group. Except for less developed countries, all this is changing in our cosmic village—mankind is in the midst of a mind-boggling transformation that offers seemingly unlimited choices and opportunities We change our environment and are changed by it. We create technology, and we are physically and psychologically changed by it. In the process traditional customs, values, attitudes, and beliefs are disrupted. Yet, as our culture and social institutions change, we *learn* to change ever more effectively and our capacity for such learning is seemingly inexhaustible. Cosmopolitan leaders are in the forefront of this phenomenon and should be on the cutting edge of innovation, while mindful of the human dimensions involved.

Change and Culture

Culture is communicable knowledge for human coping within a particular environment that is passed on for the benefit of subsequent generations. Just as mankind is unique in its capacity for creating communication symbols, so too only our species develops culture as a means of adaptation to physical or biological surroundings. For millions of years our biological evolution was marked by slow and gradual change. This leisurely pace was also characteristic of cultural adaptations in general, while specific cultures operated in relative isolation with geographic limitations. Then in the past three centuries, as the human race moved into a period of psychosocial evolution, there has been acceleration in the rate of change. The first chapter provided an illustration on the history of human development that emphasized this speed-up in change, a compression in time itself. This astronomical acceleration has weakened the traditional folk wisdom for survival and advancement. The impact of rapid change, particularly in this century, has undermined many ancient local cultures. Will this breakdown of indigenous cultures contribute toward the emergence of a planetary culture?

Some cultural systems are more open and accepting of change, while others can only integrate it in a very gradual manner, to avoid violent reaction. Furthermore, the process of innovation differs by culture. The complexities of Western cultural living would appear to stimulate creativity without inordinate attention to details. On the other hand, change in Eastern culture, as in Third World nations, is often accompanied by painstaking concern for its effect on relationships, so there is a preference for bending the cultural bonds within the existing system to avoid radical alterations.

Cosmopolitan managers must function in the midst of paradoxes involved in social and cultural change. Despite the acceleration in the change rate in the last half of this century, the pace of change varies enormously in different cultures. Yet, no tribe or group is today too remote not to experience its influence. And despite the current disturbances caused by such swift alterations, there can be patterned continuity, such as what seemingly occurs in Japan or China today. While the mainstream of civilization plunges into the superindustrial stage of human development, there still exist living laboratories of mankind's past cultural stages. Enlightened peoples are seeking to preserve these microcultures as long as possible, rather than destroy them with "progress."

There are many forces causing change in the very processes of cultural development—innovation, diffusion, acculturation, and rapid creation and disposal of new institutions. With advances in mass communication and transportation, no human group is too remote to avoid such influences. It is indeed possible for some areas to overstep literacy and industrial stages into new forms of communication and technological civilization.

Another seeming paradox of cultural change is that innovations are more likely to occur in times of turmoil and transition such as we are going through; they seem to occur in cultures experiencing social and political uncertainties, in mild ferment, as contrasted to more stable or static societies. More and more, the world's people are coming to *value* change, and to be more futuristic, rather than past oriented. Many are convinced that mankind can create its own future.

Observers of the contemporary scene realize that the massive increase in contact between and among cultures has intensified the diffusion of varied cultural elements. The cross-cultural interchange is evident world-wide whether one examines global dress and music styles, or technology and business methods. Acculturation for individuals and groups occurs from prolonged communication between two or more societies, so that all the cultures involved are changed in the process. Yet, there is the danger inherent in such contacts that cultural imposition may take place without adequate respect for the cultures involved and without mutual exchange. For example, since the fifteenth century there has been an unprecedented flow of Western cultural materials to countries outside the Euro-American orbit. Will the prolonged impact of this economic, technological, political, social, and cultural transfer into the non-Western world threaten the identity and existence of many peoples in such circumstances? The irony is that the source of such cultural transfusions was grounded in ancient Middle Eastern and Asian cultures. Only in the last few decades has the one-way Western flow begun to reverse and accept renewed contributions from Eastern thought, whether it be religion, philosophy, health services, or technological achievements. Although many revitalization movements have been spawned as a defense against Western ethnocentrism or dominance, Eastern values and influences offer vital contributions to emerging world culture, which can only benefit by the convergence of East-West thought and perspectives. Today, the People's Republic of China is especially the key crossroad for this interchange.

Modernization, in any event, uproots traditional structures, institutions, and relationships. The universal patterns of change being described here are expanding the horizons of local peoples, and fostering the "planetization" of the human race. A final paradox is that the very agents of such change are themselves changed in the process. Witness what is happening to English culture as a result of the imperial forays throughout the "commonwealth" by the former British colonialists. The English were agents of civilizing change in many countries. Today the U.K. is in a state of ferment and social change brought about, in part, by the presence in Great Britain of their former or current commonwealth members!

Developing Change Strategies

Cosmopolitan leaders should be sources of innovation, yet skillful in managing change. The *Harvard Business Review* has defined the management of change as "innovation and creativity in the achieving of goals." Agents of change may apply their efforts, in this context, to altering personal, organizational, and cultural goals. With a multinational manager operating in diverse cultures and circumstances, for example, the different circumstances require appropriate adaptation of corporate objectives and procedures. Similarly, such mangers should review their personal and personnel aims in multicultural settings. Their revision might include a goal of learning to be comfortable or at home anywhere that person happens to be located, even if it means creative circumvention of local constraints. Innovators may respect the established system, while working to bend or beat it to make it more responsive to satisfying human need.

The *New York Times* once ran an interesting advertisement as follows:

> WANTED—CHANGE AGENTS—Results-oriented individuals able to accurately and quickly resolve complex tangible and intangible problems. Energy and ambition necessary for success.

Within an organization or culture, what then would be the focus of such a change agent when employed? Probably, the initial concern would be to examine the change possibilities in six categories:

1. Structure (the system of authority, communication, roles, and work flow)
2. Technology (problem solving mechanisms, tools, and computers)
3. Tasks (activities accomplished, such as manufacturing, research, service)
4. Processes (techniques, methods, procedures, such as management information systems)
5. Environment (internal or external atmosphere)
6. People (personnel or human resources involved)

Having decided upon which category or combinations to focus one's energy for change, the leader might follow these steps:

1. Identify specific changes that appear desirable to improve effectiveness.
2. Create a readiness in the system for such change.
3. Facilitate the internalization of the innovation.
4. Reinforce the new equilibrium established through the change.

The skilled change maker is aware that any change introduced in one element of the above chain affects the other factors. The parts of complex systems are interdependent, so the innovator attempts to forecast the ripple effect. Change agents must take a multidimensional approach, considering legal, economic, and technological aspects of the change without ignoring its social, political and personal implications. They also operate on certain assumptions:

1. People are capable of planning and controlling their own destinies within their own life space.
2. Behavioral change knowledge and technology should be incorporated into the planning process.
3. Human beings are already in the midst of profound cultural change.

The implication of the latter statement is that the people to be involved in the new change process may be suspicious of simplistic solutions as a result of the information/media blitz to which they have been exposed. They may already be suffering from information overload, experiencing a sense of powerlessness and loss of individuality; and they expect innovative and involving communication about the change. Essentially, the change maker may employ three change models to bring about a shift in the status quo:

- *Power,* political or legal, physical or psychological—coercion to bring about change may be legitimate or illegitimate, depending on the purpose, the ingredients, and the method of application (legislative power may be used to promote equal employment opportunity or to prevent a disease epidemic, while the authority of role or competence may be called upon to overcome resistance to change).
- *Rationale,* the appeal to reason and the common good, but this approach must face the fact that people are not always altruistic and self-interest may block acceptance of the proposed change, no matter how noble or worthwhile for the majority.
- *Reeducative*—conditioning, training, and education become the means to not only create readiness for the change, but to provide the information and skills to implement it.

Each model has its strength and weaknesses, and sometimes the latter can be overcome in a combination of approaches.

The fields of planning, technological forecasting, and future studies provide change makers with new tools and processes for bringing about managed innovation. Through research, publications, conferences, and seminars cosmopolitan leaders can hone their skills in planned change. Some multinational corporations have their own units engaging in such studies, sometimes sharing the results of their investigations, e.g., General Electric's report on *The Future of the Business Environment*.

Security Pacific Bank in California, for instance, has a vice-president in charge of futures research. This executive searches out trends in life-styles and indicators of alternative futures to determine their implications for banking policies, procedures, personnel, and customers. Others may seek assistance from "think tanks" like the Hudson, Stanford, or Rand research institutes. Still others may attend short, intensive training sessions, such as the "Management of Change Institutes" conducted by the authors, or the workshops on "Futures Research Techniques for Corporate Planners," which is sponsored by the University of Southern California. Their Center for Futures Research announcement points out that the program is intended to explore the responsibilities of corporate leaders for the impact of technological change upon the environment, to analyze the new techniques for forecasting major organizational decisions and alternatives, and to develop more effective policies and strategies for change. They examine new tools for change makers, such as, gaming and simulation, technology assessment, social forecasting, trend monitoring system, Delphi method for gathering expert opinion, cross-impact methods, interactive modeling, relevance trees, scenarios, contextual maps, and case studies. In other words, before would-be change agents go tinkering with people's systems and cultures, there is a body of knowledge to be learned and methods to practice.

The how of planned change offers a variety of approaches. It can be as simple as "imagineering" at a staff meeting regarding the likely changes to become realities in a decade based on present trend indicators. Or it may be using the more elaborate Delphi technique, in which a questionnaire is developed with about a dozen likely situations that may occur in the future within a company or a culture. Members or experts may then be asked to rate on a percentage basis the probability of the event happening. Results are then tabulated and median percentages for each item determined. A report of results is circulated among participants, and they are asked to again rate the alternative possibilities after studying peer responses. The number of further administrations is up to the sponsor.

Perhaps one of the most practical methods of planned change for the purposes of this discussion is *force field analysis* developed by the late psychologist, Kurt Lewin. This conceptual model is based upon the understanding of "life space." Each individual lives in his or her own private world, just as employees function within a unique organizational space, and citizens within a distinctive national space. This invisible space is our perceptual *field*. There are many forces operating to influence human behavior—ideals and principles (e.g. profits or service); other people (boss, peers, family); and within ourselves (self image, needs, values, standards, ideals, or expectations that contribute to perception). Lewin's point is that the change maker must unfreeze the present equilibrium between two sets of *forces*—the driving forces for change and the resisting forces trying to maintain the status quo. For this he provides a method of *analysis* that will facilitate the establishment of a new equilibrium. One can use this technique to promote a change in self regarding diet, or to foster a change in an organization, or to lobby for a change in a nation. The United Nations can employ the method for furthering a UNESCO change on a world-wide basis, just as those in religious, educational, or criminal justice systems may affect planned change in their fields of endeavor.

Some of the steps to be taken in the process of force field analysis are:

1. Describe the change—In detail what exactly is planned in terms of the total system?
2. Identify the change—Is it a change in policy, structure, attitude, procedure, program, or combination of these?
3. Self analysis—What is your relation to the change and what needs/ motives are behind your efforts in this regard?
4. Cultural analysis—What is the present environment that requires this change and why will the organization or society (or the individual) benefit from this innovation? What are the likely related effects if this alteration is introduced? That is, the impact on the other interdependent elements in the socio-economic system.
5. Inventory resources—What material and human resources are present that would foster this change if mobilized and channeled? Who are the people likely to promote the change and provide leadership, so the instigator of the change may keep a long profile?
6. Diagnosis of D/R forces—What is the number and strength of the forces, human and nonhuman, which would promote or resist this change? How can the driving forces be mobilized, enforced, and increased in order to change the current equilibrium between driving/restraining forces? How can the resisting forces be weakened, undermined, removed or isolated? In other words, what strategies can be used to increase the driving forces, and decrease the restraining forces, possibly by converting some of the latter into the former? Remember these forces may be physical or psychological, people or events/situations, nature or acts of god.
7. Prepare the case—Why should this change be instituted and what is its rationale? Do investigation, research and development on the case for human and financial investment in this change? Anticipate arguments against the change and develop counterarguments which may be included in this presentation, or held for use at the point of decision making. Include the cost savings and budget factors.
8. Communicate the case—What can be done initially to create a readiness for change by opening up the communication system to

dialog on the proposed change? How can people who have to implement the change be involved in the planning process for it? Who should
get the complete case for the change, and on the basis of the need to
know, how can it be condensed in various versions that are appropriate
to various levels in the system? Remember to use multi, and even mass,
media as appropriate, and to be alert to intercultural communication
differences in the message transmission.

9. Channel resistance—In this tug of war between the pro/con change
   forces, have we allowed for creative dissent to cause modification or
   alteration of the change plan? Are we tailoring the case for change to
   meet the needs of individuals (e.g., for more information, ego support),
   as well as confronting those who have a vested or conflict of interest
   that causes them to oppose the change? Have we missed any strategies
   for gaining support among the reluctant?

10. Project ahead—If the goals of this change are understood and ac-
    cepted, what are some of the probable outcomes to be expected? What
    alternative plans or strategies can be undertaken if the change is re-
    jected or abandoned? What related changes might be promoted to
    strengthen this one? Will we be open to continuous changes upon the
    one being now sponsored? Should a pilot project be considered first?

11. Action plans—How can a final favorable decision be ensured? How
    can the plan for change be implemented—what is to be done, steps to
    be followed? who is to do it? where is it to be done? when is it to be
    done? Once the change is accepted and functioning, how can it be inter-
    nalized and stabilized? That is, how can it be temporarily "frozen" into
    the system and reinforced?

12. Evaluate change—Is the change actually working effectively? Does it
    need further modification or alteration? Should it be replaced? Should
    action research or follow-up study be inaugurated? Realistic fact
    finding may be in order on the feasibility of the change after its in-
    auguration, especially by those who are external consultants or had no
    part in fostering the change.

Cosmopolitan managers may find these tips for failure or success for
fostering change, especially helpful in intercultural situations. They were
prepared by Dr. Dorothy L. Harris, Associate Dean, School of Business and
Management, United States International University in San Diego, California. Failure in planning change will occur if we DON'T

1. Include in the planning process everyone concerned about the change.
2. Avoid discrepancies between words and actions relative to the change.
3. Set realistic time frames for bringing about the change, neither too
   long or short.
4. Integrate the activities involved in the change with available budget
   and resources.

5. Avoid overdependence on external or internal specialists.
6. Avoid data gaps between the change efforts at the top, middle and lower levels of the system.
7. Avoid forcing innovations into old structures incapable of handling them.
8. Avoid simplistic, cook-book solutions to the problems connected with change.
9. Realize that effective relations are a condition for change, not an end.
10. Apply change intervention strategies appropriately.

Success in planning change can be ensured if we DO

1. Identify personnel capable of diagnosing the need for change.
2. Capitalize on the pressures both from within and without the system for the change.
3. Wait for the right time when individuals or institutions are hurting enough to be ready for change.
4. Search the system at all levels for the leadership to effect the change.
5. Promote collaborative efforts between line and staff in planning and implementing the change.
6. Take calculated risks to inaugurate necessary change.
7. Maintain a realistic, long-term perspective relative to the change.
8. See to it that the system rewards people who cooperate in carrying out the change and in establishing a new norm.
9. Collect data on the situation to support the change and eventually evaluate it.
10. Set measurable objectives and targets relative to the change that are both tangible and immediate.

Change is more acceptable *when* it is understood; is related to one's security; results from previously established principles; follows other successful changes; prior changes have been assimilated; new people, departments or programs are involved; personnel share in the planning and benefits; people are trained for it.

Management in a Changing Global Marketplace

A supervisor in a major computer manufacturing firm complained to one of the authors "I am responsible for injecting the computer and state of the art opto-electrical technology into a production environment conceived in the '40s, managed by personnel hired in the '50s, if not earlier, and equipped in the '60s. Is it any wonder that resistance to change is a real, persistent, and major roadblock to the accomplishment of corporate goals." In setting up a training session on change, a key executive of IBM gave this mandate to the external consultant, "Your task is to help our middle managers break out of a mindset that is resistive to change, especially social change; otherwise they are not going to get promoted to top management!" The problem is that many leaders do not realize that they are in a whole new "ballgame"—they continue to play in the old ballpark, by the old rules, and think they have the same type of players.

It's as if there are two cultures in conflict, manifested in the perceptual differences of some in younger and older generations, or in people of any age—some of whom are openminded and others who are closeminded. Almost two decades ago, C.P. Snow put his finger on one aspect of the issue in his classic work, *The Two Cultures and the Scientific Revolution.* In it he referred to the vast communication gulf that exists between scientists and the rest of mankind, heightened by changes caused through the increasing use of electronics, automation, and atomic energy. Snow also referred to the byproduct, another cultural gap between the worldwide poor and rich peoples: it is as if rapid technological change gives truth to the adage, "the rich get richer and the poor get poorer."

Conflict between two cultures may not only occur between a majority and minority culture, or between two microcultures, as seen above in the worlds of the scientist and humanist. It may occur within an organizational culture between and among the various specializations, departments, and subsidiaries. Each of these divisions contains unique subcultures that must build bridges to each other if information is to flow and cooperation to take place. Addressing an international conference of Diebold Europe in 1979, one of the authors (Harris) cited the challenge faced by computer specialists who must manage cultural differences between themselves and general management. Each looks at organizational goals, procedures, and information systems from distinct perspectives. If the specialist is to be effective, then that person must enter into the work or life space of those to be serviced. In most social institutions, the classic separation has occurred between line and staff functions. The interdependence of the two activities suggests that skills in intercultural communication can facilitate mutual collaboration.

The same problem of intercultural relations is faced by every professional, such as physician or attorney, and the client or lay person. The challenge for that professional to move beyond a subculture is compounded when a patient/client is from a minority background.

And, the scientist and technologist must take the same leap of creative imagination into the life space of the laymen, as the affluent must do into the world of the deprived, and the Westerner into the mysterious culture of the Orient and Middle East. To further bridge the chasm between cultures, the cosmopolitan manager in the international arena needs to demonstrate (a) *openness of mind* to consider new perspectives and input, to seek more creative solutions; (b) *flexibility and adaptability in coping* with change and differences; and (c) *sensitiveness and communicativeness* in applying the methods for managing change.

Innovative managers assist people and their social institutions to build upon, yet to transcend, their cultural past. Anthropologist Edward Hall recalled that formerly one stayed relatively close to home so behaviors around us were fairly predictable. But today we constantly interact personally or through media with strangers, often at great distances from our home. Such extensions have widened our range of human contact and caused our "world" to shrink. Multicultural leaders not only have insights and skills for coping with such changed circumstances, but readily share them with their colleagues and systems. To be comfortable with changing cultural diversity and dissonance, we must literally move beyond the perceptions, imprints, and instructions of our own culture.

So, the cosmopolitan manager listens with a sensitive inner ear to catch the voices of the future thereby not missing the beat for the orderly direction of change. Through planning and research, such administrators promote a climate of renewal that avoids obsolescence. Attuned to the knowledge society, innovative leaders realize that ideas today have greater impact on people and their cultures than the invasion of armies. Thus, they seek to comprehend trends, to watch for signs of change, and to stay alert to innovative means for controlling it. These are the means for the *survival of the wisest* in the emerging cyberculture. To use them effectively is in the tradition of our innovative ancestors who climbed down from trees and walked upright, who formed tools and used tree branches as levers, who put fire to work and harnessed power, who substituted brain for brawn, who created automation and cybernation, who flew to the moon and back!

References

Beckard, R., and R.T. Harris, *Organizational Transitions*. Reading, Mass.: Addison-Wesley, 1977.

Cornish, E. (ed.), *The Study of the Future: An Introduction to the Art and Science of Shaping Tomorrow's World*. Washington: World Future Society, 1977.

Diebold, J., *Man and Computer: Technology as an Agent of Social Change*. New York: Fred. A. Praeger, 1969.

Harris, P., *Effective Management of Change*. Pittsburgh: Westinghouse Learning Corp., 1976. (Available from Harris International, Box 2321, LaJolla, Ca. 92038.)

Jantsch, E. and C.H. Waddington, *Evolution and Consciousness: Human Systems in Transition*. Reading, Mass.: Addison-Wesley, 1976.

Kahn, H., et al, *The Next 200 Years: A Scenario for America and the World*. New York: Wm. Morrow & Co. 1976.

Linstone, H. and M. Turoff, *The Delphi Method: Techniques and Applications*. Reading, Mass.: Addison-Wesley, 1975.

Lippitt, G. *Visualizing change.* LaJolla, Ca.: University Assoc./NTL Resources, 1973.

Meadow, P. *Culture of Industrial Man.* Cambridge, Mass.: Schenkman Publishing, 1974.

Ogilvy, J. *Many Dimensional Man: Decentralizing Self, Society and the Sacred.* New York: Oxford Univ. Press, 1977.

Roeber, R. *The Organization in a Changing Environment.* Reading Mass.: Addison-Wesley, 1973.

Sheehy, G. *Passages: Predictable Crises of Adult Life.* New York: E.P. Dutton, 1976.

Spindler, L. *Culture, Change and Modernization.* San Francisco: Holt, Rinehart & Winston, 1977.

Strauss, B. and Stowe, M.E. *How to Get Things Changed: A Handbook for Tackling Community Problems.* Garden City, N.Y.: Doubleday & Co., 1974.

World Future Society. *The Future: A Guide to Information Sources.* Washington: Book Service/World Future Society, 1977.

4
The Manager
As a Cultural Transmitter

In the opening pages of their book *Global Reach*, Richard Barnet and Ronald Muller tell us "the managers of the world's corporate giants proclaim their faith that where conquest has failed, business can succeed." If the end point of this "conquest" is peace and a more generous distribution of the limited resources to all persons, we support the conquest. Barnet and Muller point out that the source of extraordinary power of these managers comes not

> ...from the barrel of a gun but from control of creating wealth on a worldwide scale....In the process of developing a new world, the managers of firms like GM, IBM, Pepsico, GE, Pfizer, Shell, Volkswagon, Exxon, and a few hundred others are making daily business decisions which have more impact than those of most sovereign governments on where people live; what work, if any, they will do; what they will eat, drink, and wear; what sorts of knowledge schools and universities will encourage; and what kind of society their children will inherit.

These managers have, indeed, tremendous power. Their traditional business skills are no longer sufficient of themselves. The world view that is required of them was probably not dreamed of by their predecessors and their success or failure working in multicultural environments depends upon awareness and understanding of fundamental differences in culture. As an area of study for the international manager, it is relatively new. This is due to a variety of factors including a large domestic market, a diverse resource base that permitted a high degree of self-sufficiency and, in many cases, the lack of skill and awareness of the opportunities available in the international area. This is changing as many U.S. corporations are entering or expanding international operations.

As a result, multinational managers are required to meet, socialize, and negotiate with foreign businessmen and government officials on a regular basis. A requirement that is common to most of their activities is that the manager be able to communicate and work with persons who have grown up and who have been socialized in a different cultural environment. Customs, values, life styles, beliefs, management practices and most other important aspects of one's personal and professional life are therefore different. For the manager to be effective he must be aware of the many beliefs and values that underlie his or her country's business practices, management techniques, and strategies. These beliefs and values are so much a part of many managers' culture that they take them for granted and without challenge. They do not realize that many are culturally conditioned. Awareness of such values and assumptions is critical for managers who wish to transfer technology to another culture. This chapter will explore some of the beliefs, values, and assumptions that underlie U.S. management techniques and principles and contrast these with the values and assumptions underlying the management techniques of other cultures. Following this analysis, we shall suggest how an international manager, using the approach of cultural synergy, can integrate the contrasting values within the organization. Finally, we shall describe some of the skills found to be necessary for an American manager who wishes successfully to transfer technology to others in a different culture and society.

A recent commencement speech at Harvard University by Alexander Solzhenitsyn stirred considerable comment and reflection. He seemingly attacked American democracy which, in his opinion, has ensured that "mediocrity triumphs." He criticized the U.S. for a "deadline of courage" particularly "among the ruling groups and the intellectual elite." He spoke of the U.S. devotion to the law which paralyzes the country's ability to "defend itself." He characterized the Western press as being absorbed with "gossip, nonsense, vain talk." The response of Americans to this speech has ranged from general agreement to rejection of his analysis and Solzhenitsyn himself as an outsider who is not qualified to discuss this culture and society. Perhaps the following discussion aimed at managers will also apply to a certain extent to Solzhenitsyn.

Cultural Self-Awareness

When people communicate with one another they make certain assumptions about the process of perceiving, judging, thinking, and reasoning patterns of each other. They make these assumptions usually "out-of-awareness" or without realizing they are making them. When the assumptions are correct there is ease of communication—when they are incorrect, misunderstandings and miscommunication often result.

The most common assumption that is made by persons who are communicating with one another is one called *projective cognitive similarity*— that is, they assume that the other perceives, judges, thinks, and reasons the same way he does. Identical twins communicate with ease. Persons from the same culture but with a different education, age, background, and experience often find communication difficult. American managers communicating with managers from other cultures experience greater difficulties in communication than with managers from their own culture. However, it is possible that American managers share more interests and terms with other members of the world managerial subculture than with their own workers or union leaders. The effects of our cultural conditioning are so pervasive that people whose experience has been limited to the rules of one culture have difficulty understanding communication based on another set of rules.

An excerpt from the diary of the captain of the U.S. ping-pong team during his visit to the People's Republic of China in 1971 will illustrate this point. The example is quoted by Alfred Kraemer in his article, "A Cultural Self-Awareness Approach to Improving Intercultural Communication Skills" and is as follows:

> I seemed to have some kind of a communication gap with many of the Chinese I met. I had a number of talks, for example, with our interpreter, but we sometimes had difficulty getting through to each other. He spoke excellent English, and I used very simple words, but he often apologized and said I should get a better interpreter because "I just don't understand what you are saying." I used words like "individual" and "unique." They are words he knows, but he couldn't relate them to the idea of doing what you want to do. "Do what I want to do?" one puzzled Chinese asked me. He looked terribly confused, as if to say, "How do you do that?" I guess in China you have to do what the chairman tells you to do and then everything is cool and happy.

A number of comments can be made about his diary entry, but the most important is that the American's apparently simple question, "But what do you want to do?" implies certain assumptions about the cognitions of the Chinese interpreter. That is, that the Chinese interpreter understood and valued the idea of individual choice. However, this assumption was probably not valid, because individualism, as known and practiced in the United States, is not well understood or valued by the people of The People's Republic of China. The American was not able to see the outward cultural expression of the Chinese society and in order to do this, the American must fully comprehend the values and principles of his own culture.

In order to create cultural synergistic solutions to management problems or to transfer management techniques to another culture, a U.S. manager must identify and understand what is American about America, what common cultural traits are shared by Americans, and what values and assumptions are the foundation for their management practices. Mark Twain stated, "The only distinguishing characteristic of the American character that I've been able to discover is a fondness for ice water." There is much more.

Awareness of such cultural influences is essential for any manager who seeks to transfer management concepts or technology. Depending on the

(Text continued on page 48.)

Table 4-1
U.S. Values and Possible Alternatives

Aspects* of U.S. Culture	Alternative Aspect	Examples of Management Function Affected
The individual can influence the future (where there is a will there is a way).	Life follows a preordained course and human action is determined by the will of God.	Planning and scheduling
The individual can change and improve the environment.	People are intended to adjust to the physical environment rather than to alter it.	Organizational environment morale, and productivity
An individual should be realistic in his aspirations.	Ideals are to be pursued regardless of what is "reasonable."	Goal setting career development
We must work hard to accomplish our objectives (Puritan ethic).	Hard work is not the only prerequisite for success. Wisdom, luck and time are also required.	Motivation and reward system
Commitments should be honored (people will do what they say they will do).	A commitment may be superseded by a conflicting request or an agreement may only signify intention and have little or no relationship to the capacity of performance.	Negotiating and bargaining
One should effectively use one's time (time is money which can be saved or wasted).	Schedules are important but only in relation to other priorities.	Long and short range planning
A primary obligation of an an employee is to the organization.	The individual employee has a primary obligation to his family and friends.	Loyalty, commitment, and motivation
The employer or employee can terminate their relationship.	Employment is for a lifetime.	Motivation and commitment to the company
A person can only work for one company at a time, (man cannot serve two masters).	Personal contributions to individuals who represent an enterprise are acceptable.	Ethical issues, conflict of interest
The best qualified persons should be given the positions available.	Family considerations, friendship, and other considerations should not determine employment practices.	Employment, promotions, recruiting, selection, and reward
A person can be removed if he does not perform well.	The removal of a person from a position involves a great loss of prestige and will be rarely done.	Promotion
All levels of management are open to qualified individuals (an office boy can rise to become company president).	Education or family ties are the primary vehicles for mobility.	Employment practices and promotion

Table 4-1 (Continued)
U.S. Values and Possible Alternatives

Aspects* of U.S. Culture	Alternative Aspect	Examples of Management Function Affected
Intuitive aspects of decision-making should be reduced and efforts should be devoted to gathering relevant information.	Decisions are expressions of wisdom by the person in authority and any questioning would imply a lack of confidence in his judgment.	Decision-making process
Data should be accurate.	Accurate data is not as highly valued.	Record-keeping
Company information should be available to anyone who needs it within the organization.	Withholding information to gain or maintain power is acceptable.	Organization communication, managerial style
Each person is expected to have an opinion and to express it freely even if his views do not agree with his colleagues.	Deference is to be given to persons in power or authority and to offer judgment that is not in support of the ideas of one's superiors is unthinkable.	Communications, organizational relations
A decision-maker is expected to consult persons who can contribute useful information to the area being considered.	Decisions may be made by those in authority and others need not be consulted.	Decision-making, leadership
Employees will work hard to improve their position in the company.	Personal ambition is frowned upon.	Selection and promotion
Competition stimulates high performance.	Competition leads to unbalances and leads to disharmony.	Career development and marketing
A person is expected to do whatever is necessary to get the job done (one must be willing to get one's hands dirty).	Various kinds of work are accorded low or high status and some work may be below one's "dignity" or place in the organization.	Assignment of tasks performance, and organizational effectiveness
Change is considered an improvement and a dynamic reality.	Tradition is revered and the power of the ruling group is founded on the continuation of a stable structure.	Planning, morale and organization development
What works is important.	Symbols and the process are more important than the end point.	Communication, planning, quality control
Persons and systems are evaluated.	Persons are evaluated but in such a way that individuals not highly evaluated will not be embarrassed or caused to "lose face."	Rewards and promotion, performance evaluation and accountability

Aspect here refers to a belief, value, attitude or assumption which is a part of culture in that it is shared by a large number of persons in any culture.

cultures, there may be an overlap of values in a specific area, and therefore, the problems related to transferring ideas will be minimal. However, in some instances the gap will be significant and cause serious problems. Table 4-1 on pages 46 and 47 identifies a number of U.S. values with possible alternatives. Examples of how the cultural system might influence management are also indicated in the third column.

The order of the values and the sequence is not important. They are not mutually exclusive nor comprehensive. The ideas will be useful for a manager who will be working in a multicultural environment in the U.S. or another country. They will also be helpful to any foreign manager who is trying to understand U.S. managers and U.S. management techniques.

As indicated earlier, the purpose is not only to compare cultural values affecting management practices in culture X with those in culture Y. The purpose is also to provide a basis whereby a manager might "synergistically" relate to managers trained in another cultural system and management practices developed in other cultures. More on cultural specifics that affect international business is provided in Chapters 13-19.

The aspects of the U.S. presented in Table 4-1 have been taken from the author's own experience and from the following authors whose works are cited in the bibliography following this chapter: Theodore O. Wallin, Edward C. Stewart, William H. Newman, and Alfred J. Kraemer.

Table 4-1 illustrates how the cultural system or differences in attitude, values, assumptions, personal beliefs, interpersonal relationships, social and organizational structure affect the traditional management functions of decision-making, promotion, recruitment and development, organizing, planning, and motivation.

Given these differences, and given their profound effect upon management's functions, the international manager is constantly faced with a complex challenge: How to accommodate (and even take advantage of) these differences within the organization; and how are the diverse people in the organization going to execute their essential functions?

Cultural Synergy

Let us begin with an approach to problem-solving cultural differences in management techniques. Management is often seen as *American* management. And when we discuss international management or management systems in Japan or in the U.S. for example, we talk about *comparative* management. We ask questions such as, "How do they do it in the U.S.?" and "How do they make decisions in Japan?" We very often then attempt to discover which system is better. We look at the Japanese system and the American system and make comparisons between the two. In this age of cultural interdependence, however, there are multicultural organizations in Japan and the U.S., and in most other countries, which have members of both cultures present.

In this case, there are two basic ways to approach the interaction. One is utilizing a cultural dominance model whereby one cultural system dominates the other within the organizations. The decision, implicit or explicit, is made that the organization is either predominately American or Japanese, for example, and the organization structure and management techniques are either American or Japanese.

An alternative approach is one which is called *cultural synergy*. In the struggle for culturally synergistic solutions, an analysis of the cultures is made in terms of similarities and differences between Japan and the United States but instead of making a decision at this time—for example, does the organization utilize the American system of hiring or do we use the Japanese system of long-term employment?—the organization attempts to create a third culture solution. This utilizes aspects of both Japan and the United States and it requires a profound understanding of both cultures in order to produce integrative solutions from both cultures so that the needs and aspirations of the individuals and the organization might be met to the maximum degree possible. Examples of this approach include the Japanese managed American companies on the West Coast of the United States and the Japanese companies in Japan which are modifying their management systems as a function of interactions with American managers. Figure 4-1 on page 50 outlines the apporach to cultural synergism using Japan and the United States as examples.

In a search for aspects of another cultures management system that might be utilized by an international manager, the following steps are suggested:

1. Identify the management problems (e.g., the decision-making process).
2. Identify the area in which the problem is detrimental to the individual or the organization (e.g., the implementation of a decision in many U.S. organizations is time consuming).
3. Identify the aspects of another culture's management system that might be useful if implemented (e.g., the discussion phase of decision-making in Japanese organizations is slower but involves all persons affected by the decision—the implementation phase is therefore much smoother and less time consuming).
4. Determine a strategy for implementation.

Skills Necessary for Overseas Success

Let us now consider the question of being an effective manager in an overseas assignment. In the cross-cultural management literature, there is a lack of precise statements or criteria concerning the factors that are related to cross-cultural adaptation and effectiveness. Paul Illman in his book, *Selecting and Developing Overseas Managers*, correctly states that "effective screening of candidates at home will often prevent failures abroad." He continues and states that personality, intolerance, the inability to adjust, and having a demeanor of superiority are main causes for failure and technical

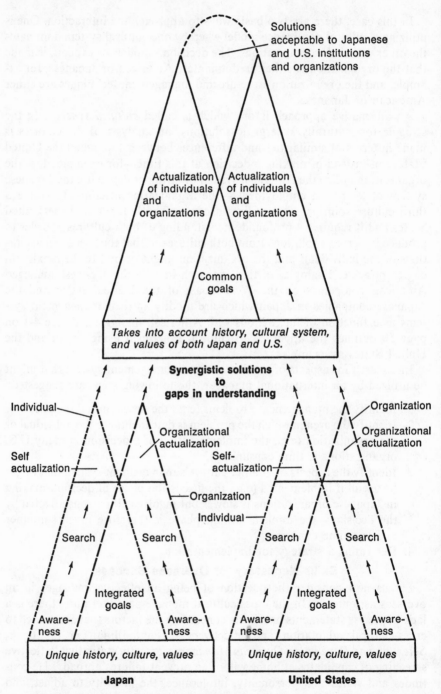

Figure 4-1. This diagram illustrates an approach to cultural synergism using Japan and the United States as examples.

skills, managerial skills, and human skills are the basis for success. Studies recently completed by Brent Ruben and others at the Institute for Communication Studies at Rutgers University have begun to identify the factors that are associated with "effectiveness" in a multicultural environment. They conceptualize the sojourner or overseas manager as a teacher possessing knowledge and skills that he wishes to share or transmit to others. As a teacher, one must have the knowledge and skills in the area of inquiry or study and one must also be able to communicate these understandings to other persons in such a way that they will be able to accept and use them. Cross-cultural management effectiveness, therefore, involves job and intercultural communication competence. The latter involves participation and skills transfer. Consider the following case:

> Mr. Rose has recently accepted a position as a technical adviser in a country in the Middle East. His company has been working in that country for a number of years and has recently signed a five-year extension of a program that was originally conceived to take five years.
>
> Mr. Rose is looking forward to his assignment. He is technically qualified, highly motivated, and his work experiences and previous success convince him there will be few problems that he cannot handle satisfactorily.
>
> Shortly, after arriving, however, he experiences frustrations and undue delays. He is working with Mr. Z., a host national, and together they have responsibilities for one aspect of the project. Working with Mr. Z. is not satisfying and Mr. Rose seriously begins to question the competence and training of Mr. Z.
>
> Mr. Rose tried to get to know Mr. Z. in an effort to determine ways of determining the problem but his attempts were not successful.
>
> From his company in the United States, Mr. Rose is receiving telexes several times a day as the project had fallen considerably behind schedule. They also became a source of frustration for Mr. Rose and he began to feel in the middle of two forces pulling in the opposite direction. In his opinion, Mr. Z. and many of his colleagues were not highly proficient or motivated to accomplish the tasks. His superiors back home did not understand or accept this situation and pressured him to adhere more closely to the timetables set earlier.
>
> Mr. Rose made a decision that the only way he could get the job done was to do it himself. He gradually assumed more responsibility and within a matter of two months the original timetable was being followed more closely.

The important question, as a manager in a foreign country, is Mr. Rose succeeding or failing? If one considers Mr. Rose's role as "getting the job done" then we could say that he was succeeding. However, if one takes the view that he was also a teacher and expected to communicate skills and transfer his knowledge, he was not doing very well.

A most unfortunate consequence also related to the decision of Mr. Rose to do it himself is the probable alienation of Mr. Z. and the almost certain reinforcement of the view that U.S. nationals in that country are often unfriendly, insensitive, and are not really too interested in the welfare and development of the country or the people.

Cross-cultural communication behaviors or skills can be learned, so a manager can function effectively with host nationals. We are making important distinctions between cognitive competency or awareness and behavioral competency at this time. Behavioral competency is the ability to demonstrate or use the skills. Cognitive competency is the intellectual awareness or knowledge base.

The following skills have been identified by Ruben as being associated with effectiveness in a multicultural environment in transferring knowledge. We shall refer to these skills as abilities. Most of these are common sense but often not demonstrated by multinational managers or supervisors of minority employees in one's own culture.

Respect. The ability to express respect for others is an important part of effective relations in every country. All people like to believe and feel that others respect them, their ideas and their accomplishments. However, it is difficult to know how to communicate respect to persons from another culture. The following are questions that should be considered in the case of an overseas' manager working in another culture with persons from that culture. What is the importance of age in communicating respect? What is the significance of manner of speaking? Do you speak only when spoken to? What gestures express respect? What kind of eye contact expresses respect? What constitutes "personal questions" as an invasion of privacy and a lack of respect? These are only a few of the many questions which could be generated relating to the important question, "How do I demonstrate that I respect the people I am working with?"

Tolerating Ambiguity. This refers to the ability to react to new, different, and at times, unpredictable situations with little visible discomfort or irritation. Excessive discomfort often leads to frustration and hostility and this is not conducive to effective interpersonal relationships with persons from other cultures. Learning to manage the feelings associated with ambiguity is a skill associated with adaptation to a new environment and effectively working with managers who have a different set of values.

Relating to People. Many Western managers, concerned with getting the job done, are overly concerned with the task side of their jobs. In transferring skills and knowledge to persons in another culture, there is a requirement of getting the job done but also the ability to get it done in such a way that people feel a part of the completed project and have benefited from being involved. Too much concern for getting the job done and neglect of "people maintenance" can lead to failure in transferring skills.

Being Nonjudgmental. Most people like to feel that what they say and do is not being judged by others without having the opportunity of fully explaining themselves. The ability to withhold judgment and remain objective until one has enough information requires an understanding of the other's point of view and is an important skill.

Personalizing One's Observations. As has been indicated many times, different people explain the world around them in different terms. A manager should realize that his or her knowledge and perceptions are valid only for self and not for the rest of the world. Thus, one would be able to personalize observations, be more tentative in conclusions and demonstrate a communication competence that what is "right" or "true" in one culture is not "right" or "true" in another. As one author said, "this is my way, what is your way? There is no 'the' way."

Empathy. This is the ability to "put yourself in another's shoes." In this context, most people are attracted to and work well with managers who seem to be able to understand things from their point of view. Mr. Rose did not seem to have much empathy for Mr. Z.

Persistence. This is an important skill for effective cross-cultural functioning, for a variety of reasons. The multinational manager may not be successful the first time and he may not be able to get things done immediately, but with patience and perserverance, the task can be accomplished.

Summary

These skills are associated with effective managing and transferring knowledge in a different culture. To the degree that managers possess these skills, they will be effective in working in a multicultural environment. Chapters 6, 9, and 12 contain more information in this area.

When working in an overseas environment as a manager, one must consider the underlying values or premises of a culture in order to function effectively. Unless one appreciates existing values in a cultural situation, and their ability to influence thought and action, one's own value system may become "cultural blinders" that prevent understanding and appreciation of other cultures.

References

Barnett, R.J. and R.E. Muller, *Global Reach: The Power of the Multinational Corporation.* New York: Simon and Schuster, 1974.

Brewer, M.B. and D.T. Campbell, *Ethnocentrism and Intergroup Attitudes.* New York: Wiley, 1976.

Illman, Paul E., *Selecting and Developing Overseas Managers.* New York, New York: Amacom, 1976.

Kraemer, Alfred J., "A Cultural Self Awareness Approach to Improving Intercultural Communication Skills," HUMRRO Professional Paper 5-73, March, 1973.

Massie, Joseph L. and Luytjes, J., *Management in an International Context* (ed.), New York: Harper and Row, 1972.

Newman, William H., *Cultural Assumptions Underlying U.S. Management Concepts*, in Massie, Joseph L. and Luytjes, J. *Management in an International Context* (ed.) New York: Harper and Row, 1972.

Ruben, Brent R., Lawrence R. Ashling and Daniel J. Kealey, *Cross-Cultural Effectiveness Intercultural Communication.* State of the Art Review, David S. Hoopes (ed.), Washington, D.C.: SIETAR, 1977.

Stewart, Edward C., *American Cultural Patterns: A Cross-Cultural Perspective.* SIETAR, 1976.

Triandis, H.C., *Interpersonal Behavior.* Monterrey, California: Brooks/ Cole, 1976.

Wallin, Theodore O., *The International Executive's Baggage: Cultural Values of the American Frontier,* MSU Business Topics Spring, 1976.

5

Understanding
Cultural Differences

Analyzing Cultural Influences

Our very way of thinking can be culturally conditioned. Eastern cultures analyze in ideograms or visualizations, whereas Western cultures tend to use concepts. Because a concept is a general notion or idea that combines the characteristics known about a subject, it provides a framework for thinking or analyzing a particular topic or experience. For example, here are actual excerpts from new stories, which can be analyzed in a particular conceptual context:

Princeton, N.J.—Girls have a hard time assuming leadership roles because there are few woman leaders to model themselves after and society treats such females as deviants, report researchers from the Educational Testing Service. . . .In classroom discussions, boys' ideas are traditionally given greater weight than girls, and teachers seldom assign females to classroom leadership roles. Such sex stereotypes need to be reversed the researchers maintain.

Quinhagak, Alaska—Natives in rural Alaska are caught in a grinding collision between two worlds, modern and traditional. Increasingly they fear that their subsistence-centered life style, the basis of their culture, will be crushed by the advancing technological society. Subsistence for such Eskimos goes beyond the definition proposed in Congress: "The customary and traditional uses in Alaska of wild, renewable resources for direct personal or family consumption as food, clothing, shelter, fuel, tools, transportation." For the native subsistence is more than support, it is really an entire way of life. It is not just food for the stomach, it is food for the soul.

Tokyo, Japan—The executives of McDonald's hamburger restaurant realized when they went into business here eight years ago that they had to adapt to Japanese attitudes rather than merely replicate their American operations. Therefore, the first McDonald's was set up in a prestigious location in order to impress the Japanese, who would have

55

considered it a second-class enterprise had it been started in the suburbs. McDonald's efforts here have been successful because they sought to understand Japanese behavior, and coped effectively with Japan's different way of doing things.

New York, N.Y.—The American businessman overseas often operates under demanding conditions. He suffers the hardship of giving up cold martinis for warm beer as one way to integrate into the English business community. He must keep his mind on business during the rounds of Geisha houses as a prelude to concluding a deal in Japan. And if he operates in Spain, he must brace himself for the rigors of 11 p.m. dinners and negotiations that may continue into the small hours of the morning!

What, then, do all these press accounts have in common which can make these commentaries more meaningful? Obviously, the concept of *culture*. It is a very useful tool for understanding human behavior around the globe, as well as within our own country.

Insights about this concept come largely from the behavioral sciences of sociology, psychology, and anthropology. Such social sciences study and inform us about how people behave, why they behave as they do, and what the relationship is between human behavior and the environment. Each of us tend to view other people's behavior in the context of our own background, that is, we look at others from the perspective of our own "little world" and are thus subjective. Cultural anthropology is particularly helpful in balancing our perspective by providing objective ways for analyzing and appreciating cultural similarities and dissimilarities. For example, in our society poverty is considered a handicap and a condition to be overcome; whereas in other parts of the world poverty is taken for granted, or even is seen by some as a special blessing.

In essence, human beings create culture or their social environment, as an adaptation to their physical or biological environment. Customs, practices, and traditions for survival and development are thus passed along from generation to generation among a particular people. In time, the group or race become unconscious of the origin of this fund of wisdom. Subsequent generations are conditioned to accept such "truths" about life around them, certain taboos and values are established, and in a multitude of ways people are informed of the "accepted" behavior for living in that society. Culture influences and is influenced by every facet of human activity.

Individuals are strongly inclined to accept and believe what their culture tells them. We are affected by the common lore of the community in which we are raised and reside, regardless of the objective validity of this input and imprint. We tend to ignore or block out that which is contrary to the cultural "truth" or conflicts with our beliefs. This is often the basis for prejudice among members of other groups, for refusing to change when cherished notions are challenged. It can become a real problem when a culture and its way of thinking lag behind new discoveries and realities. Scientific and technological advances, for instance, have outrun common cultural teachings for masses of people. This is one of the byproducts of the acceleration of change, and results in a culture gap.

Modern managers operate in multicultural settings, and need to understand what goes into the making of a culture and to develop skills in dealing with such differences. In that way their behavior will be more appropriate, sensitive, and consistent regardless of the cultural group with whom they interact. To accomplish such a goal, then, it becomes important to know the meaning of culture and the ways to analyze its diverse manifestations.

Parameters of Culture

Culture is the unique life style of a particular group of people. Unlike good manners, it is not something possessed by some and not by others—it is possessed by all human beings and is in that sense, a unifying factor. The pygmies of Africa and the Marines in the United States share distinctive forms of it. Although we all share some aspects of culture, such as language and processing food, the very diversity in human behavior is explained somewhat because we all do not belong to the same culture. At first it seems contradictory—what is one man's food in one culture, is repugnant in another culture. Thus, to facilitate intercultural relations, and delimit distortions, we must move beyond our own cultural heritage into the world of the other. That is, we should not be so locked into our own cultural way of thinking as to be unable to share other cultures.

Culture is also communicable knowledge, learned behavioral traits that are shared by participants in a social group and manifested in their institutions and artifacts. E.B. Taylor, the father of cultural anthropology defined it this way: "that complex whole which includes knowledge, belief, art, morals, law, customs, and other capabilities or habits acquired by members of a society." Its common understandings are both learned and absorbed. Each cultural group produces its own special answers to life challenges like birth, growth, social relations, and even death. As a people adjust to the peculiar circumstances in which they find themselves on this earth, a routine of daily living emerges for bathing, dressing, eating, working, playing, and sleeping. When life is formalized for humans on space stations or other planets, the species will adapt and new forms of culture will emerge.

Humans create culture not only as an adaptive mechanism to their biological or geophysical environment, but as a means of contributing to our social evolution. Our heredity combines both genes and culture traits, which influence one another. Just as the geophysical environment in which we are reared influences us, so too our social institutions—home, school, church, and government—provide a cultural context that impacts upon our behavior. The paradox of culture is evident in the matter of life cycle—all humans have some means for designating the different stages of growth and development, but particular cultures interpret these phases differently. Thus, in Western culture we often divide life into infancy, childhood, adolescence, adulthood, and possibly old age. Yet, in other societies such progression is designated by a term fitting the new role. The Andaman Islanders give a young girl a "flower name" at puberty, which she keeps until she bears her first child and is again renamed. Among the Chaga of East Africa, a new baby is referred to by a word meaning "incomplete" (literally, "without teeth"); after teeth are cut, the individual child becomes "the little one who fills the lap"; the next stage is considered infancy and lasts for approximately three years to be followed by a fourth period from age four to fifteen years old; at fifteen, the person is referred to as youth or maiden. In the Philippines, the Kalingas have ten stages of growth marked by designations connected with one's capabilities—"he creeps," "she can be sent on errands," and so forth. Variety in culture becomes the "spice of life" for earth peoples.

Culture helps us to make sense out of that part of the planet or space inhabited by us. The place is foreign only to strangers, not to those who inhabit it. Culture facilitates living by providing ready-made solutions to problems, by establishing patterns of relations, and ways for preserving group cohesion and consensus. There are many roadmaps, or different approaches for analyzing and categorizing a culture to make it more understandable and less threatening.

Characteristics of Culture

Because culture gives a people identity, how can we identify those aspects of it that make a people so distinct? One way is by studying the group in terms of certain categories.

Communication and Language. The communication system, verbal and nonverbal distinguishes one group from another. Apart from the multitude of "foreign" languages, some nations have fifteen or more major spoken languages (within one language group there are dialects, accents, slang, jargon, and other such variations). Furthermore, the meanings given to gestures, for example, often differ by culture. So while body language may be universal, its manifestation differs by locality. Subcultures, such as the military, have terminology and signals that cut across national boundaries (such as a salute, or the rank system).

Dress and Appearance. This includes the outward garments and adornments, or lack thereof, as well as body decorations that tend to be distinctive by culture. We have been aware of the Japanese kimono, the African headdress, the Englishman's bowler and umbrella, the Polynesian sarong, and the American Indian headband. Some tribes smear their faces for battle, while some women use cosmetics to manifest beauty. Many subcultures wear distinctive clothing—the "organization-man look" of business, the jeans of the youth culture throughout the world, and uniforms that segregate everyone from students to police. In the military microculture, customs and regulations determine dress of the day, length of hair, equipment to be worn, and so forth. In colonial times, the U.S. Marines wore long hair, dressed in pantaloons, and carried muskets—yes, many aspects of culture eventually do change!

Food and Feeding Habits. The manner in which food is selected, prepared, presented, and eaten often differs by culture. One man's pet is another person's delicacy—dog anyone? Americans love beef, yet it is forbidden to Hindus, while the forbidden food in Moslem and Jewish culture is normally pork, eaten extensively by the Chinese and others. In large cosmopolitan cities, restaurants often cater to diverse diets and offer "national" dishes to meet varying cultural tastes. Feeding habits also differ, and the range goes from hands and chop sticks to full sets of cutlery. Even when cultures use a utensil such as a fork, one can distinguish a European from an American by which hand holds the implement. Subcultures, too, can be analyzed from this perspective, such as the executive's dining room, the soldier's mess, the worker's hero or submarine sandwich, or the ladies' tea room, and the vegetarian's restaurant.

Time and Time Consciousness. Sense of time differs by culture, so that some are exact and others are relative. Generally, Germans are precise about the clock, while many Latins are more casual—"mañana." In some cultures, promptness is determined by age or status—thus, in some countries, subordinates are expected on time at staff meetings, but the boss is the last to arrive. Some subcultures, like the military, have their own time system of twenty-four hours—one p.m. civilian time, becomes 1300 hours in military time. In such cultures, promptness is rewarded, and in battles, the watches are synchronized. Yet there are natives in some other cultures who do not bother with hours or minutes, but manage their days by sunrise and sunset.

Time, in the sense of seasons of the year, varies by culture. Some areas of the world think in terms of winter, spring, summer, and fall, but for others the more meaningful designations may be rainy or dry seasons. In the United States, for example, the East and Midwest may be very conscious of the four seasons, while those in the West or Southwest tend to ignore such designations—Californians are more concerned with rainy months and mud slides, or dry months and forest fires.

Rewards and Recognitions. Another way of observing a culture is to note the manner and method for proffering praise for good and brave deeds, length of service, or some other types of accomplishment. When warriors are initiated into some tribes, body tattoes are then permitted—other recognitions for such fighters of valor might be war bonnets, belts of scalps, or even jewelry. At one time, long pants were a sign of maturity allowed the growing boy at a certain age. In the business subculture, there are the rewards of executive privileges—testimonial dinners and expense accounts. But in the police microculture, it may be commendations, citations, medals. The military display rank and position, as well as achievement, on their uniforms through stripes, bars, eagles, ribbons, and so forth. The celebration of achievement through eating can vary by culture—fiesta, luau, retirement dinner.

Relationships. Cultures fix human and organizational relationships by age, sex, status, and degree of kindred, as well as by wealth, power, and wisdom. The family unit is the most common expression of this characteristic, and the arrangement may go from small to large—in a Hindu household, the joint family includes under one roof, mother, father, children, parents, uncles, aunts, and cousins. In fact, one's physical location in such houses may also be determined—males on one side, females on the other. There are some places in which the accepted marriage relationship is monogamy, while in other cultures it may be polygamy or polyandry (one wife, several husbands). In some cultures, the authoritarian figure in the family is the head male, and this fixed relationship is then extended from home to community, and explains why some societies prefer to have a dictator head up the national family. Relationships between and among people vary by category—in some cultures, the elderly hold a place of high honor, whereas in others they are ignored; in some cultures, women must wear veils and appear deferential, while in others the female is considered the equal, if not the superior of the male. Books are written on business relationships, both at home and when abroad—in fact, one entitled, *The Man in the Gray Flannel Suit* was even made into a motion picture. The military subculture has a classic determination of relationships by rank or protocol, such as the relationships between officers and enlisted personnel. Even off duty, when on base, the recreational facilities are segregated for officers, noncommissioned, and enlisted personnel. The formalization of relationships is evident in some religious subcultures with titles such as "reverend," "guru," "pastor," "rabbi," or "bishop."

Values and Norms. The need systems of cultures vary, as do the priorities they attach to certain behavior in the group. Those operating on a survival level value the gathering of food, adequate covering and shelter; while those with high security needs value material things, money, job titles, as well as law and order. America is a country in the midst of a values revolution as the children of the depression days give way to the children of affluence who are concerned for higher values, like the quality of life, self fulfillment, and meaning in experiences. It is interesting to note that in some Pacific Island cultures, that as your status becomes higher, you are expected to give away or share more of your personal belongings.

In any event, from its value system, a culture sets norms of behavior for that society. These acceptable standards for membership may range from the work ethic or pleasure to absolute obedience or permissiveness for children; from rigid submission of the wife to her husband to women's total liberation. As anthropologist Ina Brown reminds us, "People in different cultures are pleased, concerned, annoyed, or embarrassed about different things because they perceive situations in terms of different sets of premises." Because conventions are learned, some cultures demand honesty with members of one's own group, but accept a more relaxed standard with strangers. Some of these conventions are expressed in gift-giving; rituals for birth, death, and marriage; guidelines for privacy, showing respect or deference, expressing good manners and so forth.

Sense of Self and Space. The comfort one has with self can be expressed differently by culture. Self-identity and appreciation can be manifested by humble bearing in one place, while another calls for macho behavior; a sense of independence and creativity is countered in other cultures by group cooperation and conformity. Representatives of some cultures, such as Americans, have a sense of space that requires more distance between the individual and others, while Latins and Vietnamese want to get much closer, almost familiar. Some cultures are very structured and formal, while others are more flexible and informal. Some cultures are very closed and determine one's place very precisely, while others are more open and changing. Each culture validates self in a unique way.

Mental Process and Learning. Some cultures emphasize one aspect of brain development over another, so that one may observe striking differences in the way people think and learn. Anthropologist Edward Hall maintains that the mind is internalized culture, and the process involves how a people organizes and processes information. Life in a particular locale defines the rewards and punishment for learning or not learning certain information or in a certain way, and this is confirmed and reinforced by the culture there. Thus, Germans stress logic, while the Japanese and the Navajo reject the Western system. Logic for a Hopi Indian is based on preserving the integrity of their social system and all the relationships connected with it. Some cultures favor abstract thinking and conceptualization, while others prefer rote memory and learning. What seems to be universal is that each culture has a reasoning process, but then each manifests the process in its own distinctive way.

Beliefs and Attitudes. Possibly the most difficult classification is ascertaining the major belief themes of a people, and how this and other factors influence their attitudes toward themselves, others, and what happens in their world. People in all cultures seem to have a concern for the supernatural that is evident in their religions and religious practices. Primitive cultures, for example, have a belief in spiritual beings labeled by us as "animism." In the history of human development there is an evident evolution in our spiritual sense until today many moderns use terms like "cosmic consciousness" to indicate their belief in the transcendental powers. Between these two extremes in the spiritual continuum, religious traditions in various cultures consciously or unconsciously influence our attitudes toward life, death, and the hereafter. Western culture seems to be largely influenced by the Judeo-Christian-Islamic traditions, while Eastern or Oriental cultures seem to have been dominated by Buddhism, Confucianism, Taoism, and Hinduism. Religion, to a degree, expresses the philosophy of a people about important facets of life—it is influenced by culture and vice versa. The position of women in a society is often the manifestation of such beliefs—in some societies the female is enshrined, in others she is treated like an equal, in still others she is subservient to the male and treated like chattel. A people's religious belief system is somewhat dependent on their stage of human development: tribesman and primitives tend to be superstitious and the practice of voodoo is illustrative of this; some religions are deeply locked into the agricultural stage of development, while many so-called advanced technological people seem to be more irreligious, substituting a belief in science for faith in traditional religions and their practices.

The ten general classifications described above are a simple model for assessing a particular culture. It is a paradigm, or mental set for evaluating the major characteristics of culture. It does not include every aspect of culture, nor is it the only way to analyze culture. This approach, and others described in subsequent chapters, enable managers to examine a people systemically. Our breakdown into ten categories is a convenient beginning for cultural understanding that can be used as one travels around the world and visits different cultures, or the model can be used to study the microcultures within a majority national culture. Just remember that all aspects of culture are interrelated, and to change one part is to change the whole. There is a danger in trying to compartmentalize a complex concept like culture, yet retaining a sense of its whole. We should look at a people's culture the way we view a beautiful jewel—we hold up different facets to the light of our consciousness, so as to better appreciate the beauty of human diversity and capability.

Systems Approach to Culture

Because there are many different anthropological approaches to cultural analysis, some readers may prefer to use this coordinated systems approach as an alternative. A system, in this sense, refers to an ordered assemblage or combination of correlated parts which form a unitary whole.

Kinship System—the family relationships and way a people reproduce, train, and socialize their children. The typical American family is nuclear and a rather independent unit; in other cultures, there may be an extended family that consists of several generations held together through the male line (patrilineal) or through the female line (matrilineal). Such families have a powerful influence on child rearing, and often on nation building. The multinational manager needs to appreciate the significance of this influence to supervise effectively minority workers like Blacks or Chicanos in the United States, or to deal in the world marketplace with businessmen from Vietnam or China. Family influences and loyalties can affect job performance or business negotiations.

Educational System—how young or new members of a society are provided with information, knowledge, skills, and values. If one is opening up a factory in India, for instance, the training plan had better include the rote method of education, whereas in some advanced societies the expectations would be for sophisticated, educational technology. Educational systems may be formal and informal within any culture.

Economic System—the manner in which the society produces and distributes its goods and services. The Japanese economic system is an extension of the family and is so group oriented that many foreigners view it as "Japan, Inc." Today while much of the world is divided into capitalistic or socialistic economic blocks, it is evident that a convergence is taking place and new regional economic cooperative entities are coming into being that cross national and ideological boundaries.

Political System—the dominant means of governance for maintaining order and exercising power or authority. Some cultures are still in a tribal stage where chiefs rule, others in the Middle East have a ruling royal family with an operating king as headman, while still others in the First, Second, Third or Fourth Worlds prefer democracy or communism, or some medium between these political extremes. Although world society seems to be in a transition that is going beyond the nation-state, the cosmopolitan manager is forced to understand and deal with governments as they presently are structured with all their diversity, and even regressiveness.

Religious System—the means for providing meaning and motivation beyond the material aspects of life, that is, the spiritual side of a culture or its approach to the supernatural. The significance of this has been alluded to earlier under "Beliefs and Attitudes." This transcending system may lift a people to great heights of accomplishment, as is witnessed in the pyramids of Egypt and the Renaissance of Europe, or it may lock them into a static past. It is possible to project the history and future of India, for instance, in terms of the impact of its belief in reincarnation, which is enshrined in its major religion. Diverse national cultures can be somewhat unified under a shared religious belief in Islam or Christianity, for example.

Association System—the network of social groupings that people form. These may range from fraternal and secret societies to professional/trade associations and the Mafia. Some cultures, like the American, are very group oriented and create formal or informal associations for every conceivable type of activity. Other societies are individualistic and avoid such organizing.

Health System—the way a culture prevents and cures disease or illness, or cares for victims of diasters or accidents. The concepts of health and wholeness, well being and medical problems differ by culture. Some countries have witch doctors and herb medications, others like India have few government-sponsored social services, while Britain has a system of socialized medicine. The U.S.A. is in the midst of a major transition in its health care and delivery system, and there is increasing emphasis on holistic health and Eastern treatments.

Recreational System—the ways in which a people socialize, or use their leisure time. What may be considered play in one culture may be viewed as work in another, and vice versa. In some culture "sport" has considerable political implications, in others it is solely for enjoyment, while in still others, it is big business. Certain types of entertainment, such as a form of folk dancing, seems to cut across cultures.

The above systems are the principal ones that might be examined by a person trying to better understand a particular culture. They offer an orderly approach to the study of major or minority cultural groupings. For business persons hoping to succeed in a foreign culture, such information and insight could make the difference between profit or loss.

Key Cultural Terminology

The specialists who make a formal study of culture use terms that may be helpful to the lay person trying to comprehend the significance of this phenomena in business or international life.

Patterns and Themes

Some cultural anthropologists, like Ruth Benedict, try to search for a single *integrative pattern* to describe a particular culture. Thus, the Pueblo Indians may be designated as "apollonian"—people who stick to the "middle of the road" and avoid excess or conflict in their valuing of existence. The pinpointing of a consistent pattern of thought and action in a culture is difficult, so other scholars prefer to seek a *summative theme*. This is a position, declared or implied, that simulates activity and controls behavior; it is usually tacitly approved or openly promoted in the society. One can note that in most Asian cultures there is a "fatalism" theme, while in the American business subculture the theme is profits or the "bottom line."

Explicit and Implicit

Some aspects of culture are overt, while others are covert. Anthropologist Clyde Kluckhohn reminds us that each different way of life makes assumptions about the ends or purposes of human existence, about what to expect from each other and the gods, about what constitutes fulfillment or frustration. Some of this is *explicit* in the lore of the folk, and may be manifest in law, regulations, customs, or traditions. Other aspects are *implicit* in the culture, and one must infer such tacit premises by observing consistent trends in word and deed. The distinction between public and hidden culture points up that much of our daily activity is governed by patterns and themes of which we may be only dimly aware, or totally unaware of their origin or meaning. Such culturally governed behavior facilitates the routine of daily living, so that one may perform in a society many actions without thinking about it. This cultural conditioning provides the freedom to devote conscious thinking to new and creative pursuits. It is startling to realize that some of our behavior is not entirely free or consciously willed by us. At times this can be a national problem, such as when a society finally realizes that implicit in its culture is a form of racism, which requires both legislation and reeducation in equal employment opportunity and affirmative action to rectify.

Micro- or Subcultures

Within a larger society, group, or nation sharing a common majority culture, there may be subgroupings of people possessing characteristic traits that set them apart and distinguish them from the others. These *subcultures* may be described in group classification by age, class, sex, race or some other entity that differentiates this micro- from the macroculture. Youth, or more specifically teenagers, share certain cultural traits, as do Blacks, Jews, or other ethnic groups. Occupationally, there are many microcultures, such as white or blue collar workers, police or the military, college students or surfers, the underworld or drug culture.

Universals and Diversity

The paradox of culture is the commonalities that exist in the midst of its diffusion or even confusion. There are generalizations that may be made about all cultures that are referred to as *universals*: age-grading, body adornments, calendar, courtship, divisions of labor, education, ethics, food taboos, incest and inheritance rules, language, marriage, mourning, mythology, numerals, penal sanctions, property rights, supernatural beliefs, status differentiation, tool making and trade, visiting, and weaning, etc. Thus, certain activities occur across cultures, but their manifestation may be unique in a particular society. And that brings us to the opposite concept of cultural *diversity*. Some form of sports or humor or music may be common to all peoples, but the way in which it is accomplished is distinctive in various cultural groupings. If we compare the Hottentots of Africa with a New Yorker of the U.S.A., there would be great discrepancies in the manifestation of cultural universals, such as, social organization, toilet habits, religious ceremonies, food preferences and preparation. The close relationship between human behavior and culture was underscored by Leslie White when he commented, "Instead of explaining cultural differences among peoples by saying one culture is phlegmatic, taciturn, unimaginative, and prosaic, we might view these behaviors as differences in cultural traditions that stimulate a respective population."

Rational/Irrational/Nonrational Behavior

Among the many definitions of culture, consider it as historically created designs for living that may be rational, irrational, and nonrational. *Rational* behavior in a culture is based on what that group considers as reasonable for achieving its goals. *Irrational* behavior deviates from the accepted norms of a society and may result from deep frustration of an individual in trying to satisfy needs; it would appear to be done without reason and possibly largely as an emotional response. *Nonrational* behavior is neither based on reason, nor is it against reasonable expectations—it is dictated by one's own culture or subculture. A great deal of behavior is of this type, and we are unaware of why we do it, why we believe what we do, or that we may be biased or prejudiced from the perspective of those outside our cultural group. How often and when to take a bath frequently is a cultural dictate, just as what food constitutes breakfast. What is rational in one culture may be irrational in another, and vice versa. Some societies send political dissidents to mental institutions for what is considered irrational behavior.

Tradition

This is a very important aspect of culture that may be expressed in unwritten customs, taboos, and sanctions. Tradition can program a people as to what is proper behavior and procedures relative to food, dress, and certain types of people, what to value, avoid, or deemphasize. As the song on the subject of "Tradition" from the musical, *Fiddler on the Roof*, extols:

> Because of our traditions, we keep our sanity. . . .Tradition tells us how
> to sleep, how to work, how to wear clothes. . . .How did it get started? I
> don't know—it's a tradition. . . .Because of our traditions, everyone
> knows who he is and what God expects of him!

Traditions provide a people with a "mindset" and have a powerful influence on their moral system for evaluating what is right or wrong, good or bad, desirable or not. Traditions express a particular culture, giving its members a sense of belonging and uniqueness. But whether one is talking of a tribal or national culture, a military or religious subculture, traditions should be reexamined regularly for their relevance and validity. Because of accelerating change, traditions must be revised or adapted to fit the changed condition of a technological age in the midst of creating a world culture.

Cultural Uniqueness

The cosmopolitan manager, sensitive to cultural differences, appreciates a people's distinctiveness, and seeks to make allowances for such factors when communicating with representatives of that cultural group. He or she avoids trying to impose one's own cultural attitudes and approaches upon these "foreigners." Thus, by respecting the cultural differences of others, we will not be labeled as "ethnocentric." *The Random House Dictionary* defines ethnocentrism as

> Belief in the inherent superiority of one's own group and culture; it may be accompanied by feelings of contempt for those others who do not belong; it tends to look down upon those considered as foreign; it views and measures alien cultures and groups in terms of one's own culture.

Through cross-cultural experiences, we become more broadminded and tolerant of cultural "peculiarities." When this is coupled with some formal study of the concept of culture, we not only gain new insights for improving our human relations, but we become aware of the impact of our native culture upon us. Cultural understanding may minimize the impact of culture shock, and maximize intercultural experiences. For the manager it represents a new body of knowledge—a tool—to increase professional development and organizational effectiveness with employees, customers, and other people encountered in the course of daily business. Certainly, it should teach us that culture and behavior are relative, and that we should be more tentative, and less absolute, in our human interactions.

To manage cultural differences more effectively, the authors contend that the first step in the process is increasing one's general cultural awareness. One has to understand the concept of culture and its characteristics before a manager can fully benefit by the study of cultural specifics and a foreign language.

References

Blair, J.G. *There is a Difference: Twelve Intercultural Perspectives.* Washington, D.C.: Meridian House, 1975.

Brown, I.C. *Understanding Other Cultures.* Englewood Cliffs, N.J.: Prentice-Hall, 1974.

Giele, J.Z. and A.C. Smock (eds.), *Women: Roles and Status in Eight Countries*. New York: John Wiley and Sons, 1977.

Hall, E.T., *The Hidden Dimension, The Silent Language*. Garden City, N.Y.: Doubleday, 1966, 1959, respectively.

Harris, M. *Cows, Pigs, Wars and Witches: The Riddles of Culture*. New York: Vintage Books, Random House, 1974.

Honigmann, J., (ed.), *Handbook of Social and Cultural Anthropology*. Chicago: Rand McNally & Company, 1973.

Levine, R.A. *Culture, Behavior and Personality*. Chicago: Aldine Pub., 1973.

Miller, G.R. (ed.), *Explorations in Interpersonal Communications*. Beverly Hills, Ca.: Sage Publications, 1976.

Otterbein, K.F., *Comparative Cultural Analysis*. San Francisco: Holt, Rinehart and Winston, 1977.

Parsons, T. *The Evolution of Societies*. Englewood Cliffs, N.J.: Prentice Hall, 1977.

Rokeach, M. *The Nature of Human Values*. New York: The Free Press, 1973.

Stewart, E.C. *American Cultural Patterns*. Washington, D.C.: Society for Intercultural Education, Training and Research, 1977.

Terpstra, V. *The Cultural Environment of International Business*. Cincinnati: South-Western Publishing Co., 1978.

6
Managing
Intercultural Business Relations

Dilemmas in International Business

We considered the concept of culture and its influence on human behavior in Chapter 5 in a general way without specific reference to the manager or management. To better understand management behavior in different cultures, let us utilize two conceptual models borrowed from the behavioral sciences. These provide a useful framework for a manager as well as a theoretical background to explain difficulties in transferring managerial concepts and technologies to other cultures. They are also practical and will provide ways for the manager to intervene in appropriate ways in other cultures so as to accomplish his objectives instead of being frustrated.

In an early chapter of his book, *Culture and Management,* Ross Webber describes the reactions of American and Korean students to a game of interpersonal conflict. In the simulation, each contestant has two strategies from which to choose with differing results. If both contestants choose strategy A, each receives $3.00; if each chooses strategy B, each receives $2.00; and if they do not agree on strategies and choose AB or BA, then each person receives $1.00.

Webber states that on repeated plays, American M.B.A. candidates generally stabilize on strategy A, with both players earning $3.00. However, when Korean graduate business students play the game under similar conditions, they tend to select strategy B and both receive $2.00.

Why is this so? Can it be said that cultural factors cause the difference? It appears that the Korean students do not or cannot cooperate. The American students cooperated and maximized their individual gain. Did the Korean students distrust each other or did they want to minimize the earnings of their competitors even more than maximize their own? If so, it would appear that relative status is more important than individual gain.

This experiment does not prove that personal noncooperativeness is a cultural characteristic of Koreans. Does it prove the cooperativeness of

Americans? If it did, there would be important implications for American managers who worked with Koreans.

In this chapter, we will propose two conceptual paradigms, frameworks, or models for understanding the behavior of persons and in particular, the behavior of managers, from other cultures. The frameworks will prove useful in assisting a manager determine "what went wrong" when there is a problem of a misunderstanding but more importantly, know how to predict with some degree of reliability the impact of his or her behavior while managing in a foreign environment and working with persons whose value systems, way of life, and management philosophy may be very different from his or her own. It will help the multinational manager understand the behavior of the other colleagues with whom he or she is working in another culture.

The Cultural Management System

Global managers function within four basic intermeshing systems of management philosophy and practice: the technical system, the economic system, the political system, and the cultural system. The first three systems are relatively easy to quantify. For example, the use of government statistics, trade association and industry figures, and other quantifiable items are readily available in most countries including lesser developed economies. The cultural system has been given the least amount of consideration of the four insofar as it relates to management practice and philosophy across different cultures. The cultural system tends to be abstract and it is difficult to make specific statements about how it influences management.

The *macro-environmental* approach in cross-cultural management attempts to identify the impact of external environmental factors on management practices. Factors such as the impact of education, politics, and law on management practices and effectiveness are considered. The assumption is that management practices depend on these external variables and the differences among organizations in various countries can be explained as a result of differences in environmental conditions. This approach is useful. However, it is incomplete, because it seems to imply that the individual passively adapts to his environment, and gives the manager little credit for influencing the environment.

Our approach will be *behavioral* in the sense that we will attempt to explain behavioral differences in managers and organizations as a function of cultural influences. The assumption is that a manager's attitudes, values, beliefs and needs are determined at least in part by his or her culture. Management practices and theories will, therefore, vary from culture to culture. Taking the behavioral approach will allow us to respond to our previous question: what are the determinants of human behavior? Or, how can I understand why a manager is acting in a particular way?

In the manager's attempt to understand himself and in his attempt to understand and predict the behavior of others, he uses a multilayered frame of explanation. As was discussed in Chapter 4, the manager and others are shaped by the systems to which they belong. If one knows the culture of the other person, then it is possible to make tentative predictions about the person's behavior. Furthermore, if one knows the other person's social roles and personality, one can predict behavior with a greater degree of accuracy.

The Anthropological Framework

In this section we shall draw largely on the works of Florence Kluckhohn and Fred Strodtbeck, *Variations in Value Orientations,* Stephen H. Rhinesmith, *Cultural Organizational Analysis,* Joseph J. DiStefano, *A Conceptual Framework for Understanding Cross-Cultural Management Problems,* and Edward C. Stewart, *American Cultural Patterns: A Cross-Cultural Perspective.*

Before considering a model for understanding management behavior in different cultures, a number of working definitions would be useful. A *formal organization* is a system of consciously coordinated activities or the forces of two or more persons who interact for the attainment of personal and common objectives. The work of the manager is to coordinate human and nonhuman resources in order to accomplish the objectives of the organization. Typical management functions involve planning, organizing, recruiting, selecting, rewarding, leading, communicating, relating, problem-solving, decision-making, conflict managing, negotiating, controlling, training, evaluating and innovating activities. "Values" is another term for which we need a working definition. As proposed in Chapter 2, a value is a conception of an individual or group of individuals that is either "implicit or explicit of the desirable which influences the selection from available modes, means, and ends of action." The concept of value is important because managers from the same culture tend to have similar values and these value systems influence their interpersonal relationship and their performance of leadership activities.

Human behavior is central to our investigation of management effectiveness. Talcott Parsons has developed a general theory of action that holds the following points as being characteristic of all human behavior:

1. Behavior is directed to the attainment of goals.
2. Behavior takes place in situations.
3. Behavior is normatively regulated.
4. Behavior involves the expenditure of effort.

With these working definitions in mind, we can proceed to describe a model for understanding human and organizational behavior. Anthropologists have, for a long time, used the concept of values for making comparisons between cultures and for making analyses of differences within cultures. The purpose was to understand differences in human behavior. In the area of managerial behavior, a number of studies have been completed with case studies illustrating the ways in which personal values influence organizational strategy choices. The paradigm developed by the anthropologist can be applied to managerial problems in cross-cultural situations.

There are three assumptions underlying the framework. The first is *that there are a limited number of common human questions for which all people at all times must seek some answer.* This assumption is simply stating that the number of questions all people experience is not unlimited and these questions arise out of human situation. The second assumption is *that while there is variability of solutions of all the questions, it is not limitless nor random but the variation is within a range of solutions.* The third assumption is *that all the alternatives of all the solutions are present in all societies at all times but are preferred differentially.* These are basic assumptions from which five questions have been identified as most crucial and common to all human groups.

The five basic questions are:

1. What is the character of innate human nature?
2. What is the relationship of man to nature?
3. What is the temporal focus of life?
4. What is the modality of man's activity?
5. What is the relationship of man to other men?

The range of solutions to these questions is illustrated in the matrix in Table 6.1. The matrix suggests that, for each culture, there is a preferred way of responding to each question from among the alternatives presented. Underlying these preferences are values, which are ideas about what is right and wrong, good and bad. Values not only influence our behavior, but provide us with a focus for understanding our own behavior as well as the behavior of persons from different cultures.

What Is the Character of Innate Human Nature?

Table 6.1 is a three-way classification for the sake of illustration, and undoubtedly further distinctions can be made. In the United States most agree that the influence of Puritan ancestors is strong and many believe that human nature is basically evil but perfectible. Control and discipline are required to achieve goodness. Others in the United States now seem to believe that man is a mixture of good and evil. There is no evidence of a society that is committed to the definition of human nature as immutably good.

Table 6-1*
Cultural Influences on Life Issues

Cultural Approaches	A	B	C
What is the character of human nature?	Man is evil†	Man is a mixture of good and evil†	Man is good†
What is the relationship of man to nature?	Man is subject to nature	Man is in harmony with nature	Man is master of nature
What is the temporal focus of life?	To the past	To the present	To the future
What is the modality of man's activities?	A spontaneous expression in impulse and desires	Activity that emphasizes as a goal the development of all aspects of the self	Activity that is motivated primarily toward measurable accomplishments
What is the relationship of man to other men?	Lineal—group goals are primary and an important goal is continuity through time	Collateral—group goals are primary. Well-regulated continuity of group relationships through time are not critical	Individual—the individual goals are most important

*Exhibit modified from Kluckhohn and Strodtbeck, p. 11ff.
†This assumes that human nature is either mutable or immutable.

What Is the Relationship of Man to Nature?

Most North Americans believe that man is master of nature. The harmony orientation can be observed in Japanese, Chinese, and many American Indian tribes including the Navajo and Hopi. Accepting the inevitable and the subjugation of man to nature is evident in societies that place a high belief in fate.

What Is the Temporal Focus of Life?

The solutions to this question (past, present, and future) are present in all societies but the ordering of one over another is what differentiates the societies. The majority of middle class North Americans are oriented to the

(Text continued on page 75.)

Table 6-2
Managerial Examples of Basic Questions

What is the character of innate human nature?

Example of management problems affected by question:	What kind of control system is necessary?		
Examples reflecting the range of solutions to management problems:	If man is evil, elaborate controls are necessary.	If man is neither good or evil, a system to avoid temptation is necessary.	If man is basically good, managers need a control system to gather information necessary for decision-making only.

What is the relationship of man to nature?

Example of management problem affected by question:	How will methods of controlling the birth rate be accepted?		
Examples reflecting the range of solutions:	Subjection to nature— no methods will be accepted. If one is to become pregnant it will happen.	Harmony with nature.	Master of nature. Any method will be okay if medically safe.

What is the temporal focus of life?

Example of management problem affected by question:	What goals should the organization have?		
Examples reflecting range of solutions:	Past—the goals of the past are sufficient.	Present—the goals should reflect the present demands.	Future—the goals should be directed toward trends and the situation of the future.

What is the modality of man's activity?

Example of management problem affected by question:	What motivates people to work?		
Examples reflecting the range of solutions	Work only as much as is necessary for the day.	A balance between work and nonwork.	Work to accomplish and to demonstrate hard work and competence.

What is the relationship of man to other men?

Example of management problem affected by question: How to select people for employment.

Table 6-2 (Continued)
Managerial Examples of Basic Questions

Examples reflecting the range of solutions:	Hire a close relative.	Hire a relative or friend of someone in in the organization.	Hire the best person.

What is the organization's responsibility to nature and the community?

Example of management problem affected by question: What is the extent of corporate social responsibility?

Example reflecting range of solutions:	Control all exploitation of nature and regulate society completely.	Within reason balance ecological and economic policies; gradual implementation of environmental controls.	Individual's right to the good life, so supply the means for unhampered employment.

future, whereas peasants in many societies focus on the "now" more than the past or the future and the Chinese orientation as well as other cultures is very much to the past.

What Is the Modality of Man's Activity?

The spontaneous expression of impulses stresses the release and indulgence of existing desires. An example is the behavior of people in Brazil at Mardi Gras. Activities that emphasize the development of all aspects of a person can be seen in Eastern culture and among Westerners influenced by Eric Fromm and others. The "doing" or activity oriented towards accomplishments is most familiar to North Americans and managers in particular.

What Is the Relationship of Man to Other Men?

In this question, a key to understanding the categorization is to ask, "whose welfare is primary?" In the individual orientation, the individual's welfare is most important. Most North Americans are in this category. The extended families of many cultures would be an example of the collateral group when the welfare of the group supercedes the welfare of the individual members. The English aristocracy would be an example of a lineal group orientation where the welfare of the group is important and the social class continues through time.

We have identified the questions and defined the solutions with a number of examples from a variety of cultures. The framework will be useful if managers are able to apply it to some of the problems they experience when working with persons from different cultures. Examples are contained in Table 6-2.

Having covered this material, the question for managers is how can it be used? The conceptual scheme can be used to anticipate problems before they occur or to analyze problems once they exist. The questionnaire included in Appendix B will also be useful in anticipating and analyzing cross-cultural management problems.

Suppose as a manager your assignment is to investigate the cultural differences in manufacturing and accounting management technology in a Latin American country. American management theory is based on the premise that each person in the organization will perform his tasks in a way which will promote the organization. Helping or hiring one's friends or relatives will be subordinated to the development of organizational objectives. To minimize the number of cultural errors a manager can examine the different solutions to all management questions that are being considered. Where differences exist, the manager can determine, in advance, when to modify a management practice to fit the situation. The manager can also know where the difference exists and will be able to intervene at that point rather than another area. The major benefit of this approach is to begin with a conceptual framework and deduce from it where specific problems might occur. This is accomplished by an awareness of the areas of difference between the two cultures at an abstract level and then generating specific and concrete management problems that might occur or have occurred as a result of the differences. If the framework is used as suggested, it will help managers avoid quick and erroneous conclusions about the causes and solutions to cross-cultural management problems.

Attribution Theory from Social Psychology

At a recent orientation session conducted for executives, managers, and their families from several European countries in the midwest, a couple from the Netherlands related the following incident. Shortly after arriving in the United States for a two-year assignment, they were invited to a barbecue by the international vice-president of their company. They arrived and within ten minutes, in their own words, "they had been insulted so often they were ready to go home." What had happened? First, from the perspective of the couple from the Netherlands; they had been invited to a meal by the international vice-president. Their expectation was that they would be the only couple present. Second, when they were introduced to the other guests many of the American women did not shake hands and "some of them shook hands with their left hand." Also, some of the men did not stand. They were incensed and "highly insulted." From the perspective of the Americans, however, the purpose of the barbecue was to provide an opportunity for the newly arrived expatriates from the Netherlands to meet several others in the company as well as a few people from the neighborhood. The American women may have extended their left hand as a friendly or warm gesture that is sometimes seen in the midwestern United States. But the important fact is that the couple from the Netherlands felt insulted and the purpose of the event from the point of view of the Americans was not accomplished. What happened?

Harry C. Triandis cites the following situation of a similar nature. In many cultures, servants and domestic help do most of the tasks around a home including the cleaning of shoes. In the United States, such employees usually do not clean shoes as part of their responsibilities. If Mr. Kato, a Japanese businessman, were a house guest of Mr. Smith, an American businessman, and asked the "cleaning person" to shine his shoes there could be a problem. It is, or at least could be, an inappropriate request. However, the crucial question is, what *attributions* does the cleaning person make concerning Mr. Kato's request? There are probably two possibilities. One is that he or she could say Mr. Kato is ignorant of American customs and in this case the person would not be too disturbed. The cleaning person could respond in a variety of ways, including telling the Japanese guest of the American custom, ignoring the request, and speaking to his or her employer. However, if the cleaning person *attributes* Mr. Kato's request to a personal consideration (he is arrogant) then there will be a serious problem in their interpersonal relationship. If a person from one culture is offended by a person from another culture and one believes it is because of culture ignorance, this is usually forgiven. If one "attributes" the offense or "error" to arrogance there will be serious problems. Two other illustrations at the end of this chapter will provide examples of how attribution theory can be used by managers.

Attribution theory is concerned with how people explain things that happen. It is a way of explaining to ourselves why things happen in the world. It helps to answer such questions as:

1. Why did Mr. Kato ask the cleaning person to shine his shoes?
2. Why did I pass or fail an examination?
3. Why can't Molly read?
4. Why has the Soviet Union agreed to on-site nuclear inspection?

There are many ways of perceiving the world and given the many possibilities we all take certain cues from the environment and interpret them in meaningful ways to each of us. There are too many cues for any person to pay attention to all of them at the same time. Thus, each person has many ways of reducing the number of stimuli and organizing them into meaningful pieces of information. The ways that we take information from the environment become subconscious and habitual. We also interpret behavior in terms of behaviors appropriate for a role. The couple from the Netherlands expected to be the only persons invited to the barbecue and once there, expected other guests to use their right hand and to stand when being introduced. Mr. Kato expected that it would be acceptable to ask the cleaning person to shine his shoes. From the perspective of the cleaning person, this is not acceptable. When each one's expectations were not realized they attributed motives to the "offender" based on their cultural construct.

Attribution theory helps to explain what happens and is applicable to cross-cultural management situations for the following reasons:

1. *All behavior is rational and logical from the perspective of the behaver.* (At a recent seminar involving Japanese and American businessmen, an American asked a Japanese what was most difficult for him in the United States. The Japanese replied that "the most difficult part of my life here is to understand Americans. They are so irrational and illogical." The Americans present listened, and were both amused and surprised.)
2. *Persons from different cultures perceive and organize their environment in different ways, so that it becomes meaningful to them.*

To be effective in working with people from different cultures requires that we make *isomorphic attributions* of the situation. Isomorphic attributions result in a positive evaluation of the other person and it means that we can correctly infer the meaning of the other's behavior (verbal or nonverbal) *from the perspective of the other.*

The following example is quoted from Harry C. Triandis and is taken from the files of a Greek psychiatrist. As background information it is important to remember that Greeks perceive supervisory roles as more authoritarian than Americans who prefer participatory decision-making. Read the verbal conversation first then the attributions being made by the American and the Greek.

*Verbal Conversation**	*Attribution†*
American: How long will it take you to finish this report?	American: I asked him to participate.
	Greek: His behavior makes no sense. He is the boss. Why doesn't he tell me?
Greek: I do not know. How long should it take?	American: He refuses to take responsibility.
	Greek: I asked him for an order.

---

* This is the spoken dialogue between the American and the Greek. It could be tape recorded, written, or videotaped. It can be measured.
† The "attributions" made by the American and the Greek are not externalized and cannot be recorded.

American: You are in the best position to analyze time requirements.

American: I press him to take responsibility for own actions.

Greek: What nonsense! I better give him an answer.

Greek: 10 days.

American: He lacks the ability to estimate time; this time estimate is totally inadequate.

American: Take 15. Is it agreed you will do it in 15 days?

American: I offer a contract.

Greek: These are my orders: 15 days.

In fact the report needed 30 days of regular work. So the Greek worked day and night, but at the end of the 15th day, he still needed one more day's work.

Behavior	*Attribution*
American: Where is the report?	American: I am making sure he fulfills his contract.
	Greek: He is asking for the report.
Greek: It will be ready tomorrow.	Both attribute that it is not ready.
American: But we had agreed it would be ready today.	American: I must teach him to fulfill a contract.
	Greek: The stupid, incompetent boss! Not only did he give me wrong orders, but he does not even appreciate that I did a 30-day job in 16 days.
The Greek hands in his resignation.	The American is surprised.
	Greek: I can't work for such a man.

Also consider the following situation. Read the verbal conversation first then the attribution. A French businessman and an American businessman are discussing politics. The statements were overheard in actual conversations between an American and Frenchman. The attributions were developed by discussing the verbal conversation with the American and Frenchman following the conversation.

Verbal Conversation	*Attribution*
American: What do you think of the new movement to "Buy French?"	American: I'll see if it's true that the French are prodduct chauvinists.
French: Well, I generally buy products made in France anyway because of quality considerations.	French: Doesn't he know that the best products are made in France? The Americans always try to get rid of their inferior products in France.
American: I read recently that Giscard d'Estaing announced that buying an imported product is a vote against employment. Don't you think this move will hurt your credibility with other EEC countries?	American: I'll find out what he thinks of the EEC.
	French: Why is he butting into EEC problems? Americans think they own Europe.
French: Well, you know that France is the strongest country in the EEC and exerts sufficient power to offset any public opinion difference. Besides, unlike the British and the Germans, we are not just a satellite of Uncle Sam.	French: Where would the EEC be without France?
	American: The French never consider the Germans as equals.
American: Yes, but is protectionism really going to help France in the long run?	
French: Oh, don't worry about France. I predict that by 1982 she will surpass the U.S. in GNP. Besides why is the U.S. keeping Concorde out of New York if not protectionism?	French: These Americans never learn to "cultivate their own gardens." They claim they are protecting their environments . . . but if Concorde were their development, it would be landing allover the world.
American: Maybe you're right. But public opinion is opposed to SST.	
French: Perhaps, but public opinion can be bought in the U.S.	French: Americans are all alike, they only think what T.V. tells them to think.

The two examples illustrate, that at almost every place in the intercultural conversation, the statement of one person leads to an intimation that does not match the attribution of the other. These are extreme examples of non-isomorphic attributions, and they are working to the detriment of the relationship.

The intercultural skill to be developed by managers working with persons from another culture is the ability to make isomorphic attributions; that is to be able to infer or attribute the same meaning to the verbal conversation or behavior that the other person does. Another extreme example is directing the soles of one's feet towards a person from the Middle East. This does not have any particular meaning in the United States, but in the Middle East it is insulting.

Conclusions

In this chapter we have proposed two specific conceptual paradigms that culturally sensitive leaders can use in managing human resources in pluralistic work environments. The first approach—the anthropological model—offers a conceptual framework that can provide insight for determining, in advance, where specific management problems might occur. The second approach—the attribution paradigm—will assist a manager in putting the same meanings, inferences, or attributions to a verbal or nonverbal communication that the other person intends to convey. Both of these approaches can enhance a manager's effectiveness in intercultural business relations.

References

DiStefano, Joseph J., *A Conceptual Framework for Understanding Cross-Cultural Management Problems.* London, Ontario: Unpublished class discussion notes, 1972.

Kluckhohn, Florence R. and Strodtbeck, Frederick L., *Variations in Value Orientations.* Evanston, Illinois: Row, Peterson and Company, 1961.

Lloyd, L.H. (ed.), *Communication Assessment and Intervention Strategies.* Baltimore, Md.: University Park Press, 1976.

Rhinesmith, Stephen H., *Cultural Organizational Analysis.* Cambridge, Mass.: McBer and Company, 1971.

Triandis, Harry C., "Culture Training, Cognitive Complexity and Interpersonal Attitudes" in Brislin, Richard W., Bochner, Stephen and Lonner, Walter J., *Cross-Cultural Perspectives on Learning.* New York: John Wiley and Sons, 1975.

Triandis, H.C. (ed.), *Variations in Black and White Perceptions of the Social Environment.* Urbana, Ill.: University of Illinois Press, 1976.

Webber, Ross A., *Culture and Management.* Homewood, Illinois: Richard D. Irwin, Inc., 1969.

7
Managing
Cultural Shock

Coping with Transitional Challenges

Increasingly we interact with people who are very different from us, or with situations that are very unfamiliar to us. Even when we share a common nationality, we may have to deal with citizens who are indeed "foreign" to us in their thinking, attitudes, vocabulary, and background. Or we find ourselves encountering conditions that are totally unexpected and cause us to be very uncomfortable.

It is not just an issue of going abroad to a strange land that calls for innovative coping, but we may have challenges within our enviroñment to move beyond our upbringing or local cultural conditioning. These are called *transitional experiences* that urge us to go forward and succeed in a new unknown, or to regress back into the safe past. Depending on how we answer such challenging opportunities, growth or disruption may follow. Such experiences happen to minority students who enter college, or to white supervisors of minority workers; to prison parolees, or to returning veterans; to married couples who divorce, or to families who move from one geographic area to another location within a nation; to those who change their careers in midlife, or have major alterations in their roles; to foreign students who come to our universities, or to multinational managers and technicians going overseas.

To get a sense of the transitional experience that can cause cultural shock, consider the following scenarios.

First to Third World. You board a jet for a year's assignment abroad in a country radically different from your own, in which you will be perceived as "the foreigner." You leave a so-called advanced nation—an urban technological society, and in a matter of hours find yourself in an ancient, agricultural land. The mass of people live as rural peasants in villages, with a scattering of immensely populated cities. You have been raised in a Western culture in the Judeo-Christian tradition, but your hosts are in Eastern culture, from a Hindu-Môslem tradition with a bewildering variety of minor religions (from Parsi who leave their dead on high places for the vultures to consume to Jains who will not kill any living thing from flies to insects.) Depending on your host's religious affiliation, beef or pork are forbidden foods, so poultry and fish will be your main diet. You must now cope with an Oriental mindset; an Asian sense of time, place, and face. The population is multicultural and multiracial, speaking fifteen different languages and over five hundred dialects. Suddenly, you are aware that beneath a veneer of modernity, you realize that what you once read about in the Bible or history, is now real—bullock carts, sacred animals, dung used for building material, widows throwing themselves upon their husband's funeral pyre, and poverty like you did not know still existed. All the things you took for granted in your "developed" country are not available—from radio or television at any hour, to filing cabinets and electric appliances, to convenience packaging and frozen foods. All your reference points and groups are off. Simple actions at home become horrendous operations here. Now make the most of this opportunity and enjoy your visit!

Majority to Minority Culture. Your company transfers you and your family to a section of your country where you feel like an "immigrant." From the Northeast you come to this Sunbelt that is so different and unique. In fact, your boss suggests you enroll in Rice University to take a course entitled, "Living Texas." She says it will help you and your family to get introduced to the myths and mannerisms of Texans, so you will not be so culturally isolated among these boisterous, unusual natives. It teaches newcomers how to adapt to this former republic, rather than have you try to recreate the environment you just left. You are considered "people from the outside" in this land of rapid growth and petropower, which Easterners tend to stereotype as a center of rightism, repression, and racism. It is a state of contrasts from huge ranches and high technology to Bible-belt mentality and laws. So you sign up for the course that covers everything from "Talking Texas" and Texas cooking to the Mexican side of the Texas revolution and Texas folk heroes. If you can adapt, you will probably fall in love with these friendly people, their jalapeño lollipops and chili pepper dishes and even discover their diverse ethnic mixture and the "Austin sound" of music. Oh, by the way, a current popular recording here is "Freeze a Yankee," which berates Easterners for waiting to develop their oil off the Atlantic Coast!

Mainland to Island Mentality. You are an American of Puerto Rican descent, one of many thousands born or reared on the U.S. mainland. As a second-generation "Neorican," you decide to go back to the Commonwealth for college. You are enrolled in the Catholic University of Ponce, but you are having trouble assimilating to the land of your ancestors. As an ex-New

Yorker, you learn you have no edge in getting a part-time job because of your better education. Yes, you are resented in an economy with an average 20% unemployment. When you get a position, you get paid less than NYC; high-paying jobs are scarce. Furthermore, you realize that you also speak Spanish poorly in comparison with the natives, and in this culture you are perceived as an "outsider." As one of more than a million Neoricans here, you are seen as a group to be more independent and aggressive—you think, act, and talk *differently*. Some of you have not been able to adjust and so returned to the States. You are somewhat ridiculed by the locals because you are unfair competition for scarce jobs among a growing population, you speak "Spanglish" (a mixture of English and Spanish), you have odd cultural traits, and you come from a "drug culture" (metropolitan New York). Furthermore, when you do speak English well, your fellow students and workers think you are "showing off!" In fact, although you had a normal, happy home life on the mainland, here you have to fight an *image* of Neoricans as "drug addicts, immoral, overly aggressive, and undereducated." Although you avoid politics, you are accused by your presence of helping to speed up the cause of statehood. Yet, you love the climate, the beaches, the life-style, and the people. You know that upon graduation, your temporary job with the airline can be turned into a permanent one as a customer representative. So you decide to plant roots and join "Neoricans in Puerto Rico, Inc."

Utilizing Cross-Cultural Opportunities

The above three incidents are transitional experiences that are real and true. Having indepth, intercultural encounters can be stimulating or psychologically disturbing, depending on your preparation for them and your approach to them. The process of adjustment or acculturation to a new living environment or a different kind of people takes time, usually some months, for we have to learn new skills for responding and adapting to the unfamiliar. Moving to California can be somewhat traumatic for someone from a small Midwestern town, but the adjustment period will probably be shorter than for the average American who is assigned on business to another country. The more strange the environment or indigenous population, the longer it may take the "foreigner" to adapt and the more that individual may be "thrown off" by the situation. When abroad, the extent of the trauma depends on whether one lives on the economy, or in a military/diplomatic/corporate compound with his or her own kind. The experience of coping with human differences around this globe can be renewing or devastating.

Recall our previous reference to the musical, *Fiddler on the Roof*, about a Jewish family in Russia that eventually emigrates to the United States? Tevye, the father of this family, sings a wonderful tune entitled, "Tradition," which provides two helpful insights into this issue of transitional experiences. He observes, "Because of our traditions, we have kept our balance for many years. Because of our traditions, everyone of us knows who he is and what God expects of him." When we are in a place where the traditions and customs are foreign and unexpected, we may lose our balance and become unsure of ourselves. The same thing can happen within our own society when change happens so rapidly that all the old traditions, the cues we live by, are suddenly undermined and irrelevant. Stress, tensions, frustrations can build up when we go outside our own culture, or even within our own society when it is in the midst of a profound transition, as it is in the last part of the twentieth century. Under such circumstances our very sense of self becomes threatened.

Transitional experiences offer us two alternatives—to cope or to cop out. We can learn to comprehend, survive in, and grow through immersion in a different culture. The positive result can be further self development and movement toward a higher level of personal awareness and growth. Whenever we leave home for the unfamiliar, it involves basic changes in habits, relationships, and sources of satisfaction. Inherent in cultural change is the opportunity to leave behind, perhaps temporarily, one set of relationships and living patterns, and to enrich one's life by experimenting with new ones. Implicit in the personal conflict and discontinuity produced by such experiences is the possible transcendence from environmental or family support to self support. Intercultural situations of psychological, social, or cultural stress also stimulate us to review and redefine our lives; to see our own country and people in a new perspective. Or, we may reject the changes or new culture and possibly lose a growth opportunity.

Identity Crisis in Change

Each of us lives in our own private world. We formulate a mindset, or psychological construct by which we read meaning into our daily events and experiences. It is the basis by which we perceive our unique reality. It contributes to our sense of identity. But each of us experiences the world through his or her own culturally influenced values, assumptions, and beliefs. Many of us are unaware of what these attitudes and perceptions are until a transitional experience causes us to reflect on and reexamine our values, priorities, life styles. Just as adolescence or a life crisis, such as divorce or heart surgery, may trigger profound reevaluation and change, so too may intercultural experiences. The process of cultural shock may lead to progressive or destructive changes in one's sense of self. Prior to that, our culture and families helped us to answer that fundamental question, "Who am I?" Both contributed to identity that provides us with the ability to predict expectations and events, and our relationship to them. We learn over many years how to project this sense of self in a way that is acceptable to those with whom we live. But when we go abroad into a totally uncertain scene, we experience discomfort and possible rejection of this self because we do not "fit in." Thus,

Table 7-1
Identity Crisis Syndrome

Phase 1 Awareness	Phase 2 Rage	Phase 3 Introspection	Phase 4 Integration
Nothing about his/her ethnic/racial/cultural identity—drifts along as a minority in majority culture.	Equality with the majority culture is a myth.	Super-heightening of psycho-social sensitivity.	Comparatively quiescent.
Begins to sense a difference, vague dissatisfaction, asks "Who am I?"	Near-constant, overwhelming anger and hostility toward majority culture which put self in this condition; minority culture for submitting to the ascribed social rules of the majority.	Need to know and understand minority/majority differences—questioning.	Below surface some rage in control (but the wrong cues can set it loose).
Loses reference points with own group—flounders.	Inner conflict, bitterness, and sullenness.	Serious introspection.	Situation in hand (majority associates may be mislead to believe the identity crisis is over).

we can be threatened by transitional experiences and perhaps act inappropriately. Then, an identity crisis may be produced. It is similar to what many females are going through under the impact of the women's liberation movement, or what hispanic or black minorities in America experience as they struggle to move into the country's mainstream.

Perhaps two models of social scientists will help us to understand the phenomenon, as well as its special significance for acculturation. Both conceptual frameworks recognize fundamental human needs for a sense of personal and social worth, as well as to be needed by others, to belong, to be recognized by others, and to be a unique self. The first on *Identity Crisis* was adapted from the work of Dr. Chester A. Wright, a social psychologist at the Naval Post Graduate Institute in Monterey, California. Let us examine this paradigm in terms of a minority person, such as Puerto Rican/Black/Indian,

Table 7-1 (continued)
Identity Crisis Syndrome

Phase 1 Awareness	Phase 2 Rage	Phase 3 Introspection	Phase 4 Integration
Gets curious about own minority or heritage, "What are *my* people like?"	Negative, self-destructive behavior heightens and over-taxes an already battered ego, possibly to the point of open irrationality—	Possible insomnia symptom.	Must seek firm knowledge about *my* people (e.g., reads group's history, searches for roots and inquires about ancestry).
May adopt a distorted and incongruous self-image of minority identification that produces anxiety, extremes of behavior; majority/minority swings of identification, back and forth to extremes; results in more anxiety.	Deep personal conflict over minority status in majority culture.	Need to "ventilate" with fellow minority members (e.g., "soul blowing sessions of blacks"). Need to be active, against the majority and with the minority; insists on being heard as a representative of this minority.	Begins to be more comfortable with self—builds congruent self-identity; majority/minority conflict recedes. Needs channeling toward positive personality building; if not, may lapse back into the first stage and begin the cycle all over again.

Goal: To perceive self as a unique person, accepting of own heritage and culture and its contribution toward one's distinctive personality, so that the image one projects to others is in harmony with the inner person. That is, to be congruent and self accepting— comfortable with self. (NOTE: This is a goal for American culture; in Japan, the goal might be expressed as to experience self as a worthwhile member of a family/company.)

in the majority American culture. In the process of striving to resolve one's identity from the perspective of a citizen representing one of these three minority microcultures, the person might pass through four stages. Table 7-1 describes the behavior symptoms of someone moving through these developmental phases. Although it is typical for most individuals to pass through these stages in sequence, it is possible for a person to get fixated in one phase, or to regress back to a previous stage. The intensity of the experience and the time in each phase differs with each unique person. The process is not unlike what adolescents go through, so some teenagers never move beyond the rage stage, while others experience it as a short, mild adjustment. Some researchers believe that the more intelligent the person, the more prone to this identity crisis syndrome. For example, the model can be helpful to explain the behavior of a thirty-five year old housewife who is bright and the mother of three children. As she becomes aware of the women's liberation message and literature, then gets involved in the National Organization of Women, she might very well experience a role crisis and pass through these developmental stages.

However, the major reason for providing this conceptual model is for those who go abroad and experience some degree of cultural shock. As a foreigner in a different culture, uncertain of local expectations, it is very possible for one's sense of self, especially in terms of nationality, to come into question. Readers who may have suffered cultural shock, may appreciate the relationship of the previous four stages and what happens to the expatriate struggling to find him- or herself in a strange culture.

The second model concerns the *Transitional Experience* from a state of low self and cultural awareness to high self and cultural awareness. It is adapted from Dr. Peter S. Adler, a counseling officer at the East-West Center, University of Hawaii. Table 7-2 on pages 90 and 91 describes five stages of transition that can ensue in the cultural shock process. There is no particular time sequence to each phase of adjustment, nor does each presume that one must pass through the previous stage automatically. It is simply a description of learning experiences that persons may have in making a major transition, such as to another foreign culture.

Both the *Identity Crisis* and *Transitional Experience* models provide insight into what happens to people in change, caused by a life crisis or living in a different culture. The transitional experience, for example, begins with an encounter of another culture, and evolves into an encounter with self. It requires the giving up of the familiar to take risks with the unknown. It can be the means to greater consciousness and awareness, to appreciation for human diversity and unique cultural systems. It can be the mechanism for helping the individual to be less culture bound and more culture free, to increase interpersonal effectiveness, and to cope better with future shock.

Culture Shock

Grammatically, the term should be "cultural shock," but popularly it is known as culture shock. The phenomenon may, and often does, occur during a major transitional experience. But, what is it exactly? Perhaps a few quotations may help us to get a fix on the concept.

Dr. Kalervo Oberg, an anthropologist, referred to it as a generalized trauma one experiences in a new and different culture because of having to learn and cope with a vast array of new cultural cues and expectations, while discovering that your old ones probably do not fit or work. More precisely he notes:

> Culture shock is precipitated by the anxiety that results from losing all our familiar signs and symbols of social intercourse. These signs or cues include the thousand and one ways in which we orient ourselves to the situations of daily life: how to give orders, how to make purchases, when

and when not to respond. Now these cues which may be words, gestures, facial expressions, customs, or norms are acquired by all of us in the course of growing up and are as much a part of our culture, as the language we speak or the beliefs we accept. All of us depend for our peace of mind and efficiency on hundreds of these cues, most of which we are not consciously aware.

For the average person going for some length of time into a strange culture is like being a "fish out of water"—the props are knocked out from under that individual, so frustrations and tensions increase until one adjusts to the new situation.

Professor Lawrence Stessen, author of *Managerial Styles of Foreign Businessmen*, summarized the problem faced by United States managers abroad:

> In the age of hangups, the American entrepreneur venturing into overseas lands soon discovers his. It is what the anthropologists call "culture shock," a series of jolts that await even the wariest American when he encounters the wide vartiety of customs, value systems, attitudes, and work habits which make it difficult for him to move comfortably in a foreign commercial environment. Some adjust and survive, others retreat to the familiar atmosphere of a service club, Hometown, U.S.A.

As modern managers become more cosmopolitan in their attitudes and life styles, the impact of culture shock may be lessened.

Research is underway to try and identify those individuals who are more prone to suffer from this malady, especially severe when one must live for a long time in another culture. Professor W.J. Redden, a Canadian now living in Bermuda, developed a *Culture Shock Inventory* for this purpose. His premise is that:

> Culture shock is a psychological disorientation caused by misunderstanding or not understanding the cues from another culture. It arises from such things as lack of knowledge, limited prior experience, and personal rigidity.

Therefore, he seeks to assess persons going on foreign deployment on eight measures:

1. Western Ethnocentrism—the degree to which the western value system is seen as appropriate for other parts of the world.
2. Intercultural Experience—the degree of direct experience with people from other countries, through working, traveling, and conversing; also learned skills, such as language and culture studies.
3. Cognitive Flex—the degree of openness to new ideas, beliefs, experiences, and the ability of the individual to accept these.
4. Behavioral Flex—the degree to which one's own behavior is open to change or alteration; the ability to experiment with new styles.

Table 7-2
Transitional Experience Adjustments
Stage of Transition

Contact	Excitement, euphoria of new experience. Second culture perceived as intriguing, enchanting. Perceptions screened and selected.	Stimulated and playful—sense of discovery. Attuned to similarities, not differences.	Functionally integrated with own culture—interested, assured, and impressionistic.	New environment viewed from insularity of one's own ethnocentrism. Differences are perceptually deselected since person has few psychological mechanisms for dealing with radically new stimuli. The similarities between new and home culture are validation of own cultural status, role, and identity. Provides rationalizations and confirmations of own cultural behavior.
Disintegration	Significant differences in host/home cultures are noted and begin to impact. Present cultural realities cannot be screened out, so contrasts are observed.	Sense of increasing confusion, loss, disorientation. Experiences isolation, apathy, loneliness and inadequacy.	Periods of depression, withdrawal, severe "homesickness." Increase of tension and frustration.	Cultural differences begin to intrude, and loss of self esteem may grow because of awareness of one's difference from host culture. Experiences loss of own cultural ties and supports. Begins to misread new cultural cues; unable accurately to predict social expectations of Locals. Alienation may set in; inability to "fit in" may lead to undermining of sense of identity and personality.

Reintegration	Differences in second culture may be rejected, possibly through generalizations, stereotyping, evaluations, and judgemental attitudes and behaviors.	Manifesting anger, rage, nervousness, some anxiety and frustration.	Behavior characterized by suspicion, hostility, exclusiveness, opinionatedness rebellion, and rejection.	Rejection syndrome with second culture demonstrated by preoccupations with likes and dislikes, and a projection of the latter upon the locals. Negative behavior evident in overcompensation, greater self-assertion, and growing self-esteem for coping.
Autonomy	Differences and similarities are legitimized and accepted. Begins to overcome previous defensiveness. Rising sensitivity.	More relaxed, self-assured, warm, empathetic and accepting with indigenous population. Begins to communicate nonverbally.	Demonstrates self-control, confidence, independence, and like an "old hand."	Capable of negotiating, socially and linguistically, in the second culture. Can cope with differences, and is assured of ability to survive new and unfamiliar experiences. Significant growth in personal flexibility.
Independence	Differences and similarities in second culture valued. More independent, yet giving.	Experiences with locals trust, humor, love and other emotions.	Person becomes more expressive, creative, and self-actualizing.	Social, psychological, and cultural differences are accepted and even enjoyed. Capable of exercising choice, responsibility and meaning in the second culture. Able to profit from further transitions.

5. Cultural Knowledge: Specific—the degree of awareness and understanding of various customs, beliefs, and patterns of behavior in a specific other culture.
6. Cultural Knowledge: General—the degree of awareness, sensitivity, and understanding of various beliefs and institutions in other cultures.
7. Culture Behavior: General—the degree of awareness and understanding of patterns of cultural differences and human behavior.
8. Interpersonal Sensitivity—the degree of awareness and understanding of verbal and nonverbal human behavior.

The above categories are interesting for they provide clues to the kind of personality to be cultivated if a professional or manager is to successfully cope in the international arena.

Studies have shown that children are more adaptable to new cultural challenges, while spouses, usually wives, are more prone to experience cultural shock—its impact is lessened on their partner immersed in the foreign business experience. However, upon return to the home culture, the manager, professional, or technican is likely to confront "reentry shock."

When in a strange culture, our concerns that may disturb or frustrate, may be real or imagined. Those in culture shock manifest obvious *symptoms* as our previous conceptual models indicated. Some of the signs evident while on an overseas assignment may be as follows: excessive concern over cleanliness, feeling that what is new and strange is "dirty;" this may be seen with reference to water, food, dishes, and bedding, or it might be evident in excessive fear of servants and shopkeepers relative to the disease they might bear. Other indications of the person in such trauma are feelings of helplessness and confusion, growing dependence on long-term residents of one's own nationality, constant irritations over delays and minor frustrations, as well as undue concern for being cheated, robbed, or injured. Some become mildly hypochondriac, expressing overconcern for minor pains and skin eruptions—it may even get to the point of real psychosomatic illnesses. Often such individuals postpone learning the local language and customs, dwelling instead on their loneliness and longing for back home, to be with one's own and to talk to people who "make sense."

Some anthropologists, like Kalervo Oberg, consider culture shock a "malady, an occupational disease which may be experienced by people who are suddenly transported abroad." He notes that in the process of acculturation—adaptation to the second culture—the victim may experience depression, annoyance, confusion, disorientation, withdrawal, hostility, and paranoia toward the "foreign" people among whom he or she resides. For persons who seek international assignments as a means of escaping "back home problems" with career, marriage, drugs or alcoholism, it should be obvious that the experience abroad will probably only exacerbate personal problems that might be better resolved in one's native culture.

Culture shock is neither good or bad, necessary or unnecessary. It is a reality that many people face when in strange and unexpected situations. For personal reasons, an individual might seek to minimize the dysfunctional effects, and to maximize the opportunities of another cultural experience. For world corporations, government agencies, and international foundations, the focus on foreign deployment of personnel might be concentrated on delimiting the culture shock in order to be more cost effective, to promote the employee's productivity abroad, or to improve client and customer relations with host nationals. What can be done to facilitate acculturation when business or pleasure take one for an extensive stay in another country or continent? Such answers are equally valid for foreign students brought to another country for study or training, as well as to bicultural exchanges or third country nationals who are brought to one's homeland for business or public service.

Organizations responsible for sending others abroad should be careful in their recruitment and selection of their own nationals for foreign service. Surveys have shown that those who adjust and work well in international assignments are usually well-integrated personalities with qualities such as, flexibility, personal stability, social maturity, and social inventiveness. Cosmopolitans either have fewer prejudices, or are at least aware of their own biases, and can be more tolerant of the objects of their bias. Such candidates for overseas work are not given to grandiose or unrealistic expectations, irrational concepts of self or others, nor do they have tendencies toward excessive depression, discouragement, criticism, or hostility.

On the other hand, one should also be realistic about the difficulties that may be experienced when living abroad. Intestinal disorders and exotic diseases *are real*, and may not always be avoided by innoculations or new antibiotics such as doxycline. In some countries, water, power, transportation, and housing shortages *are real*, and one's physical comfort may be seriously inconvenienced. In other nations at various stages of development, political instability, tribal wars, ethnic feuds, and social breakdown may make such places undesirable, for a time, in which to accept or seek an assignment. Real difficulties can arise from not knowing how to communicate in a land that is foreign to a person, or in trying to cope with strange climates or customs. But we are born with the ability to learn, to adapt, to survive, to enjoy. After all, human beings do create culture, so the shocks caused by such differences are not unbearable or without value. The intercultural experience can be most satisfying, contributing much to personal and professional advancement. One can discover neighbors everywhere, and develop friends in the world community.

Implications for Other Traumas

The phenomenon and process of culture shock has applications to other life crises. The descriptions and information provided in the above section have transfer value for the person going through a divorce, or recovering from near-death illness. For example, there is the matter of *role shock*. Each of us choses or is assigned or is conditioned to a variety of roles in society and its organizations—son or daughter, parent or child, husband or wife, teacher or engineer, manager or union organizer, man or woman. In these positions, people have expectations of us and we have expectations of them, and such expectations often differ for a role in different cultures. A woman, for instance, may do in one culture what is forbidden in another. In some societies, senior citizens are revered, while in others they are ignored. In some places, youth regard teachers with awe, while in others they treat them as inferiors or "buddies."

But that role perception is subject to change, even accelerated change, so that for some today they are experiencing role crisis within their own culture. The person who has been brought up to a particular understanding of what a manager is and does, may be upset when he or she finally achieves that role and finds it to be changed, so that one's traditional views of the function are suddenly obsolete. Role shock has been used to describe the discrepancies between what the individual views as the ideal role, versus what he or she discovers to be the actual or relevant role—there is a gap between the role one expects to play and what one must actually do to succeed. It can be very disconcerting, and the shock may be severe or even last for a long period. It can be related to identity crisis if one's life meaning is found in a job or role, so the description in the previous model can be applicable here. A cross-cultural assignment can accentuate role shock. Many technicians sent abroad find themselves in totally different role requirements than back home—for example, they may be asked to do less themselves, and to devote more time to training, consulting, and supervising.

When individuals return from foreign deployment, possibly having experienced long times as expatriates, there is another form of reverse culture shock that can be faced. Having perceived their own culture from abroad, more objectively, one can have a more severe and sustained jolt through *reentry shock*. Robert Maddox, writing in *Personnel*, a publication of the American Management Association, maintains that the problem is growing in the multinational marketplace, and that managers need special counsel to assist their reintegration into their native country and parent organization. Life for the manager while abroad, especially working in an international division or foreign subsidiary, can be radically different than in the more traditional home organizational and social culture. Some returning "expats" feel a subtle downgrading and loss of prestige and benefits. Others bewail the loss of servants and higher social contacts, as well as other overseas "perks" or prerequisites. Many feel uncomfortable for six months or more in their native land, frustrated with their old company, bored with their narrow-minded colleagues. They seem out of touch with what has happened in the country or corporation, and no longer seem to fit in. The phenomenon can be temporary and the person assisted with reorientation programs. But for some, culture and reentry shocks can be the means for major choices and transitions—to a new locale, new job or career, and new life style. Other "expats" never do make the necessary adjustment, and live as strangers in their own homes.

Just as individuals can experience culture shock, so institutions may experience *organization shock*. Companies or agencies that operate on obsolete organizational models, such as the traditional bureaucracy, instead of the more relevant, emerging "adhocracy," can experience all of the disorientation, disturbance, and dislocation used in the previous section to describe people in culture shock, or the transitional experience, or identity crisis. Increasingly, corporations with archaic policies, structures, and procedures experience this phenomenon.

In a sense, future shock now being experienced by many inhabitants of this planet is like mass culture shock. An emerging cyberculture is rapidly impacting upon the traditional societies. People throughout the world are finding it increasingly difficult to cope—everything "nailed down" seems to be coming loose. As Alvin Toffler wrote in his best-seller, *Future Shock:*

> In three short decades between now and the end of the century, millions of psychologically normal people will experience an abrupt collision with the future. Affluent, educated citizens of the world's most rich and technically advanced nations will fall victim to tomorrow's most menacing malady—the disease of rapid change. Unable to keep up with the supercharged pace of change, brought to the edge of breakdown by incessant demands to adapt, many will plunge into future shock. For them the future has come too soon!

> The symptoms of future shock range from confusion, anxiety, and hostility to regression, excessive authority, physical illness, seemingly senseless violence, and self-destructive apathy . . . Its victims feel constantly harassed and attempt to reduce the number of changes and decisions with which they must cope. The ultimate causal ties of future shock terminate in cutting off the outside world entirely—dropping out, spiraling deeper and deeper into disengagement.

So many people are saying, "stop the world, I want to get off"; many are succumbing to escapisms like alcoholism, drug addiction, terrorism, or hedonism. Many who cannot "shift their gears" to the new culture and lifestyle, who cannot make the transition to a different society of the future, will not make it into the twenty-first century, either figuratively or literally. It is the authors' contention that people who are more cosmopolitan, have experienced culture shock, have profited from opportunities to deal with human differences, are, as a result, likely to cope more effectively with future shock. As human society moves beyond industrialism and creates a new civilization, Toffler urges people to become more anticipatory, as well as participatory in the decisions that shape their future; to channel our destiny in humane directions and to ease the trauma of transition!

Fostering Acculturation

Stress or tension is no respecter of time, place, or persons. In today's "pressure-cooker" world, some tension is almost normal. A society in transition, such as ours, is bound to produce more stress than previous generations experienced in the world of the past. In a changing environment that is fast-paced, change itself can lead to stress and frustration. The need today is for modern persons to learn to defuse stress, to reduce tension to controllable levels, and to alleviate pressures. Otherwise, insecurity, instability, and insomnia take over.

Characteristic of American culture is the drive for success, and a low tolerance for failure. Thus, when such nationals go abroad, they find it more difficult to evaluate progress and to measure their success. The encounter with a different culture can not only heighten stress, but cause such personal confusion that a vicious cycle is set in motion. In the process of attempting cultural adaption, the increase of stress can lead to frustration, which contributes to greater anxiety, sometimes leading to hostility—thus the cycle can repeat itself. What, then, can be done to better manage the expected stress and strain of intercultural living and working? Meditation, biofeedback, and exercise are certainly preferable to tranquilizers.

Writing in *Mental Hygiene* some years ago about "Family Adaptation Overseas," H. David and D. Elkind pointed out that stable, healthy family relationships abroad can make the differences between success and failure in the foreign assignment. Families trained to interact in mutually supportive ways can provide themselves with their own resources for adjustment in an alien environment. In other words, an innovative family community can provide the ego support that may not, at first, seem evident in the second culture. But suppose a manager, technician, or professional is sent abroad without family for some length of time? Here are ten tips that anyone may employ to deflate the stress and tension of culture shock wherever and whenever it may be confronted:

Be Culturally Prepared. Forewarned is forearmed. Individual or group study and training are possible to understand cultural factors in general, as well as cultural specifics. The public libraries will provide a variety of material about a particular culture and nationality, if one has the motivation to read beforehand about the people with whom he or she will soon be living. The public health service can also advise about required innoculations, dietary clues, and other sanitary data about the land of one's hosts. Before departure, the person scheduled for overseas service can experiment with the food or restaurants representative of the second culture. Furthermore, one might establish contact in his or her homeland with foreign students or visitors from the area to which one is going.

Learn Local Communication Complexities. By all means, study the language of the place to which one is assigned should it be different from one's native tongue. At least, learn some of the basics that will help in exchanging greetings and shopping. In addition to courses and books on the subject, audio tapes, cassettes, and records can advance one's communication skills in the second culture before and after departure. Sometimes a class can be attended or a tutor obtained for additional language study upon arrival. This is important to ascertain the nonverbal communication system in the country, such as the significant gestures, signs, and symbols. Published guides of culture specifics can be most helpful to learn expected courtesies, typical customs, and other niceties that improve intercultural relationships. Not only does the new foreigner need a local dictionary, but also must learn what newspapers and magazines will provide the best insight into this people.

Mix with the Host Nationals. Socialization with people from the nation to which one intends going is essential, both before departure and upon arrival. Those met in one's home culture may provide introductions to relatives and friends in their native land. Try and live on the economy. But if one is forced into living within a company or military colony of one's own kind, then avoid the "compound mentality." Immerse oneself in the host culture: Join in, whenever feasible, the artistic and community functions, the carnivals and rites, the international fraternal or professional organizations. Offer to teach students or business people one's language in exchange for knowledge of their language; share skills from skiing to tennis and it will be the means for making new international friends.

Be Creative and Experimental. Dare to risk, try, and learn, and perhaps even to fail, which also can lead to wisdom. Truly, nothing ventured, nothing gained. It takes social imagination to leap across cultural gaps, and to put oneself in the other's private world. Innovations abroad may mean taking risks to get around barriers of bureaucracy and communication in order to lessen social distance. This principle extends from experimenting with the local food to keeping a diary as an escape to record one's adventures and frustrations. Tours, hobbies, and a variety of cultural pursuits can produce positive results in a strange land. In a sense, one needs to be open and existential to the many opportunities that may present themselves while abroad to know more about the locals who are seemingly so different.

Be Culturally Sensitive. Be aware of the special customs and traditions which if followed by a visitor, will make one more acceptable. Certainly, avoid stereotyping the natives, criticizing their local practices and procedures, while using the standard of one's own country for comparison purposes. Recognize that in some cultures, such as Asia and Iran, saving face and not giving offense may be considered very important—sometimes, invitations or agreements will seemingly be given as a social grace, when a local may have no intention of following up on the matter. It takes great sensitivity to make such fine distinctions, so that one senses when the natives are merely being polite or gracious rather than hurt us with a "no." Americans, for instance, are quite pragmatic and like to organize. It may be a real challenge, then, for such persons to relax and endeavor to get into a different rhythm of the place and people they are visiting.

Recognize Complexities in Host Cultures. Counteract the tendency to make quick, simplistic assessments of situations in a country foreign to a visitor. In most complex societies, its composition is made up of different ethnic or religious groupings, stratified into social classes or castes, differentiated by regions or geographical factors, separated into rural and urban settlements. Each of these may have distinct subcultural characteristics over which is superimposed an official language, national institutions, and peculiar customs or history that tie this people together. Thus, avoid pat generalizations and quick assumptions—the particular people you meet there may not be representative of the majority culture. Instead, be tentative in one's conclusions, realizing one's point of contact is a limited sample, within a multifaceted society.

Perceive Self as a Culture Bearer. That is, each person bears his or her own culture, and distortions, when going abroad. Thus, one views everything in the host culture through the unique filter of one's own cultural background. The cause of disturbances in one's experience in a foreign land may be in the visitor's upbringing or culture, or in lack of understanding of the second culture. If the visitor comes from a culture that is impersonal, then that person can expect to be startled in a culture in which "personalism" is esteemed. So too, if one is raised in democratic traditions, that individual may be jolted in a society that values the authority of the head male in the family and extends this reverence to national leaders.

Be Patient, Understanding, and Accepting of Self and Hosts. In strange situations, one must be more tolerant and flexible. In the unfamiliar environment, an attitude of healthy curiosity, of willingness to bear inconveniences, of patience when answers or solutions are not forthcoming or difficult to obtain, is valuable to maintain mental balance. Such patience must be extended from self to other compatriots who struggle with cultural adjustment, to the locals who may function at a different pace. Time can be a great healer and work wonders in foreign cultural encounters which may vex and irritate.

Be Most Realistic in Expectations. Avoid overestimating oneself, his or her hosts, or the cross-cultural experience. Disappointments can be lessened if one scales down expectations and needs as appropriate for the local scene. Thus, one may be pleasantly surprised when things happen beyond one's expectations. This is most sound advice when one moves from the First World to the Third or Fourth Worlds. It applies to everything from airline schedules to renting rooms. Multinational managers, especially, must be careful in new cultures not to set unreasonable work expectations for themselves or their subordinates until both are more acclimated. At least, make allowances for jet fatigue before mounting the parapets!

Accept the Challenge of Intercultural Experiences. Anticipate, savour, and confront the psychological challenge to adapt and change as a result of a new cross-cultural opportunity. Be prepared to alter one's habits, attitudes, values, tastes, relationships, or sources of satisfaction. Such flexibility can become a means for personal growth, and the transnational experience can be more fulfilling. Of course, a deep interest and commitment to one's work—professionalism—can be marvelous therapy in intercultural situations, counteracting isolation and strangeness when living outside one's culture.

Conclusions

No particular culture is inherently better or worse than another—just different and unique. Every culture provides its adherents with a sense of identity, and has a profound influence on their behavior and life space. Thus, a transitional experience beyond one's culture can contribute to a heightened sense of self, or can deeply threaten the ego. Each individual going into a second culture can benefit, or suffer, or experience both realities through such encounters. But intercultural contacts are more satisfying when people make the effort to communicate, to enter into interpersonal relationships, to perceive and deal with differences, to behave reasonably well in situations in which there is no personal precedent. Transitional experiences require change from monocultural to a multicultural frame of reference, and are essential to the working through of one's self concept. The tensions and crises of such change demand an individual answer to life's confusions, which may reaffirm one's uniqueness in relation to others, especially when they are strangers.

References

Boulding, K. & E., *Introduction to the Global Society; Interdisciplinary Perspectives.* New York: Learning Resources in International Studies, 1977.

Brislin, R., Bochner, S. and Lonner, W., *Cross-cultural Perspectives on Learning.* New York: John Wiley & Sons, 1977.

Council on International Educational Exchange, *Whole World Handbook.* New York: CIEE (777 UN Plaza), 1978-79.

Darrow, K. & Palmquist, B., eds., *Trans-cultural Study Guide.* Denver: Volunteers in Asia (via Bookstore, Center for Research and Education), 1975.

Fersh, S., *Learning About Peoples and Culture.* Denver: McDougal, Littell (via Bookstore, Center for Research and Education), 1974.

Frieg, J.P. and S.G. Blair, *There Is a Difference: 12 Interculture Perspectives.* Denver, Colo.: CRE/Meridan House, 1975.

Huston, P., *Message from the Village* (Female Role Change in Third World), Epoch B. Foundation, P.O. Box 1972, Grand Central Station, New York, N.Y. 10017, 1978.

McNeill, Allen, Schmidt, *Cultural Awareness for Young Children.* Detroit: R.H. Stone Products (13735 Puritan), 1978.

Matthiasson, C., *Many Sisters, Women in Cross-Cultural Perspective.* New York: Macmillian/Free Press, 1974.

Pursel, J.J., *The Effectiveness of Classroom Instruction in the Attitudes Toward Overseas Culture Shock Issues.* (Doctoral dissertation, United States International University) Ann Arbor, Michigan: University Microfilms, 1973.

Redden, W., *Culture Shock Inventory—Manual.* Fredericton, N.B., Canada: Organizational Tests Ltd., 1975.

Spielbergen, C.D. and Guerrero, R.D. (ed.), *Cross-Cultural Anxiety.* New York: Wiley, 1976.

Stessen, L., "Culture Shock and the American Businessman Overseas," *International Educational and Cultural Exchange.* U.S. Advisory Commission on International Education and Cultural Affairs, Washington, D.C. 20520. Summer 1973.

Toffler, A., *Future Shock.* New York: Random House, 1970.

Tyler, L. et al, *Intercultural Communicating.* BYU Language and Intercultural Research Center, Provo, Utah, 1976.

8
Managing
Organization Culture

Coping with Organizations' Cultural Differences

What have these people in common?

- Sally has just graduated from college and is hired as a management trainee for a multinational corporation.
- Hari just received his MBA from an American university and is employed in his own country of Pakistan for a Middle Eastern Airline.
- Frank has been an American expatriate for six years and has been reassigned to corporate headquarters in Boise, Idaho.
- Mohammed, an Egyptian who was educated in Britain, is posted temporarily for additional training at a factory of his transnational employer in Fort Wayne, Indiana.
- Patricia, of New England Yankee stock, is transferred by her company, A.T.& T., to their offices in Macon, Georgia.
- Lee is leaving his native Korea to supervise a construction crew of his fellow nationals in Saudi Arabia where his company has a subcontract with the U.S. petroleum manufacturer.
- Brett is a senior vice-president with an Ohio company that has just been acquired by the nineteenth largest multinational corporation in the world.
- Alicia, a Hispanic high school graduate, has just been recruited under an Affirmative Action plan to work in a government law enforcement agency that has been dominated until now by white Anglo males.

Each of these individuals is faced with the problem of integration into an unfamiliar organizational culture. Perhaps, it would be better to think of it as the challenge of acculturation. They must learn the accepted cultural behavior in a unique organizational environment which will ensure their entry, acceptance, and effectiveness in that setting. Their approach to the different institutional contexts can facilitate their success or failure in the corporation or agency. Writing on "The Organization as a Microculture," Dr. Leonard Nadler reminds persons in situations such as were described above, that their own "cultural baggage" can impose limitations on their own creativity. One may have a "tunnel vision" based on past experience that hampers adequate adjustment and performance in the new scene. Whether one is a recruit in the organization, transferred within the company domestically or internationally, or an employee of a subsidiary owned by a larger entity, each must learn to cope with a unique subculture.

There are many dimensions to be examined relative to this concept of the organization as a microculture, influenced by the larger macroculture in which it operates. Everything the reader has learned previously in this text about culture in general, can be applied to organizational culture. The various ways to study a national or ethnic culture that are described in Chapter 5 are equally valid for the subculture of any human system that employs people for a specific purpose. Furthermore there are related concepts, even synonyms, that amplify the subject under consideration, such as organizational environment, climate, or atmosphere. Each organization also has a distinctive psychological and even physical *space* that it occupies in a society or macroculture. The organization's culture is intertwined with its sense of space, and each influences the other. It carves out its own "territorial imperative" with reference to an industry and competitors. Some corporations, for example, provide a psychological space that is unhurried and uncluttered, while others provide a situation that is stressful and crowded. The cultural behavior of the organization can be further manifested in the space allocations for executives and workers, for departments and divisions. Organizational space becomes a consideration in making many management decisions, such as the site for training programs, what public tours are to be shown, what areas are designated as "security" and entrance there is limited, what external structures and appearance communicate to a community. When planning change, the invisible space of the organization must be examined in terms of forces therein that influence employee behavior. Within the "private world" of a company or agency, one studies the driving forces, for example, which would facilitate the proposed change in the culture, as well as the resisting forces that would perpetuate the status quo. Institutions, like individuals, have their own perceptual fields or base from which they operate in the larger culture.

When anthropologists study a people, they examine how a group defines and delineates itself. A related concept is organization *boundaries*. Human systems demarcate themselves from the larger environment by physical or psychological barriers between internal and external activities, or by differences in terminology, norms, and expectations for people associated with them. Such boundaries, whether they be visible or invisible, serve as buffers between the macro- and microcultures, as well as filtering and coding functions for the screening of inputs into the organization. Finally, as Drs. Hamner and Organ remind us in their book, *Organizational Behavior*, these boundaries protect the integrity of the system, preventing it from being absorbed by the external environment, or from losing its distinctive character. Every organization interacts and is interdependent with larger social systems which surround it. The organizational boundaries help to focus human energies in the accomplishment of specific mission, in delimiting human interactions, and in pointing up significant organizational relationships.

The organizational culture should be responsive to both internal and external forces for change. In fact, the whole new behavioral science technology called *organization development*, not only studies a system's culture, but creates strategies for its planned renewal or alteration. The accumulated cultural wisdom of an organization that began with its entrepreneurial founders, is refined and developed by subsequent management and employees, as a means of ensuring that entity's survival and growth. In the private sector, for instance, organizational culture should facilitate effective operations and profitability. But if the system is to remain relevant in serving human need and in avoiding the impact of "organization shock," then it must engage in a process of continuous planned change, including in cultural practices

The organization's culture affects employee, supplier, and customer behavior, as well as community relationships. The reader of this material would do well to consider these ideas in terms of one's own organizational culture, its client's or customer's organizational culture, as well as related organizational cultures (such as contractors, competitors, or government regulators). Furthermore, the issues of this chapter have implications regionally, nationally, and internationally. The corporate culture of Coca-Cola influences and is influenced by the regional culture wherein are located its headquarters and principal activities, Atlanta, Georgia. That same corporate culture interfaces with American culture in its domestic marketing, as well as when it produces and sells its soft drinks abroad, whether that be China or Mexico. Coca-Cola's culture has impacted upon the Mexican people, for instance, and it has adapted to the Spanish culture of the United States' adjoining neighbor on its southern border.

The organization's culture has a powerful impact on the worker's or member's morale and productivity. It even influences the organization's image of itself which, in turn, is communicated to its public. Those associated with the organization can either accept or reject its culture. If it is the former, then the member may conform or modify that culture. If it is the latter, then its personnel become frustrated or leave that organization.

Analyzing Organizational Culture

An organization's culture is multidimensional. It encompasses a body of ideas and concepts, customs and traditions, procedures and habits for coping in a particular macroculture. It is an interwoven fabric that helps people in the microculture to achieve its objectives and preserve its values. It represents an interplay of diverse subsystems, such as economic, technological, educational, and political, in addition to social, value, and belief systems.

There are aspects of an organization's culture that are formal, explicit, and overt, just as there are dimensions that are informal, implicit, and covert. Fundamentally, the organization is an energy exchange system. There are inputs into the social system of information and resources. Physical and psychic energy pours into the organization, along with capital, to be transformed into output. In attempting to achieve its goals and mission, the organizational culture is further influenced by leadership practices, norms and standards, rules and regulations, attitudes and principles, ethics and values, policies and practices, structures and technologies, products (artifacts) and services, roles and relationships. To facilitate these activities, cultural mandates or traditions are established concerning dress codes, work hours, work space and facilities, tools and equipment, communication procedures and special language, rewards and recognitions, as well as various personnel provisions. The resulting cultural behavior and activities are manifested in the outputs, such as products, services, personnel, or public information (Figure 8-1).

An organization as large as General Motors, for example, has many subcultures in the form of divisions for manufacturing, marketing, and other functions or models of cars. It may have many domestic and foreign subsidiaries that also have unique subcultures. The largest transnational corporations adapt themselves to the culture and circumstances in which they operate, while trying to retain that which gives them their distinctiveness and accomplishments. The GM culture is quite different from that of competitors within one's own country, such as Ford Motors or American Motors, but it is especially different from a comparable company abroad, such as Datsun in Japan or Volvo in Sweden. The formal aspects of GM's culture are like the tip of an iceberg—its overt activities are written objectives, technological processes, raw materials, and manpower skills; the informal or covert elements involve attitudes and feelings, values and group norms that dominate the organization and affect both productivity and quality control. When General Motors, for example, opens a subsidiary plant in Juarez, Mexico, it develops a Mexican-American management team to create a plant culture appropriate to that community. It provides the Mexican and American managers, and their spouses with language and cultural training to enhance the success of the intercultural operation.

One way of diagnosing an organization's culture is to use an approach like Rensis Likert, described in Table 8-1. Dr. Likert examines six critical factors of management—leadership, motivation, communication, decisions, goals, and control. Then he characterizes these in terms of four systems—the first two types are traditional or classical (almost like Douglas McGregor's

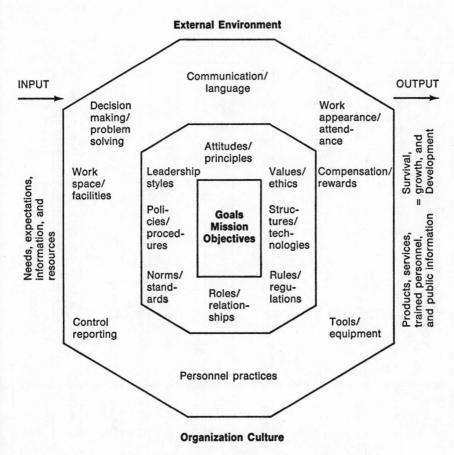

Figure 8-1. Shown here is a conceptional illustration of the many aspects of organizational culture.

Theory X Style of Management), while the next two types are more democratic and participative (comparable to McGregor's Theory Y.) The differences in the organizational cultures of the industrial age or disappearing bureaucracy, and that of the emerging superindustrial entity, the adhocracy, is evident in Table 8-2. This reprint from Dr. Phillip Harris's text, *Organizational Dynamics*, points up the direction of change in organizational culture as one reads the left column in contrast to the right column that describes cultural behavior in the organization of the future.

(Text continued on page 109.)

Table 8-1
Profile of Organizational Characteristics

INSTRUCTIONS: For each variable, place an "x" in the position that best describes conditions as they currently exist in your organization.

Issues	Systems: 1	2	3	4
LEADERSHIP				
How much confidence is shown in subordinates?	None	Condescending	Substantial	Complete
How free do they feel to talk to superiors about job?	Not at all	Not very	Rather free	Fully free
MOTIVATION				
Are subordinates' ideas sought and used, if worthy?	Seldom	Sometimes	Usually	Always
Is predominant use made of 1 fear, 2 threats, 3 punishment, 4 rewards, 5 involvement?	1,2,3 occasionally 4	4, some 3	4, some 3&5	5,4, based on group
Where is responsibility felt for achieving organization's goals?	Mostly at top	Top and middle	Fairly general	At all levels
COMMUNICATION				
How much cooperative teamwork exists?	None	Little	Some	Great deal
What is the direction of information flow?	Downward	Mostly downward	Down and up	Down, up & sideways
How is downward communication accepted?	With suspicion	Possibly w/suspicion	With caution	With a receptive mind
How accurate is upward communication?	Often wrong	Censored for the boss	Limited accuracy	Accurate
How well do superiors know problems faced by subordinates?	Know little	Some knowlege	Quite well	Very well
DECISIONS				
At what level are decisions made?	Mostly at top	Policy at top, some delegation	Broad policy at top, more delegation	Throughout but well integrated
Are subordinates involved in decisions related to their work?	Not at all	Occasionally consulted	Generally consulted	Fully involved

Issues		Systems: 1	2	3	4
DECISIONS	Decisions are based on adequate information and use of sound decision models.	Rarely	Sometimes	Often	Usually
	Financial factors, as opposed to consideration of whole system, control most decisions.	Usually	Often	Sometimes	Factors are Balanced
GOALS	Is the organization "activity" or "goal" oriented?	React mostly to "in" basket	Do what we are told	Have some goals	Acitivity relates to system of goals
	How are organizational goals established?	Orders issued	Orders, some comments invited	After discussion, by orders	By group action (except in crisis)
	How much covert resistance to goals is present?	Strong resistance	Moderate resistance	Some resistance at times	Little or none
	At what level are goals set?	Not at all	Top level only	Through divisional department level	Through branch/section level
	How often are individual goal and performance conferences held?	Never	Rarely	Semi-Annually	Quarterly or Monthly
CONTROL	Is delegation of responsibility and authority adequate?	Two levels too high	One level too high	Adequate	Just right
	Is there an informal organization resisting the formal one?	Yes	Usually	Sometimes	No, same goals as formal
	What are cost, productivity and other control data used for?	Policing, punishment	Reward and punishment	Reward, some self-guidance	Self-guidance problem solving

By permission of Dr. Rensis Likert (Rensis Likert Associates, Inc., 630 City Center Bldg., Ann Arbor, Mi. 48108), as reprinted from *Organization Dynamics* by P.R. Harris, 1973.

Table 8-2
Change in Organization Cultures

Disappearing Bureaucracy	Emerging Adhocracy
(Industrial Age Model—the "factory" system comparable to McGregor's Theory X Management and Likert's System 1/2.)	(Superindustrial Age Model—the "cybernated" system comparable to McGregor's Theory Y and Likert's System 3/4.)
Old Culture—a system characterized by more permanence, hierarchy and division of labor.	**New Culture**—fast-moving, information-rich, kinetic organization of the future.
Traditionally, workers labored in sharply defined slots or roles with narrow specializations. The operated within a chain of command from the top down. Somewhat intractable structures and departments . . . . Slow to change, usually as a result of external influences. Somewhat static in operations . . . Primarily concerned about self-interests of organization . . . . Functions well in a stable society where problems are routine and predictable, environment is competitive and undifferentiated.	Modern systems with transient units, mobile personnel, and continuous reorganization . . . . Workers roles more hazy and temporary in a setting where talents and disciplines converge to accomplish task . . . . Fluid, participative arrangements with changing organizational roles, relationships, and structures. Characterized by disposable divisions, task forces, project teams, and adhoc units . . . . Sense of corporate social responsibility. . . . Dynamic, self-renewing, continuously adapting . . . . Functions best in a superindustrial society of cyberculture characterized by accelerating change.
Vertical power concentration among a few at top levels who make all important decisions for lower echelons . . . . Organizational communication is vertical, slow, and delay is normal . . . . Simple problem-solving mechanisms for routine issues and low speed decisions . . . . Staff/ line arrangements between support and operative units . . . . Requires mass of moderately educated workers for routine performance . . . . Emphasis on efficiency, profitability, plant/ equipment maintenance, and capital expansion.	Horizontal disbursement of power with a shift of decisions sideways and to lower levels of responsibility . . . . More sharing of decision-making with workers and consumers, and wider input . . . . Organizational communications circular or lateral with fast information flow and computerized systems; delay costly . . . . Complex problem-solving for meeting increasingly non-routine, novel and unexpected problems requiring high speed decisions . . . . Team approach with convergence of specializations . . . . Requires fewer knowledge workers and technicians . . . . Emphasis on people maintenance and human resource development.

Old Organization Man—Frequently a white male who employs his energies and skills for the good of the organization to whom he is loyal and committed. Considers executives and managers the "brains," while workers are the "hands." Labors within a hierarchical pyramid in which rank and role are clearly defined. Looks to the corporation or agency for approval and recognition, reward and punishment. He is conditioned somewhat to subserviance and paid to conform; he is discouraged from displaying creativity or deviancy. Concerned about economic security and status in the organization, subordinating individuality for the good of the organization. Joins in corporate emphasis on competition, success, and achieving quantity production. Usually a narrow specialist with limited education who fears change, and advocates the status quo. By his past orientation, he is ripe for future shock . . . . The exceptional among this type were the free-swinging enterpreneurs who built vast enterprises, fiercely defending rugged individualism and independence, in the spirit of Western pioneers.

New Associative Person—Varied competent people, including many women and minorities, who employ their energies and skills for self-actualization, often in temporary groupings. Mobile, self-motivated persons who take economic security for granted, and seek personal and professional development. See executives and managers as coordinators/consultants of mixed, temporary work teams. Operate in complex setting, within a matrix requiring flexibility and functional skills. Often creative deviants who look within self and profession for approval and fulfillment. Knowledge workers who respect only the authority of competence. Skilled in human relations and group dynamics so as to be capable of quick, intense work relationships on a temporary team, and then disengaging for another challenging assignment. Agents of change who find transience liberating and emphasize cooperation and quality production or service. Individuals who create and plan their futures, envisioning change as a challenge for new learning . . . . These superindustrial persons are often part of enterpreneurial groups, sometimes within large, complex systems in which interdependence is the norm. Unafraid to enter into new fields, and even to pioneer the universe.

Many organizations are now in a state of profound transition between the disappearing bureaucracy and the emerging adhocracy. Some will disappear before the turn of the century, while others will adapt for the twenty-first century. To help one assess further the status of the social institutions in which he or she may be involved, the reader is referred to Appendix C where an "Organizational Culture Survey Instrument" has been provided.

Possibly the simplest way to analyze an organization's culture is in terms of the ten basic classifications provided in Chapter 5.

Communication and Language. Each human system may have unique interaction processes or lexicon, in addition to that of the macroculture. The military subculture, for instance, has its own terminology, codes, and acronyms. If the organization is of a scientific, technical, or research nature, it may employ a whole scientific vocabulary. Similary, various professions, such as law, medicine, and psychology, have their own specialized languages. To facilitate the work process, many trades and occupations have their own jargon and abbreviations. The more physical the work, the more likely a specialized speech pattern may develop. Some jobs characteristically involve much swearing or sexual references. Other careers, such as in the criminal justice systems, require a coded system of speech. Social status inside the organizational culture can be observed in terms of language analysis—blue-collar workers may not speak as sophisticatedly as managers; supervisors generally have, for example, a better command of grammar and correct expression, as well as more word power. The cultural orientation of an organization, its formality or informality, can be determined in the way people address one another—"Sir," "Mrs.," "Dr.," "Professor," or first names, as well as the use of ranks and titles.

In this category, one might analyze both verbal and nonverbal communication, especially the body language. With new emphasis on equal opportunity, the changing organizational culture is evident in new job titles, positions, or references which avoid sexist connotations—from a male orientation, the trend is toward a more general or impersonal designation. Even within the same country when new plants or offices are opened, management must seek to learn the regional or geographic language patterns of the area. Just as whole industries may have unique communication systems, so new products, services, and equipment may spawn new forms of communications such as computer languages. An organization's culture, furthermore, can be assessed in terms of its major communication systems—internal/external, formal/informal—and the various combinations of these.

Dress and Appearance. Another characteristic of organizational culture is manifested in the customs, rules, regulations related to one's attire and appearance. Some require uniforms, business suits and ties, and have many requirements or taboos on female clothing (e.g., length of skirts, use of slacks, cosmetics, etc.). Other organizations are very informal and permissive regarding employee garments and adornments. Some professions and occupations delineate themselves through a particular garb, such as a white medical smock or hard hat. In some organizations, all supervisors must wear shirt and tie, while the blue-collar employee has standard work clothes. Dress and appearance at work not only differ by country, but by geographic area within a nation. In the United States, for example, people tend to dress more conservatively on the job in the East, while in the West they may be more informal and colorful in their attire.

Food and Feeding Habits. Some organizational cultures differ radically in their eating procedures—when it is permitted (e.g., length of lunch and coffee breaks), where the employees eat (e.g., executive dining rooms, cafeteria, or from a lunch box), what they eat (e.g., hero sandwiches, fast foods, or lavish menus), and how they eat (e.g., on the run, extended two Martini lunch, "brown bag" with discussions). Many personnel problems or grievances center around food and feeding procedures—frequency of coffee/tea breaks, allowances for overtime dining, office parties, provisions for special foods on the menu (e.g., "soul" and diet foods). In the military subculture, dining may be in the mess or the field, and special rations may be provided in the latter situation. All such factors can have a powerful influence on employees' morale.

Time and Time Consciousness. Some organizations place a high priority on exact promptness, while in others it is relative. Traditional organizations work within a tight time frame of an eight hour day, and all employees are expected to be on duty at 7, 8, 9 a.m., and to depart at 4, 5, or 6 p.m. In some modern enterprises, they are experimenting with flexitime, as well as a variety of approaches to the work week (e.g., one week on and one off, or three- or four-day weeks with longer work days). The forty-hour week is giving way to thirty hours of labor, and some institutions are permitting job sharing (e.g., one job shared by two employees, including husband and wife). Organizations may operate on a variety of time shifts throughout a twenty-four hour day. Some microcultures like the military and police may have their own time system where precision in timing is rewarded. Others operate in a more relaxed time frame where the hours put on the job are incidental to proper accomplishment of tasks. Unions' contract negotiations with employers frequently center around time issues, such as length of work days, holiday schedules, vacation and sick leave. However, the whole industrial age concept of time and work hours is giving way to more flexible, innovative approaches. This becomes an increasingly vital issue as cybernation replaces people, so less work available must be shared by more employees. Furthermore, in the superindustrial age, the fine line between work time and leisure time is eroding. There is also less "clock-watching" in American organizations, and the spreading out of formal work into the evening hours.

Rewards and Recognition. Various organizations use a variety of means to recognize and reinforce achievement, accomplishment, productivity, performance, and experience. In some such microcultures, there are commendations, citations, or visible tributes of all types. There may be markings on uniforms, pins and other adornments to point out the exceptional employee. The whole issue of rank, roles, status, promotions, and fringe benefits can be viewed in this category. Sales personnel who succeed may get free trips or other such ego boosts, while executives get company cars, villas, or stock options. The size, place, and decorations of one's work space can be designated as a means of reward and recognition. The range of procedures in this regard within corporations and government agencies may go from incentive and compensation plans to special perks and retirement dinners.

Relationships and Bisexuality. The organizational chart and structure may indicate much about formalized relationships in such microcultures (e.g., departments, divisions, subsidiaries, or territories). In military organizations rank influences the type of relationship, and people may be divided into squads, companies, battalions, etc. The type of work one does may segregate him or her from others in the organization—those in marketing do not mix with those in manufacturing, or those in research avoid fraternizing with clerical help. One of the authors once worked in a corporation in which the factory workers were never permitted to mix with the office workers, because the latter had status, but only earned half as much. The organizational culture may consciously or unconsciously classify work relationships. There was a time when there were clear cut men's jobs and women's work, but now Equal Employment legislation is overcoming such sex discrimination—male-dominated fire or police departments, for instance, are now opening up to women employees. There was a time when one would call a company or association, and if a female answered, the caller would assume it was a secretary—now it may be a female manager or professional at the other end of the line. Cultural assumptions, distortions, and biases can delimit whole classes of people to underemployment. Today, superindustrial enterprises tend to be more open, informal, and flexible regarding organizational relationships. Such relationships have significant impact on work atmosphere, employee rapport, loyalty and morale, as well as motivations.

Values and Norms. Organizational needs eventually cause the setting of priorities as to what is important in order to satisfy those concerns for survival and development. Thus, an institutional value system emerges regarding customs, practices, and activities that the organization's people highly esteem. Such measures of worth may be positive or negative, written or unwritten, but these values have a powerful influence on employee behavior. The observer of organizational culture should determine what is the relative merit attached to working hard, doing one's duty, observing the rules, teamwork, reliability, customer service, and other such value indicators. These company maxims or value systems may be further reinforced by established standards for worker behavior and performance. Such norms may be found in personnel manuals, performance criteria, union contracts, work conventions, and even management pronouncements. They affect job retention, career development, profitability, and organizational excellence. The values and norms of an organization sometimes are evident in corporate logos, slogans, and symbols, as well as in the literature for internal and external consumption. Statements such as "People are our most important product" or "Service is our name" are among such indications. It can even be expressed in the corporate title such as this La Jolla, California firm's designation—"The Innovative Group, Inc."

Sense of Self and Space. Another aspect of a system's culture is its sense of organization identity, which also can be evident from the above indicators, or in its trademark and public relations program. Older, well established and financed corporations may have a sense of congruence and steadiness. They calmly go about the business of making profits and offering quality service. Other companies have a sense of inferiority or may lack confidence, and struggle to prove themselves even to the point of overcompensation. Still other entities have a real or false sense of superiority, and may be given to exaggeration with their various publics. All of this is manifested in organizational image which can be positive or negative, and is a matter of focus for management consultants who might be called into a social system to improve its effectiveness. Earlier in this chapter we already have discussed this dimension of this category, organizational space, which deals with institutional territoriality. This can range from keeping a sense of distance between the organization and other entities in an industry, or high cooperation with suppliers and other manufacturers. It is shown in organizational space relations and requirements.

Organizational Processes and Learning. Organizational cultures can also be studied in terms of the reasoning, human relations, and manufacturing or technological processes utilized to accomplish tasks. An R & D firm, for instance, might place great emphasis on the scientific method of inquiry. A banking or engineering institution might employ logic, while a company of art dealers or management consultants might make greater use of experience and intuition. Possibly the most important aspect of this is the way the organization processes information—how much and how quickly, who gets it, and for what purpose. In the emerging information-rich, knowledge society with its technicians and knowledge workers, this may turn out to be the most vital process of all to analyze in this regard. Undergirding all these are the means or methods for learning or changing the organizational culture. That is, how well does the organization use its inputs, feedback, and experience? How much energy and finances does it devote to its human resource development? What is the scope, methodology, and quality of its employee training and educational processes? How does informal and on-the-job training complement the formal plan for personnel or career development? Chapters 9-12 explore these issues in greater detail.

Beliefs and Attitudes. One of the most elusive elements of organizational culture to ascertain is the dominant belief system for the institution as a whole. Some organizations, for instance, are success and win oriented—there is nothing they cannot accomplish if they devote their collective energies to a specific task; this, in turn, influences group and individual employee attitudes. Obviously, those in sales and marketing have such convictions about their organization, its products, and services. Organizational ideals and principles are usually subtle and informal, but they impact on employee behavior.

The driving themes can range from "profits," "integrity," "innovate," to "don't rock the boat," "the customer is always right," or "the customer be damned." Attitudes of pride, loyalty, snobbishness, exclusivity, professionalism, sloppiness, client concern, secretiveness, and even paranoia may be manifested in a variety of ways throughout a human system. Analysis of the organizational culture may reveal deep beliefs in the Puritan work ethic, "up-by-your-bootstraps," opportunity for all, private property, human rights, sexual distinctions, superstitions, and so forth. The United States Marines obviously relish their belief in "esprit de corps." A transnational corporation, such as 3M, has high regard for creativity and innovation, and confirms this in their advertising programs. Other employers and their employees reflect the organization's strong attachment to a particular ethnic or religious heritage. Some executives with a long military background affect their organizational culture with great stress upon security, whether their contracts warrant this or not.

In another company, the attitude may be that work should be challenging, fun, and that employees should be aided by the organization to stay in good physical and mental health. In fact, many corporations back up such beliefs by major investment in preventative health programs for personnel.

The organizational image projected through public and community relations programs provides much insight on an institution's attitudes and beliefs.

The above analytical method can provide many insights on ways of evaluating organizational culture in order to deal with such more effectively.

Cross-Cultural Differences in Organizational Cultures

Because the microculture is a reflection of the macroculture, it stands to reason that the location of an organization will be affected by the culture of the community that surrounds it. Even within a country, such as the United States or India, this would be a significant factor affecting worker behavior. There is an interaction continuously between the majority and minority cultures, each influencing the other. Thus, when a manager goes abroad, outside his or her native culture, the organizational culture which that person represents should adapt to local circumstances. Furthermore, the organizational cultures in the host country with whom the expatriate interfaces are quite unique manifestations of the indigenous culture. Should this person who is a foreigner in a strange land go to work for one of the local companies or government agencies as a consultant or even an employee, the individual should expect that things will be done quite differently from "back home" and that people in the native organization will behave very differently from colleagues in one's own country.

The state of technological, economic, and social development of a nation will also affect the organizational cultures. First World nations, for instance, may have more organizations using the emerging adhocracy model, while

Third World countries might still use the industrial or traditional organizational modes. Typical managerial activities such as planning and innovating, organizing and controlling, recruiting and selecting, evaluating and rewarding/punishing, leading and relating, communicating, problem-solving and decision-making, negotiating and managing conflict, supervision and training are all conducted within the context of the dominant local culture. Thus, that unique people's perception of their world and of human beings, their motivational orientation, their ways of associating, their value and activity emphasis, will be reflected in the social institutions they establish. A corporation or government agency mirrors the images and imprints of the indigenous population to various degrees.

Perhaps some examples of such cross-cultural differences in organizations and their workers will best illustrate this point that requires such sensitivity upon the part of visitors or expatriates. In a traditional Latin organization that is rapidly disappearing, the supervisor-subordinate relationships are such that an employee would never *directly* approach a foreman or manager to discuss a problem—in the old authoritarian mode, one does not question the boss. In Japan, where the GNP is beginning to surpass the United States, the corporation's first duty is to its employees, and it is not considered demeaning for the worker to identify with the organization that employs him or her. In Japanese industry, the adversary labor-management relationship is considered unhealthy and uneconomic, the survival of an elitest attitude from the industrial revolution. For the most part, corporate, not government, enterprises provide for employee welfare more efficiently and less bureaucratically. In fact, corporate elitism is frowned upon, and group harmony is accented. Interestingly enough, part of this new organizational culture in Japan resulted from the American occupation of their country. In Arab organizational cultures, personal relations and trust are paramount. Thus, Westerners who try to negotiate with Middle Eastern firms and their representatives, especially when attempting to act as a "middle man," do well when: (1) they are genuine and sympathetic while clarifying the options; (2) they present the possibilities so that everyone is a winner and saves "face"— maximize gains for each contestant, minimize risks and costs, and present opportunities for compromise; (3) they are a trust broker, so that the two parties can trust the "midwife" until they can learn to trust each other.

Every item in the last section on categories for analyzing organizational culture thus takes on an *intercultural* connotation. For instance, in the classification *Language and Communication*, consider that a language is a means of communicating within a particular culture. There are 3,000 different languages approximately, and each represents a different perceptual world. A number of nations may share an official language, such as English, but have a variety of versions of it, such as British or American. In India, the official language is Hindi, but English a "link" language among fifteen major languages and innumerable dialects; organizations in that country may be expected to speak the official language, but only 30% of the population do so, and personnel in many companies will probably speak the local language and all that it implies. Thus, in the matter of organizational communications, a social institution may reflect the nation's language homogeneity or heterogeneity.

To further illustrate this point, take the previous classification in organizational culture of *Time and Time Consciousness* and consider its cross-cultural implications. In some countries, company representatives may start a meeting within an hour of the time agreed upon, and the sequence of one's arrival at that staff conference may depend upon one's status in the organization, or one's age. The length of work days have great diversity in different cultures—in some starting and stopping is exact, and may be spelled out in a union contract, whereas in others it goes by the sunrise and sunset, or the heat of the day, or the seasons. The idea of coming late is very relative in macro-/microcultures. The time for training may depend on such cross-cultural factors as availability of people on their own, not company time; on the use of new educational technology; on new concepts of human resource development. The rhythm of life for a people is determined by their stage of human development; therefore for populations in the pre-industrial nations, time is shaped by the natural cycles of agriculture; whereas in industrialized nations, the artificial time of the clock and the assembly line regulate workers. In the superindustrial society, time becomes a scarce resource, while in underdeveloped nations time is abundant. Sociologist Daniel Bell reminds American "clock-watchers" that the computer with its nanoseconds is considered a time saver in organizational cultures of high technology. For some populations, the rhythm of life is linear, but for others it is cyclical.

Anthropologist Edward T. Hall observes that culture is the organization's medium, the way a particular people express themselves. It is also the basis of management information systems. In Chapter 2 reference was made to Hall's concept of context cultures. Thus, in an organization within a high context culture, there is a likelihood that much of the human behavior will be covert or implicit, whereas in the low context it may tend to be more overt or explicit. Hall envisions, for instance, West Germany and the United States as on the lower end of the context scale often characterized by coded information, formal transmitted messages, limited involvement and relationships with fellow workers, fewer distinctions between insiders and outsiders, and change that is relatively easy and rapid. On the other hand, he would suggest that China and Japan would fit the description of high context, and in such cultures information is either implicit in the physical context or internalized within people, rather than explicit coding and transmitting; bonds between people tend to be strong and there is deeper involvement with coworkers; greater distinctions are made between those outside or inside the culture; and cultural patterns are more long-lived. These observations from his book, *Beyond Culture*, remind us of the management challenges that face multinational corporations. Their representatives from a low context culture can get into grave business difficulties when they operate in a subsidiary within a high context culture, or vice versa.

Yet, when multinational managers are sensitive to cultural factors in international business, a synergy may take place between two macrocultures within the organizational microculture as in the case of Sony in California. In fact, the managerial style that emerges has been dubbed "Z," the synthesis of Japanese and American management approaches.

Los Angeles Times—August 4, 1978—Synopsis of Published Article:

FACTORY BLENDS U.S., JAPANESE STYLES: MANAGEMENT OF SONY'S SAN DIEGO PLANT KEYED TO FLEXIBILITY

Sony Corporation's sprawling color television plant in Rancho Bernardo Industrial Park is the company's most successful overseas venture. . . . A look at Sony here shows a style different from many American companies, especially in the more paternalistic treatment of workers. But it also reveals management far from pure Japanese and in the forefront of Japanese firms that are successfully adapting to the American environment. "Sony is above all an example," says Stanford professor, Richard Tanner Pascale, "of what a well-managed firm does, particularly a multinational. It is only secondarily a Japanese company.". . . Part of the adaptation is that Sony does not expect life-time loyalty from its American workers, only loyalty as long as they are signed up with the firm. Thus, there is a higher annual turnover of employees in San Diego than in Japan. . . . The employees have voted twice to remain non-union. A Sony senior vice-president, Shiro Yamada noted, "To run a plant effectively, it is necessary to keep morale high and have good close communications. When a union intervenes, it is hard to maintain these good relations."

Other observations in the feature include: low absenteeism, high performance, friendly and non-hierarchical relations with management, well disciplined employees, family atmosphere, mixed management team of Japanese and Americans with avoidance of rotation of the Japanese managers every two years, group consultation on decision making, and plans for including Americans in top management.

Professor Michael Yoshino of Harvard Business School said that Sony is more innovative and international-minded than the typical Japanese firm. He believes that other Japanese firms in the multinational marketplace must evolve a hybrid system along the line of Sony's.

Multinational Organizational Cultures

The transnational corporation that moves beyond the culture of a single country and operates comfortably in the multicultures of many nations, obviously will develop a very unique microculture of its own. Its organization model and environment will reflect the synergy of the diverse macrocultures in which it functions, as well as the varying managerial approaches to business, government, and people. John Lutz, a principal in McKinsey and Company of New York, pointed up the pragmatic approach of multinational corporations in international business:

> How can management organize to deal with worldwide opportunities? First, worldwide enterprises organize themselves to carry out their international activities in different ways, *depending on their traditions*, the nature of their business, and the balance of centralized or decentralized decisions that stem from the particular marketplace they are serving.

Lutz further observed that to meet the challenge of geographic dispersion, organizational changes were necessary in terms of *corporate planning* regarding diversification of product line for world enterprise; in *finance*, where new systems for managing cash flow, as well as currency exchanges, to and from corporate headquarters; in *logistics*, relative to purchasing and traffic of material resources; in *personnel functions*, for the recruiting, development, transfer, promotion, and compensation of competent employees in all corners of the world regardless of nationality; in *public affairs*, so that actions are undertaken that integrate community concerns in both base and host country operations. Thus, far-flung business activities require a new organizational culture that is able to accommodate itself to cross-cultural realities.

The multinational entity becomes a conglomerate of organizational cultures. For example, through acquisitions and mergers, the mother corporation may develop a variety of overseas subsidiaries. The central base operation then impacts considerably upon the organizational culture of its affiliate, but that company abroad inputs and influences the headquarter's culture.

The multinational enterprise adapts to the larger culture in which it functions, depending on its experiences with the external environment. Vern Terpstra identifies five factors to be considered in international business:

Cultural Variability—the degree to which conditions within a macroculture are at a low or high, stable, or unstable rate. The more turbulent the macroculture, for instance, the more unpredictable are business operations. The internal structure and processes in that situation requiring rapid adjustment to change, would demand open channels of communication, decentralized decision-making, and predominance of local expertise.

Cultural Complexity—that is the issue of high and low context cultures to which we previously referred. It requires a response from corporate leaders that takes into consideration the covert and overt approaches of the macroculture.

Cultural Hostility—the degree to which conditions locally are threatening to organizational goals, norms, values, et al. Depending upon how the transnational corporation is perceived, the indigenous environ may range from munificent to malevolent in terms of acceptability, cooperation, political climate, material and human resources, capital and good will. In response, the organizational culture may range from integration and collaboration to tightening up and finally being forced to leave.

Professor Terpstra maintains that the above three dimensions occur within cultures, but that the next two can be observed among macrocultures. Figure 8-2 attempts to depict these concepts in terms of a continuum that affects the organization's culture and its conduct of international business.

Cultural

Independent	— Interdependence —	Interdependent
Homogeneous	— Heterogeneity —	Heterogeneous
Munificent	— Hostility —	Malevolent
Simple/low context	— Complexity —	Complex/high context
Low/stable change rate	— Variability —	High/fluid change rate

Continuum

Figure 8-2. This is a continuum of cultural concepts that affect an organization's culture and its conduct of international business.

Cultural Heterogeneity—the degree to which cultures are dissimilar or similar. It is easier for a transnational corporation to deal with a culture that is relatively homogeneous, or like the base culture (e.g., English-based multinationals would have an edge possibly in British Commonwealth nations). But when a culture is diverse and disparate, then it is difficult for the central headquarters to coordinate the behavior of subsidiaries and their employees. Management may have to be more differentiated, semiautonomous, and decentralized units may have to be established. Expatriates from the base culture may be more prone to culture shock on assignment in the host culture.

Cultural Interdependence—the degree of sensitivity of the culture to respond to conditions and developments in other cultures. This dimension may range from economic dependence on other nations for raw materials, supplies, and equipment, to adaptation and adoption of new technology and processes from other interacting cultures, to being subject to scrutiny in the host culture for attitudes and actions that occurred on the part of the corporation in another culture.

Thus, all such factors impact upon the multinational's organizational culture, influencing decisions, planning, information systems, and conflict resolution. Terpstra cites a variety of strategies that a transnational corporation can utilize to cope with the vagaries of international operations—environmental impact assessments, comparative and/or cluster analysis, cultural scanning and intelligence systems, computer simulations, social cost/benefit analysis, systems dynamics and modeling, social indicators/quality-of-life monitoring, risk analysis and scenario writing, trend extrapolation and technological forecasting, and establishment of external affairs units. For a multinational to be effective, a synergy should take place between the host, base, and international business environments. It requires adaptations within the transnational organization's culture to factors of language and communication, law and politics, values and beliefs, education and training, technology and material resources, and local social organization.

Future Organizational Cultures

As organizations go through the transitions from an industrial to a superindustrial mode, the direction of tomorrow's organizational cultures is already evident. The harbingers are today's task force, matrix, and project management approaches. A review of the previously described emerging adhocracy also provides insight into what might be expected to happen. Because culture is a dynamic process of adaptation, the organization that becomes static, begins to stagnate and possibly regresses. Contemporary systems must continuously alter their organizational cultures, or organization shock will set in. Such institutional crises is characterized by confusion, doubt, rigidity, and even disruption. The signs of these difficulties are manifest in excessive adherences to corporate customs and traditions; lack of planning and forceful decision-making; sharp drops in sales, services, or memberships; high turnover and absenteeism among personnel, especially at the management level, and an inability to attract competent, knowledgeable workers; irrelevance in programs, processes, or products with decreasing income and profits; widening communication gaps between younger and older employees with a polarization between activists and traditionalists; increasing dissatisfaction and confrontation over lack of progress, particularly in the light of diminishing units and subsidiaries.

When organizations utilize adequate feedback mechanisms within their microcultures to monitor input and regulate output, then the entity is alert and aware, sensitive to the larger environments in which it functions. To better meet human needs requires relevant organizational responses. New realities relative to the economy, resources, and technological innovations challenge human systems to planned renewal.

The shape of organizational cultures to come is becoming evident from the writings of various behavioral scientists. Dr. Raymond Forbes of the Naval Postgraduate School maintains that the organizations of the future will be less self-contained and more ecologically in tune with their environment—not just the natural environment, but the technical, economic, regulatory, and human context in which they function. He believes they will develop scanning mechanisms so that the internal environmental factors of structure, technology, task, and personnel will operate in harmony with external environment from which it draws its raw data and cues. Forbes envisions a holistic view with dynamic interactions and relationships between the micro- and macrocultures.

Dr. Burt Nanus of the University of Southern California predicts that corporations will become more future-oriented and take responsibility for creating their own tomorrows. His forecasting includes organization norms incorporating planned change and adaptability, more long range planning and futures research, development of more sophisticated early-warning systems to anticipate crises before they become unmanageable. Nanus also sees organizations taking a more global perspective, and considering the interface between the corporate and environmental systems before making decisions. Information gathering, exchange and rapid response to this data will be characteristic of such innovative corporate cultures.

Author Don Fabun writing in *Kaiser News*, "The Corporation As a Creative Environment," sums up the trends: profound transition from a monolithic, bureaucratic hierarchy to an increasingly free form team cooperation. He prophesizes that organizational cultures will be more responsive and rewarding of creativity and innovation on the part of members, and focus the energies of its personnel toward more meaningful goals and objectives. Fabun reports that the most prevailing organizational image will be that of an energy exchange system—input of energy from the external environment, transformed into output by patterned internal activities—that makes maximum use of human energy, more psychic than physical. The energy exchanges in this open system of subsystems are transactions that take place in a field of force, operating in space/time, and made up of the activities of people in both the internal and external environments. Fabun foresees greater corporate social responsibility and organizational interdependence, and a diminishing of the dividing lines between public and private sectors.

Assessing organizational cultures after the transformation into a transindustrial society, Willis Harman of the Stanford Research Institute expects a shift from the central theme of material progress to projects that enlist the energies and commitments of both the society and organization's members. He sees social institutions emphasizing spiritual, as well as technological development, and that organization culture will focus upon materials conservation and individual enhancement. The trend toward greater corporate social responsibility is already evident.

Relative to the people in tomorrow's organization, it is obvious that these will be largely knowledge/technical workers of multicultural backgrounds. Because managerial skills will be scarce and in demand, one can envision the development of a cadre of executives and administrators capable of being transferred across the traditional boundaries of nations, industries, and public/private sectors. Dr. Chris Argyris of Yale University believes that the organizational culture of the future will include personnel policies that

1. Encourage employees to be authentic with one another and management.
2. Fully appreciate the value of human resources, as well as other factors which contribute to organization success.
3. Foster individual responsibility for career development.
4. Take a holistic approach to promoting organizational health.

Significantly, management consultants are beginning to appreciate that the informal culture of an organization has as much influence on corporate effectiveness as the formal structure of jobs authority, technical and financial procedures. Thus, the target now for planned change must be the organizational climate, along with the work attitudes and habits of employees. Organizations of the future will be excellent to the extent that they maximize their human energy assets, and minimize their human energy losses. They must be able to capitalize on ad hoc, unstructured relationships among people, to cope effectively with uncertainty and accelerating change, and to cooperate in multicultural environments.

In the Corporate Environment Program studies of the Hudson Institute, Herman Kahn presents a scenario for the world macrocultures that will have profound positive impact on organizational microcultures. He predicts that the transition to the post-industrial society will feature:

1. Expanding resource utilization with global increases in productivity, wealth, and affluence.
2. Increasing technological and capital investments while trying to protect and improve the environment, and fewer, long-term serious shortages of necessary resources and raw materials.
3. Systematic internalization of management information and practices, so that organizations can function well with only average managers.
4. Resources will be able to support a world population of 20/30 billion at 20/30 thousand-dollar per capita levels (1974$) for centuries.
5. World population and GWP (gross world product) should stabilize in the twenty-first century.
6. New innovation and discoveries in terms of resources and technology will solve problems, produce crises, and upgrade the quality of life.
7. The next century will see a decrease in absolute poverty and in income gaps—the rich and poor will get richer.

8. Industrialization of the Third World will continue to expand.
9. Internalization of appropriate and adequate internal costs will contribute to a gradual improvement in the quality of life for all—growth need not be destructive.
10. The post-industrial economy of the twenty-first century will have resolved the basic problems that plague mankind today relative to survival needs, and a humanistic utopia is just beyond the horizon.

If only part of the optimistic prognosis comes into being, organizational life, now in crises, should vastly improve in the next hundred years. Behavior in organizational cultures will be radically altered to meet these new, emerging realities. Theodosius Dobzhansky, the prominent geneticist, commented that life was the result of neither design or chance, but the dynamic interaction of living substances with their changing environment. As people interact more through global human systems, we can look forward to the decades ahead with some enthusiastic anticipation. Expanding efforts to use organizational development technology should help to transform existing organizational cultures, and create the patterns for tomorrow's social systems.

Furthermore, Dr. Krishna Kumar of Hawaii's East-West Center intimates that today's organizational microcultures are already having profound influence on their macrocultures. He cites the multinational corporation as perhaps the most important transnational actor whose emergence is transforming the international economic system, with great political and social consequences. Therefore, Kumar has underway a research project to examine the cultural effects of multinational corporations on host societies, and the set of cultural problems encountered by multinational corporate personnel as a result of their functioning in a cross-cultural environment. It is our hope that these observations will alert the reader to the importance of Unit 3 on "Organizational Responsibilities and Cultural Differences."

A study jointly undertaken in 1978 by the Society of Manufacturing Engineers and the University of Michigan casts some light on the challenge of future organizational cultures. It reported that workers will expect more variety and responsibility in their jobs, and in the near future will work a 32-hour, 4-day week. Furthermore, by 1990 workers in major industries will labor alongside robots and other automatic devices. The development of sensory techniques will enable robots to approximate human capability in assembly. Obviously such advances have staggering implications for the work environment, as well as man/machine relations.

The new organizational culture should enable people to

1. Spend their lives on something worthwhile that will outlast them.
2. Live a life of consequence without stress and undue cultural restraints.
3. Preserve for tomorrow what we can use up today.
4. Value the worth as much as we did the work ethic.

5. Accept differences and appreciate similarities.
6. Seize opportunities for personal and professional development, while overcoming the disadvantages to developing one's potential.

References

Beckhard, R. and Harris, R.T., *Organizational Transitions: Managing Complex Change*. Reading, Mass.: Addison-Wesley Publishing Co., 1977.

Cass, E.L. and Zimmer, F.G., *Man and Work in Society*. New York: Van Nostrand and Rheinhold Co., 1975.

Feldman, D. and Harris, D., *A Day to Day Key to Successful Employee Negotiations*. Phoenix, AZ.: General Cassette Corp., 1978.

French, W.L., Bell, C.H., and Zawacki, R.A., *Organizational Development*. Dallas: Business Publications/Irwin-Dorsey Ltd., 1978.

Gladwin, T.N., *Environmental Planning and the Multinational Corporation*. Greenwich: JAI Press, 1977.

Hamner, W.C. and Organ, D.W., *Organizational Behavior*. Dallas: Business Publications/Irwin-Dorsey Ltd., 1978.

Harris, P.R. and Harris, D.L., *Leadership Effectiveness with People*. Phoenix, AZ.: General Cassette Corp., 1978.

Hutzel, J., *Strategy Forumations in the Multinational Business Environment*. San Jose, CA.: Institute for Business and Economics, San Jose State Univ., 1975.

Kahn, H. and Scalera, G., *The Future of World Economic Development*. Croton-on-Hudson, N.Y.: Hudson Institute, 1978.

Nadler, L., "The Organization as a Micro-Culture," *Personnel Journal*, Dec. 1969 (48, 12, 949-955).

Rhinesmith, S.H., *Cultural-Organizational Analysis*. Cambridge, Mass.: McBer & Co., 1970.

Rogers, E.M. and Shoemaker, F.F., *Communication of Innovations: A Cross-Cultural Approach*. New York: Free Press, 1971.

Terpstra, V., *The Cultural Environment of International Business*. Cincinnati: South-Western Publishing Co., 1978.

Williams, J.C., *Human Behavior in Organizations*. Cincinnati: South-Western Publishing Co., 1978.

9
Cultural
Training for HRD

- Hank Jones, an agricultural graduate, left his native Wisconsin to join the Peace Corps. Subsequently, he was assigned to an Agricultural Extension Agency in Bolivia. Within three months after his arrival in that country, he returned prematurely to the United States.
- Sam Seeley was a foreman for a national cannery in San Diego, California. The majority of the workers in his tuna processing section were of Mexican origin. Since he knew a few basic Spanish words, and was a friendly fellow himself, Sam expected no problems with his people.
- Doris Lang, a management information specialist, loved her job with an international computer corporation. She was very competent, but had never traveled outside her native Canada. In preparation for an overseas assignment to Kenya, she was sent to corporate headquarters in New York for a month's technical training.
- Harry Brown worked for the U.S. Department of Commerce and was assigned to head a trade mission to Romania. With a team of department and business representatives, he had his first experience behind the "Iron Curtain." After three weeks of frustrating negotiations, his colleagues began to notice signs of "culture shock."
- Harriet and Tom Hayes were having strained relations after 15 years of marriage. Harriet hoped that a change of scene might do them both good. She was delighted by his new company assignment as a helicopter technician in Iran. She has read many stories about the fabulous ancient Persia and really looks forward to an exciting experience abroad.
- Seth Long is a U.S. Customs agent assigned to one of the ports of entry on the U.S.-Mexican border. Every day he must communicate with many North and South Americans. Furthermore, many of his colleagues are Mexican-Americans.

The Why of Cultural Awareness Training

Each of the characters in the above critical incidents would be an excellent candidate for cultural awareness training. Otherwise, each might fall prey to a malady cited by Fali Chothia, Director of the Center for Orientation of Americans Going Abroad: "Ignorance of cultural differences is one of the chief causes of misunderstandings in a world that is getting more and more interdependent on the one hand, and increasingly torn with strife on the other." If the people in these situations had taken part in an educational experience in cultural awareness, stress and strain would have been reduced, and human energy constructively utilized in more effective intercultural relations. A rationale can be developed to warrant cross-cultural learning that extends from the efforts of multinational corporations in the world marketplace to urban school systems engaged in bilingual programs for minority youth. Intracultural interface should be an enriching experience.

The justification for such human resource development was expressed well by the poet, Walt Whitman, when he remarked: "Surely whoever speaks to me in the right voice, him or her I shall follow." From a manager's viewpoint, consultant Peter Drucker stated the case for this type of training, "The purpose of a business is not to sell products or services, but to buy customers." In Chapter 1, reasons were offered why organizations should make cultural awareness training an integral part of ongoing human resource development. Over a decade of research by the authors with such diverse clients as Westinghouse Electric Corporation, the U.S. Customs Service, the American Management Association, J.I. Case, Chase Manhattan Bank and General Motors Corporation substantiates this line of reasoning.*

Cultural awareness training is not just for the employee going overseas. It has numerous applications domestically that will increase organizational effectiveness. Findings indicate that it should be a regular part of personnel training, especially management development. The realities of a more pluralistic society and international business make this a necessity for superindustrial organizations. The goal is to help representatives toward more appropriate, sensitive, and consistent behavior in their human interactions.

At the 1978 World Congress on Human Resource Development in Washington, D.C., the delegates from the International Federation of Training and Development Organizations agreed that transcultural education programs should be placed within the context of general human resource development (HRD). Various presentations on worldwide HRD provide

---

* P.R. and D.L. Harris, "Preventing Cross-Cultural Shock," *Management and Training/Audio-visual Communications,* May 1976, 10 (5), 37-41; "Intercultural Education for Multinational Managers," *International and Intercultural Annual,* Dec. 1976, 3, 70-85.
R.T. Moran, "Dress Rehearsal for a Cross-Cultural Experience," *Exchange,* 1974, X (1) 23-25; "A Threshold Model of Flexibility in Cross-Cultural Adjustment," University of Minnesota Report, January 1977.

some insight as to why cultural awareness training is valuable. Key points from the IFTDO conference are:

1. HRD means "people growth" by offering more options in individual lives through learning. In this manner, personnel will become more effective in their current positions, prepare for new career assignments, and be readied for the future in terms of their occupations, organizational environment, and social change. Thus, in this sense, the human resource specialist provides employees with "vision" and is a "revolutionary" agent of change.
2. People normally seek to identify their capacities and develop their potentialities. There is a mutual benefit to them and their organizations when the latter invest in their training.
3. HRD has different cross-cultural connotation. In some nations, it refers to changes in attitudes, expectations, structures, and applications. In others, the emphasis is on learning as a skill for development, and a life-long process. In Japan, for instance, there is equal concern for non-technical (tea serving, flower arrangement, etc.), as for technical training.
4. HRD is a critical need for people who are underdeveloped or underemployed; industrial development cannot take place unless whole parts of a population are liberated culturally through educational change and opportunity. Thus, training may very well be a central force for social change (e.g., women and minorities).
5. HRD should promote a social revolution in human attitudes toward work and training, as well as toward the nature of the worker and the work environment. Many present conceptualizations on such matters will not be appropriate for the future.
6. There are lesser developed countries, as well as lesser developed people in so-called advanced nations. Thus, HRD aims to liberate people from ignorance and dependency, giving them instead, hope, opportunity, and responsibility.
7. Multinational corporations are unaware of the implications of their HRD programs—"development" in its fullest sense means more than personnel management, training, and utilization. They provide too much technical training without ample personal/cultural training. They lack a holistic approach in the capitalization of human assets, and thus fragment and undercut HRD.
8. The Third World provides basic raw materials that keep the technological societies advancing. The United States, in turn, exports more to Third World nations than it does to Europe. It stands to reason that the least the First World can do is invest finances and talent into HRD within the Third and Fourth Worlds. Technology transfer to such areas helps to satisfy their rising expectations and expanding popula-

tions. It should permit such people to adapt, not adopt, advanced systems to meet their own unique needs.

9. HRD experts need cross-cultural orientation to adapt training objectives, technology, and methods to the cultural differences in the people they seek to develop. To avoid a clash in cultural assumptions and training disasters, an *intercultural synergy* is required (a) between trainer and trainee values, assumptions, attitudes, and information; and (b) between HRD needs and delivery systems.

It is hoped that by translating these points to the more specific area of cross-cultural education, a positive conclusion for such training can be reached. The first stage should be general in approach, rather than oriented to a specific culture. In other words, drawing from the fields of cultural anthropology, communication, group dynamics, and comparative management, personnel need training to understanding cultural influences on human behavior. The trainee then applies this to differences in a variety of cultural groups and intercultural experiences. Such basic preparation can be supplemented for employees going into specific intercultural challenges at home or abroad. Such interpersonal experiences are becoming increasingly frequent in the U.S., as described by the following:

> Some of the most attractive opportunities for American executives today are with foreign companies in the United States. The influx of foreign firms into the U.S.A. is intensifying, and to compete effectively, they must rely on American expertise. . . .Activity by European firms in recruiting American executives has tripled over the past two years. . . .Not many Europeans have the in-depth experience and knowledge required to deal with the highly competitive market factors, government regulations, and labor negotiations found here in the U.S. . . .Generally foreign firms lean toward executives who have some experience in how European companies operate. . .some knowledge of the corporations's native language.*

Regardless of the type of cultural awareness training undertaken, there is similarity in the general objectives for management or personnel development. Goals of these programs include:

1. To encourage greater sensitivity and more astute observations in areas and situations, as well as with people, who are culturally different.
2. To foster greater understanding in dealing with representatives of microcultures within one's own country.
3. To improve customer and employee relations by creating awareness of cultural differences and their influence on behavior.
4. To develop more cosmopolitan organizational representatives who not only understand the concepts of culture, but can apply this knowledge to interpersonal relations and organizational culture.

---

* Reprinted from *ASTD International News*, No. 11, April 1978.

5. To increase managerial effectiveness in international operations, especially with regard to cross-cultural control systems, negotiations, decision-making, customer relations, and other vital administrative processes.
6. To improve cross-cultural skills of employees on overseas' assignment, or representatives of microcultures in our own country.
7. To reduce culture shock when on foreign deployment, and to enhance the intercultural experience for employees.
8. To apply the behavioral sciences to international business and management.
9. To increase job effectiveness through training in human behavior, particularly in the area of managing cultural differences.
10. To improve employee skills as professional intercultural communicators.

A related approach to this type of training is an intercultural communications workshop or course. The Human Resources Research Organization tested such a workshop for the U.S. Army. Its objective was to improve participant skill by increasing the ability to recognize cultural influences on thinking. Specifically, the program was successful in helping trainees diagnose their difficulties in intercultural communication, especially the culturally-biased elements which lead to false assumptions about foreigners or minorities, and thus handicapped interaction with others. It sought to counteract ethnocentric dialogue, and the peculiarities of the home culture.

Another intercultural communication course for employees of the U.S. International Communication Agency sets forth these erudite aims:

1. Identify and define the basic constructs and paradigms of intercultural communication, including various theories of communication, the relations between culture and communication, the concepts of similarities and differences, the relation of thought-patterning, language, and non-verbal codes.
2. Diagnose the problems which arise in interpersonal, interethnic, international, and cross-cultural communication, and apply relevant theory on the issues to identify causes and possible solutions.
3. Compare and contrast the roles of the media in various national settings, the formation and measurement of public opinions in different societies, and the role of satellites in developed and developing countries.

The Canadian International Development Agency conducts a predeparture program for their overseas volunteers which includes learning modules in intercultural communication and transfer of skills. Daniel Kealey of CIDA maintains that "Transfer of Skills" means more than education, teaching, or training—it implies both technical and communication competences. In such cross-cultural situations, he believes the *how* of the communication may be as important, if not more so, than the *what*. Their training aims to instill seven skills (see Chapter 4) that could be offered as the objective of all cultural awareness learning:

1. *The capacity to communicate respect*—to transmit, verbally and non-verbally positive regard, encouragement, and sincere interest.
2. *The capacity to be nonjudgmental*—to avoid moralistic, value-laden, evaluative statements, and to listen in such a way that the other can fully share and explain self.
3. *The capacity to personalize knowledge and perceptions*—to recognize the influence of one's own values, perceptions, opinions, and knowledges on human interaction, and to regard such as relative, rather than absolute, for more tentative communications.
4. *The capacity to display empathy*—to try and understand others from "their" point of view, to attempt to put oneself into the other's life space, and to feel as they do about the matter under consideration.
5. *The capacity for role flexibility*—to be able to get a task accomplished in a manner and time frame appropriate to the learner or other national, and to be flexible in the process for getting jobs done, particularly with reference to participation and group maintenance or morale.
6. *The capacity to demonstrate reciprocal concern*—to truly dialogue, take turn talking, share the interaction responsibility, and in groups, promote circular communication.
7. *The capacity to tolerate ambiguity*—to be able to cope with cultural differences, to accept a degree of frustration, and to deal with changed circumstances and people.

With the internalization of such skills, CIDA finds that a more effective transfer of skills and intercultural communication occurs.

There has been limited research on cultural awareness training in multinational corporations, but several studies on various aspects are underway now. One graduate thesis study by Martin Waxman, an IBM Systems Analyst, surveyed 180 American companies doing business in Latin America. In 1977, he reported that in Group One, which did not completely reply to his questionnaire, the typical overseas representative spent 3.5 years abroad. Of these firms, 69 percent had no courses to train, indoctrinate, counsel, or prepare personnel for assignments. When asked why there was no cross-cultural training, 37 percent said they previously had not considered its importance, 32 percent reported that there was not enough time available, 15 percent pleaded the costs for such training were too high, and 10 percent admitted they did not have, or know how to get, resources for such training. It is a sad commentary on international business in the light of attrition rates and costs, as well as the limited success by Americans in the overseas market.

With Group Two, which unanimously responded to the survey, the average range for an overseas assignment was 4.5 years, and 77 percent provided cross-cultural preparation in general. Of these respondents, only 39 percent reported training in the culture and customs of target countries prior to departure; 24 percent offered culture specific training while overseas.

Although the sample is small, the responses show why cultural awareness training is the missing ingredient in the development of managers, technicians, and sales personnel for international business.

The What of Cultural Awareness Training

There are a variety of approaches relative to the content and methodology of cultural awareness training. One strategy is an intensive three-day workshop which centers around the eight concepts described in Chapter 1— cosmopolitan, intercultural communication; changing intercommunication; cultural sensitivity, acculturation; cultural management influences; effective intercultural performance; changing international business; and, emerging world culture. Such training is seen as one phase of orientation prior to going overseas. Other elements of this Foreign Deployment System are discussed in Chapter 12.

Another approach is a five-day course for the American Management Association entitled, "Management Skills for International Managers." Its major themes are: managing in the international field; understanding the people-side of the overseas job; motivating the work force at home and abroad; improving communication skills domestically and overseas; avoiding pitfalls in local customs; developing policies for international business that get the job done; and studying special areas.

Based on the above experiences, the authors designed a three-day public seminar. The international version of the program centers around six learning modules of 3½ hours each. The principal topics are managing in the international field, understanding cultural differences, effective cross-cultural communication, intercultural communication clues, doing business with the Japanese, and insights into transnational business relations. In a domestic version of the same seminar, a co-trainer, preferably female, is needed to deal with the issues of women in management, which is also a cultural difference. The same themes are utilized, but emphasis is on the changing society, minority cultures, equal employment opportunity and affirmative action, organizational culture and its impact on behavior, and improving employee relations. The methodology involves a variety of techniques such as those described in Chapter 10.

The principal strategies to this aspect of human resource development are:

1. *Cognitive*—the emphasis here is upon knowledge of other peoples and their culture, especially customs, values, and social institutions.

2. *Awareness*—the emphasis in this strategy is either on *self* awareness for better adjustment outside one's culture, including insight into the impact of one's native cultural conditioning, or the alternative focus is upon *cultural* awareness in the sense of being sensitive to the cultural factors which influence both parties in human interaction, especially when one is a "foreigner" or "stranger." (This learning involves culture general information and being alerted to the differences in cultural systems.)

3. *Behavioral*—the emphasis in this training is upon learning about specific cultural behaviors and expectations in host cultures for which the trainee is being prepared; modeling of appropriate host culture behavior, simulating host culture environment, and experiential exercises about the host culture.

4. *Interaction*—the emphasis is upon actual interaction with representatives of host or other cultures to increase awareness of the others' backgrounds, values, and learned behaviors, as well as exploring one's own culture in the same regard. (Foreign visitors and students are usually utilized for this purpose, or visits to subcultures within one's country or neighboring cultures.)

5. *Area Simulation*—the emphasis is upon creation of a particular cultural environment or situation comparable to a host culture to which the trainee is going, even as to similar physical climate and conditions. (Cultural assimilator exercises are programmed on target cultures.)

6. *Relationship Systems*—the emphasis is upon intercultural relations or human response in terms of a systematic approach that can be applied across culture. (The U.S. Navy, for instance, utilized the KEEPRAH SYSTEM of Dr. Jack Donoghue, United States International University, San Diego, California. It involves analysis of eight interrelated systems in every culture—kinship, educational, economic, political, religious, recreational, associational, and health.)

7. *Language Studies*—this approach focuses upon the study of a specific foreign language *and* the cultures of the peoples who speak that particular language (e.g., English, Spanish, or French speaking peoples).

8. *Cross-Cultural Communication*—emphasis is on the study of communication theory in general, and of intercultural communication in particular. (The focus is upon improving skills and competencies in cross-cultural communication.)

9. *Confrontation/Contrast*—these related approaches involve either confronting or contrasting differences between one's own culture and that of another which may be role played or represented by a native. In such cross-cultural encounters, the trainee observes responses and evaluates behavior for improved performance. These are culture general approaches related to the previously described "awareness" and "interaction" models. HumRRO (Human Resources Research Organization)

uses videotapes with host nationals or actors doing the role play. An alternative approach developed by Robert Humphrey employs a "Dual-Life Value System" for intercultural interactions that plays upon the mutual preserving or surviving inclinations of one person and another, despite cultural differences. Research on self-confrontation approaches indicate a rapid acquisition of cross-cultural skills which are retained at a high level following training.

There have been many variations on these generalized approaches to cross-cultural training. One called DA-TA (Demonstration through Action with Theoretical Analysis) is combined with *Scouting* (taking an observer role with a cultural community before entering it as a participant), *Access* (seeking entry by authentic self presentation), *Exploration* (discovering and understanding the goals and needs of the host community), *Interest-Interaction* (development of mutual interests between the host and participant communities), *Termination* (summary of dialogue by the trainee with clarification of future role and obligations to the host community), and *Evaluation* (debriefing for assessment of the positive and negative aspects of the intercultural experience). This is discussed further in Chapter 10.

U.S. military services have been most innovative in actions research on large-scale intercultural training efforts. Purposes of such undertakings with enlisted personnel are: to improve race relations within the military unit that brings together people from diverse multicultural/ethnic/racial backgrounds; to improve relations between military personnel and members of the community in which they operate (communities within the nation and those in other countries); and, to improve the international and intercultural experience of the individual service-person.

For more than a decade, the U.S. Navy has been a pioneer in the area of intercultural training. It now includes this training as a part of its Human Resource Management Support System, referring to it as "overseas diplomacy." Major research for the Navy was performed by the Center for Research and Education in Denver, Colorado, which develops very creative learning methods and materials for cross-cultural training. CRE recommends these strategies:

1. *Behavioral*—before entry and during visits to a target culture, listen to its music and experience its media; go on a pleasure excursion with a national from the host culture; learn to cook their recipes and experience their food; play their games in a typical locale for such; learn about matters of local interest and talk to nationals about same; read their newspapers and magazines; spend time alone in the company of host nationals.
2. *Affective*—respond to stimuli and activities of the target culture, by use of a Verbal Semantic Differential and Activities List, stimulation by aversive activities and conditions found in the culture.

3. *Cognitive*—trainee develops questions about the host culture, is provided a resource list on the culture, tandem cultural activities with language training, field stay exercises.

The Center for Research and Education has also successfully tested this model with the Peace Corps and other organizational representatives. A system for measuring the cross-cultural learning and change has been designed.

The Peace Corps, now a part of the federal agency called *Action*, provides one of the longest and most comprehensive cross-cultural preparations for volunteers going overseas. The program is based upon a detailed task analysis of specific positions in specific locations, and an understanding of the volunteer's role in the host culture. The emphasis is on self-development, and the orientation is primarily experiential. In describing a Peace Corps training program in Escondido, California, Dr. Richard McKenna noted that the focus was on cultural adaptation through problem solving and behavior modification, as well as area studies. The training model emphasized the acquisition of self-management skills.

The Foreign Service Institute (FSI) is responsible for conducting specialized cross-cultural training for several U.S. agencies. Its three week course includes learning units on host cultures, including the operations of its legal system, family roles, and behavior expectations, and cross-cultural interaction. An interesting feature is a module on "Meet the Critic" which explores 150 questions frequently asked of Americans overseas and the issue of American stereotypes. In addition, FSI sponsors courses in area studies and languages.

Obviously, there is a need for cross-cultural training of foreign nationals coming into a country on temporary duty or student exchanges. The International Training Institute in Washington, D.C., provides "Transition Seminars" in English for such persons entering the U.S., as well as tutorial programs. The subject matter on the American environment covers comparative government, economy, education, and cultural and social problems. The four-week seminar, which includes field trips, is aimed at helping the trainee gain confidence in dealing with North Americans.

For those engaged in designing cross-cultural training programs, the content should be based upon the needs of the participant and the organization represented.

The trainer's approach is likely to be eclectic. This review may provide insight into subjects and strategies that should be the focus of endeavors to customize cultural awareness training. On the other hand, for a concerned leader, this overview may provide criteria for evaluating intercultural programs offered by external organizations for public participation.

Perhaps a 1973 UNESCO study, Internationalizing Management Education, offers the best summary when it identified the "Skills Required for Effectiveness Overseas":

1. Language ability, both oral and written
2. Understanding of geopolitics, economics, social structure, and culture of the area
3. Ability to relate well with new kinds of peoples
4 Ability to negotiate, bargain, resolve conflict in intercultural settings
5. Ability to manage autonomous units dealing with foreign markets, governments, unions, financiers
6. High tolerance for ambiguous situations, along with adaptability to new situations and conditions
7. Ability to develop talents and potentials of staff while abroad
8. Strength of personality to act forcefully but sensitively in unfamiliar contexts

The When of Cultural Awareness Training

Diverse opinions exist on when it is most appropriate to provide cultural awareness input, and how long it should take. Some argue that it belongs in elementary and secondary schools as a separate course, culminating in college with studies in cultural anthropology. Trainers are beginning to realize that it is the missing element in executive, management, and supervisory training, and should be an integral part of all human resource development. Many maintain that such educational programs belong in professional schools and continuing education classes, especially for those in a "people" profession requiring diverse human interaction such as medicine or law. For graduate studies in international business, for instance, the curriculum should have some input on the subject, if not a separate course, then at least as a part of comparative management.

It is essential study for teachers in the field of bilingual education or international relations, but it could be incorporated as a regular element in any teacher preparation. In many school systems, some form of intercultural relations is a necessary component of inservice training, especially for teachers in the inner cities.

For implementation of Equal Employment Opportunity and Affirmative Action programs, many companies and government agencies are routinely requiring some form of cultural awareness training relative to women and minorities. Certainly, specific occupations would seem to demand such training before the individual undertakes full-time work, with additional reinforcement training from time to time. For example, those working in the U.S. border management program dealing with foreign visitors, those in public service to ethnic or minority communities, those in government foreign service or commerce activities, those engaged in sales and marketing, or those in an industry which operates on an international scale, such as petroleum or gas, need cultural awareness training.

The real issue, however, involves organizational representatives assigned outside their native culture for short- or long-term visits. When engaged in international relations work, service, or business, cross-cultural knowledge and skills are integral to the role requirements. Some believe cultural training should be given before going abroad, while others opt for such training only after arrival in the host culture. Still others insist that it must be a combination of before, during, and after the overseas assignment. In the Waxman study of 180 companies doing business in Latin America, approximately 40 percent of those with formal courses of preparation included the training on culture factors prior to departure. About 22 percent provided additional training overseas. Approximately 49 percent of these companies included the employee's family in intercultural preparation. A small percentage made it optional.

The length of time devoted to preparation for foreign deployment varies according to the organization and the availability of time and finances for training. Some nonprofit agencies devote a year prior to departure for such preparation, beginning with self-study and weekly meetings, and gradually accelerating the amount of time devoted to cross-cultural and related training in group settings. A year would seem desirable in the case of foreign language studies with cultural specifics accompanying the education. One major multinational corporation devotes three to six months to getting the employee and the family ready for assignments abroad.

Program planners in the Canadian International Development Agency believe timing is a critical factor. If too close to departure, trainee anxiety may block learning. Without foreign experience, the volunteers find it hard to focus on the input. Therefore, CIDA prefers to emphasize recruitment and selection for the overseas tour, and concentrate on in-country training.

Whether circumstances or opinion dictate a long- or short-term approach to cross-cultural training, it is the quality of that training that is important. Some feel that the intensity of the educational experience is important, arguing for intensive language or cultural training in terms of weeks and days. Meaningful insight is gained from one or two learning modules of several hours, but for busy career people, a three- to five-day program is valuable. General facts of culture and ways to improve intercultural relations can be explored. The Monterrey Institute of Foreign Students has a bicultural program for managers of American plants in Mexico. It includes four weeks of Spanish language training and five days intensive cultural orientation.

The Where of Cultural Awareness Training

The place cultural awareness training occurs can influence the depth of learning and behavior change. An organization, therefore, must decide: to conduct the program themselves, or send participants to an external training center or university campus; to have the training on organizational premises, or use an off-site facility; and/or, to have the educational experience in their country or abroad. Depending upon trainee and organizational needs, a case can be made for each position. It would, of course, be ideal to get a group away from office or plant and into a well-equipped conference center; to utilize a staff of both internal and external resource personnel; and, to train both in the home and host culture. Realistically, time, task, and financial constraints may cause management to settle for less, unless superior facilities and staff are found within the organization or within a particular country. The involvement of the employee's family may dictate the site. Or, part of the intercultural training might be conducted within the home by means of a self-instructional media program, or within an ethnic or geographic community within the home country.

Thus, to train personnel for Latin America, a U.S. organization might use a location in Puerto Rico, Florida, or the Southwest. Interestingly, in the Waxman study of comparable corporations, 46 percent used off-site training facilities.

Tips for International Trainers Going Abroad

The ASTD's International Division surveyed its membership about a *Guide for International Trainers*, and the following questions were compiled as a check list for international trainers preparing to conduct sessions abroad:

1. Country and location?
2. Native language and other languages commonly used for training and human resource development?
3. Political or customs restrictions that might affect a consultant entering the country to conduct training?
4. Influence of trainee's sex, age, race or role that might interfere with acceptance of training presented?
5. Cross-cultural situations that might affect acceptance of training presented?
6. Situations to be avoided by foreign training consultants?
7. Unusual customs or etiquette or protocol to be observed?
8. Availability of American produced tape, films, and other audio-visual equipment?
9. Can and should American tapes, films, et al be adapted?
10. Influence of trade unions on the training given or the trainer?
11. Laws or policies on manpower, training, and HRD in that country which external consultants should know?
12. Printed information available for trainer indoctrination before entry?
13. Location of HRD personnel in government agencies?
14. Incountry organizations that trainers should be in contact?
15. Presence and location of National Productivity Center, if any.

The Who of Cultural Awareness Training

The issue of who should be trained can be viewed from the perspective of the cultural awareness trainer or trainee. Those in leadership positions, particularly on an international level, are most in need of cross-cultural input, as well as skills. Also, there are times when total or partial family involvement is desirable. When a race relations or integration plan is introduced into an American school system, teachers, students and their families can benefit from intercultural training. When an employee is sent abroad for a long period of time, it affects spouse and children. If the family accompanies the worker, they too are subject to "culture shock," and can influence a premature return. Thus, family involvement in cross-cultural orientation can have real benefits. Some oil companies do not send the technician's family to hardship posts, but locate them in a more developed country nearby or in the home culture. The worker is rotated home to his family every few weeks. A family should be prepared to cope with the situation created by the employer.

In terms of presenters, a variety of alternatives are available for live or media training in cultural awareness. Such resource persons may be professionals who understand cross-cultural education and challenges—psychologists, communications specialists, cultural anthropologists, or inter-HRD specialists, trainers, and facilitators. They may acquire skills and information on culture which can be shared with trainees. Representatives of the host culture, foreign nationals experienced in a particular culture, and local professors with specialized, relevant knowledge can all be called upon for assistance with a cross-cultural program. There are consulting organizations, universities, and government agencies that specialize in cross-cultural education. Some of these are listed at the end of this chapter. Others are included in Appendix D. The key issue is whether to utilize the organization's personnel for culture training, contract external consultants, or combine both types of resources.

Finally, in planning for cultural awareness training, it must be decided whether to include strangers in the sessions or limit them to personnel. Would the organization do well to send a group away for training, or mix them with representatives from other entities going to the same host culture? There are advantages to both positions.

When only a few persons are sent abroad in one year, it is well to mix the training class with other representatives from home culture organizations who are going to the same location. Companies working on the same project or contract in the Middle East, for instance, may engage in joint culture specific training.

Competency in the subject matter and experience in the host culture are principal factors to consider with regard to trainee and trainer.

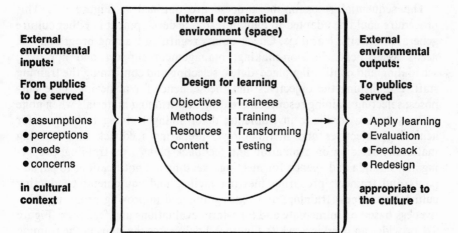

Figure 9-1. This diagram shows how a systems process can be applied to cultural awareness training.

The How of Cultural Awareness Training

Cultural awareness training is best accomplished by a variety of methods and techniques. That is, what best fits the situation, and what proves to be the most effective. Chapter 10 describes the principal means used today in this type of adult education. In intercultural workshops for different human systems and participants, the methodology can include audio-visual presentations (films, slides, audio/video cassettes); instrumentation for data gathering and sensitizing (inventories on communication, change and personal growth, and a Cultural Shock Test); group dynamics (brainstorming and imagineering case studies and critical incidents, various simulation games and exercises); and illustrated lectures with various conceptual models and paradigms.

The case study method is one of the most effective techniques for conveying culture specific information in a short time, and for stimulating group discussion, as illustrated in Unit 4 on culture specifies. In a previously cited study, Westinghouse managers requested more case studies and problem solving. These were subsequently developed and tested successfully. (Examples of this type of approach are discussed in Chapters 15, 16, 17, 18, and 19.)

The methods utilized should be the result of a needs assessment and planning process. Figure 9-1 offers a systems process for cultural training.*

---

* Request *Designing Developmental Workshops:An Open System Approach,* Working Paper Series, February 1978, from Dr. Raymond L. Forbes, Human Resource Management Research Program, Naval Postgraduate School, Monterey, California 93940.

The sequential steps in the process are outlined in Figure 9-2. This procedure could be adapted to human resource development in either culture general or specific learnings. Check-points regarding training programs are: needs assessment; decision-making; management support and approval; scheduling and confirming place/dates; selecting and confirming the training staff; establishing the objectives and the sequence for achieving these purposes; selecting training resources; creating new training materials when none exist; selecting feedback instruments; determining training techniques for achieving objectives and methodology; preparing feedback and learning materials; deciding on evaluation and feedback plans after training; preparing memoranda and agenda for meetings; sending out notifications to participants and trainers; preparing meeting facility and equipment; conducting cultural awareness training; and redesigning and improving program effectiveness based on immediate and long-term evaluations and feedback. Figure 9-1 provides an overview, while Figure 9-2 delineates the steps in the training system.

Many innovative techniques have been employed by consultants to facilitate learning both in culture general and culture specific information and insights. HumRRO's Alfred Kraemer did a project for the U.S. Army entitled "Cultural Self-Awareness Approach to Improving Intercultural Communication Skills." Maintaining that intercultural communication is hindered by culturally-conditioned assumptions about the other, he designed a series of self-awareness exercises involving video recordings of staged "excerpts" from cross-cultural dialogues for trainee analysis.

Videotape role playing of critical intercultural incidents in the daily work of customs officials has been used for problem-solving. Jack Hayes and Bruce Qualset of La Jolla's The Innovative Group use videotape with top performers to gather data on organizational culture. Denver's Center for Research and Education has created a measurement system for determining adaptation potential of Peace Corps Volunteers. The instruments include a Gestures Test, a Factual Information Test, a Verbal Semantic Differential, an Activities List, and a Structured Interview. Dr. Richard McKenna of Dimensions in San Diego reported his experiences with the Peace Corps training methods. The techniques involved simulations, role playing, sociodrama, situational exercises, Spanish dialogues and gesture exercises, local and Mexican field trips, demonstrations, case studies and critical incidents, vignettes about foreigners, and other types of group dynamics.

The model for student exchanges between cultures perfected by Stephen Rhinesmith for the American Field Services can be adapted for worker, manager, or family exchanges, especially within organizations that have worldwide operations. The AFS orientation of students to go abroad and return could readily be applied to the needs of multinational families involved

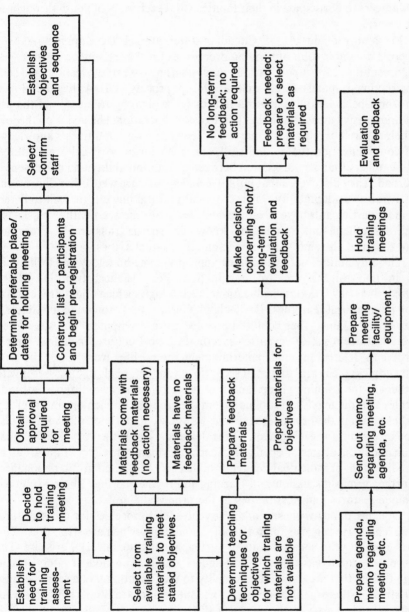

Figure 9-2. These are the sequential steps in the systems process outlined in Figure 9-1.

in international transfers. He has also designed a program for training volunteers to participate in their multicultural exchanges of youth throughout the world.

Pri Notowidigdo of the Canadian International Development Agency reports a combination of training procedures for those going on overseas assignment that focus upon learning modules using case study, lecture, and self-instructional material, as well as group process. CIDA has developed pre/post-behavioral observation indices for evaluating trainees, and the use of unobtrusive measures in the field to assess operational behavior on the job. Their experience indicates a marked difference between a trainee's knowledge of communication theory and skill, and behavior in cross-cultural settings. Researchers found a correlation between adaptation ability and effectiveness abroad. They discovered that initiative and persistence were other dimensions of a trainee's adaptability. Their cross-cultural training efforts seek to determine if participants have adequate qualities of openness, empathy, respect for self and others, and personalized knowledge that is transferable. Programs are designed to reinforce such personality characteristics.

The only limitation to developing appropriate methodology and techniques is in the trainer's creative imagination. For instance, two San Diego researchers have proposed educational technologies which might prove useful for intercultural learnings. Dr. Roland Werner wants to create a "Cultural Sensitivity Game" that could be adapted to the computer. The simulation would utilize a list of scenarios specific to a host culture, including typical problems related to food, entertainment, home life, work, etc. The first player picks a cultural universal scenario at random, reads it, discusses it with others in the training group, and then secretly marks two different attitude scales that distinguish his opinion from the group's. As each one in the group takes a turn in the process, the two scales allow computation of a cultural dissonance score for each player. Three deviation scores then provide information about the degree of openness of each individual, the effect of the group in modification of individual behavior (ability to adapt), and group dissonance. Further group discussion and learning follow the scoring. There are many unique features and possibilities in the proposed simulation.

Douglas Bailey wishes to adapt psycho-social processes for cross-cultural awareness. He suggests man-machine simulations which are structures to involve real psycho-social threats to participants in "teamwork" exercise. The purpose is to increase intercultural understanding. The model centers around ego threats that are damaging in reality to the functioning of a team because of stress in the organizational or host culture, or, are life-like for the team represented in part by members of different cultures. This can be done if some team members are machines programmed to respond differently than human correspondents.

The stressed-based approach to cultural awareness involves machine games designed to culturally-appropriate signals. Human members can learn a response vocabulary appropriate to a simulated cultural context. The threat situations would be emotionally charged interactions with representatives of social, financial, and governmental institutions. The aim is to learn appropriate responses in an "alien" culture.

Audio-visual aids can help in the process of culturally reorientating an individual. There are few films or videotapes that provide a culture general approach. However, there are many motion pictures to aid in teaching culture specifics.*

What is needed is a self-instructional system on culture which a manager and family may study and discuss in their home prior to a major intercultural experience. Two experimental systems on "Increasing Cultural Awareness" have been designed (Harris International, Box 2321, La Jolla, Ca. 92038). Each involves the use of colored slides, audio cassette, and manual. Audiovisual learning packages to orient personnel and their families to live, work, or study in a second culture have also been developed (Orientation & Media International, Box 242, Pacific Grove, Ca. 93950).

Associates of the National Training Laboratories Institute of Applied Behavior Science (P.O. Box 9155, Rosslyn Station, Arlington, Va. 22209) have used the laboratory method of education for intercultural training. They believe human relations type sensitivity training ("T" groups) can improve race relations within a country, and aid those going on overseas assignment. When the "unstructured" group process is used with mixed nationalities or race representatives, this intensive learning experience becomes a cross-cultural microcosm. Such strategy helps integrate the substantive content of culture learning with the situational requirements for behavioral change.

Not much is written about evaluating cross-cultural training designs and methods. Existing information is often outdated or incomplete. What is available comes from external contractors working for the U.S. Armed Forces, or researchers for the Peace Corps, CIDA, and volunteer agencies. The principal methods used to assess program effectiveness and trainees' learning in intercultural education are:

1. Pre/post evaluation instruments with participants upon completion of training, and subsequent follow-up questionnaires (three, six, or twelve months hence).
2. Use of control groups for comparison studies on impact of training.
3. Observers to measure results during and after training sessions, and/or when trainees go into the field (observations by instruments, videotape, interviews).
4. Ratings by peers and supervisors of trainees after training is completed and they return to the job or go on overseas assignment.

---

* Dr. Jean Marie Ackerman edits a two volume, *Films of a Changing World/A Critical International Guide* which is available from the Society for International Development (1346 Connecticut Ave., NW, Washington, D.C., 20036, USA).

Writing for the International Division of the American Society of Training and Development in 1977, the late Milton Feldman cautioned:

1. Cognitive learning strategies alone may have limited effectiveness because behavioral change is difficult to obtain.
2. Many cross-cultural training programs and practices have not been validated by research, and those that have been subjected to controlled studies have measured largely cognitive and attitude change, not behavioral change.
3. Communication skills, both verbal and nonverbal, take considerable time to develop. Language training should relate to the appropriate vocabulary for the job situation abroad, and the type of persons with whom the trainee will interface in the new culture.
4. Alert trainees to the possibility of building new stereotypes based on limited information received in training or experience about the behavioral, values, and customs of a complex host culture; modal behavior is not to be observed merely as a result of a training course or interface with individuals or subcultures who are not representative.
5. Seek a balance of content and process within the constraints of time, finances, and circumstances.

Professional Development

Many organizations and publications can help managers or human resource specialists increase professional effectiveness in intercultural training, especially for foreign deployment. These resources are listed in Appendix D.

One way for managers and trainers to keep abreast of trends in intercultural education and deployment is to develop personal links to counterparts in other organizations and countries. These people have similar concerns about facilitating cross-cultural interventions and assignments.

The international network of HRD specialists is a loose, participative system for exchange of information and skills. It can be established within a multinational corporation or agency that operates in more than one nation, or within different industries, product lines, or career classifications. Personnel managers, for example, may link up with those in similar positions in other cultures. Consultants engaged in global practice do the same through the International Consultants Foundation. Those in cross-cultural communication and training activities make contact with one another at the annual conferences of SIETAR (Society for International Education, Training, and Research) and IFDTDO (International Federation for Training, Development, and Organization). Those in organization development services can contact colleagues through NTL and ASTD.

Jan Margolis, Director of Management Education and Organization Development for The Bristol-Myers Company, has reported on several international networks established by training specialists within multinational corporations that resulted in sharing training methodology, learning materials, and mutual services. Eventually, this international cooperation within one corporate entity lead to joint programming and productions, including establishment of regional training centers throughout the world. These, in turn, became separate profit centers and focused upon both culture specific and cultural general factors. The centers became focal points for training trainers, especially in major market areas.

Margolis believes that this synergy of professionals with similar interests has certain characteristics when international networks are formulated:

1. Communication constellation of peers in a two-way interaction flow.
2. Influence of individual member competence, rather than position.
3. The smaller the grouping, the more effective.
4. Relationships develop that are more intense in a locality, whereas those at a great distance maintain occasional contact.
5. Based on shared superordinate goals, power, and self-interests.
6. Interconnections can be strengthened with the support of proper organizational philosophy (e.g., corporate encouragement).
7. Open system with shared, changing leadership, consensus decision-making and goal setting, multicultural approaches, and multi-sources of financial support requiring collaborative efforts.

References

Batchelder, D. and E. Warner, (eds.) *Beyond Experience: The Experiential Approach to Cross-cultural Education.* Brattleboro, Vt.: The Experiment in International Living, 1977.

Brislin, R.W. and S. Bochner, *Cross-cultural Perspectives on Learning.* New York: Sage/Wiley-Interscience, 1975.

————, (ed.), *Translations: Applications and Research.* New York: Halsted, 1976.

Chothia, F., *Other Cultures Other Ways.* Denver: Center for Orientation of Americans Going Abroad, 1978.

Feldman, M.J., *Coping with Problems in Meeting Training Needs for Cross-cultural International Training.* Madison, Wi.: American Society for Training and Development, International Division, 1977. (Also by the same author and source, "Training for Cross-Cultural International Interaction in the Federal Government" of Special International Training Edition of *Training and Development Journal,* Nov. 1976, 30 (11), 19-26.)

Ferguson, H., *Survival Manual for the Innovative Leaders in Multicultural and Ethnic Studies.* Thompson, Conn.: Interculture Associates, 1977.

Fersh, S., *Learning about Peoples and Cultures.* New York: McDougal, Little, 1974.

Goldstein, I., *Training: Program Development and Evaluation.* Belmont, Ca.: Wadsworth, 1975.

Jain, N.C. and R.L. Cummings, (eds.), *Proceedings of the Conference on Intercultural Communication and Teacher Education.* Milwaukee: Urban Laboratory, 1975.

Lippit, G.L. and D.S. Hoopes, *Helping Across Cultures.* Washington, D.C.: International Consultants Foundation, 1978.

Learning Resources in International Studies (60 E. 42nd St., New York, N.Y. 10017) Conference Proceedings Series on "Education in the 21st Century" (1974):
    Anderson, C.A. (ed.), *International/Intercultural Education for Teachers;*
    Morehouse, W. *Agents of Change: Case Studies of Organizations and Programs in International/Intercultural Education in Schools;*
    Ponce, J.M., *Intercultural Education in the Two-Year College;*
    Williamsen, M. and C.T. Morehouse, *International/Intercultural Education in Four-Year Colleges.*

McNulty, N.G., *Training Managers: The International Guide.* New York: Harper & Row Publishers, 1969.

Mager, R., *Preparing Instructional Objectives. . . .Goal Analysis. . . .Developing Attitudes Toward Learning.* (3 Vols.) Denver: Fearon/Center for Research & Education Book Store, 1975.

Noer, D.M., *Multinational People Management: A Guide to Organizations and Employees.* Washington, D.C.: Bureau of National Affairs, 1975.

Rhinesmith, S.H., *Bring Home the World: Management Guide for Community Leaders of International Programs.* New York: AMACOM, 1975.

Schnapper, M., *Experiential Intercultural Training for International Operations.* (Doctoral Dissertation, University of Pittsburgh) Ann Arbor: University Microfilms, 1972.

————, "Nonverbal Communication and the Intercultural Encounter," *1975 Annual Handbook for Group Facilitators.* La Jolla, Ca.: University Associates.

Seelye, H.N., *Teaching Culture: Strategies for Foreign Language Educators.* Denver: National Textbook/Center for Research and Education Book Store, 1974.

Smith, G.R. and G.G. Otero, *Teaching About Cultural Awareness.* Denver: CITR/Center for Research and Education Book Store, 1977.

Vansina, L.S., "Improving International Relations and Effectiveness Within Multinational Organizations," *New Technologies in Organization Development.* (Vol. 2) La Jolla, Ca.: University Associates, 1975.

Von Klemperor, L., *International Education: A Directory of Resource Materials on Comparative Education and Study in Another Country.* Garrett Park, Md.: (02115): Garrett Park Press.

10
Methods for
Cross - Cultural Training

Commitment to Intercultural Preparation

Time and money are wasted if employee training for functioning in a multicultural environment is deficient. A study made at Columbia University in 1975 by Alison Lanier asked companies if cultural training was provided for employees sent overseas, 33% said they did not provide preparation of any kind. Of the companies that did, 60% said they used in-house staff who had no real qualifications for orientation training. When questioned further, most companies considered preparation to be one or more interviews "covering compensation, travel procedures, company medical plans, and how to get a passport." Of the companies that prepared their personnel, 43% did not include the spouses.

A study by Rob Jones and Sherman Tingey, reported at the 1978 SIETAR Conference revealed that less than half of the 60 multinational corporations they surveyed provided pre-departure training for managers.

What are cross-cultural orientation programs? What is cross-cultural training? Cross-cultural orientation programs according to Brislin and Pedersen, are "designed to teach members of one culture ways of interacting effectively, with minimal interpersonal misunderstanding, in another culture." This is a general definition and can be applied to most cross-cultural orientation or briefing programs. Specific training objectives must be developed according to specific needs and purposes of the organization. George Renwick, vice-president of Intercultural Network, Inc. made the following assumptions concerning the training of persons to function effectively in another culture:

1. Individuals with responsibilities for the formulation, administration and evaluation of policies and projects must increasingly deal with the special problems and possibilities of multicultural environments. In the

147

private sector, managers must select, train, and coordinate the efforts of multicultural staffs to meet the complex objectives of the corporation and the demands of a culturally diverse clientele. Members of corporate staffs must anticipate, appreciate, and adjust to each others' differing values, expectations, and patterns of behavior if their efforts are to be satisfying for them and advantageous for the corporation. In the public sector, officials must anticipate, and plan to meet, the needs of multicultural constituencies.

2. The knowledge and skills essential to carrying responsibility, exercising authority, and working productively in multicultural environments can be learned. The appropriate attitudes can be cultivated. Through proper training, perception can become more penetrating and discernment more accurate; judgments can therefore be made with more confidence. Relationships become more cooperative and therefore more conducive to the achievement of individual and organizational objectives.

3. Competence in multicultural management is learned most effectively through interaction, experimentation, and discussion within a structured, supportive, information-rich, low-risk environment.

4. Technical competence is of primary importance for international executives, managers, and others in this area. However, cross-cultural communication skills are also required.

Awareness and recognition of personal and professional failures in many international organizations have led to the establishment of programs designed to prepare persons to interact and communicate effectively with persons from different cultures. The programs are often called cross-cultural orientation programs. These are either programs that give information (briefings) about specific countries and customs, programs that provide practice in developing specific skills (training), or a combination of briefing and training. A combination of briefing and training is most effective for managers who will be functioning in a multicultural environment. A listing of resources for orientation programs is included in Appendix D.

Cross-Cultural Orientation Programs

Attempts by individuals and agencies to prepare persons for communicating and interacting across cultures have ranged from laissez-faire attitudes, "let them learn from their own experience and mistakes," to detailed and explicit training in specific skills. Technical competence and language training are, of course, prerequisite skills. But persons involved in the area are becoming convinced that these skills alone, without the interpersonal skills necessary to establish communication, are insufficient.

Most literature describing and evaluating cross-cultural training programs has been written in the past 15 years. The establishment of the Peace Corps in

1961 served as an impetus for program development at that time. Prior to 1961, writings and research on cross-cultural training in the international field focused on international political relations and intercultural artistic exchange programs.

In an effort to provide a framework for the categorization of cross-cultural training programs since the Peace Corps. James Downs lists the four models of training as: the Intellectual Model; the Area Simulation Model; the Self-Awareness Model; and, a new training trend called the Cultural Awareness Model.

The *intellectual model* consists of lectures and reading about the host culture. It is assumed that an exchange of information about another culture is effective preparation for living or working in that culture.

The *area simulation model* is a culture-specific training program. It is based on the belief that an individual must be prepared and trained to enter a specific culture. It involves simulation of future experiences and practice in functioning in the new culture.

The *self-awareness model* is based on the assumption that understanding and accepting oneself is critical to understanding a person from another culture. Sensitivity training is a main component of this method.

The *cultural awareness model* assumes that for an individual to function successfully in another culture an individual must learn the principles of behavior that exist across cultures. In 1973, Kraemer developed a cultural self-awareness approach to cross-cultural training. It is based on the assumption that an individual's effectiveness in intercultural communication can be improved by developing the individual's cultural self-awareness—the ability to recognize cultural influences in personal values, behaviors, and cognitions. This ability, according to Kraemer, has several beneficial results: (a) it should enhance a person's skill at diagnosing difficulties in intercultural communication; (b) it should be easier to suspend judgments when confronted with behavior that appears odd and (c) it should make individuals aware of their ignorance of other cultures and correspondingly, increase their motivation to learn about it.

Although different in methods and assumptions, each training program's purpose is to train individuals to effectively interact and communicate in other cultures. The programs prepare individuals to work with people who think differently, behave differently, and hold different beliefs and values. The most widely used cross-cultural training methods are described and evaluated in the following sections.

The Culture Assimilator

The culture assimilator is an area simulation program which is culture specific. It was developed in 1971 by social scientists (Fiedler, Mitchell, and Triandis) at the University of Illinois. Its basic goal is to prepare persons to respond to specific situations in a particular country. Culture assimilator training programs have been established for the Arab countries, Iran, Thailand, Central America and Greece.

The culture assimilator is a programmed learning experience designed to expose members of one culture to the basic concepts, attitudes, role perceptions, customs, and values of another culture. To develop assimilators, first determine the major dimensions of social perception and cognition that are used in each culture, and the extent to which these dimensions influence responses. Themes, or culturally-determined viewpoints, are then isolated as representative generalizations about that culture. The end product is a programmed instruction simulation exercise that has the learner interpret, evaluate, and then assimilate immediate feedback. The program explains why an answer is correct or incorrect. If incorrect, the learner reviews the episode and reinterprets.

Feedback exposes the learner to major themes characterizing the two cultures, home and host. New concepts are developed from concrete incidents or assimilators. The culture assimilator can be validated by asking persons of the host culture to answer to the interaction incidents without seeing prepared alternatives.

The following example is from the Thai assimilator. It was developed after a U.S. student reported being bothered by the Thai teachers' lack of punctuality. The student asked fellow Thai students if they were similarly disturbed. The students indicated they were, but said they would never show these feelings to their professors. The assimilator incident was refined from this episode and was written by Triandis and his colleagues at the University of Illinois.

> One day a Thai administrator of middle academic rank kept two of his assistants waiting about an hour for an appointment. The assistants, although very angry, did not show it while they waited. When the administrator walked in, he acted as if he were not late. He offered no apology or explanation. After he was settled in his office, he called his assistants in; they all began working on the business for which the administrator had set the meeting.

> If the incident is observed exactly as it is reported in this passage, which one of the following best describes the chief significance of the behavior of the people involved?

> 1. The Thai assistants were extremely skillful at concealing their true feelings.
> 2. The Thai administrator obviously was unaware of the fact that he was an hour late for the appointment.
> 3. In Thailand, subordinates are required to be polite to their superiors, no matter what happens, nor what their rank may be.
> 4. Since no one commented on it, the behavior indicated nothing of unusual significance to the Thais.

> The first description is not entirely true, although it is characteristic of Thais to try to appear reserved under any circumstance. If the assistants

were skillful at concealing their true feelings, there would be no doubt about their feelings. Also, the reference to the chief significance of the behavior of the people involved may limit it to the assistants.

Number two is a very poor choice. While the administrator behaved as if he were unaware of his tardiness after observing the hour's wait, it is possible that he was acting.

The third choice is the correct one. The information in the episode is utilized to its fullest extent. This "deference to the boss" may be observed anywhere in the world, but it is likely to be carried to a higher degree in Thailand than in the U.S. Certain clues indicated number three—the assistants' concealed feelings, the administrator failed to apologize, no one mentioned the tardiness subsequently, the appointment was kept.

Number four is completely wrong. While the behavior reported in the passage does not seem as significant to the Thais it might to Americans, why was nothing said about the tardiness? And why were the assistants "very angry" although they "did not show it?" Is there a more significant level of meaning for this behavior?

The culture assimilator has been subjected to more empirical study than any other training method, and several studies support its usefulness in decreasing adjustment problems. Two laboratory studies, one using the Arab assimilators and the other, the Thai assimilator, compared U.S. nationals who had been trained with the assimilator method and others who had been trained only in the geography of the country. Data from both studies indicated that assimilator training lessened interpersonal and adjustment problems between the trainees and persons of the host culture.

A field study was conducted in Honduras using the culture assimilator. Results indicated that the assimilator-trained subjects were higher on adjustment measures than a control group of subjects who had not received assimilator training.

Although these studies indicate the usefulness of the culture assimilator as a method of cross-cultrual training, there are a number of problems with the approach. The program is ethnocentric in the sense that it focuses on the foreign culture and that culture's peculiar characteristics and differences. It is essential to identify the values of a culture and recognize the influence of these values when encountering a person from that culture. Other problems concern the lack of field assessment, long-range evaluation of assimilator-trained persons, and the best content for the assimilators. There is also the question of the subjects which are probably highly motivated persons, atypical of those actually involved in an intercultural experience.

The Contrast-American Method of Cross-Cultural Training

The contrast-American method is a culture-general approach rather than culture specific (e.g., the Thai assimilator). It is essentially a cultural awareness method of cross-cultural training. Stewart, Danielian, and Foster described the contrast-American method in 1969. It consists of role-playing encounters between a U.S. national and a person of another culture (this person represents a composite culture) who holds contrasting values. By interaction in the role-play, U.S. nationals develop greater awareness of their own values. The assumption underlying this method is that to function effectively in another culture, an individual must understand cultural differences in terms of behavior and values. To do this, individuals must first know their own culture.

The technique was developed to simulate psychologically and culturally significant interpersonal aspects of the overseas situation in a live role-play encounter. Stewart, Danielian, and Foster outlined four steps in the simulation construction:

1. Literature describing American cultural patterns was reviewed and analyzed, and American values and assumptions were identified.
2. These dimensions were extended to derive differences of cultural characteristics that contrast with American ones.
3. A series of overseas advisory situations was then constructed to elicit spontaneous culturally derived behavior from an American trainee.
4. Role-players were trained to reflect the contrast-American values and assumptions in an emotional confrontation between the role-player and the trainee.

The following role-playing situation is an example and illustrates the American desire to get the work done, while the contrast-American's desire is to preserve the status relation between the officer and the men. Following the role-play situation, the trainees receive feedback from the trainers. It demonstrates how this method brings out contrasting and often conflicting values.

> One of the scenes was designed around the topic of leadership. During one of the simulations of this scene, Captain Smith, the American role-player, tried to persuade the Contrast-American, Major Khan, to take measures to improve leadership in his battalion. Captain Smith found fault with some of the techniques utilized by some of Major Khan's second lieutenants.
>
> American: And I know that . . . if they are allowed to continue, the efficiency in the duties that they're performing, or their soldiers are performing, will be reduced.
>
> Contrast-American: What kind of duties are they performing which are not good?
>
> American: They have an inability, I think, to communicate with the noncommissioned officers and to properly supervise the accomplishment of the task. They almost have the attitude that this work is the type of work which they should not take part in; they should merely stand by and watch. I know you have a big respect for General George Washington

and I should point out this example. One time during the American Revolution, there was a sergeant with some artillery pieces which were stuck. He was standing by, very neat and clean in his uniform, cajoling his soldiers as they looked at him, and shouting for them to push harder to get this cannon out of the mud. General Washington rode by on his horse, noticed this situation and stopped. His rank was not showing for he had a large cape on over his uniform; it was rather cold that day and had been raining. He asked the sergeant what the problem was, and the sergeant told him, "Sir, the soldiers cannot get this cannon out of the mud." Then General Washington dismounted from his horse, walked over and assisted the soldiers in pushing the cannon out. Afterward, he walked over to the sergeant and said, "Sergeant, tell your commander that General Washington has assisted your men in pushing the cannon from the mud."

Contrast-American: Yes.

American: He was willing to assist his men and do anything that they were doing if it were really necessary.

Contrast-American: Perhaps if he were not in a disguise, not wearing a cape, if he were in his uniform of a general, he would never have dismounted the horse. He would have waited there as a general.

American: I think . . .

Contrast-American: . . . people would have gotten extra energy while pushing that cannon, they would have looked at him, that big, tall, towering general sitting on a horse, they would have looked at him and derived all inspiration and strength from him, and then pulled out the cannon without his assistance. His very presence would have been enough.

American: Perhaps this may have taken place. However, I think the point that he was trying to make, the same point that I'm trying to make, sir, is that many times the presence of an exalted ruler or an officer is adequate, but other times it is not. As you have pointed out on several occasions, I have assisted with my hands on this project, because the situations there, I thought, just required help. I don't think that it lowers the soldiers' opinions of officers, if the officer gives them some assistance on occasion.

Contrast-American: Yes, I agree, but you see, Captain, one thing leads to another. You start with a small thing. The moment we resign to it, we say, oh, it doesn't matter, it's such a negligible thing, it won't make much damage to my soul, my virtuous life. The moment you give in one place you know, it grows. It grows, yes.

American: Do you think helping soldiers on occasion could perhaps damage your virtuous life?

Contrast-American: No, today you do that, tomorrow you do a larger concession to something else, you lose your integrity and virtue as an individual. You're not doing justice to your person, to your position, to your status."

The Contrast-American Method of cross-cultural training was evaluated by using four instruments in a pretest/post-test assessment. Thirty-five Westinghouse executives who had a high probability of being sent overseas were the subjects. Preliminary evaluation indicates that the simulation exercises effectively increased cultural awareness.

A problem with the method concerns insufficient instructions to the role-players unless the players are professionals. When Stewart demonstrates this technique, he uses professional actors. When the role-players are not well trained, the technique is less effective. Another problem concerns the culture general approach and the applicability and transfer of concepts to a particular situation.

Peace Corps Training Programs (ACTION)

The agency most involved in preparing persons for cross-cultural living situations is the Peace Corps. Presently, the training programs are being reduced, but in 1965 the Peace Corps used 58 universities as training centers as well as several nonacademic organizations. These programs lasted an average of 11 weeks and cost $2,345 per participant. These training programs vary and are eclectic in nature. They cannot be categorized using Downs' framework. Rather, the programs employ techniques from all models.

The original training philosophy, methods, and learning experiences used by the Peace Corps to prepare volunteers to work in other countries are described in the four volume *Guidelines for Peace Corps Cross-Cultural Training* (Wight and Hammons, 1970). This manual identifies effective methods and materials.

The goals of Peace Corps training are:

1. Prepare the volunteer to accept and to be tolerant of values, beliefs, attitudes, standards, behaviors, and a style of life that might be quite different from one's own
2. Provide the skills to communicate this acceptance to another person
3. Provide the sensitivity and understanding necessary to effectively interact with a person from another culture
4. Teach appropriate behavior responses in situations where characteristics of the other culture prevail
5. Prepare the volunteer to understand, anticipate, and cope effectively with the possible reactions to him/her as a stranger or as a stereotype of his/her own culture
6. Provide an understanding of one's own culture and the problems cultural bias might create
7. Provide the adaptive skills to cope with one's own emotional reactions in the new and strange situation and to satisfy one's own culturally-conditioned behavior.

8. Provide the skills needed for continued learning and adjustment in the other culture
9. Help develop an orientation toward the sojourn in the other culture as a potentially interesting, enjoyable, and broadening experience

Peace Corps training also provides language training, training in technical skills, if necessary, and the interpersonal skills and sensitivities necessary to live and work effectively with persons whose ways may be different and, therefore, difficult to accept. Conditions essential for learning these skills are detailed, and programs are based on the assumption that the trainee will assume the major responsibility for learning. As the trainee learns from experience, the learning process should become a way of life.

Most evaluations of Peace Corps training programs are conducted after the training period, but before the trainees begin assignments in other countries. However, in order for the evaluations to be accurate, they should be performed after the trainee enters the host culture.

Prior-to-departure training should be complemented by additional training in the country of assignment. Trainees are more likely to complete their assignment if such in-country training is provided.

Self-Confrontation Training Techniques

The use of videotape in therapeutic and educational situations is becoming widespread and its success is well-documented. As a cross-cultural training technique, a method called *self-confrontation,* was developed by psychologists of the Training Research Laboratory at Wright-Patterson Air Force Base. A trainee plays a role with a person from another culture in a simulated cross-cultural encounter and the situation is videotaped. Following the interaction, the encounter is played for the trainee and trainer to point out strengths and weaknesses in both the verbal and nonverbal behavior of the trainee. The trainee can observe responses and evaluate behavior for improved performance in future role-play situations and for actual performance in a different culture. This is a culture general approach, although the situations can also be specific to a particular culture. Following Downs' categories, this is essentially a self-awareness model of cross-cultural training.

This technique uses a psychological principle of stimulated-recall that is useful in rapid learning. After replaying the behavioral situation on videotape, trainees are able to relive the scene and recall their thoughts at the moment, thus permitting complete utilization of the psychological impact of self-confrontation.

This approach enables trainees to retain skills for at least two weeks. Retention and application of these skills over a longer time period has not been demonstrated. Another problem concerns the videotaping of the experimental and the control group. The experimental group subjects may have done better on the criteria measure because they were more at ease with the videotape equipment. Experimental group subjects were videotaped twice, and the control group subjects once. This could account for the difference in performance.

Other Cross-Cultural Training Programs

Several cross-cultural training programs have not been evaluated. A number of these have been prepared for conference or seminar presentations. For purposes of comparison, a summary of some of these programs is presented. It is hoped the developers will evaluate the programs for their effectiveness as a method of cross-cultural training.

The DA-TA Model of Learning and the SAXITE System of Dialogue

A method of cross-cultural training that combines demonstration through action with theoretical analysis (DA-TA mentioned earlier in Chapter 9) and scouting, access, exploration, interest-interaction, termination, and evaluation (SAXITE) was developed by Wedge (1971). The purpose of the model, which is derived from the principles of psychiatric interview, is to train leaders in cross-cultural interaction.

In the training programs, five concepts are emphasized: (a) the idea of social communication, the flow of information from one person to another in the form of signals which are assigned meanings by the participants (b) the idea of perception as a transactive process (c) the idea of communicating culture as a system of shared habits and channels of communication (d) the idea of community as a boundary-maintaining system of social organization with which persons identify themselves as members and within which non-members are perceived as outsiders (e) the idea of dialogue as a process ability to become more independent of external sources of information and problem definition; the development of the ability to deal with feelings created by value conflicts; decision-making skills in stressful situations; and, the ability to use one's own and others' feelings as information. Contrast is made between university education and cross-cultural education.

The program has been used by the Peace Corps in training volunteers for assignment in Ecuador, Chile, and Bolivia, but unfortunately, there has been no research on the impact of the training program.

Intercultural Communication Workshops

Although the methods and goals of the Intercultural Communication Workshop (ICW) have been employed in a number of settings over the years, the formal use of Intercultural Communication Workshops began at the University of Pittsburgh in 1966 under the direction of Davıd S. Hoopes and Stephen H. Rhinesmith. As a part of orientation programs for new foreign students attending U.S. institutions of higher learning, some of the recently developed themes and techniques of intercultural communication were applied. Language and orientation lectures were supplemented by workshop programs led by individuals trained in cross-cultural communication theory and practice. The focus was on the process of communicating. The content was the problems the participants had previously experienced and were presently experiencing in communicating their ideas and feelings.

The goals of the early workshops varied according to whether the foreign students had recently arrived in the U.S. or had been attending a U.S. institution for some time. For new arrivals, the fundamental goal was to provide an atmosphere and framework within which they could begin the process of organizing and understanding their experience at both a cognitive and an emotional level, and thus help them in the process of adjustment and adaptation to the U.S. society and culture. Films, group discussions, and communication exercises were used to provide a stimulus for the interaction. In all groups, U.S. students were included. Foreign and U.S. students were encouraged to exchange information and feelings about themselves as individuals and as persons from a particular culture. It was assumed that this sharing at the cognitive and emotional level would help the foreign student understand differences in behavior and value throughout his sojourn in the United States.

Goals for foreign students who had been in the United States for some time included these same objectives, but with the additional purpose of helping students understand and integrate into their social behavior the experiences they had in this culture. In addition, the workshops provided opportunities for participants to express their feelings concerning their life in the United States.

Goals for the U.S. student were twofold: to provide an opportunity to get beyond the formality that frequently characterizes verbal exchanges between foreign and U.S. students; and to provide feedback on behavior from a different cultural perspective. First, a deeper relationship was expected to develop that would enable U.S. students to communicate with, understand, and accept individuals from another culture. Then, U.S. students could better understand their own culture and its effect on their behavior.

Other U.S. institutions were experimenting with similar intercultural communication workshop programs. In an attempt to create a common base of information and experience and to train more ICW facilitators, the National Association for Foreign Student Affairs, the Regional Council for International Education, and the U.S. Department of State conducted the first Intercultural Communication Workshop leadership training program at Wheeling, West Virginia in January, 1969.

Many of the goals of an intercultural communication workshop are similar to those of the T-group and other training methods. Each ICW will emphasize its own set of learning objectives. Goals common to all are: increased self-insight; increased awareness of others; increased awareness of one's impact on others and greater interpersonal competence. In addition, there are goals unique to the ICW that distinguish it from other forms of human relations training. At an abstract level, these are: an understanding and appreciation of the life styles of persons from various cultural groups; an increase in cultural sensitivity; the ability to adjust to new environments; and the ability to function effectively with persons from different cultures. At a more specific and measurable level, three goals distinguish the ICW from other forms of training:

1. Increase ability to identify the cultural dimensions of verbal and nonverbal behavior as well as other learned characteristics of oneself (This refers to a very basic goal of gaining an awareness of the role one's own cultural background plays in influencing one's behavior and values.)
2. Increase ability to identify the cultural dimensions of verbal and nonverbal behavior as well as other learned characteristics of persons from different cultures (This goal is similar to the first except it is directed towards gaining information and knowledge about others in the group as persons from a particular culture.)
3. Increase ability to identify areas in which differences cause difficulty in communicating interpersonally with persons of different cultures (This refers to the typing together of knowledge of others and oneself, and the areas of similarity and of difference as they cause difficulty in communicating interpersonally with persons from another culture.)

The exclusion of cognitive and affective goals from these objectives does not imply that these objectives do not exist. It does indicate, however, that in cross-cultural communication, as in any interpersonal communication, only behaviors are observable; and, therefore, the separation of the behavioral from the cognitive and the affective.

In each ICW there is a differential emphasis in attempting to accomplish the three objectives, and this constitutes an important element among the varieties of ICW experiences. Some groups, for example, emphasize the goal of increasing participants' ability to identify cultural aspects of their own behavior. For U.S. participants, exercises would be developed to help them recognize the great variety of manifestations of the cultural influences in their lives. Exercises demonstrating aspects of American culture such as individualism, egalitarianism, action and problem orientation, and reasoning in terms of probability would be developed. No attempt is made to select mutually exclusive cultural aspects of American life, as the resulting list would be short and at a high level of abstraction. In the process of discussion and interaction it becomes evident that these aspects are also present in varying degrees within other cultures.

The intercultural communication workshop combines the two polarities that have developed in the human relations training movement. Traditional forms of sensitivity training, for example, generally ignore the cultural differences of the participants and focus primarily on the personal. This is true even if participants are from different cultures. On the other hand, black/white sensitivity programs tended to focus exclusively on the cultural, attempting to teach white people about black people or black people about white people, while ignoring the unique aspects of the white and black participants. The ICW approach considers each participant as a person in the context of a culture and as an individual. An attempt is made to help participants understand how their socialization has influenced the development of their values and behaviors.

The facilitator in an ICW plays a more active leadership role than a sensitivity group trainer who does not accept and often overtly rejects a leadership role. The ICW facilitator steers the discussion and intervenes to keep the focus of the interaction on the personal and the cultural. The facilitator also structures the discussion so that an atmosphere of openness and trust can be established (a group maintenance function). During an ICW, the facilitator presents topics for discussion that focus on the "there and then" (recollected experiences and feelings) as well as the "here and now" (the behavior emitted in the group). This is in contrast to most sensitivity training groups where the focus is on the "here and now."

Specific methods used to accomplish the goals of the ICW include:

1. Readings related to the field of intercultural communication. Often articles or portions of a book are given to participants prior to the workshop to provide a cognitive framework for the experience. Materials are also given to participants during the workshop.
2. Communication exercises which are designed to facilitate the process of communicating interpersonally with persons from different cultures and to identify some of the variables involved in human communication.
3. Critical incidents (originally developed by Flanagan, 1954) which consist of brief descriptions of difficult and often conflict situations that occur between people from various cultural backgrounds. These incidents are presented to the group for discussion and identification of appropriate and nonappropriate responses from different cultural viewpoints.
4. Role-playing exercises allow participants to play the role of another person, or of themselves. Participants experience the feelings of a person from another culture, and experience themselves as a product of their own culture.

Cross-Cultural Simulations

An educational strategy that is being utilized in cross-cultural orientation programs now, much more so than in the past, is simulation (not to be confused with the area simulation model). The best known simulation is perhaps Bafá Bafá, which was developed by R. Garry Shirts for Simile II. Bafá Bafá is a simulation in which participants are divided into two cultures, Alpha and Beta. After learning the "rules" of their culture, they are required to interact with members of the other culture. The Alpha culture is a warm, friendly and patriarchal society speaking English. The Beta culture does not use English and are hard working, and their task is to accumulate as many points as possible. Once the participants in the two cultures learn the rules and the language, they are to interact with each other. Visitors to the other culture are often confused (as they are in an actual cross-cultural situation) by the strangeness of the foreign culture. This confusion often becomes frustration and hostility.

In the debriefing of the simulation, participants come to realize the rationale behind the behavior they had observed during the activities. A discussion of their reactions and the specific skills that are associated with effective interactions are also discussed.

This simulation has been used in academic and business settings and in other programs in which it is important for the participants to have an experiential understanding of the meaning of culture. After playing Bafá Bafá, according to Garry Shirts, participants report they have learned the following:

1. What seems logical, sensible, important and reasonable to a person in one culture may seem irrational, stupid, and unimportant to an outsider.
2. Feelings of apprehension, loneliness, lack of confidence are common when visiting another culture.
3. When people talk about other cultures, they tend to describe the differences and not the similarities.
4. Differences between cultures are generally seen as threatening and described in negative terms.
5. Personal observations and reports of other cultures should be regarded with a great deal of skepticism.
6. One should make up one's own mind about another culture and not rely on the reports and experience of others.
7. It requires experience as well as study to understand the many subtleties of another culture.
8. Understanding another culture is a continuous and not a discrete process.
9. Stereotyping is probably inevitable in the absence of frequent contact or study.
10. The feelings that people have for their own language are often not evident until they encounter another language.

11. People often feel their own language is far superior to other languages.
12. It is probably necessary to know the language of a foreign culture to understand the culture in any depth.
13. Perhaps a person can accept a culture only after he or she has been very critical of it.

Other simulations such as The Owl, Rafa Rafa, Baldicer, Majorians and Minorians are available and useful in orientation programs.

Training Programs for International Organizations

In a paper presented at the 1978 IFTDO Conference in Washington, D.C., Mel Schnapper distinguishes several kinds of training that are necessary for a manager who will be working in a multicultural environment:

1. Managerial training, which focuses upon the managerial function (such as leading, planning, etc.) regardless of the language, cultural differences, or the business
2. Intercultural training, which focuses upon cultural differences such as values, perceptions, and assumptions
3. International business, training which focuses on business practices and functions across national boundaries such as production, marketing, and finance
4. Language training, which focuses on developing language skills in the social and technical areas

In training programs for international managers going to a variety of countries, the authors have found that case studies and critical incidents are among the most effective methods for conveying specific cultural information in training. Examples are presented in Chapters 15-19. Other valuable techniques include background readings, simulations, films, and video tapes.

Dr. Robert Kohls has done research on an instrument for evaluating cross-cultural trainees' readiness to function in a foreign environment. He believes it can be used as a tool for feedback and self-assessment. It provides a forty-two-point role model and paired behaviors that are grouped into the following categories:

1. Trainee self-awareness
2. Trainee and others
3. Trainee ability to become "other" (empathy)
4. Trainee and job
5. Trainee and life-style
6. Trainee and the foreign culture

Upon direct inquiry, Dr. Kohls will share this instrument for further research—537 7th Street, S.E., Washington, D.C. 20003.

Conclusion

Cross-cultural training programs are designed to prepare individuals for life in another culture, and greater effectiveness with microcultures within one's native land. It is hoped that more international organizations will utilize these methods in the training and preparation of their personnel for overseas assignments, thereby reducing business losses and personal trauma.

References

Brewster, E.T. and E.S., *Language Acquisition Made Practical: Field Methods for Language Learners.* Colorado Springs, Colorado: Lingua House, 1976.

Brislin, Richard W. and Pedersen, Paul B., *Cross-Cultural Orientation Programs.* Gardner Press, Inc. New York, 1976.

Fiedler, F., Mitchell, T., and Triandis, A., "The Culture Assimilator: An Approach to Cross-Cultural Training." *Journal of Applied Psychology,* 1971, 55, 95-102.

Hoopes, D.S., Pedersen, P.B., and Renwick, G.W. (eds.), *Overview of Intercultural Education, Training, and Research,* Vols. I-Theory; II-Education and Training; III-Special Research Areas. Washington, D.C.: Society for Intercultural Education, Training, and Research, 1978.

James, Rob and Tingey, S., *Intercultural Education for Overseas Managers: An Empirical Study and Proposed Model.* Paper presented at the 1978 SIETAR Conference. February 1978.

Kraemer, A.J., "A Cultural Self-Awareness Approach to Improving Intercultural Communication Skills." HumRRo Professional Paper, 5-73, 1973.

Lanier, Alison, "Planning for the Human Factor in Your Overseas Moves, *International Business.* May/June 1977.

Schnapper, Melvin, "Multinational Training for Multinational Corporations/International Organizations." Paper presented at the 1978 IFTDO Conference, June 1978.

Stewart, E., Danielian, J., and Foster, R., "Simulating Intercultural Communication through Role Playing." HumRRo Professional Paper, 65-73, 1973.

Stewart, E.C., *American Cultural Patterns: A Cross-Cultural Perspective.* Pittsburgh, Pennsylvania: RCIE, 1971.

Wedge, B., "Training for Leadership in Cross Cultural Dialogue: the DA-TA Model of Learning and the SAXITE System of Dialogue." *Readings in Intercultural Communication,* Vol. I, D. Hoopes (ed.), University of Pittsburgh, 1971.

Wight, A.R., and Hammons, M.A., *Guidelines for Peace Corps Cross-Cultural Training.* Estes Park, Colorado: CRE, 1970.

11
Cross-Cultural
Family Preparation

Survival or Growth Abroad

This chapter has two themes. The first suggests what happens to most families when they go overseas—they survive. That is, the couple does not get a divorce, no one becomes addicted to alcohol or drugs, the employee has a position to return to in the organization, and there is no substantial financial loss resulting from the assignment. The second theme suggests what happens to some families—they grow. That is, they mature and grow emotionally and intellectually, and their whole person benefits from the experience. They become a closer family. Consider the implications of the following observations:

> It's definitely not a place to come if you've got a problem of any kind. I don't care if it's alcohol or marital problems. A lot of people have come over here thinking, "A new life, we'll start over. . . . Well, they find it worse.

> I know a lot of mothers that don't speak the language and sit home every day, and you can't sit in the house every day . . . being scared to go out of the house or not wanting to go out of the house because you don't know the language . . . and they turn to alcohol. And it's just terrible, because it gets on the kids, too.

> If you took a vote of the 30,000 Americans here in Iran, are they disappointed or happy? Do they want to stay or go? Which way would they vote? I think they would go.

> From *CBS 60 Minutes*
> "Yanks in Iran" Broadcast
> over the CBS Network
> Sunday, January 2, 1977

The Gilded Cage: Life in Singapore is Comfortable, Dull.

> *Wall Street Journal*
> September 1, 1978

Many employees and their families sent overseas by the multinationals can't stand the strain of alien ways and are brought back at great expense to the companies. Cross-cultural training may be the answer."

Across the Board
Conference Board Magazine
February, 1978

In Chapter 12, important questions and procedures concerning the selection of persons for an overseas assignment are considered. Decisions about the most suitable candidates for expatriation are faced regularly by many multi-national corporations and international organizations. In a comprehensive study completed in 1974 by the Center for Research and Education (CRE), it was found that the "adjustment problems of Americans abroad are severe, and adjustment failures are costly in terms of economics, efficiency of operations, intercultural relations, and personal satisfaction with duty abroad."

Exact statistics concerning the number of Americans who are "failures" overseas and return early are difficult to determine and vary from country to country. In the CRE study, the figure given most frequently for outright failures of families who return early was 33 percent. Besides those who return prematurely, there are many who remain abroad, but perform marginally in their overseas assignment. The cost to an organization to bring persons back ahead of schedule ranges from $20,000 for those assigned to London to in excess of $150,000 for senior managers assigned to the Middle East. Family units cost as much as $210,000 to relocate depending on geographic area and employee status. In this chapter, some factors involved in moving a family to another culture are considered.

Entering a New Culture

When families leave their homeland for a temporary assignment in another country, or leave one city in their own country for a move to another city, the phenomenon of "cultural shock" is experienced by most persons involved. The term basically describes the impact of a new and different environment on an individual, and was explained in detail in Chapter 7. Children begin new schools that sometimes use a different curriculum. They leave behind old friends and have to initiate making new friends. For some children, and especially teenagers, this is a difficult task. Spouses of employees assigned overseas must begin a whole new life style. At home perhaps they were working and pursuing a career. In many other countries, finding gainful employment is difficult for a spouse because of local regulations. The employee generally finds that his or her productivity and effectiveness is considerably below what was experienced in their native country. These factors may exact a heavy toll of suffering in a family. If family relocation within one's country is usually traumatic, consider what occurs when relocation is outside the family's native culture. Perhaps careful use by the family of the checklist in Appendix A will lessen the shock of an alien culture.

Cultural shock may occur because the experiences of all family members are not what they were accustomed to in their native country. Their worlds, small though they may be, are not as predictable as they were. When this is happening, cultural shock is experienced. Symptoms are varied, but the following are examples: excessive anger over delays or changes in plans, preoccupation with cleanliness, writing letters home about how awful the people are, blaming the host nation for things that go wrong, a superstitious attitude towards host nationals, using labels of "good" and "bad," a reluctance to learn even a few words of another language, feelings of hopelessness, and a general desire to be with persons from one's own country.

These feelings are reactions to new situations, and are not experienced initially. When individuals first enter another culture, some are given the red carpet treatment. They are met at the airport, taken by limousine to their lodgings, and wined and dined. Excessive delays at customs, delayed shipment of household goods, and other inconveniences are usually overlooked. They are on a high. This feeling of enthusiasm lasts from a few hours to a number of weeks or even months. But sooner or later, the basic reality of living in a new country comes home. The *honeymoon* phase of the transition is over.

Welcome to the second phase called *the party's over*. A family is in this phase when they complain more frequently than before about their life in the new country. There is also the desire to be with other countrymen. This is a critical phase, and new families should be cautious of the kinds of countrymen they become friends or acquaintances with at this time. Americans who are having bad experiences in a particular country seem to have a missionary zeal towards newcomers to warn them of the perils and evils they will shortly experience. They are looking for new arrivals from home who will join gossip sessions about how awful it is to be here and how great it is back home. This kind of unhealthy conversation may distort the overseas experience. Families should associate as much as possible with people who are having positive experiences.

The third phase is the *turning point*. Will the family be able to stop complaining and get on with life and responsibilities, or will they continue to sit around and complain? A good sign is when a sense of humor returns. Can they laugh at themselves and the kinds of experiences they are having or is everything deadly serious? Once a family begins to learn about the host nationals and the kind of people they are, as well as some customs, things do not seem so uncomfortable and strange.

The final stage is *healthy recovery*. For example, an American family may accept the new life style as just another way of life. Host nationals are not defective Americans. They have their way, and Americans have theirs. Americans have had different teachers, and therefore are different in many

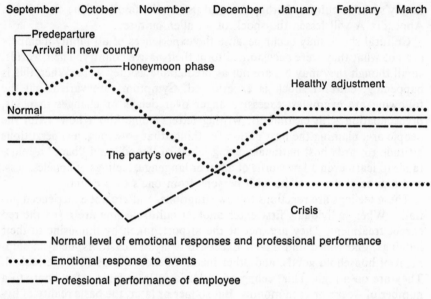

Figure 11-1. Shown here are the various phases a family will experience upon entering a new culture.

respects. There will still be moments of pain, misunderstanding, and tension, but these are experienced everywhere. Figure 11-1 indicates the various phases of adjustment.

The Expatriate Couple

At the moment, the typical employee sent abroad with a family is male. Female personnel sent overseas tend to be single, but a trend is likely for more female managers, professionals, and technicians with families to be assigned overseas.

Relationships between the couple and other members of the family, if they are present, are of critical importance to the success of an overseas experience. When looking at the traditional expatriate American family, for instance, it is probably true to say that the typical worker invests more time on the job, has achieved a higher level of education and expects and experiences faster promotion. Those in management or technical posts usually earn more money and derive more prestige and personal satisfaction from their job.

Robert Seidenberg in his book, *Corporate Wives—Corporate Casualties,* states that an executive expects support from a spouse in order to successfully fulfill social and other responsibilities. In an overseas job situation, often the assignment is not clear, and the length of stay depends on a variety of factors. The expatriate needs the spouse's support as home becomes an unofficial retreat where customs are familiar, the language is understood, and the environment is not strange. Sidney Werkman quotes children of persons working overseas to illustrate the problems:

> My father works extremely hard and very long hours, so I never have known him very well. We never share any real family life with him.
>
> I don't have any recollection of my father when we lived in Europe and Asia . . . my mother was around a good deal and I divided my time between her and the maid.

These statements are meaningful, and they are made frequently. A father may become excessively busy and lose contact with his family. But for the experience to be successful for all members, it is critical that the father be involved with spouse and children, and spend a significant amount of time with them.

A wife does not have the same kind of support and reinforcement that a husband has. The husband usually functions in English, or his native language, has a support system and experiences himself, and is seen by others as important. His long hours often prevent a wife from receiving the emotional support that she requires to function effectively in situations that are often more difficult than the husband's. If there is a problem at school she usually handles it. If the telephone does not work, she is at home. If the gas runs out or the power is shut off or a brown-out is experienced, she handles the situation. The problems of home repairs and services often escalate abroad.

In these difficult times, very often there is no one to turn to. When she becomes confused, lonely, bored, or depressed, her husband may be out of town or even out of the country. He may be away on a field trip or keeping regular foreign office hours from 7:00 a.m. until 8:00 p.m. She may experience a bind in priorities between the corporation and the family. Negative feelings and frustrations may stay bottled-up inside.

What is left to do? She may remember things that her mother did when she was frustrated and alone—rearrange the furniture, work in the garden—or she may find out-of-the-home activities to occupy her time. Finding meaningful and gainful employment is almost impossible.

The couple abroad has come a long way since their proclamation of equality and a desire to achieve what is best for both of them. The results are painful for the individuals and include divorce, chemical dependency (drugs and/or alcohol), serious depression, mental breakdown, suicide, or a failure to be effective in most situations. If children are involved, the implications and disruptions in their lives are obvious.

What can the couple do? At this stage, it is important to spend time together. Possibly, they should not have gone overseas in the first place.

An overseas assignment is not for everyone. If there are marital, mental, or chemical dependency problems, going overseas will not help. It will only increase the problem. If there are other kinds of family problems such as learning disabilities of children or severe behavior disorders with teenagers or preteens, then it is preferable that the family not go overseas. The problem will likely only get worse. If anyone in the family is emotionally unstable (e.g., needing tranquilizers to get through a day), compulsive about having things done in a certain way, then the family should think seriously about rejecting the overseas' assignment.

Problems which are small in the home culture generally become larger overseas. Big family problems in one's native land become disasters in most other countries. Going overseas to start anew is questionable strategy.

Preparation for Overseas Assignment

Appendix D contains a list of organizations that provide training for persons and families going overseas. For most multinationals, the selection for international assignment centers around: (a) Is the employee technically qualified? and (b) Is the employee willing to expatriate?

If the answer to both of these questions is yes, then the person becomes a candidate for an overseas assignment. If the individual has moved several times in the home nation, the assumption is made that he and his family probably will not have any great difficulties in a foreign country. However, some corporations and organizations are beginning to question this. Just because a person is successful in the home culture, he or she may not be successful in another country. Furthermore, effective service in Japan does not guarantee doing a good job in Nigeria.

Whenever feasible, spouses and teenage children should participate in intercultural briefing and training sessions, as described in Chapters 9 and 10. In a program recently completed by 200 employees and their families assigned to Iran, a learning activity called RAYRAN was developed by George Renwick, Nancy Adler, and Robert Moran for American Graduate School of International Management which designed and conducted the program. This simulation helps participants prepare for some of the factors that are critical to their success in Iran. Parts of the RAYRAN learning activity are included to illustrate how a family might be prepared for a specific culture:

> The purpose of this sequence of integrated exercises is to provide an opportunity for the participants to reflect upon, discuss, and make decisions on some of the fundamental cultural dimensions of their work in Iran. The variety of activities in which they will engage will enable the participants to do the following:
>
> 1. Visualize as immediately as possible the specific situations in which they must function in Iran.
>
> 2. Identify the personal and professional qualities necessary for successful adaptation and effective performance in Iran.

3. Clarify their personal and professional objectives which will give direction to their efforts in Iran.

4. Anticipate some of the specific difficulties they may experience in Iran, both on the job and outside the job.

5. Clarify their expectations of their Iranian students, as well as the students' expectations of them.

6. Identify what additional knowledge and skills they would like to have in order to fully accomplish their mission in Iran.

Having engaged in these activities, the participants will be acquainted with the subjects to be developed more fully during the remainder of the program. They will, therefore, be able to take fullest advantage of the program.

Phase One—Selection

Situation

An American company is planning to send an American instructor and his family to Iran. The family will live in Iran for an extended period of time—probably two years. Part of the time the man may live in a city, but he will probably live most of the time and do most of his work in an undeveloped rural area. The subjects he will teach are technical. His students will be Iranian military personnel. Most of them will be reasonably fluent in English.

His position will require him to work closely with a limited number of students over an extended period of time. It will also necessitate frequent association with other Iranian military personnel and with Iranians in the area where he lives.

Instructions

There are three candidates for this position overseas. Only one will go. A profile of each candidate follows. Please read each profile, consider the qualities of each candidate carefully, and then decide which one you think should be sent to Iran. When you have made your decision, write on the line provided the name of the man who, in your best judgment, should go. (You will have about ten minutes to do this part.)

Candidates for Assignment in Iran

Bill

Bill has had extensive experience overseas; he has lived and worked in foreign countries for more than six years. He is extremely curious about Iran and thoroughly knowledgeable about the customs of its people. He is fully aware of the differences between American and Iranian cultures. He has little idea, however, about the particular, personal difficulties he himself would experience while trying to adjust to life in Iran. Although he is pretty well sold on the American way of doing things, he is somewhat open to other ways of doing things and sometimes respects them.

Bill is an acceptable teacher. He understands what his students expect of him. He is usually sensitive to his students' level of ability, their frustrations, aspirations and customary ways of education. He is able to understand his students through carefully observing their behavior; they don't have to explain themselves to him.

Bill's technical knowledge is adequate. His ability to speak Farsi is fair. He is married. Going to Iran would be all right with his wife. She would have some difficulty adjusting to life in Iran, but would be able to do it fairly well. Bill and his wife have always had a very close, comfortable relationship with one another. Their teenage daughter, who is very shy, is very reluctant to move to a new city. Bill, himself, wouldn't mind going to Iran. Earlier in his life, he failed at some things he had attempted, and he learned a lot from his failures. He now has a very realistic sense of his strengths and weaknesses, both personal and professional. He has assessed somewhat realistically the difficulties he would have in transferring his skills to his Iranian students. While he is not on the job in Iran, Bill would keep pretty much to himself; he would not mix much socially with Iranians or Americans. He is a very serious fellow who seldom finds much to laugh about.

Chuck

Chuck has a great sense of humor; it seems that the more difficult the situation, the more easily he laughs. During his hours off work, Chuck would spend a lot of time with both Iranians and Americans; he would mix easily with them and enjoy being with them. They, too, would enjoy being with him.

Chuck has had no experience overseas. He has very little curiosity about Iran and very little knowledge about Iranian customs. His awareness of the differences between American and Iranian cultures is minimal. He does have some idea, however, about the personal difficulties he would have while adjusting to life in Iran. He likes American ways of doing things, but he is very open to other people's ways of doing things and very tolerant of them.

Chuck's technical knowledge is fairly good. He has little knowledge of Farsi. He is married. His wife has little desire to go to Iran and would have considerable difficulty adjusting to life in Iran. He and his wife have had some difficulties in their relationship. They have no children. As far as his own desire to go to Iran is concerned, Chuck is very enthusiastic; he has wanted to go overseas for a long time. Chuck has been successful in everything he has ever attempted. His assessment of his strengths and weaknesses, either professional or personal, is quite unrealistic. He is very clear, however, on some of the difficulties he would have to deal with in transferring his skills to his Iranian students.

As a teacher, Chuck is all right. He understands to some extent what his students expect of him. He is somewhat able to gauge their level of ability and has some sense of their frustrations, aspirations and customary ways of education. He is somewhat able to understand his students through observing their behavior, but must rely to some extent upon their own explanations of themselves to him.

George

George's Farsi is excellent and he knows some things about the customs of the Iranian people. He has some awareness of the differences between American and Iranian cultures. He has assessed carefully and accurately the personal difficulties he would have in adjusting to life in Iran. George has had some experience overseas—about three years. He is confident that American ways are the best and has little tolerance for any other ways.

George's technical knowledge is outstanding; he is one of the most competent men in the company. He is married. His relationship with his wife over the years has been all right. They have two young children; their oldest is three, the other is two. His wife would like to go to Iran; she studied Persian art and is interested in international cooking. George, himself, has little desire to go to Iran.

As a teacher, George is quite good. He has a good understanding of what his students expect of him. He has a sense of his students' level of ability, and is aware of their frustrations, aspirations and customary ways of education.

He has had many years of military experience and was well regarded by both officers and enlisted men. George has some idea of his personal and professional strengths and weaknesses. His estimates, however, regarding the difficulties he would have in transferring his skills to his Iranian students, are quite inaccurate. While not on the job, George would sometimes mix with Iranians and Americans and he would get along all right with them. George has some sense of humor; he sometimes enjoys a good laugh with others, if there is not much pressure on him at the time.

Write on the line below the name of the man who you believe should be sent to Iran: _____

Consider how the single most important reason why you think this man should be sent. Write your reason in the space below. Please be specific. Instead of stating simply that he is most qualified, explain exactly why he is most qualified:

Stop at this point. Wait until all the members of your group have made their decisions. After all the members have made their decisions and written the reasons for their choice in their handbook, then continue on.

Selection Committee

Your group has been appointed by the company to be a selection committee. Your responsibility as a committee is to select the man who will be sent to Iran with his family to instruct the military personnel there. You have each given some thought to the three candidates for this position, and have decided which one you think should be sent. Your task now is to decide, as a committee, which one will be sent. The man you select will leave for Iran with his family in two weeks. (You will have twenty minutes to complete your work as a committee.) Begin with Step 1:

Step 1

Reporting: Each member of the committee is to write on the top line below the name of the man you yourself thought should go to Iran, and then list the names of the men the other members of the committee thought should go:

_____

_____

_____

Step 2

Decision: If there is disagreement among your committee members as to which man should go, the committee should discuss the reasons for each member's decision. During the discussion, the qualities of the two or three candidates still under consideration should be reexamined and reevaluated. The objective is to come up with a consensus among the members of the committee regarding the man to be sent to Iran.

When one candidate has been agreed upon (or if there was complete agreement at the beginning), each committee member is to write the name of the man selected on the line below:

_____

The Committee's Choice

Step 3

Explanation: Your committee should now discuss the reasons why you selected the man you did, and decide upon the two most important reasons. Write these two reasons on the lines below. Please be specific. Indicate the particular qualities that persuaded you to select the man you did.

1._____

2._____

Step 4

Select one member of your group to represent you in the large group. Stop at this point. Please do not go on. Return to the large group.

Large Group
Reporting and Discussion

As each group reports on its selection, record the name of the man selected and the reasons for their selection on the lines below:

First Group:

Name: _____

Reasons: 1._____

_____

Second Group: etc.

Reasons:_____

Phase Two—Objectives

Your company has recently put you through a selection process, perhaps somewhat similar to the one we just put Bill, Chuck, and George through. You yourself were the one chosen to go to Iran.

For the purposes of the remaining exercises, assume that you are actually in Iran now. You have a place to live, the complications and hectic pace of the move are pretty well behind you and you are beginning to settle in. This is an appropriate point to consider your objectives for your time in Iran.

Step 1

Personal Objectives: What you, yourself, get out of your experience here in Iran depends in large part upon your own objectives for yourself. During the next few minutes, please give some thought to your personal objectives. (You will be asked to consider your professional objectives later.) After identifying some of your personal hopes and objectives, please write them on the lines below. (Your personal objectives are for your own reference only; you will not be asked to discuss them with other participants or members of the staff unless you would like to.)

My Major Personal Objectives

1._____
2._____
3._____

Step 2

Professional Objectives: Now that you are here in Irán and are somewhat settled, you will begin your work immediately. You will walk into your first meeting with your daneshju (students) Monday morning at 8:00 a.m. Their names are Farshid, Moji, Kamal, Reza and Yahia. You will be working with them closely for an extended period of time.

The professional objectives which you carry into your work are critical. The objectives you have set for yourself will shape (1) what you teach Farshid and the others, (2) the methods you use to instruct them, and (3) the results of your (and their) efforts.

Please give some thought to your professional objectives during the next few minutes. If they are not already clear, take this opportunity to begin to formulate them. Then write on the lines below the two objectives you have set for yourself which you consider to be most important:

My Major Professional Objectives

1._____
2._____

Stop at this point. Wait until all members of your group have finished writing their professional objectives. After they have finished, continue on to Step 3.

Step 3

Report: For the interest and information of the others in your group, tell them what your major professional objectives are. They will write your objectives in their handbooks. As they explain their objectives to you, record these in the appropriate spaces below. If you do not understand what someone means by a particular objective, or why an objective was chosen as important, ask the person for clarification. (This step should take no more than five minutes).

Our Group's Major Professional Objectives

First Person:

1._____
2._____

Second Person: etc.

The four groups discuss, with the help of a resource person and a discussion guide:

1. Expected and possible difficulties on the job
2. Expected and possible difficulties outside the job
3. American expectations of Iranians
4. Iranian expectations of Americans

Such a learning activity helps a family focus on their objectives for going overseas as well as some of the specific problems they may experience. Although the program itself was not designed to "deselect" anyone, a few families decided not to relocate following the program. If the wrong family has been selected, it is very difficult or impossible to prepare them to be effective.

In retrospect, perhaps such simulation exercises should raise the issue of major crises the family may face in the target culture. How, for example, would a family cope with riots, anti-foreigner campaigns, political kidnappings of foreign managers or violent revolution that may force the family to abandon their house and belongings because of a forced evacuation?

Ensuring Overseas Success

In a study of thirty-three U.S. multinationals, the Conference Board, in 1976, identified the following elements of a successful orientation program. The Board's recommendations have been adapted to illustrate critical aspects of family preparation for foreign deployment:

1. Assure candidate self-disqualification will not destroy his or her career.
2. Allow enough time for orientation of candidate and family.
3. Get the foreign subsidiary to participate in the orientation program design, including on-site activities.

4. Assign responsibility at headquarters and the field for relocation and preparation.
5. Customize the specific orientation program to the candidate and his family.
6. Use pictorial as well as written materials; experiential as well as cognitive input.
7. Engage consultants for special needs when in-house resources are inadequate.
8. Include cultural and economic counseling.
9. Provide language instruction for the candidate and family.
10. Make provisions for educational and recreational needs of the family during training, as well as when abroad.
11. When feasible, offer candidate and spouse a pretransfer visit to the foreign location.
12. Pay special attention to processing details related to relocation entrance to foreign country, and adequate housing and transportation.
13. Assign a seasoned expatriate family to help ease the initial adjustment after arrival.
14. Audit the results of each orientation effort.
15. Make adjustments at headquarters and in the field as needed to accommodate the needs of expatriate families.

Medical, Household, and Critical Considerations

Helen L. McNulty, vice-president of Intercultural Communications, Inc., a Minneapolis based organization, has worked with many families going overseas and has the following suggestions for those preparing for expatriation:

Official documents—Apply for passport and any necessary visas. It is advisable to have separate passports for each family member. If the children are on the mother's passport, neither mother nor children can travel outside the country independently.

Doctors—Make appointments for medical examinations for each family member well in advance, three months ahead if possible, in order to be finished with series immunizations a month before departure date.

Request copies of any important records, x-rays, or prescriptions. Have prescriptions written in generic terms rather than with brand names. Bring an adequate supply of neccessary medications.

Be sure to have each person's blood type in case a transfusion is needed.

Inquire about gamma globulin shots as a preventive measure against hepatitis, and the antibiotic "doxycycline" to thwart diarrhea.

Arrange to have copies of eyeglass prescriptions, as well as an extra pair of glasses for those who wear them.

Make dental appointments for each family member well in advance, so all needed work can be completed by the family dentist. Request instructions on fluoride treatment abroad for children. Ask for copies of records, x-rays and statement of any recommended orthodontic treatment.

See a veterinarian for required shots and certificates if taking a pet. Write ahead to the United States Embassy in the country for current information on pet entry requirements. Consult with a veterinarian about preferred travel arrangements for the pet. Determine whether it will be necessary to inform someone abroad if the pet is to arrive in advance of the family. Reexamine whether it is even advisable to take a pet abroad (e.g., dogs are food, not pets in some cultures, whereas in others they are considered offensive).

Lawyer—Each adult member of the family should have an up-to-date will, properly witnessed and signed with the original placed in a safety deposit box, a copy for the lawyer, and a copy in the family's possession.

Draw up a power of attorney and leave it with a responsible relative or friend so that someone can act legally in your behalf.

Bank—Arrange with a home bank to mail monthly statements via air mail. Get copies of any papers that might be needed. Original naturalization papers can never be replaced so it is best to travel with copies of these documents. Arrange power of attorney for someone to have access to your safety deposit box. The bank will need to register authorization and signature.

Carry enough foreign currency to cover porters' tips, taxi fares, etc.

Purchase travelers' checks (preferably in small denominations) to cover hotel, restaurant, and sightseeing expenses while in route.

Put credit cards in safety deposit box except for the department store cards needed for ordering from abroad.

Schools—Notify the children's teachers of departure date in case special examinations must be scheduled to allow completion of term work. Request sufficient grade reports, test results, teacher evaluations, samples of work, etc. to facilitate grade placement in the new school.

Write schools in the new city for information, or if a school is selected prior to arrival, notify the school of the children's date of arrival, their grade level, and request space be held for them.

Insurance—Arrange for adequate insurance for household effects and luggage. A floater policy will cover belongings wherever they are, as well as injury to persons on the property, or injury caused by a member of the household. Marine insurance for automobiles should be especially specified. If keeping automobile insurance from this country, check if it covers the country of assignment. Some insurance companies abroad will give reduced rates if a letter showing a no accident record is presented.

Get appropriate health insurance coverage. Even if full medical care is available through the company, coverage is desirable for home leave or emergency travel.

Post Office—Remember to fill out change of address cards so mail will be forwarded. Notify magazines, newspapers, charge accounts, and the Internal Revenue Service of the address change. Provide family and friends with specific information on how to mail letters and packages. In some countries, the duty will exceed the value of the package.

Department Store—Pay a visit to a personal shopper at one or more department stores. Register and the process for ordering from overseas will be clarified.

Miscellaneous—Check absentee voting procedure in case any special registration is required.

Obtain an international drivers license through the American Automobile Association (AAA).

Give notice of your moving date to all utility companies—gas, oil, water, electricity, telephone, etc. and discuss arrangements for billing and discontinuation of service. Also notify the milkman, drycleaners, and any other delivery service.

Keep records of official expenses involved in the move.

Draw up a list of instructions for survivors in case of death. Make three copies—keep one, give one to a state-side lawyer, and put one in a safety deposit box. Include:

1. Name, address, and date of birth for each member of the family.
2. The location of the will, the name and address of the executor, the name of the lawyer and bank officer with whom the families should get in touch.
3. The location of birth certificates, marriage certificates, veteran's discharge certificate, divorce papers.
4. Proof of citizenship if a naturalized U.S. citizen.
5. The location of safety deposit box and key.
6. The location and types of insurance policies, the issuing companies, the amount and beneficiary of each policy, their names and addresses. (Insurance companies generally require certified notification of death within 30 days, together with proof of birth and citizenship.)
7. The location and total amount of stocks, bonds, deeds, and other securities owned, and the name and address of broker.
8. The location and important details about mortgage papers, and nature of financial agreements.
9. The location of bank accounts and bank books.
10. Vital data on social security, the social security card number, the location of the card, the name and address of former employers.
11. Location of income tax papers and significant tax records.
12. Names of debtors and/or creditors and a complete description of the accounts and what each involve.

13. Name, address, and telephone number of a lawyer and law firm, and a list of the papers in the lawyer's possession.
14. The name and address of the person or bank who has power of attorney.
15. Pension arrangements.
16. Funeral arrangements preferred. In this connection, checked preparations already made.
17. Names and addresses of relatives to be notified at once.
18. Names and addresses of any friends to be notified in case of death.
19. Names of organizations to which belonged. Make a note here about any benefits that may be coming to the family from these organizations.
20. Significant information about children's medical records including data which they might have difficulty collecting if parents are not around.

Important Items to Take Along—You should have easy access to: passport; vaccination records; internationally recognized credit cards; and national and international driver's licenses. In a secure, hand-carried container there should be copies of insurance policies, school records, medical and dental records, power of attorney, wills, inventories of personal luggage, air freight, and household shipments, extra passport photos, and car motor and serial number.

A first aid kit is a good idea. Items to include are a thermometer, tweezers, scissors, a first aid manual such as Red Cross, eye dropper and eye cup, sterile gauze, (squares and roll), adhesive tape/bandages, cotton, sterile cleanser (alcohol or iodine), foot powder, foot fungus ointment, Terramycin ointment for eyes, ointment for burns, cuts, minor abrasions, aspirin, laxative, antacid for stomach such as Kaopectate, dry skin lotion, and dental floss. A physician may recommend antidysentery medication, antifungus ointment, sore throat and cough preparation, ear and nose drops, and Benadryl or antihistamine. For certain climates, insect repellant, sunburn protection, and suntan lotion are appropriate.

Conclusion

The transition is difficult for most persons moving overseas. Adequate preparation and training are required to meet the challenges, not only to survive, but to grow professionally and personally. If the institution or corporation does not have the necessary resources to select and prepare families, they should use external consultants. The attrition rate would thereby be reduced, and personal suffering lessened. Benefits to the corporation, both in money saved and human resources is obvious.

A family must be prepared to be self-reliant and to operate without the support systems to which it is accustomed. On the other hand, if the family abroad lives at a higher socio-economic level than is customary, there is a problem of readjustment to their own culture.

The family can do much to assume responsibility for its own cross-cultural preparation. It begins with reading about the host culture and people. Interviews with persons who have lived in the target country, especially host nationals, can be conducted. Attending family learning groups or similar interpersonal training sessions in one's church or community may help. Certainly, discussions within the family are in order. The subjects might include (a) supplementing children's formal education; (b) recreational substitutes in the absence of familiar facilities and game opportunities; (c) providing mutual support when faced with unusual stress abroad; and (d) making the most of growth opportunities available through travel and learning a new way of life.

References

Alexander, William Jr., "Mobil's Four Hour Environmental Interview," *Worldwide P & I Planning*. January-February, 1970.

"Executive Suicide—Too High Goals," *Harvard Business Review*. July, 1975.

Hays, Richard D., "Expatriate Selection: Insuring Success and Avoiding Failure," *Journal of International Business Studies*. Spring, 1974.

Heenan, David A., "The Corporate Expatriate: Assignment to Ambiguity," Columbia Journal of World Business. May-June, 1970.

Ivanavich, John, "The Study of American On-The-Job Performance Failures," *University of Washington Business Review*. Winter, 1969.

Lanier, Alison R., *Your Manager Abroad: How Welcome? How Prepared?* New York: Amacom, 1975.

Leontiades, James, "The Uprooted European Manager in America," *European Business*. Winter, 1973.

Seidenberg, Robert, *Corporate Wives—Corporate Casualties*. New York: Amacom, 1973.

Shabaz, Wayne O., "Cross-Cultural Orientation for Overseas Employees," *The Personnel Administrator*. May, 1978.

————, "Successful Repatriation Demands Attention, Care and a Dash of Ingenuity," *Business International*. March 3, 1978.

Teague, Burton W., *Selecting and Orienting Staff for Service Overseas*. New York: The Conference Board, Inc., 1976.

Tucker, Michael F., "Who Should Be Assigned Overseas?" *Bridge*. Vol. 3, No. 1. Spring, 1978.

Werkman, Sidney, *Bringing Up Children Overseas*. Basic Books, Inc., 1977.

Wood, Ralph C., " 'Innocents Abroad' No More," *The Christian Century*. July 5-12, 1978.

Children's Intercultural References

Africa Sketches and *Les Guides Aujourdi* (English Series). The Book Store, Bridge, 1800 Pontiac, Denver, Colorado 80220.

Festivals in Asia. New York: Kodansha International, 1975.

Games Children Sing Around the World. World Leisure and Recreational Association, 345 E. 45th Street, New York, New York 10017.

Japan Through Children's Literature: A Critical Bibliography. Center for International Studies, Duke University, Durham, North Carolina.

Nichols, M.S., and P. O'Neill, *Multicultural Resources for Children.* Box 2945 Stanford, California 94305.

Schmidt, N.J., *Children's Books on Africa and their Authors: An Annotated Bibliography.* New York: Africana, 1979.

12
Foreign
Deployment

Human Intercultural Exchange Policy

In today's global village there is a vast migration of people from one nation to another for the purpose of study and work. Some go on temporary or short term assignments, while others remain abroad for long periods. Thus, foreign deployment may be for days, months, or years. Some corporations have a corps of international employees who get transferred from country to country, remaining away from their native land, except for short vacations or business trips, literally for decades. There are many citizens who leave their motherland on their own initiative to seek employment abroad, or as a result of an invitation of a foreign government. Consider this item from a Southern California newspaper in 1978:

> SAUDI CITY LURES SECOND OFFICIAL. Escondido, Ca.—City Utilities Director Larry Michaels announced Tuesday that he would quit his job here to assist with the planning and construction of a city for 150,000 in Saudi Arabia. Michaels, 43, thus becomes the second official from San Diego County in recent weeks to join the Pasadena-based Ralph M. Parsons Company, an international engineering and construction firm under contract to the Saudi Arabian government to build a new community on the shores of the Red Sea. . . .Del Mar City Manager Wayne Dernetz previously announced he will leave his post for the same purpose to participate in the construction of Yanbu, 120 miles north of Jidda, and envisioned as a major industrial and refining complex.

The need for immediate and vast transfers of knowledge and technology from developed to less developed societies is immense. It has been spurred by the discoveries of tremendous natural resources, especially gas and oil, in Third World countries. The superindustrial nations need the natural resources and raw materials of less developed countries to refine and manufacture, as well as to supply energy to their own affluent consumers.

Preindustrial nations usually have human or natural resources, but need the brain power and technology of the advanced countries to capitalize on their own assets. Therefore, human intercultural exchanges and international business will increase as world culture and homogenization progresses.

The issue, then, is can these transcultural interchanges be facilitated for the benefit of both the expatriate and the indigenous population, as well as for the enhancement of both home and host cultures? For this reason, there should be a foreign deployment policy and system.

Any organization—government, corporation, or association—has a responsibility to carefully select and prepare representatives being sent abroad. Obviously, any enterprise which undertakes an international operation would ensure that their employee or member is technically qualified to perform in the new environment. But is the individual psychologically suitable and ready to function normally in the strange culture? Employee effectiveness and productivity can be undermined, in addition to international goodwill and customer relations, if the answer is no. The focus of this chapter is on why organizations should assume responsibility for its overseas representatives, and what activities should be undertaken to provide adequate intercultural preparation and support before, during, and after foreign deployment. The case for such corporate efforts can be justified on financial grounds alone. According to John Habberto, president of the Business Council for International Understanding, in the late 1970's, U.S. firms estimated a $60-75,000 investment to send a middle manager abroad with family on a two-year assignment. If that person is ineffective or aborts the foreign assignment, the losses could total a quarter of a million dollars. (Refer to Chapters 6, 7, 9, 10, and 11.)

Technically, assignments that take an individual from one geographic location and subculture within the individual's own country can be considered foreign. In other words, the observations presented here would be valid for a person being relocated from New England to the rural south of the United States. Cross-cultural preparation and adjustment is necessary even within an individual's homeland. However, most of this chapter is directed toward the employee who is being sent by an organization to a second culture for business purposes.

Deployment in this context refers to the transfer from home to host culture for a long or short time period. The dictionary defines this term as "to arrange, place, or move strategically." An organization should have a system for doing this, especially when many people are involved. To better understand, look at the dictionary definition of *system*, "an ordered, comprehensive assemblage of facts, principles, and practices in a particular field; a coordinated body of methods, plans, and procedures" for accomplishing an objective. Such strategies are vital, profitable, and effective in preference to a haphazard approach to cross-cultural transfers.

Several key questions must be asked to determine if an organization needs a foreign deployment policy and system. Does the company, agency, or association:

1. Experience a costly premature return rate for many employees and their families when assigned outside the country?
2. Experience continuing complaints from its foreign service personnel regarding problems of cross-cultural adjustment, especially in their interactions with host nationals?
3. Experience lowered morale, productivity, and cost effective utilization because of personnel problems of a personal and intercultural nature while abroad?
4. Experience undue concern about employee, customer, public, or government relations at the foreign site operations?
5. Experience readjustment problems when overseas personnel return to the home culture and corporation?

If the answer to any or all of these inquiries is positive, and the organization wants greater capitalization of its human assets involved in international business, then the major issues to be confronted in terms of policies and procedures are:

1. How to choose and train the foreign deployment staff—those individuals responsible for recruiting, training, and processing employees for assignments abroad
2. How to select, develop, and prepare personnel for foreign transfer, or to work domestically in international business activities
3. How to facilitate the acculturation of foreign personnel coming to the parent company culture, such as the United States, for orientation, training, consultation, or temporary duty (This refers especially to overseas representatives of subsidiaries abroad, or licensees who come to corporate headquarters on short-term visits.)
4. How to apply the insights and programs developed for foreign deployment to domestic operations where appropriate (That is, redesign of policies and systems for internal transfer within the parent culture, as well as in the recruitment, selection, development, and supervision of minority employees.)

Figure 12-1 provides an overview of the Foreign Deployment Cycle. There are fifteen steps that an individual might take when going through the major stages of entry to and exit from a second and different culture. The entry process begins with the sponsoring organization making a careful selection and preparation of the foreign deployment staff—recruiters, processers, and trainers. The second step is recruitment of candidates who are suitable for assignment abroad. The third step involves selection of the best personnel for foreign service, which might include assessment, interviews, simulations, and

Host culture integration

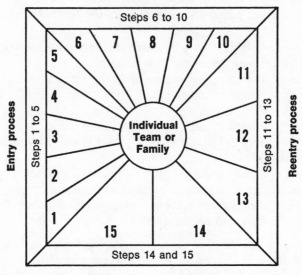

Figure 12-1. This foreign deployment cycle illustrates 15 steps an individual might take when entering and exiting another culture.

1. Selection and preparation of F.D. staff
2. Recruitment of overseas candidates
3. Selection of personnel for foreign service
4. General cultural or area training
5. Specific culture and language training
6. Departure and travel
7. Onsite orientation and briefings
8. Culture shock/adjustment
9. Overseas monitoring and support services
10. Acculturation-making host friends
11. Withdrawal, psychologically anticipating going home
12. Exit-transition, travel home or visit other countries
13. Reentry shock
14. Readjustment
15. Reassignment in parent organization

evaluation of personal data gained from personnel records, tests, and instrumentation.

In preparation of these individuals, and possibly their families, the fourth step is general cultural awareness training or geographic area studies (e.g., Asia, Europe, Africa). The process of host culture integration begins at home with the fifth step of culture specific and language training. It might include contacts with nationals of the second culture.

The sixth step is departure preparations and travel to the new culture. After arrival, the seventh step is orientation and briefings on the indigenous population and society, as well as on the organizational culture to which an individual is assigned.

The eighth step is initial culture shock to a great or lesser degree, and the inevitable adjustments to the differences in the strange culture. The ninth step is acculturation—adapting to the second culture, making progress living there, developing acquaintances and even friends among the locals.

The next stage is the reentry process to the native land. It begins abroad with the eleventh step—psychological withdrawal from the host culture and people. The twelfth step is exiting, including the transition afforded through travel. Hopefully, it permits visiting other countries and cultures for a gradual transfer back to the homeland.

The last stage of home culture reintegration involves three final steps. Thirteen, is reentry shock, most prevalent among managers as they experience the changes in their organization and society since they left. Fourteen, is gradual readjustment to the changed situation. This may take up to six months or a year. Fifteen is reassignment to a post in the parent organization, a looking back with satisfaction at the personal and professional growth which occurred during the overseas assignment, and the impact of that learning on the individual's career development.

All of these steps should be considered by the organization that is responsible for sending people abroad. They should become facets of the system that must be established for the purposes of foreign deployment. It is a continuing cycle for the exchange of people, and for effective intercultural relations.

In Chapters 1 and 11 reference was made to the high cost of premature return of expatriates and their families. Any investment in foreign deployment programs and culture awareness training is miniscule in comparison to the financial, human, and productivity loss resulting when employees fail to adjust on an overseas assignment and must be brought home ahead of schedule.

Gus Lanzo, Director of Career Education and Development for the Grumman Aerospace Corporation, estimates a $100,000 per person loss for premature return of their personnel from Iran. This figure includes travel, housing assistance in home and host culture, training, and replacement expenses.

Bell Helicopter had a 50 percent turnover of workers at one point on an Iranian contract. Profits are very much undercut already, and the price of sending culturally unprepared employees abroad may go even higher in terms of customer and public relations. Writing in the *Washington Post*, Richard T. Sale reported on "The Shah's Americans" from Bell Helicopter who were assigned to Isfahan. The Americans (some 31,000 in 1978 in Iran) complained of a hardship post, housing and food inconveniences, excessive security, and tax disadvantages under the new U.S. rules (January 1, 1976). The Iranians criticized the American expatriates for not having the courtesy to learn their language, eat their food, travel in their country, or attempt to understand their religion, Islam. A Bell personnel official admitted that most technical employees were "ex-military professionals, the mid-level fellows who don't

know any other way of making a living. The money's good, so they came."
His friend observed:

> I don't know why we seem to have chosen to recruit so many of our peo-
> ple from the jails of Texas and Tennessee. It's a rough, knock-'em-back,
> country-music, Coors beer-drinking crowd. They are arrested frequently
> for starting fights, for public drunkenness. They have ridden their motor-
> cycles through the great Shah Mosque, one of the most sacred Moslem
> shrines.

A language instructor on the scene summed it up this way: "Most Bell
employees are out of their depth. They're poor white trash here only for one
reason: to make beaucoup bucks." The lack of an intelligent foreign deployment policy and system cost Bell money, as well as future sales and good will.
Sadly, it is a classic example of the "Ugly American" syndrome which is now
being replicated by Japanese, Germans, and other nationalities.

Lanzo maintains that the influx of foreign workers into Iran overpowers
the local population, and causes the native systems to breakdown.
Meanwhile, Iran's industrialization is so drastic and sudden that it has contributed to the recent social and political unrest. Lanzo cites planning as an
example of cultural differences that can cause serious problems. When the
Iranians state that the housing for overseas' workers is ready, they mean "in
a year and a half, God willing." Rather than lose face and reveal that the
locals are behind the schedule established by Grumman Aerospace, the Iranians reply, "We will be ready." Thus, those engaged in foreign deployment
must anticipate delays and build it into their planning; the planners must anticipate culture problems and prepare for them in advance.

Organizations can undertake certain policies and actions to facilitate the
adjustment and performance of employees abroad. Policies may state that no
pets may be taken overseas, or a bonus may be given for staying an extra
year. Actions that a corporation or agency can take to improve foreign adjustment are:

1. Form an information network on the local culture/situation among
   multinational representatives who have served or are in the host area.
2. Rotational assignments by employees without families to permit them
   more home visits.
3. Job sharing of overseas tasks by two workers, so that one can be rotated
   home regularly.
4. Develop country or area manuals for employees to supplement the standard commercial publications.
5. Screen out early in recruitment, selection, and training, the nonad-
   justers (those with allergy, drinking, marital problems, etc.).
6. Use media reports of the overseas work scene in training to encourage
   or discourage personnel preparing for deployment.

7. Avoid making statements in training that are contrary to onsite experience.
8. Counterbalance the stress and strain of cultural adjustment with the opportunity for an enriching personal and professional experience.
9. Allocate housing abroad on a numbered, first-come, first served basis.

Such pragmatic deployment strategies can do much to foster employee integration into the strange culture, as well as to help them get control of their new job situation.

Jerry Hooper, President of Organization Development Resources, Ltd., reports that one client, Morrison-Knudsen Company (MKI), asked for an onsite interview study of overseas employees. The purpose was to develop a new foreign deployment policy and system. Prompting the investigation was a 37 percent turnover worldwide of their international personnel with an average replacement cost directly of $45,000, and indirect costs estimated as high as a half million dollars for key overseas employees. The findings caused a reorganization of policies and programs for foreign operations. Their principal conclusions were: recruitment, selection, and training of international personnel were antiquated and inconsistent, as well as informal; and, international operations lacked systematic international personnel programs and procedures. Investment in correcting these deficiencies proved more cost effective than wasting human and financial resources on high turnovers.

The reforms ranged from increasing base pay and overseas living allowances to improved information on the foreign living environment and choice of two-to five-year assignments. Many engineering and technical tasks are done at remote locations throughout the world. Thus, preventative programs were instituted to counteract the problems of extreme isolation, such as depression, abuse of alcohol or drugs, and loneliness.

In the article "American Expatriates Abroad," *The Bridge*, Winter 1977/78, Dr. Lenny Snodgrass and Graig Zachlod observed that more than a quarter million Americans are living outside the United States, and others think the figure may be greater and will certainly rise. Snodgrass and Zachlod observe:

> The complexity of difficulty to adjust to an alien culture bears heavily upon the responsibility of organizations which select personnel. The assessment of a person's technical competence may prove far easier than measuring those characteristics which may or may not make him and his family adaptable to an overseas assignment. . . .Family assistance and training are thus essential.

In another article, "Preparing Managers for Work in Other Countries," *Journal of European Training*, Summer, 1972 by Dr. Bernard Bass and K.M. Thiagarajan, states:

> Although the basic function of management is the same the world over, the management practices and social norms, as well as cultural values, in-

evitably affect the behavior of managers both on and off the jobs because they differ vastly between countries. Thus, a manager who is well qualified and has proven competence in one functional area of business cannot be automatically assumed to be effective while working in a different country. The manager who is assigned outside his native land, needs to increase awareness and understanding of differences in managerial beliefs, values, and practices in the host culture, and develop some degree of ability to adjust to them.

Dr. Melvin Schnapper, Director of Training and Development for G.D. Searle & Company, maintains that the world of the multinational corporation is too vast, complex, and changeable for one training model to have universal application. He believes that multinational management development should focus on four major areas: managerial; intercultural; local business issues and practices; and language. Not knowing of cultural and business differences in the host country can lead to unnecessary waste, costly mistakes, and career failures. Schnapper finds that "experiential" training prior to departure is the best way to confront managers with the requirements of intercultural coping and personal change process.

Deployment Plans and Procedures

General and specific culture orientation for foreign deployment are described throughout Chapters 13-21. Perhaps, a brief insight to the policies and practices of three major multinational corporations on foreign deployment will summarize this section most appropriately. The Grumman Aerospace Corporation has established policies for international assignment covering certain personnel needs, not unlike those proposed in Chapter 11: recruiting; selection procedures; training; housing allowances; medical services; educational facilities and allowances; tax allowances; transportation allowances; travel arrangements; overseas salary compensation; and pets. Their planning for employee deployment abroad includes: (a) defining scope of tasks overseas; (b) personnel planning and scheduling; (c) site preparation; (d) recruiting and selection; (e) personnel preparation; (f) administration of physical moves.

The cultural orientation includes the employee family and takes from three to six months on the average. In addition, simultaneous planning, training, and scheduling onsite is offered to local nationals who will be working with the Americans.

Frank Lee, a consultant on the Fairchild Overseas Orientation Program, reports that aircraft manufacturers seek personnel with appropriate skills to accomplish the task and meet the social requirements of the job. Fairchild's experience is typically three to four months from the time a position opens to the point of getting the proper individual onsite. For example, in the case of an employee and his family selected for assignment in Brazil, the program design features:

1. Conference between family and trainer/consultant for information purposes (the book, *Living Overseas,* a Brazil area handbook and country specific kit, and a Sao Paulo city kit); the session also identifies the family's specific training/orientation needs, U.S. resources relative to the company and government (employees who have lived in Brazil, Brazilian students, libraries, university aids), and problems to anticipate with reference to intercultural communication and cultural transition
2. Implementation of family orientation plan (e.g., visit Brazil's consulate; go to dinner with a Brazilian student; collect information about the country and its people; meet with the trainer to consider cultural differences relative to values, beliefs, and customs; meet with international personnel specialist of the corporation relative to company policies, benefits, and resources in-country
3. Integration meeting with trainer and family to synthesize and summarize data acquired about Brazil, review expectations, and develop an in-country follow-up plan for personal growth in intercultural relations

This approach is highly cognitive and lacks experiential opportunities. Yet it is individualized to the employee and family, and is suitable for deployment of small groups. It does not seem to utilize much media, and depends heavily on directed self-study with emphasis on reading. But it does put the responsibility for facilitating adjustment on the family, and involves each member in the process.

The third model is more comprehensive and is from Bechtel Corporation. The policy manual, *Corporate Orientation for International Assignments,* considers all facets of selection, training, and orientation of employees for service abroad. Nessa Loewenthal from the Office of International Personnel reports that Bechtel's orientation program utilizes multimedia, guest specialists, group participation, and resource materials that are accurate and current. (Bechtel produces a series of booklets on specific countries and cultures for employees.) The goal is to standardize the plan so that any corporate office may utilize the training aids. The orientation policy is quite explicit. Four major areas covered by corporate trainers and processors are:

1. Cross-cultural (culture, customs, and people of the area to which assigned)
2. Job orientation (specifics of project scope and organization, employee position and responsibilities, company formalities and procedures, supervisory responsibilities, review of the local work situation relative to manpower training needs, safety, labor relations, and local employees onsite)
3. Area specific (employee/family concerns, medical care, insurance and benefits, compensation and employment conditions, taxes and housing, transfer of household and personal effects, local schools and education allowances, local facilities for transportation, rest/recreation/vacation opportunities)

4. Human relations (especially for management level, this deals with local government, U.S. representatives abroad, clients and their needs, roles with Bechtel employees and dependents onsite)

As noted in Chapter 10, the Peace Corps has one of the most sophisticated training programs for representatives going on overseas assignments. One-third of its annual budget is devoted to such preparation. Because it involves volunteers, the Corps experiences a 22 percent attrition rate in training, and a 35 percent rate overall.

Strategies of foreign deployment should encompass: the staff engaged in recruiting, selection, and training; the employee and dependents assigned abroad; and the host culture managers who are responsible for organizational personnel in the strange environment. The focus should be on the opportunities afforded by the international assignment for personal growth, professional exchange and development, and effective representation of country and corporation. In summary, the orientation stage for foreign deployment might be divided into five phases as described in the following plan. It outlines what the employee's responsibilities are for his or her own preparation for service abroad.

Personal Plan for Foreign Deployment Orientation

Phase One—Organizational Resources: Data Gathering

(It is assumed that large multinational organizations will acquire informational resources that employees may utilize when they have been selected for a specific foreign assignment. With the assistance of the office of international personnel, the data are made available on a "need-to-know" basis.)

- Consult the organizational data bank for relevant cross-cultural information about the country and culture to be entered (e.g., input on housing, education, customs, food, etc.). Be prepared while on foreign deployment to make personal notes for additional contributions to this computer bank upon return from abroad.
- Consult the organizational directory of returned employees from the country to which assigned. Prepare to contact and interview some of these fellow workers for personal insights on their experiences in the host culture.
- Consult the organizational data bank on resources to be contacted at home and onsite that would enable employees and dependents to become more effective in the new cross-cultural opportunity (e.g., language training possibilities, geographic area studies and economic information, universities and research centers with required specialists and information).

- Consult the organizational library for international personnel to review pertinent books, periodicals, and brochures, as well as any self-instructional media programs.
- Keep a personal reference notebook for significant data gathered relative to the search undertaken in this phase.
- Check the organizational data bank, manuals, or files on company policies for overseas employees (e.g., conditions of employment, compensation, termination, grievances and discipline, paid sick leaves, vacation, leaves of absence, insurance and disability, relocation allowances to and from site, travel time, legal liabilities, educational and local travel opportunities, continuation of employee benefits abroad—credit unions, employee assistance, company publications on-site).
- Seek necessary immunizations and medical aid from organizational health services.

Phase Two—General Culture/Area Orientation

- Become culturally aware of the factors that make a culture unique, and the characteristics of the home culture that influence employee behavior abroad.
- Seek local cross-cultural experience and engage in intercultural communication with microcultures within the homeland, so as to sensitize self to cultural differences and how to cope with them.
- Encourage spouses to develop programs and experiments that foster more cosmopolitan attitudes in the family, and counteract ethnocentrism—cook national dishes of other countries, attend cultural weeks or exhibits of foreign or ethnic groups, socialize with people from a different cultural or racial background, try folk dress or dances of other people.
- Read, understand, and practice, the corporate policies on equal employment opportunity and affirmative action.

Phase Three—Language Orientation

- Undertake 60 to 80 hours of formal training in the language of the host country to which assigned.
- Supplement classroom experience with 132 to 180 hours of self-instruction in the language—listen to audio cassettes or records in the foreign tongue, read newspapers, magazines, or books in the new language, speak to others who have this language skill, listen to music in the language.
- Build a 500 word survival vocabulary.
- Develop specialized vocabularies—on the job, with the maid, in the

marketplace, etc.

- Seek further education in the language before departure, but most certainly, upon arrival in the country of assignment.
- Practice the language at every opportunity, especially with family members.

Phase Four—Culture Specific Orientation: Training and Learning

- Learn about the specific culture of the country to which assigned, preferably during the six months prior to departure. Gather data about the size of the country and its population (demographic facts), the customs, mores, values, taboos, history, social systems, and communication patterns. Learn what is necessary regarding the host culture's family, educational, political, and social system; history and laws; regulations and taxes; food and housing; recreational and travel prospects. Understand and prepare for "culture shock."
- Check out specific company policies for the assigned country, relative to allowances for transportation, housing, education, expense accounts, and provisions for salaries, taxes, and other fringe benefits including medical service and emergency leave.
- Find out and obtain necessary transfer documents (passports, visas, et al), and learn customs policies and regulations, as well as currency restrictions, for entry and exit of both the assigned country and the nativeland.
- Interview fellow employees who have returned from the host country. Get practical information about banking, shopping, currency, climate, mail, and law enforcement.
- Read travel books and other information about the country and culture, especially that provided by the sponsoring organization.

Phase Five—Job Orientation: Information Gathering

- Obtain information about: the overseas job environment and organization; the clients and contractors: key personnel; the work schedule and hours; hiring status and contract monitoring; job drawings, specifics, or other papers; purchasing and field procurement; project procedures and progress reports; quality control and job-site security; and labor relations, especially with third country nationals (TCNs) and host country nationals (HCNs).
- Learn of the local population's attitude toward the project to which assigned, especially the government officials. Know what customs and restrictions to observe relative to the job.
- Arrange for necessary technical training to assure high performance abroad.

Components of Deployment System

Stage One—Employee Assessment

The first major component in the foreign deployment system is concerned with evaluation of individuals who are sent abroad, as well as evaluation of the organizational program responsible for the transfer and reentry process. From the perspective of the organization's responsibilities, a complete foreign deployment system should:

1. Ascertain the adaptability of key personnel for foreign service, including their ability to deal with the host nationals effectively.
2. Summarize a psychological evaluation of the candidate's skills in human relations within an intercultural context, as well as the candidate's ability for coping with changes and differences; the candidate's proneness to severe culture shock.
3. Identify specific physical and intellectual barriers to successful adjustment in the foreign environment, if possible, to correct any deficiencies.
4. Highlight any specific technical or management factors which need strengthening before the cross-cultural assignment.
5. Find out any family problems or situations with dependents that would undermine employee effectiveness abroad.
6. Provide this assessment for top and middle management personnel on a priority basis, then supervisors and foreman, and finally technical and hourly employees.
7. Offer portions of the evaluation for any employee on a temporary assignment out of country, such as short business trips or project assignment abroad.
8. Provide special review of individual suitability for foreign deployment in remote sites with limited input and support services.
9. Adapt the process to meet the needs of foreign nationals brought on assignment to domestic operations, or for Third World nationals (TCN) brought to the foreign work site.
10. Interview candidates for foreign deployment with questions by psychologists and international personnel specialists.
11. Provide group meetings for candidates, possibly including employees who have returned from the foreign site, or host country nationals, to study interactions and determine suitability of the prospects.
12. Use instrumentation for data gathering about the candidates' attitudes and competencies regarding change, intercultural knowledge and relations, and communication skills—may involve commercial or homemade questionnaires, inventories, check-lists, e.g., culture shock tests.

13. Use one-way mirrors, video or audio tape, closed circuit television, simulation games and other educational or personnel technology as a basis for observation.

The overseas assessment process might investigate:

1. The tasks or activities the candidate might engage in, and the candidates' ability to accomplish them.
2. The people with whom the individual will interact and the individual's ability to deal with representatives of the indigenous population.
3. The extent to which the official position requires social interactions with host and third country nationals, as well as expatriates, and the capacity of the candidate to deal with such variety of human relationships.
4. Whether the work can be handled by an individual or requires team collaboration, especially with persons outside the company, if the work is to be done in a remote location, and how the candidate is likely to cope with the situation.
5. The language skills required (English or a foreign language) and the capacity of the candidate to meet them (how skillful must the candidate be in speaking the foreign language).
6. The situational environment of the foreign assignment, and the likelihood of this particular candidate to cope effectively under these circumstances. For example, is the culture like or very unlike the home culture, does it require the individual to operate in a manner quite different from a similar position in the home environment?
7. Whether the individual is provincial in outlook, or has that person demonstrated prior interests in things foreign—how cosmopolitan in attitude is the candidate, and what is the individual's experience outside the home culture?
8. If the candidate possesses a realistic concept of life overseas—job requirements, incongruities, opportunities, and frustrations—and if the candidate has previously visited the job site, what reactions did the candidate have?
9. The candidate's ability to operate autonomously, to deal with differences, and to cope with discontinuity
10. Hypothetical situations, critical incidents, or case studies that approximate the new assignment and how the candidate responded, especially when there was job or social friction.
11. How the person envisions the absence of several years from the homeland while on foreign assignment. (Is the individual realistic on how it will affect and change his or her personal life and that of dependents, as well as impact on career development and life plans?)
12. How the candidate would be rated on overall assignment suitability relative to knowledge of the demands to be made upon him or her by the foreign job and society.

The assessment process should provide the candidate with factual information about the host country and assignment. Having seen films, slides, or videotapes of the onsite situation, and having discussed the salary adjustment, housing provisions, tax problems, and other such realities, the candidate should be given the opportunity to choose. This may result in the candidate refusing the foreign assignment.

The Assessment Center, popular in current personnel practice, may adapt their program and practices to assist with recruitment and selection of overseas personnel. Or, if an Office of International Personnel does not exist, the organization may have to utilize an external resource, such as an international executive/management/technical search firm, or hire "job shoppers." Some organizations use a selection review board made up of their own employees or members, qualified volunteers, and people who have served in the target culture. Existing specialists in corporate health and personnel services can provide valuable data if the candidate is already an employee, or they may assist with the testing of those who come from outside.

Dr. Michael Tucker, in his article, "Who Should be Assigned Overseas?" *The Bridge* (Spring 1978), maintains that the organizations responsible for foreign deployment have not invested enough time and effort to develop valid indicators of overseas success, nor have they created the screening methods needed to identify such indicators in candidates. The overseas selection process, he notes, is further hampered by a lack of observable and measurable factors that define adjustment or maladjustment. Dr. Tucker has considerable experience with the program that the Center for Research and Education developed for the United States Navy. It reduces overseas failures by using a personal selection system based on proven success criteria.

The qualities described as the outcome of cross-cultural training in Chapter 9 could also be the criteria for selecting candidates for overseas service—empathy, openness, persistence, sensitivity to intercultural factors, respect for others, role flexibility, tolerance for ambiguity, and two-way communication skill. Research indicates that possession of these characteristics is correlated to adaptation and effectiveness outside an individual's home culture.

Paul W. Russell, Jr. of Colorado State University did a doctoral study on "Dimensions of Overseas Success in Industry" (1978). He reviewed the literature for the last two decades on what factors are associated with successful international corporate assignments. The following section indicates 80 traits cited in 10 categories. Those with an asterisk are the characteristics sought more often in candidates foreign deployment.

Dimensions of Overseas Success in Industry

1. Technical Competence/Resourcefulness
   *Technical skill/competence
   Resourcefulness

Imagination/creativity
Demonstrated ability to produce
  results with limited resources
Comprehension of complex relationships

2. Adaptability/Emotional Stability
  *Adaptability/Flexibility
  Youthfulness
  Maturity
  Patience
  Perseverance
    *Emotional stability
    Variety of outside interests
    Ability to handle responsibility
    Feeling of self-worth/dignity
    Capacity for growth

3. Acceptability of Assignment to Candidate and Family
  *Desire to serve overseas
  Willingness of wife to
    live abroad/family status
  Belief in mission/job
  Stable marriage/family life
  *Adaptability of spouse/family
  *Previous experience abroad
  *Motivation
  Willingness to take chances
  Willingness to travel
  (Negative trait: overly strong ties with family in home country)

4. Planning, Organization, and Utilizing Resources
  *Organization ability
  Self-sufficient as manager
  Ability to build social institutions
  Management skills
  Administrative skills

5. Interpersonal Relationships/Getting Along with Others
  *Diplomacy and tact
  Consideration for others
  Human Relations skills
  Commands respect
  *Ability to train others
  Desire to help others
  Ability to get things done through others
  Sense for politics of situations

6. Potential for Growth in the Company
  *Successful domestic record
  *Promotability
  Company Experience
  Industriousness

*Educational qualifications
*Mental alertness
Intellectual
Dependability

7. Host Language Ability
   *Language ability in native tongue

8. Cultural Empathy
   *Cultural empathy/sensitivity
   *Interest in host culture
   Respects host nationals
   Understands own culture
   Open-minded
   Area expertise
   *Ability to get along with hosts
   *Tolerant of others' views
   Sensitive to others' attitudes
   Understands host culture
   Not enthnocentric/prejudiced
   Objective

9. Physical Attributes
   *Good health
   Sex gender acceptability
   Physical appearance

10. Miscellaneous
    *Character
    Generalist skills
    Independence on job
    Social acceptability
    *Leadership
    Friendliness
    Initiative/energy

Some organizations try to circumvent the selection problem by hiring for overseas assignment personnel with successful international experience and language skills, or host and third country nationals. Obviously, to assure effectiveness, some type of evaluation process should be utilized even in choosing such persons.

Writing in *Omega*, an international journal of management science (Vol. 5, No. 2, 1977), two Isreali scholars, Yoram Zeira and Ehud Harari examined "Structural Sources of Personnel Problems in Multinational Corporations: Third Country Nationals." They found that these people had morale problems centering around blocked promotions, transfer anxieties, income gaps, unfamiliarity with host culture, adaptability difficulties, avoidance of long-range projects abroad, innappropriate leadership styles, and inability to participate in decision-making and screening management information. Furthermore, investigations indicated that third country nationals (TCNs) with high potential and a desire for promotion are not always anxious to serve abroad, especially after one or two international transfers. Zeira and Harari discovered that variegated international experience is not necessarily translated into managerial behavior compatible with local environmental needs and headquarter expectations. They believe that no multinational staffing policy is free of serious dysfuntional aspects, but means must be sought to diminish such effects.

The final aspect of the assessment cycle after the individual evaluation is corporate. That is, periodic objective assessment of the current status and practice in selection, orientation, training, and onsite assistance provided to employees who are transferred outside the home country of the organization. There might be an advantage in having external consultants study how effectively the program/system prepares personnel to deal with intercultural differences related to both management and life styles. For example, a large international construction firm had an elaborate department and plan for human resource development of employees sent abroad. When the corporation president arrived onsite in Saudi Arabia, he was besieged by workers and their families with personal and personnel problems. Obviously, the deployment program was not working. He fired the Vice President of Human Resource Development on his return to the United States.

The corporate assessment process might include a survey of employees overseas regarding their special needs and problems related to foreign assignment, and how well their orientation program helped them to cope with the onsite reality; or the investigation might be limited to expatriates who have returned home.

As previously indicated, some evaluation would be in order for the staff involved in recruitment, selection, and training of overseas personnel as to their appropriateness for these tasks, and the validity of their assumptions and practices.

Stage Two—Employee Orientation

The second component in a foreign deployment system is some type of self-learning/training in culture general and specifics. In the general program for increasing cultural awareness, several alternatives are possible. The first, group training, in the general factors of culture is described earlier in this chapter, as well as throughout Chapters 9, 10, and 11. Group training is intended for an organization's managers, technicians, and sales and marketing personnel engaged in international business, as well as their families when they are assigned abroad.

Another alternative is a longer program called an Intercultural Management Seminar. This might be six consecutive days, or one day a month for six months. It is intended for executives, management, or supervisors with responsibility abroad, or for foreign nationals. It includes learning modules on cross-cultural communications and change, understanding culture and its influence on behavior, culture shock and cross-cultural relations, improving organizational relations and intercultural effectiveness. Additional topics to be covered are: transnational management of responsibility; intercultural performance appraisal; intercultural concepts of productivity, leadership, conflict management; and the changing role of multinational managers. Essentially, it is in-service training in comparative management.

Still another approach to replace or supplement formal group instruction, is individualized learning packages for the employee and the employee's family. This is a programmed learning and media instructional system on cultural differences in general, and for the specific country to be visited. For example, simulations, slide/cassette, and videotaped presentations on cultural awareness are combined into a standarized presentation that serves those assigned abroad singly or in small groups where group training is not feasible. Such a self-instructional program could be utilized at home with one's family. It might also serve as a preparation for classroom instruction.

Specific area programs can be developed for orientation purposes. That is, a cultural briefing program for personnel assigned to a particular geographical area or country that is foreign to them. Thus, the Middle East could be a subject of area study with particular emphasis on Saudi Arabia and Iran. A learning program of twelve or more hours can be designed that consists of videotape or film cassettes inserted into a teaching machine, and a discussion guide or self-instructional manual for individual study. The same material could be projected on a large screen for use in a group training situation. Chapter 10 reviewed a number of methods that organizational trainers can utilize in this orientation.

When presenting the culture specifics of a particular country, a number of fine publications are available to assist employees going abroad. Appendix D provides a list of such resources.

Obviously, no foreign deployment orientation is complete without adequate language and technical training to fit the employee properly for an overseas assignment. However, the focus here is on cultural training and preparation. Foreign student advisors in various American universities can be a helpful resource to those planning orientation programs for employees abroad. They may not only assist with student speakers for country specific information, but they design orientation programs for foreign students coming into the United States. Many of their techniques and approaches can be adapted to corporate cross-cultural programs, and the National Association of Foreign Student Advisors can be a helpful resource in this regard.*

*Read Robert T. Moran's "Dress Rehearsal for a Cross-Cultural Experience," *International Educational and Cultural Exchange*, Vol. 10, No. 1, 1974, a publication of the U.S. Advisory Commission on International Educational and Cultural Exchange, Department of State, Washington, D.C. 20520.

Margaret Anne Horan has been involved in extensive orientation of Americans going abroad and of foreigners coming to the U.S. In the article, "Cross/Trans/Intercultural Communication Training," *Training and Development Journal,* (November 1976), she observes:

> Intercultural training programs should meet the expressed needs of participants through research prior to and immediately after the sessions. Data gathered in such needs/attitudes surveys indicated the need for input on difficulties experienced abroad—such as, homesickness, confusion, anxiety, difficulty sleeping, knowing expectations of host nationals, intriguing/irritating aspects of life in the foreign culture, expression of emotions.

Bernard Bass and K.M. Thigarajan in "Preparing Managers for Work in Other Countries" maintain that the orientation should focus on sensitivity to people in general, the recognition of cultural differences, and the issue of stereotyping:

> At the first level, people assume the host culture is similar to their own and relate to the host nationals as if they were no different from their associates at home. At the next level, the individual recognizes the cultural differences and forms stereotypes of other culture groups. . . .The third and highest level of interpersonal understanding occurs when an individual recognizes cultural differences and proceeds further to *differentiate* between subcultures and specific individuals within the context of the other cultural system.

Both professors also believe that most multinational organizations are now including the spouse, at least, in the cross-cultural training. Because wives, in particular, seem most affected and challenged by culture shock, it not only helps their adjustment abroad to include them in the training, but provides them with insights to share with dependents. It also helps them understand their husband's problems in the foreign work situation.

Perhaps a few specific corporate practice in overseas orientation may best make the point. In the Fairchild company approach the training of employees is considered:

1. A start in the learning process about the other culture/country with emphasis on proper attitudes, tools, and skills to be effective in the other culture.
2. A means for developing realistic expectations about the assignment and the foreign country.
3. An opportunity to experience and test the mindset and coping skills necessary for effectiveness abroad.
4. An intensive learning period to acquire information about intercultural communications, cultural adaptation, area studies, and specifics of processing, moving, and transporting personal effects.

Consensus of experienced trainers is that cross-cultural orientation should be flexible, experiential, individualized, participative, and integrated with home and onsite situations. The Grumman Aerospace Corporation believes the essential elements of indoctrination to prevent culture shock encompass these aspects of a target country: geography; climate; history; religion; social customs; schools; politics; law; language; working conditions; and the standard of living. Morrison Knudsen International has ascertained that the ten most important concerns of expatriate employees are: base pay; overseas salary living allowances; information on housing/food/medical care abroad; married versus single status overseas; foreign premium/differential; work conditions onsite; and skill and leadership ability of project supervisors.

Working as a training consultant for an Indonesian government owned fertilizer manufacturer, Walt Tait points out some of the realities that should be included in culture specifics preparation:

> To feel like an albino among all the host nationals of brown skin and dark hair, so that some natives see you as "sick"....To raise one's thumb and indicate o.k., whereas the extended little finger means "bad"....To learn never to touch or pat an Indonesian on the head because it is the resting place of the soul and therefore inviolable. . . .Always to give and receive with the right hand, never the left unless one apologizes with "Ma' af". . . .Since they are a gentle people, one never raises the voice; to become angry or to lose your temper is considered improper and rude. . . .Although it is proper to shake hands on meeting Indonesian males, it is impolite to do the same with females. . . .Be prepared for individuals who must report on the job to multiple managers at different levels.

As a result of his Peace Corps training endeavors on behalf of Denver's Center for Research and Education, Dr. Albert R. Wight suggested the Experiental Learning Model for cross-cultural orientation (see Figure 12-2). In reviewing the research literature, Dr. Wight confirms that innovative, experienced-based training models are needed to provide adequate preparation for trainees to live and work effectively in another culture. The design of such programs must be structured to achieve increased participant involvement in and responsibility for the learning process. The orientation should be trainee-centered, especially on problem solving, in contrast to the memorization of facts. Appendix D contains a partial listing of widely-used organizations of external consultants that assist corporation, associations, and government agencies in preparing personnel for foreign deployment. Included is a directory of foreign language schools.

Stage Three—Onsite Support and Monitoring

An effective foreign deployment system should include a component with various human resource support services, as well as a method for continuous

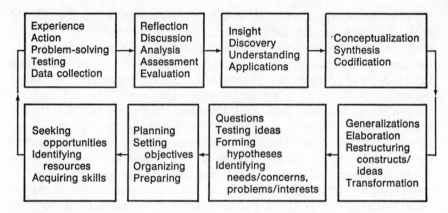

Figure 12-2. Cross-cultural orientation can be achieved by means of an experiential learning module, such as this one developed by Dr. Albert Wight.

monitoring of the worker's performance. Now that employees have been recruited, selected, trained, and transported abroad, the personnel responsibility should be to: (a) facilitate their integration into the strange work environment and host culture, (b) evaluate their needs and performance, and (c) encourage morale and career development. Toward the end of the person's tour of duty, the office of international personnel should assist in an orderly transition to the home culture and the domestic organization.

As a follow-up to the predeparture training, some type of orientation and briefing should take place regarding the local situation soon after the family arrives in the foreign country. Back home there might have been a lack of readiness to listen to details about the job and new community. Now that the expatriates are faced with the daily realities of coping in a strange country, there may be a greater willingness to utilize helpful hints. Also, the family may have many questions that they wish to ask of those with experience on the scene.

Within a week to three months after arrival, this onsite accultural program should get underway. Volunteers are likely to come from workers' families, as well as the foreign community to assist in this "indoctrination." The consulate staff may provide resource professionals for this purpose. In any event, the onsite orientation should be pragmatic, and meet the needs of the expatriate family. It should demonstrate that the company cares about its people. It should aid the new worker or family to (a) resolve immediate living problems; (b) meet the challenge of the host culture and the opportunities it offers for travel, personal growth, and intercultural exchange; (c) attempt to reduce the culture shock, and to grow from that experience; (d) provide communication links to the local community and the home organization. Much of this can be accomplished in a systematic, informal, friendly, group setting.

Three formal steps that the organization's human resource development staff should take abroad are:

1. *An adjustment survey*—Using a paper/pen instrument (questionnaire, check-list, inventory) approximately three to six months after arrival, request that the employee supply feedback on the foreign deployment situation. That person, possibly with the aid of other family members, should carefully fill out the form so as to identify their special needs, problems, and advantages found in the alien culture. An envelope may be provided to return the information directly to an external consulting firm or to corporate personnel officials in the home culture. Greater cooperation and authenticity might be forthcoming if onsite management does not have access to the individual responses. If third-party anonymity is desirable, then the external resource might be utilized to collect and analyze the data gathered. A second administration of the inquiry form might be considered twelve or eighteen months after arrival, or just prior to completing the assignment.

2. *Data analysis and reporting*—The information is analyzed from two viewpoints: individual need, and foreign deployment policies and practices. The material would be "massaged" for the identification of problems and the recommendation of solutions. Reporting enables back-home management to monitor its foreign deployment system, while onsite management can improve the quality of working life for the expatriated employees. As group data is compiled and stored in a computer, a profile is drawn on overseas employee needs and concerns relative to foreign deployment at a particular location. This collection of significant information is then used in future orientation and training programs for planning. Data stored from deployment groups over a period of years provides insight into the requirements of overseas personnel in a geographic area, such as the Middle East. The results from such inquiry studies, whether used on a short- or long-term basis, have preventative value relative to problems of cultural adjustment, and lead to considerable savings in financial and human terms.

3. *Organizational communications*—To counteract alienation, loneliness, and feelings of being "cut off," a corporation, association, or agency needs to establish vital communication links with its representatives abroad. Newsletters, and other company publications are only a first step in this regard. The corporate office of international personnel could regularly send audio cassettes to expatriates and their families. In addition to internal news and communication items that keep overseas' employees up-to-date, morale-booster messages from key officials could be incorporated into this informational system. More importantly the cassette media could be used to continue the cross-cultural training undertaken in the predeparture and onsite briefing sessions. It can also

be used for professional development of employees in technical matters. The taped lessons would be for re-inforcement of previous learning, and ego building at the foreign location. The program aims to "plug in" the worker to domestic company operations, and build confidence in the employee relative to the importance of the overseas assignment. The cassettes can be played in the home for family discussion, or with small groups of employees in a training session with the onsite supervisor.

The cassette player can also be used for a series of structured questions presented by the office of international personnel. Such interview tapes can ascertain the status of the foreign deployment experience. The employee is given an opportunity between questions to respond and record answers on the issues raised. An alternative in this feedback process is to supply a list of printed questions and a blank cassette or tape for the worker to use. If employee anonymity is a factor, an envelope could be provided for direct return of the cassette to the corporate personnel office. The same approach can be used for supervisors to report on the adjustment of new employees abroad, thereby providing some evaluation on the foreign deployment preparation.

Any material gathered from the feedback instruments or cassettes is analyzed by corporate personnel or external consultants to improve the cross-cultural training program, and gather data that can eventually be used in case studies, critical incidents, and other training aids.

Part of the onsite support service should include language training, whether in formal or informal group learning situations. Tutors, or home study cassettes, tapes, or records and closed circuit television can be valuable media for this purpose. Local nationals might be employed for this language and cultural instruction.

Gus Lanzo of Grumman Aerospace Corporation believes that the success of overseas sales efforts is very dependent on the calibre of predeparture and in-country training of personnel. His company's follow-on efforts range from meeting the family at the overseas destination to providing temporary and permanent accomodations, and information on available schooling, transportation, and communication. In remote areas, the corporation takes on the responsibility of providing such things as a bus service, a motor pool, telex, news bulletins, and even school and shopping systems.

Ideally, at least six months before completion of the foreign assignment, the employee should be getting assistance relative to departure, transition, and re-integration into the nativeland and domestic work environment. Grumman's program takes into consideration these practical needs of the returning family: (a) transportation to the airport; (b) stopover vacation enroute based on length of overseas duty; (c) interim housing, if necessary, while the family is "settling in" to the United States; (d) financial adjustments to reward successful foreign performance; and (e) guidance on new job assignments within or without the company. The whole Grumman foreign deployment policy is to give recognition, stature, and status to the program and the personnel involved.

Snodgrass and Zachlod in the article, "American Expatriates Abroad," (*The Bridge*, Winter 1977/78) point out some special problems that those assigned outside the United States experience:

> ....Termination of participations by American in any bi-national situation is more related to unsatisfactory family adjustments than unsatisfactory work relationships. There may be a single pivotal factor which accounts for an unsuccessful adjustment, e.g., the wife's inability to adapt to a role other than a domestic housewife, or women who have previously enjoyed a career and suddenly find themselves without meaningful identity. Other studies have found that the problem of American identity becomes quite serious after the third or fourth year for the children and parents. This problem is compounded when they are forced to return to the States, or when teenagers go home to college and university work. ....Families trained to interact in mutually supportive ways can provide themselves with resources for adjustment in the alien environment.

Onsite support services cannot be just for the first year abroad, or take for granted that the adjustment is satisfactory if the family manifests no overt problems in the first two years of a five-year tour of duty overseas. There needs to be a continuing follow-up and undergirding of the foreign deployment program with reinforcement inputs, "hotline" alerts and counseling, and other innovative means to reduce family stress and strain. A positive, preventative program can be launched to reduce dependents' anxiety when one parent's assignments require extensive travel. The same approach is required when a parent is like an itinerant because of frequent absence such as occurs in offshore drilling jobs.

Corporate leadership is required to help the overseas employees and their families develop a sense of community, organizing to supply necessary services to their offspring. For instance, it is obvious that many American teenagers need help finding outlets for their energies when overseas, especially when the social supports (e.g., drive-in theaters and restaurants), rapports, fashion, and dating opportunities are severely restricted or nonexistent in a remote location. Creative parents and corporate personnel can join with local resources to provide American adolescents with a place to belong to and activities they enjoy.

Furthermore, Snodgrass and Zachlod believe that more emphasis should be given to mental health services in both the selection and support of overseas personnel. They recommend an overseas counselor for family adjustment problems, supportive assistance from American community service organizations (e.g., Rotary), improved psychological screening by American businesses sending personnel overseas, and increased orientation and training of adolescents returning to the United States. It is interesting to note that the problems of a Japanese family returning to their homeland is often exacerbated after a long tour abroad, and the children find it most difficult to reintegrate into the closed school and employment systems in Japan. Obviously, organizations that disrupt normal family life by a foreign deployment assignment have some responsibility to facilitate the tour of duty abroad and the return to the homeland.

Yoram Zeira states that rotation of expatriates among managerial positions is common practice in most multinational corporations. In an article in *Management International* (1976/No.3), he recommends the following to overcome some of the disadvantages of such policies:

1. The rotation program should be "customed" to each manager's background, attitudes, needs, aspirations, and prospects, so that each prospective expatriate is prepared realistically for the assignment and is better motivated to take the hardships involved.
2. Predeparture briefings should provide details about desired managerial patterns abroad, as well as the results of diagnostic studies of host national employees (e.g, morale, job attitudes).
3. Host country nationals need coaching about the rotation policy and purpose, so they will cooperate with the rotated expatriate managers.
4. The Expatriate managers' evaluation criteria should include their capacity to cope effectively with the human problems caused by MNC's (the multinational corporation's) rotation policies and with HCN (host culture nationals) personnel.

Zeira believes that many of the problems experienced in the rotation of multinational corporation managers would be delimited if corporate policy and practice were less enthnocentric. In any event, the in-country support system for expatriate employees and their dependents should accomplish the following:

1. Help them enter and enjoy the local environment and culture while they are living abroad
2. Enable them to bridge the culture gaps with the indigenous population and institutions
3. Facilitate their getting into the local infrastructure
4. Provide preventative programs and corrective services for dealing with human failings in a strange situation (e.g., abuse of drugs, alcohol, depression)

A total system of transcultural personnel services should offer counseling and community services to expatriate families. Frequently, a group of organizations in the same industry, or multinational contractors working on the same project or in the same region can best meet this objective. For example, thirty companies in the petroleum field have banded together in the informal Overseas Industrial Relations Discussion Group to deal with common concerns in foreign deployment. Similarly, giant corporations in overseas construction and engineering have formed the International Occupational Program Association. IOPA is a structured vehicle for confronting the alcohol, emotional, and related family problems within employee populations overseas.

Stage Four—Reentry Program

The last component in the foreign deployment system is centered on reintegrating the expatriate into the home society and domestic organization. For a person who has been abroad for sometime, the homeland and the organizational culture have changed in the meantime. The reentry process begins overseas with the psychological withdrawal of the expatriate faced with returning home. The organization provides services to facilitate the employee's exit from the foreign assignment—travel and transition assistance. Upon return, reentry shock may occur for six months or more, as the person struggles to readjust to the life style and tempo of the changed home and organizational cultures. Apart from the challenge of reestablishing home and family life is the issue of reassignment in the parent company or agency.

For many expatriates, it is a time of crises and trauma, the last stage of the culture shock process. The experience abroad for those who are sensitive and who got involved in the host culture was profound. It causes many people to reexamine their lives, values, attitudes; to assess how they became what they are. It prompts others to want to change their life style. The reentry home becomes the opportunity to carry out these aspirations. Individuals are not satisfied to return to old neighborhoods, old friends, or the same job or company affiliation. Many wish to apply the new self-insights, and to seek new ways of personal growth. The organization that sent them abroad in the first place should be empathetic to this reality, and be prepared to deal with it.

The problem is exacerbated when internal political turmoil in the host nation suddenly forces an employee and family to return home. Recent experiences of Americans in Vietnam and Iran provide "horror stories" of expatriates forced to abandon jobs, personal savings, and belongings because of a change in the foreign government. Harrassed, exhausted, frightened families are occasionally air lifted back to the United States. One wonders about the degree of responsibility their sponsoring organizations assumed for their integration into the U.S., as well as for financial losses.

Writing in the American Management Associations' publication, *Personnel* (January-February 1971), Robert Maddox discussed "Problems and Trends in Assigning Managers Overseas." He first raises the issue of the quality of managers sent to foreign subsidiaries, noting that in the past, the overseas operation was the dumping ground for mediocre managers who had more problems on returning stateside than they encountered abroad. Maddox agrees with today's trend of sending the organization's most competent personnel abroad because, among other reasons, it costs 2½ times what the same manager costs the company at home, and 4½ times what it costs to employ a local national counterpart. The policy, he notes, is to assign managers who are on their way up in the organization. After a few years in the international operation, they are brought back to the home office with a more cosmopolitan viewpoint, and knowledge of world business realities. However, Maddox discovered through interviews with multinational corporation executives that the major problem in this regard is "reentry."

Sometimes the problem is accentuated by small-minded domestic management that downgrades the managers brought home to the United States. Because of high salaries, bonuses, servants, and other benefits overseas, some expatriates are discontented with the lowered expectations and compensation at home. For some, there is a distinct change in the level of social life; they do not have the social privileges and contacts, the perks and emoluments of the foreign situation. They may return to the life of a middle manager in middle-class suburbia without movement in prestigious circles and involvement with high-level government officials. Often their role in the domestic organization is less exalted, and the scope of their decision-making authority is restricted. Furthermore, the returned manager is somewhat out of touch with American culture, for their native society is different from when they left. This difficulty is found in the public, as well as the private, sector—missionaries, government officials, Peace Corps volunteers, and other such persons subject to lengthy assignments abroad are prone to re-entry shock and all that it implies. It is an old syndrome—"how are you going to keep them down on the farm after they have seen Paris!"

The foreign deployment system is incomplete unless it helps returning employees to fit into the home culture and organization. The system may involve group counseling with personnel specialists, psychologists, and former expatriates. Ideally, the family should be included in the discussion whether they have been abroad or not. For some, the personal crises is so severe that intensive individual psychological counseling is in order.

To capitalize on human corporate assets, the organization should further close the deployment loop. Special assistance such as financial aid to obtain a home mortage, or outplacement advisement because a position is no longer available in the home organization or the person wishes a change of affiliation and career. For a few, it may be legal assistance because a divorce is inevitable. In such ways the sponsoring organization fulfills its responsibility toward the overseas employee reassigned home.

However, expatriates coming back from an overseas assignment are a valuable resource. The corporation can learn much from their cross-cultural experience. The information can be used to improve the whole foreign deployment process. Some possibilities to consider are:

1. Data gathering from all employees who return from either temporary or longer relocations abroad. A standardized questionnaire or interview

procedure can be developed and the results stored in a computer for future use. Separate records can be kept on those in the premature return group.

2. Data analysis and application of the information obtained from employees upon re-entry would be carried out by the office of international personnel or external consultants. Findings would be studied for ways to improve recruitment and selection of personnel for overseas assignment; employee training programs for foreign deployment; management policies and practices at foreign sites; consumer, customer, public, and employee relations in target countries; and relocation assistance for the returning expatriate employees.

3. Consultation with foreign deployment specialists and policy changes should follow as a result of the findings. The results have implications for corporate manpower policy and practice, especially relative to cost reductions and effectiveness of the international business operations.

4. Human Resource Development programs in multinational organizations should benefit from these procedures, and special undertakings may be stimulated by the findings and recommendations of specialists' reports on the foreign deployment situation. For example, some of the data may have lateral application to domestic management practice or development, particularly with minority personnel. It may be helpful in understanding company reports that come to headquarters from international subsidiaries. It may prompt a systematic inventory of skills in the international work force, encourage the design of an international or in-country performance review and appraisal system, show the need for an International Managerial Replacement Planning System, foster the development of strategies for the interim utilization of expatriate technicians and managers before their next overseas assignment, and bring to management's attention the need for a system that brings host or third country nationals into the domestic operation.

Conclusion

Dr. Bernard Bass of the University of Rochester has worked with numerous managers throughout the world. He believes that the impact of reverse culture shock can be lessened. It can be a positive growth experience for individuals to rediscover their identity in work and social enviornments where most others have not had similar cross-cultural experiences and opportunities. Organizations can assist employees to anticipate and prepare for the threat of the home culture, and to see it as a similar challenge for personal and professional development, as was the change previously to the host culture.

Foreign deployment issues are universal, and not limited to one nationality. Murray and Smetanka did an interesting study of Japanese managers and their families assigned to Canada. Under the auspices of the Widsor International Business Studies Research Unit, their findings were reported in *The Bridge* (Summer 1978) as "Cultural Shock: The Japanese Executive in Canada." Their sojourn was documented through both the expartiation and repatriation process. Murray and Smetanka concluded:

> In summary, it is probably safe to say that the Japanese executive in Canada feels the same cultural shock—anxieties, apprehensions, tense situations—that a North American feels in Japan. The question is whether this problem would be alleviated with more information about the country of assignment is difficult to answer. At the present time, a number of companies have packaged programs for their executives going abroad. Mitsubishi provides guide books, films, and workshops conducted by overseas experts to prepare the executive and his family for his new home. The success of these have yet to be tested, but it would appear that such efforts are a step in the right direction. It is also suggested that companies start to look at re-entry workshops, preparing the executive and his family for the repatriation phase.

A broad-based foreign deployment system must be an integral part of an organization's international operations. Only then will cultural synergy occur to the benefit of the human family. One indicator of the importance of the issues raised in this chapter can be viewed in terms of rising investment funds abroad. For example *Time* magazine (February 12, 1979) reports that in the past three years European industry investments in the U.S. rose 60% and total $30 billion, while U.S. multinational's investments in Europe are more than $60 billion and continue to climb. If a fraction of these sums were invested in intelligent foreign deployment systems and exchanges, personnel on both continents would benefit and profitability would be enhanced.

References

Aitken, T., *The Multinational Man: The Role of the Manager Abroad.* New York: John Wiley & Sons, 1973.

Angel, J.L., *American Encylopedia of International Information, Vol. 2: Directory of American Firms Operating in Foreign Countries.* New York: World Trade Academy Press Publication, Simon & Shuster, 1979.

Beeth, G., *International Management Practice: An Insiders View.* New York: American Management Associations (AMACOM), 1973.

Council on International Educational Exchange (777 United Nations Plaza, New York, N.Y. 00017). *Handbook on International Study for U.S. Nationals.*

Center for Research and Education. *Improving Cross-Cultural Training and Measurement of Cross-Cultural Learning.* Denver: The Center for Research and Education, 1973.

Holmes, B., *An Exploratory Study of Intercultural Contacts of Americans in Other Cultures.* (unpublished doctoral dissertation, Department of Communications, University of Colorado (Summary available from Dr. Holmes, 3801 S. Spruce St., Denver, Colorado 80237.) Ann Arbor, Mich.: University Microfilms, 1978.

Humer, S.N., *The International Operations of National Firms: A Study of Foreign Investments.* Cambridge, Mass.: The MIT Press, 1976

Humphrey, R.L., *Succeding Overseas: A Model for Solving Cross-Cultural Conflicts at Home and Abroad.* San Diego, Ca.: Grossmont Press.

International Federation of Training and Development Organizations. *1978 IFTDO Conference Cassettes Catalog from the World Congress on Human Resource Development.* Available from the American Society for Training and Development, P.O. Box 5307, Madison, Wisconsin 53705.

Johnson, M.B., *Training Needs of American Workers Overseas as Perceived by Americans Who Have Worked in Asia.* (Doctoral disseration University of Wisconsin) Ann Arbor, Mich.: University Microfilms, 1970.

Kuman, K., *The Social and Cultural Impacts of Transnational Enterprises* Honolulu: East-West Center, 1978. Available from the East West Culture Learning Institute, Honolulu, Hawaii 96822, U.S.A.

Pierce, E.B., *All You Need to Know About Living Abroad.* New York: Pan American Airways, 1978. (One of several foreign deployment publications available from this airline on living overseas.)

Robuck, S.H. and K. Simmonds, *International Business Management and Multinational Enterprises.* Homewood, Ill.: Richard D. Irwin, Inc., 1973.

Robinson, R.D., *International Business Management.* New York: Holt, Rinehart, & Winston, 1973.

Thiagarajan, K.M., et al, *Managing the Multinational Firm: A Behavioral Science Approach.* Englewood Cliffs, N.J.: Prentice Hall, 1977.

Vansina, L.S., "Improving International Relations and Effectiveness within Multinational Organizations." *New Technologies in Organization Development,* Vol. 2, Ed., J.D. Adams. La Jolla, Ca.: University Assoc., 1978.

Waxman, M.N., *Practical Sensitization and Adjustment Raining for Business Effectiveness in Latin American Environments.* (Master's Thesis, University of Bridgeport) Ann Arbor, Mich.: University Microfilms, 1977.

(European multinational corporations send employees scheduled for overseas' assignment to these central facilities for training in culture specifics: Center for International Briefing, Farnham, Surrey, England; Royal Tropical Institute, The Netherlands.)

13
Cultural Themes
and Patterns

Key Cultural Insights

It is impossible to study in detail every culture, and to make comparisons with similarities and differences from our own native culture. In this unit, specific cultural traits for several areas of the world are covered in a limited fashion. We begin with the theoretical underpinning of the national character or basic personality concept.

Developed by Dr. Abram Kardiner and Dr. Ralph Linton, the concept rests on the following premises:

1. That an individual's early experiences exert a lasting effect on his personality.
2. That similar early experiences tend to produce similar personality configurations in the people who experience them.
3. That the childrearing practices and socialization techniques of a society are culturally patterned and tend to be similar (although not identical) for the various families within the culture.
4. That these practices and techniques differ from culture to culture.

A wealth of evidence has been provided by anthropologists, sociologists, psychologists, and others to support these premises. Therefore, it follows that:

1. Members of any culture have many elements of early experience in common.
2. They also have many elements of personality in common.
3. Since the early experience of individuals differs from one culture to another, the personality characteristics and values differ from culture to culture.

The *basic personality* of a culture is the personality configuration shared by most members of the culture, as a result of early experiences that they have in common. This does not mean that behavior patterns of all members of a culture are similar. There is a wide range of individual differences, but there are many aspects that most of the people share to varying degrees.

This chapter looks at cultural variations for Africa, Europe, the Middle East, the Eastern European Bloc and Latin America. Special cultural differences—"the differences that make a difference"—are discussed. These local customs and practices can serve as guidelines for managers who must determine appropriate and inappropriate ways of interacting. They are illustrative of geographic themes and patterns that can be identified to facilitate international business.

As in previous chapters, the nontechnical aspects of business are considered. These pragmatic observations, subject to change with time, circumstances, and the personalities involved, are proposed as hints for facilitating international business. As Edward T. Hall says in *Beyond Culture*:

> Deep cultural undercurrents structure life in subtle but highly consistent ways that are not consciously formulated. Like the invisible jet streams in the skies that determine the course of a storm, these hidden currents shape our lives; yet their influence is only beginning to be identified.

Africa

Africa, a large continent of many nations and cultures, is currently undergoing rapid change and development. In many areas there is an increasing amount of interaction with Western businessmen while in some countries, there is very little contact. The following cultural considerations apply, in general but with appropriate changes, to all nations in Black Africa. Excluded are the countries under Islamic influence (Arab countries), Rhodesia, and South Africa, whose business practices and customs are more reflective of European culture.

The Family

The basic unit of African society is the family, which includes the nuclear family and the extended family or tribe. In traditional African society, the tribe is the ultimate community. No unit has more importance in society. There may be some loose confederations, but they are temporary and limited in scope. In political terms, the tribe is the equivalent of a nation. It does not have fixed boundaries, but on its sanction rests the law (customary law like the English Common Law). All wars were fought on the tribe's behalf, and the division between "them" and "us" lay in tribal boundaries.

In some ways, the tribe is more than a nation. In Europe and America, ethical and moral standards are not given by national sanctions, but rest on religious and cultural traditions common to the whole continent. But in traditional Africa, except for areas under Islamic control, the tribe provides the guidelines for accepted behavior. The tribe bears a moral connotation and provides an emotional security. It is also a source of social and moral sanctions as well as political and physical security. It provides its members with rules governing responsibilities, explanations of the responsibilities, and guidelines for organizing the society, and hence, the culture.

The following quotations from *Business International Research Report* suggest the importance of the tribe.

> The basic sociological unit in Africa is the tribe, which inhabits one village or a series of villages, or (in the case of nomadic tribes) is widely scattered. A feeling common throughout Africa is the sense of tribal responsibility and brotherhood. When tribal members go to the cities for jobs or education, their enhanced stature brings the responsibility of assisting tribal brothers. This obligation often imposes a burden on the successful member far in excess of his income.

> In such a situation, the successful African is unlikely to resist the pressures of his society. He is thus forced to augment his income, often by means regarded by foreigners as theft and corruption. In the Western sense, it may be. In the African context it is not.

The presence of tribalism may be giving way, but its importance cannot be ignored. The article "Nigeria," *Atlantic* (December 1976) states:

> Tribalism is a major factor in who gets what job, especially in the civil service, even though jobs in an office seldom go to members of the boss's tribe, as they used to. Some businessmen refuse to hire members of their own tribe because they think it encourages demands for favors and militates against good performance, and younger men fight tribalism harder than the older generation. But tribalism is also a major factor in the rebirth of Nigerian politics. In each of the seven states I visited, people spoke only of their own tribe's candidates for leadership and predicted that the national parties would be alliances of tribal leaders.

The tribe is broken down into different kinship lines. The concept of kinship is important to understanding African societies. It constitutes the primary basis for an individual's rights, duties, rules of residence, marriage, inheritance, and succession.

Kinship refers to blood relationships between individuals, and is used to describe relationships in a narrow, as well as a broad sense. Parents and their children are a special kind of kin group. The social significance of kinship covers a wide social field in most African societies. In Western culture, its significance usually does not extend beyond the nuclear family, but in the African culture, it embraces a network of people including those that left the village for the urban areas.

The family—father, mother, children—is the ultimate basis of the tribe. But the tribal and family unit organization is being disrupted by changes in the economic organizational structure. The economic organization has tied reward to individual effort, and developed road, rail, water, and air communication networks that have increased the range and speed of contact and, therefore, the rate of intercultural contact and change. The reorganization has also brought tribes together as territorial units, thereby increasing opportunities for migration from one area to another and weakening family bonds.

As this new found mobilization moves more people to the large urban areas, they try to maintain some family ties. This involves a responsibility to support family members still in the villages. It also affects Africans' business relationships with managers from abroad in terms of hiring practices and the need for extra income to support those at home. Earnings from business transactions are often used for this purpose.

Trust and Friendship

Trust and confidence are essential elements needed for successful enterprise in Africa. It is very important to get to know co-workers as individuals before getting down to actual business activities. Friendship comes first. Often, a friendship continues after specific business activities end. Socializing outside of the office is common. It is under those relaxed conditions that managers talk politics, sports, and sometimes business.

Contrast this with American businessmen who are interested primarily in getting the job done. There is some socialization outside the office, but only for business purposes. As soon as the job is done or the contract fulfilled, the U.S. manager moves on to other things. A friendship that develops outside of the office and continues for an extended period of time is unique.

Business International Research Report states that:

> No amount of capital, know-how, goodwill, or energy will guarantee success for multinational corporations if they cannot win the trust and confidence of the governments and people with whom they deal. . .such trust and confidence is sadly lacking in Africa today.

In Africa, interpersonal relationships are also based upon sincerity. African societies are warm and friendly. People generally assume that everyone is a friend until proven otherwise. When Africans smile, it means they like you. When smiles are not seen, it is a clear sign of hate and distrust.

Africans believe strongly in friendship and once a person is accepted as a friend, the person automatically becomes a member of the family. A friend can pop into a friend's place anytime. In African societies, formal invitations and appointment making are not common. Friends are readily prepared to entertain fellow friends anytime.

One of the most important factors to remember when doing business in Africa is the concept of friendship before business. Normally before a meeting begins, there is general talk about events that have little or nothing to do with the business at hand. This can go on for some time. If the meeting involves the coming together of people who have never met, but who are trying to strike a deal (an African and a foreigner), the African will try to reach out for friendship first.

Essentially, the African culture is still friendly and warm to strangers. Making real friends in Africa is an easy task. In addition, friendship and trust must come before an African enters a business deal. A close bond must develop between the two people involved. If an African tries to reach out but receives a cold response, he may become alert and suspicious, and lose interest in the deal.

Time

The way an individual views the concept of time has a major impact on any business situation. If two businessmen enter a situation with complementary goals, abilities, and needs, a successful arrangement can be thwarted if each has different ideas about time. The U.S. manager tends to be inflexible when it comes to time. Everything is done according to a schedule with little or no deviation. Meetings must begin on time and end on time. The entire day is segmented into time slots, and the American becomes uneasy or nervous if the schedule is interrupted or if little is accomplished.

In Africa, time is viewed as flexible, not rigid or segmented. People come first, then time. Anyone in a hurry is viewed with suspicion and distrust. Since trust is very important, individuals who follow inflexible time schedules will have little success. The African wants to sit and talk—get to know the person before discussing business.

In the larger cities of Africa, the concept of time is changing. Punctuality is becoming more important. Contact with Western businessmen has brought an increasing awareness and acceptance of the segmentation of time and its consequent inflexibility. But away from the capital city, time is still viewed in a relaxed and easy-going manner. Businessmen in outlying areas like to talk politics and hear the latest news when city businessmen come to visit.

Time is not seen as a limited commodity. What cannot be done today can always be accomplished tomorrow. Among friends, people who know one another, meetings are not held promptly. People may arrive several hours late. Many times foreigners misinterpret this as laziness, untrustworthiness, lack of seriousness in doing business, or even lack of interest in the venture. However, lateness in meetings is seen as very much a part of life. It is understood among friends that even though everybody agrees to meet at a given time, they will not actually gather until much later. This lateness has become known as "African time." However, when Africans are dealing with foreigners, they normally try to be on time out of respect for the non-Africans' concept of time.

Corruption

Corruption in Africa is often a result of tribal responsibilities that individuals carry with them when leaving the village for a job or schooling in the city. The enhanced stature of city life brings a responsibility of assisting tribal brothers. This obligation often imposes a financial burden on the successful member far in excess of income. The worker is unlikely to resist the pressures of society, and is thus forced to augment income, often by means regarded by foreigners as corrupt. However, to the African, it is not. As long as great disparities in income and standards of living continue, the bribe system is also likely to continue as it has in many countries. In Africa, extra income is swiftly distributed through the extended family system to remote relations living in remote places. The tradition of sharing continues even as individuals move away from their tribal origins.

One of the greatest problems in Nigeria, for example, is the corruption in government on all levels. General Obasanjo recently declared: "It is gross and destructive indiscipline on the part of any society to accommodate cheating by any member of that society. It is alien to our African traditional society." In the same address, he publicly admitted that "it is a matter for regret that most public servants tend to subdue their political discipline in the face of personal aggrandisement." The following is an example:

> The company, Jones & Smith Food Company, is located in the capital of a large African country. However, they want to expand their headquarters to another state capital. To do this, they need approval from the federal government and the state government. The company sent in a written application a few months ago, but did not get any response.
>
> The manager of the project went several times to the Federal Ministry of Trade and Economic Development but was always told to come back the next day. Mr. Jones became frustrated and mad at the clerks and officials involved. However, in the process of the argument, one of them said, "This is not America. It's Africa. If you want anything done on time, you've got to give a bribe. Kind of like a gratuity tendered before, rather than after a service is performed."
>
> Mr. Jones, who is not accustomed to such practices, angrily stormed out of the office. In the car, he narrated the incident to the driver who advised him to give the "gratuity" or have the proposal denied.
>
> In emergency meeting, the company's board of directors decided to offer the gratuity. To the company's surprise, the proposal was approved the next day.

But back in Jones' home culture a board of directors may frown upon such payments, and home country laws may consider such bribes illegal.

Task Orientation

If a foreigner appears too task-oriented, the African counterpart interprets it as planned foul play. If hurried through business negotiations, the African suspects cheating. In addition, Africans might brand the task-oriented approach of Americans as a demonstration of their superiority complex. They may even associate Americans with the previous British colonial masters. Some natives believe that European imperialists kept Africans down, humiliated and ridiculed, and exploited Africa's resources. If that happens, there is very little chance for the business deal to succeed if contemporary foreigners get lumped with the mistakes of their predecessors.

Respect for Authority

Age is another important factor to consider in Africa. It is believed that the older one gets, the wiser one becomes—life has seasoned the individual with varied experiences. Hence, in Africa, age is an asset. The older the person, the more respect the person receives from the community, and especially from the young. Thus, if an American is considerably younger than the African, the latter will have little confidence in the American. However, if sincerity, respect, and empathy are shown, the American will receive a positive response.

Respect for elders tends to be the key harmony in African cultures. Elders are generally respected as wise people. Young people may not oppose the opinion of elderly people. They may not agree, but they must respect the opinion. In some cases, especially in rural areas, young people are not expected to offer opinions in meetings. The informal and formal interpersonal relationship in Africa is based on cultural norms of various African societies.

Business and Common Courtesies

Business is normally discussed in the office or in a bar or restaurant—always outside the home. When an African is the host of such meetings, he will pay for everyone. The opposite should be true if an American is the host.

Home matters are not discussed in business meetings. What happens in the home is considered private.

When invited to someone's home for a meal, do not discuss business. All business is done outside the home, and men are expected to be away from home on business matters much of the time.

As indicated earlier, age commands respect. Age and wisdom are seen as the same, and the norms of the elders must be followed in order to ensure smooth business dealings.

In traditional Nigerian culture, the woman is a domestic helper for the man.

Summary

When comparing the American and African cultures and how they affect the business environment, it is necessary to understand that the U.S. is a low-context culture. It is technologically oriented with emphasis on individual achievement rather than group participation. In the communication process, a low-context culture places meaning in the exact verbal description of an event. Individuals in such a culture rely on the spoken word. This is typified by the common statement, "say what you mean."

Africa is a high-context culture. In the communication process, most of the meaning is not from the words, but is internalized in the person. Meaning comes from the environment and is looked for in the relationship between the ideas expressed in the communication process. High-context cultures tend to be more human oriented than low-context cultures. The extended family fits into the high-context culture.

Businessmen from Africa and the U.S. can profitably work together if they accept the differences between them and work to create an atmosphere of nonjudgmental acceptance. On the part of the American, it means slowing down; not being tied to a time schedule.

Europe

Cultural differences related to the business process in France are discussed in this section, and contrasted with typical American practices. By implication some of these social and business customs may be extended to other countries in Europe that will assist multinational managers in doing business in that part of the world.

Europe is a continent divided into two geo-political spheres. It is obvious that business practices will also vary if a country is based on capitalist or socialist systems. Although Western European countries struggle for united and cooperative action in the Common Market, it is a complex of distinctive nations and cultures. Thus, it is difficult to generalize about Europe. Detailed information on England and Ireland, for example, is provided in the case studies in Chapter 16.

Doing Business in France

> ...the French constitute the most brilliant and the most dangerous nation in Europe and the best qualified in turn to become an object of admiration, hatred, pity or terror, but never of indifference.
>
> Alexis de Toqueville

Idealism

The French tend to believe that the basic truths on which life is based derive from principles and immutable or universal laws. They are concerned with the essence of values. The motto of the French Republic is "Liberty, Equality and Fraternity." To the French, values such as these should transcend everything else in life. They behave in an individualistic manner. "Chacun defend son beef-steak" (everyone protects his own steak). Sometimes they are frustrated. They find it hard to live by these ideals in everyday life, yet the hunger for these altruistic ideals is still present and deeply ingrained in most French people.

Social Structure and Status

Social classes are very important in France. The French social classes are: the aristocracy, the upper bourgeoisie, the upper-middle bourgeoisie, the middle, the lower-middle, and lower classes (blue-collar workers, peasants). Social classes categorize people according to their professional activities (teachers, doctors, lawyers, craftsmen, foremen, and peasants), as well as, their political opinions (conservative, left-oriented).

Social interactions are thus affected by these social stereotypes. It is extremely hard for a French individual to be rid of social stereotypes. They affect personal identity. Unlike an American who can theoretically attain the highest levels of social consideration by working hard and being professionally successful, a Frenchman finds it difficult to do so. If professionally successful, a Frenchman can expect to climb one or two stages of the social ladder in a lifetime, but often nothing more.

The French are very status conscious. Social status in France depends on one's social origins. Outward signs of social status are the level of education, a beautiful house with a well-designed, tasteful facade (not a gaudy one), knowledge of literature and fine arts, and the social origins of one's ancestors.

Cooperation and Competition

The French are not basically oriented towards competition. To them, the word competition has a very narrow meaning—practicing a sport at the highest level of international excellency. For example, for the French, only superstar athletes such as Bruce Jenner, O.J. Simpson, or Jean Claude Killy are involved in competition.

The average Frenchman does not feel affected by competition. This attitude can be dangerous. For example, in a 1978 New Year's Eve television speech, President Giscard d'Estaing tried to educate the French and make them face the fact that competition really should affect their lives. He said competition is not just what the French soccer team experiences during the Soccer World Cup. The economic welfare of the French people actually depends on how competitive French goods are on international markets. He tried to awaken the French to the notion of competition, so that they would motivate themselves to work harder and be more productive.

A consequence of these different attitudes is that when Americans interact with French people, they may manifest their competitive drive. The French may interpret their American interlocutors as being antagonistic, ruthless, and power-hungry. They may feel threatened, and overreact or withdraw from the discussion.

Personal Characteristics

French people are friendly, humorous, and sardonic. Americans may also be friendly, but they are so friendly that they are seldom sardonic. Americans need to be liked. French people do not. Americans tend to like people who agree with them. French people are more likely to be interested in a person who disagrees with them. Because they want to be liked, Americans try to impress others. On the other hand, the French are very hard to impress, and impatient with those who try. A Frenchman, when trying to get a sense of a person, looks for qualities within the person and for personality. An American looks at the person's achievements. Frenchmen tend to gain recognition and to develop their identity by thinking and acting against others, while Americans increase their self-esteem by acting in accord with the actions and expectations of others. French people are more inner-oriented, and base behavior and evaluations upon feelings, preferences, and expectations.

Trust and Respect

A Frenchman trusts a person according to inner evaluation of the personality. An American trusts a person according to past achievements and upon other people's recognition, and ranking of that person.

French people tend to respect an individual according to character. Americans tend to respect an individual according to professional accomplishments. Because social stereotypes are so vivid, an average Frenchman cannot earn respect from members of other social classes merely through work accomplishments and performance.

Style of Conversation

Many Americans use superlatives like most, best, and largest. The reason may be the importance of competition as a social value for the Americans, along with the importance of quantified measurements in assessing standards of excellency. American conversations usually include numerous pronouns such as "I" or "my." French interlocutors seldom put themselves forward or try to make themselves look good in conversations. If they accidentally do, they will usually add, "Je ne cherche pas à me vanter mais. . ." ("I do not want to boast but. . ."). Boasting is often considered a weakness, a sign of self-satisfaction and immaturity. In conversations with French people, Americans may ask their French counterparts questions about themselves. The French will probably shun such questions, and orient the conversation towards more general subjects. To them, it is not proper to show characteristics of self-centeredness.

The French often criticize institutions, conditions, and people they live with. A conversation where disagreements are exchanged can be considered stimulating by a Frenchman, while an American will likely be embarrassed. It is not uncommon to see two Frenchmen arguing with each other, their faces reddened with what seems to be anger, exchanging lively, heated, and irreconcilable arguments. Then later, they shake hands and comment, "That was a good discussion. We should do it again sometime!" The French tend to think that such arguments are interesting and stimulating. It is also a meaningful outlet for tension.

Humor

Americans and French enjoy and appreciate humor. However, the French tend to use humor in more numerous situations than Americans do. They also often add a touch of cynicism to their humor, and may not hesitate to make fun of institutions and people.

Consistency and Contradictions

Americans prefer consistency and predictability, and expect role-conforming in their relationships. The French on the other hand abound in contradictions and are not overly disturbed by them. They profess lofty ideals of fraternity and equality, but at times show characteristics of utmost individualism and selfish materialism. For example, the things that occasionally seem to matter most are owning a little car, a little house, and cashing in on one's little retirement pension. On the political scene, they seem continuously restless, verbally criticizing the government and capitalism, yet are basically conservative. They have supported a conservative government for the last 20 years.

Attitudes Toward Work

Attitudes of the French toward work depend on whether they are employed in the public sector or in the private sector. In the French bureaucracy and in public concerns, there is little incentive to be productive. Quotas are rarely assigned, and it is virtually impossible to lay-off or dismiss employees on the basis of job performance.

In the private sector, the situation is different. It is true that French workers do not respect the work ethic as much as many American counterparts do. They are usually not motivated by competition or the desire to emulate fellow-workers. They frown on working overtime and have the longest vacations in the world (between four to five weeks a year). However, they usually work hard in their allotted working time. French workers have the reputation of being productive. Part of the explanation for such productiveness may lie in the French tradition of craftsmanship. A large proportion of the French work force has been traditionally employed in small, independent businesses where there is widespread respect for a job well-done. Many Frenchmen take pride in work that is done well because traditionally they have not been employed in huge, impersonal industrial concerns. They often have a direct stake in the work they are doing, and are usually concerned with quality.

Authority

French companies contain many social reference groups that are mutually exclusive. Tight reins of authority are needed to ensure adequate job performance. The lesser emphasis on delegation of responsibility limits accountability and contributes to a more rigid organization structure. As a consequence, decision-making is more centralized in French companies, and it may take longer before decisions are reached and applied. This may be a source of frustration for American executives (especially lower- and middle-management executives) who are working with French executives from a comparative management level. Americans may resent the amount of time that is necessary before their recommendations are considered and dealt with by top-management. Americans are accustomed to executives having a higher degree of responsibility. The flow of communication is improved if American executives have direct access to two or three top executives of a French company. This is where the actual decision-making power is.

The highest executives of large French companies also differ from their American counterparts in their conception of authority. The top two men of a French company are accountable to a lesser extent than their American counterparts. It takes poor performance for them to be challenged in their functions by a board of directors or by subordinates. Patterns of authority are more stable in French industry. Therefore, because they do not need to justify their actions to the same extent, the very top French executives tend to be more autocratic in their managerial style.

Executive functions, also, have more overtones of social leadership. For example, one often depicts industry leaders, such as Mr. Dreyfus, the head of Renault, or Mr. Michelin, the head of the tire company, as ruling their empires in the same way as Napoleon ruled his. In their professional activities, these very top industry executives are autocratic leaders of men, but in addition, they have a high social, and even political, status.

It is interesting to compare French and American business magazine interviews of executives. Along with professional experiences and activities, top French executives usually mention details concerning their personal lives such as former professors who had an impact on them, enriching social and personal experiences, books that influenced their outlook on life, and what their convictions on political and social issues are. On the other hand, top American executives will more likely emphasize the progression of their career in terms of professional achievements.

Organizational Structure and Decision-Making

The organizational structure of French companies tends to be more rigid than that of American companies. The French put less emphasis on control of individual performance. The Americans, on the other hand, tend to favor a flexible organizational structure with greater delegation of responsibility, and greater control of individual performance.

Americans attach much importance to achievement. Therefore, decision-making in U.S. companies occurs at levels where the results allow managers to reach quantifiable goals.

The decision-making process is more centralized in French companies. Important decisions are made by only the top executives.

Motivation

Most Americans put high value on professional accomplishments. Their self-esteem derives largely from these accomplishments, and so does their social status. They are motivated to work hard in order to earn money, particularly in light of the fact that there is little job security and social security in America. As a result, most Americans are very ambitious and expend considerable energy in their work.

However, there is a major difference between the motivations of Americans and French people concerning work. Although the French appreciate the Americans' industriousness and devotion to their work, they do not believe it is worthwhile. To the French the *qualitè de la vie* (quality of life) is what matters. In the present French government, there is even a Minister in charge of the quality of life. The French attach a great importance to freetime and vacations, and are seldom willing to sacrifice the enjoyment of life out of dedication to work.

Conflict

Americans do not like conflict, especially interpersonal conflict. They feel uncomfortable, and are concerned about what others think when they are involved in conflict. Because most Americans are pragmatic, they think of conflict as a hindrance to achieving goals.

However, the French, partly because they live in a more closed society with relatively little social mobility, are used to conflict. They are aware that some positions are irreconcilable, and that people must live with these irreconcilable opinions. They, therefore, tend not to mind conflict, and sometimes enjoy it. They even respect others who carry it off with style and get results. The French are also less concerned about negative reactions from those with whom they are in conflict.

Tips for Working in France

A firm and pumping handshake is considered uncultured. A French handshake is a quick shake with some pressure in the grip.

A French woman offers her hand first.

Punctuality in business and social invitation is important. If invited to a person's home for a social occasion, it is polite to bring a gift of flowers, but not roses or chrysanthemums.

At mealtime a French person enjoys pleasant conversation, but not personal questions or the subject of money.

Snapping the fingers of both hands and slapping an open palm over a closed fist have vulgar meanings.

Great importance is placed on neatness and taste.

Generalizations regarding the manners and customs of Europeans are:

1. Do not ask the price of something; never inquire about the income of a person.
2. Perfume is never given as a business gift. It is considered too personal.
3. Flowers are extremely important. Give them to the host and hostess when invited to dinner.
4. Do not talk about firing a person because it is extremely difficult to do.
5. Reward is generally given by means of a bonus, extra trips, or gifts.
6. Become aware of the staff-line differences between European companies and American companies.
7. In many European countries, coffee and dessert may come before drinks—opposite of the U.S. custom.
8. American female executives may have difficulty in Europe because only a few European women hold high positions in industry and government.
9. There is a relatively high degree of nationalism in Europe at this time, particularly in France, despite supranational aspirations in the West.
10. When traveling in Europe, be constantly aware that customs are different in each country. Do not assume things are done the same in Europe as in the United States, or even the same in western versus eastern Europe.

Managing Cultural Differences

The Middle East

Doing Business in Saudi Arabia

In 1977 Saudi Arabia furnished to the United States close to a million and a half barrels of oil every day. Other Arab and Gulf States imports of oil to the U.S. provide nearly 45 percent of all U.S. oil imports which is almost a fifth of all oil that is used by Americans. At the same time U.S., Saudi trade has burgeoned. In 1976 American firms sold over $4 billion in goods and services to the Kingdom and many more billions have been awarded for future delivery.

Because there is so much business transaction between the United States and the Middle East, for purposes of a general introduction to the area the following practical points are important and presented at this time.

Things to remember when negotiating with Arabs throughout the Persian Gulf are:

1. Not all peoples in "The Middle East" are *Arabs*—for example, Iranians and Israelis.
2. Not all Arabs are *Moslem*—for example, Lebanese Christians and Greek Orthodox.
3. Not all Middle Easterners are Semites, something many Arabs and Jews have in common.

The modern Saudi world was founded by the late King Abdulaziz Ibn Sàud, who gave the country its present name in 1932. The country itself occupies 2,240,000 square kilometers of the Arabian peninsula and from the 1974 population and housing census, preliminary statistics indicated there were over seven million people in Saudi Arabia, but this included the foreign nationals living in that country.

Saudi Arabia carries a unique religious responsibility for it is the keeper of Islam's two holiest places: Mecca, the birthplace of the greatest prophet, Muhammad, and Medina, the city of the Prophet's burial. Each year over a million faithful followers make a pilgrimage, or Haji, which each faithful Moslem is required to perform in his lifetime.

The five rules which are the pillars of Moslem faith are:

1. The recitation of the profession of faith
2. Canonical prayer repeated five times a day
3. The fasting during the month of Ramadan
4. Payment of the tax of purification on certain kinds of property
5. The pilgrimage of haji to Mecca

Arabic is a divine language since it is the language of the Koran and the Koran is the word of God as revealed by the last and greatest of his prophets, Muhammad. Poetry and eloquence are regarded as among the highest skills and poets are in great demand as all persons enjoy the subtleties of rhyme and meter in Arabic. Here are some linguistic factors to be aware of in working with Arabs:

1. Arabs love the spoken word, tend to ramble and don't get to the point quickly. It is unwise to exhibit impatience or annoyance at this. Arabs may be offended at your lack of appreciation of their eloquence.
2. Arabs are masters at flattery and appreciate compliments.
3. Don't accept a mere "yes" or "no" as a promise from an Arab. Here are some clues at the meaning:
   - Only if it was repeated and emphasized numerous times was it meant at face value.
   - To an Arab, a mere yes/no means "maybe," or even the opposite, so the foreigner would do well to repeat and emphasize his answers, following the Arab practice.
   - Arabs find bluntness very disrespectful, which is why they usually respond in the most agreeable manner, regardless of truth.
4. Any effort the foreigner makes to use Arabic will be received enthusiastically by Arabs, and create much good will. Therefore, find occasions to compliment Arabs on their language's beauty and expressive characteristics.

What do Saudis think of Americans? Generally, Americans are well thought of and liked by Saudis. This may well be a result of the success story of Arabian American Oil Company (Aramco), which is a creation of four major oil companies—Texaco, Mobil, Exxon and Socal—to secure the exploration concessions that resulted in the tremendous oil discoveries as well as the positive continuing relationships that Americans have had with Saudi Arabians. Furthermore, many Saudis have been educated in the U.S., and hold fond memories of their visits.

The following are some physical factors to be aware of when working with Arabs.

1. Maintain strong eye contact. The eyes are the windows to the soul.
2. Don't gesture with left hand. It is the "toilet" hand. Don't eat with the left hand.
3. Don't cross your legs so that sole of foot points towards someone. It is impolite.
4. Arabs like close proximity to persons they converse with. Americans prefer about 30 inches for face-to-face impersonal conversation. Arabs prefer about half that distance.
5. Yes is "said" nonverbally by swiveling the head from side to side. No is "said" by tilting one's head back and clicking one's tongue.

For Successful Intercultural Relations—

1. Don't express admiration for an Arab's possessions, or he'll feel honorbound to give them to you. To refuse such a gift would constitute an insult as it is refusing the person.
2. Arabs are very emotional people and are easily outraged by even slight provocations. Don't regard these emotional displays as having serious implications for a relationship with an Arab and don't feel you have to act calmly 100% of the time yourself. Arabs like expressive, assertive persons and expect periodic displays of emotion from others, including foreigners.
3. Don't launch a full-scale verbal assault on a negotiating opponent in front of others; you will wound his dignity and possibly make an enemy. Criticisms of an Arab should be done tactfully, and do any serious criticizing in private on a one-to-one basis.
4. Never publicly criticize a colleague or a member of your own negotiating team. The Arabs will sympathize with his shame and lose respect for you because of your apparent lack of loyalty.
5. Don't try to "break the ice" by making polite inquiries about an Arab's wife or daughters, or discuss your own wife or daughters with Arabs.

Some things to know:
1. Arabs are emotional and their dignity is important to them.
2. The loyalties of an Arab are: family, community, country, friends, and then outsiders.
3. Arabs are hospitable and their offers should not be refused.
4. Arabs are honest but love driving a hard bargain.
5. Demonstrating respect is important.
6. A Saudi shakes hands frequently, but it is not a firm handshake.

Chapter 19 provides other culture specifics about the Middle East.

The Eastern European Bloc

Doing Business in Communist Cultures

The following are factors that must be considered by the Western businessperson dealing with executives from Eastern Bloc countries and were derived from materials written by Myron Vretsky.

Economic Factor—Rigid Economies in Eastern Bloc. All Eastern Bloc countries prohibit the export and import of their currencies. Therefore, transactions are made either by means of hard currency or through bilateral trade agreements (under which one country agrees to supply another with fixed quantities of goods over an extended period of time in return for other goods, rather than currency).

Organization of Industry—Communist Party Plays Important Role.
Enterprises in Eastern Bloc have specialized product lines generally; well-established, formal and enforced lines of *communication*. The Communist Party acts as a large and powerful labor union unknown to Western counterparts.

Planning—The Five-Year Plan Is Established by Party Congress of the Country. Five-year plan formally is based on proposals from various ministries, and deals with political, social and economic goals of the country. These goals are then filtered down through individual enterprises where management prepares one- and five-year plans as U.S. companies do. These plans are submitted to Party Congress for revision and/or approval.

Selection of Management—Opposite to that in U.S. Primarily, Eastern Bloc managers have engineering degrees. Party membership is almost essential in top management and often in middle management. There is very little mobility between job functions and between organizational entities. In case of promotion, *past* is emphasized more than *potential* in the future (as U.S. bases on potential).

Means of Motivation—Bonuses. Whereas in the U.S., relatively few workers qualify for bonuses, the Eastern Bloc places more emphasis on bonuses because there are few other motivational options. It is based on percentage of total salary in Eastern Bloc.

Western representatives may encounter difficulty in consummating business deals with executives in Eastern Bloc countries. For example, in Eastern Bloc countries:

1. More people are involved in business discussions.
2. Negotiating process is much more formal than in U.S.
3. Eastern businessmen insist upon specificity in order to avoid risk.
4. The governments may be more directly involved.

The potential for increased economic dealings with Eastern Bloc creates need for American businessmen to understand the rigid and highly-enforced organizational patterns of enterprises in the Eastern countries. Basically, a conservative strategy is more wise in accomplishing long-term goals for development.

The adherence to a totalitarian form of government with its impact on business practice varies in the Eastern Bloc countries. Some nations such as Hungary and Yugoslavia differ in their carrying out of Soviet Orthodox Communism and its planned economy. Although Eastern European and other communist states are closed systems, the "party line and loyalty" is greatly influenced by the indigenous culture. In fact, the growth of Euro-communism is demonstrating a break from rigid orthodoxy and a trend toward more independent economic actions. A convergence is underway between the communist and capitalist systems, especially with regard to economics.

Latin America

Diversity in Pan America

This continent of Central and South America is made up of many nations and cultures. The Spanish heritage and language dominates except in Brazil where the Portuguese language and culture reigns supreme. Other European influences (German, Irish, Italian), as well as African influence, are evident across the Americas. Some countries, such as Columbia and Mexico, have strong manifestations of ancient Indian cultures. Now for a few guidelines and cautions. They have been modified from briefing materials prepared by Alison Lanier, president of Overseas Briefing Associates (see Appendix D for description of services).

Social Customs

Shaking Hands. This is the same as in Europe. If there are several people in the room enter with a little bow and then go around to each person and shake their hands. The "hi everybody" is considered rude and brash. "So long, see you tomorrow" is equally poor.

The abraco is the usual greeting but don't use this unless you know the person and your relationship is ready for the abraco.

Pleasantries. Nobody rushes into business. As a foreign businessman take your time and ask about your colleague's family's health, or make a few compliments about the weather. The local sports team is a good beginning point of conversation.

Thank-you notes. Use these often after any courtesy that is shown to you and send promptly. Flowers are often presented as a thank you.

Time. Latin Americans are often late according to North American standards but expect North Americans to be on time. Their offices close about 6 and dinner usually begins after 8. As a guest never arrive exactly on time.

Party Traditions. The old tradition is for women to congregate on one side of the room and for men to be on the other but this is changing.

If you visit a Brazilian's home, cafezinho (demi tasse) will be served you and you should do the same for guests in your home.

For large formal affairs, invitations are written by hand. Flowers are often sent before a large affair. At a smaller party you should take them to your host or hostess.

Women. South American countries are conservative for the most part. It wasn't long ago that women did not go out without a chaperone. Visiting females should be careful not to be noisy or conspicuous in any way and drink only light drinks.

As a foreigner be prepared for Latin men to flirt with all wives, but men should be careful not to flatter or flirt with a South American wife. Also be aware that a Latin may have a public wife (legal) and a private wife (mistress).

Privacy. There are closed doors, fences and high walls around their home. Wait, knock, and wait to be invited in. Don't drop in on neighbors. This is not a custom.

What About Questions? North Americans begin getting to know people by asking a lot of questions. However, it is safer to talk about local things. Questions are often interpreted as prying.

Space. Latin speaking distance is closer than North American speaking distance. They may also break our "bubble" without saying "excuse me." Instead of handshakes men often embrace.

Class and Status. People may not be served on a first come, first served basis. Their place in society may determine the order of preference.

Doing Business. The pace in Latin America is traditionally slow especially when negotiations are under way. Decisions are made at the top. Brazilians, for example, do not like quick, infrequent visits. They like relationships that continue. This implies a long term commitment to Brazil.

Deals are never concluded over the telephone, usually not even by letter, but in person.

Don't call anyone by his or her first name unless the person has made it clear they are ready for it. When in doubt, be formal.

Dress conservatively and use calling cards of good quality.

While waiting, learn more about the culture.

Themes In Understanding Latin Americans

Themes are basic orientations which are shared by many or most of the people. They are beginning points.

Personalismo. For the most part, a Latin's concerns are his family, his personal friends, his hobbies, his political party, possibly athletics such as the local bullfight, but transcending all these is his concern for *himself*. So to reach a Latin, relate everything to him in those terms: himself, his family, his town, his country and above all his personal pride. To be successful, everything should be personalized for the male.

Machismo. It means "maleness" and is an attitude that men have towards women. The macho is aggressive and sometimes insensitive and machismo represents power. Machismo is made up of virility, zest for action, daring, competitiveness, and the will to conquer. How is it translated into daily business life? A man must demonstrate forcefulness, self-confidence, visible courage, and leadership with a flourish. The machismo concept is implanted early in childhood and is impressed in both sexes. Yet, the female may actually control the home, children, and husband.

Desires to Get Rich Quick—Fatalism. There is instability in many Latin American economies and as a result there is a boom or bust attitude. Many desire to make it rich by speculation, manipulation or gambling. As a result, businessmen are not as interested in stable growth as U.S. businessmen.

Wagley, in the *Latin American Traditions,* says that for Latin Americans wealth comes and goes—you can be rich today and poor tomorrow and vice versa.

Related to this is the Latin American tendency to let *chance guide their destiny.* Most are convinced that outside forces govern their lives.

They are willing to "accept the inevitable" Don Quixote who followed his quest whether or not it appeared hopeless seems like a foolish man to many Americans. To most Latin Americans he is heroic. He was "bowing to fate," "taking what comes" and "resigned to the inevitable."

Good Manners and Dignity. Latin Americans are much like Europeans in this respect. They are more formal, and more elaborate. They shake hands on meeting and departing. Helping in the home is something a Latin American would not do because such a task would lower their dignity. In Latin America, the work one does is directly related to the social class one is in.

One is born "high" or "low." Latin Americans are by and large stratified societies. Aristocratic values plus late industrialization and strong central governments have combined to create an imbalance in manpower needs of South America and the supply. Seventy percent of South American workers have no industrial skills at all. In the remaining thirty percent there is an over supply of professional and white collar workers and an acute shortage of managers.

In the more advanced Latin American nations, such as Venezuela, all this is changing.

Latin Americans are born with a sense of place but the two class society (very rich and very poor) is giving way to a growing middle class.

Hospitality. Latin Americans are warm, friendly and hospitable. They like to talk, and want to know about a visitor's family and your interests.

Mañana Concept. It means to a Latin American an indefinite future. Here is an example from Liebman: A small bookkeeper will willingly promise to have ready for you something at a particular time. He knows he will not have it ready at that time. Why does he promise? A prominent Mexican psychiatrist offers the following explanation:

1. The promiser may die before the time promised and thus be relieved of the obligation.
2. The recipient of the promise may die and thus not require fulfillment of the promise.
3. The customer may renege on the contract and thus end the transaction.
4. Others whose work had priority may cancel their orders and thereby fulfillment may be possible.
5. The promisee may wait to inquire until the day following the day promised for delivery. This allows an extra day. An explanation of sickness or emergency can absolve the delay and a new date can be set.
6. Who knows? A miracle may happen and the work can be completed.

Meanwhile, you are happy. This is important. To make people happy is to exercise power.

Authoritarianism. There are signs of respect in both tone of voice and manner that denote grades of inferiority and superiority in a hierarchical society. It is present in the rich who believe that the poor are poor and that the rich are rich because God ordained it that way.

The *caudillo*, owner-manager, is master in his own domain. He has power and authority, and believes that the poor want a strongman who can give orders. The caudillo will jump when someone stronger pulls his string.

The *patron* is the man of power or wealth who sustains loyalty from those of lesser status. He can be the employer, the politico, the landowner and in other cases the money lender or merchant. Decisions are therefore difficult. They have to be made by the one in authority, and the Catholic priest or bishop often had a role in this in the past.

Authoritarianism does not allow for questioning. The patron knows everything and is all powerful. To play these roles, one has to be respectful in a subservient position.

Latin America is going through a social revolution in which agricultural and traditional societies are giving way to modern industrial nations. The impact of Roman Catholicism is strong in the Latin cultures but lessening as a force in the daily lives of people especially in the urban areas.

Further insight into the Latin American mentality is provided in the case study in Chapter 15 on Puerto Rico.

Conclusion

Cultures and business practices change. The "hints" provided in this chapter were meant to be helpful to the multinational manager without falling into the trap of making too many overgeneralizations. Generalizations need to be checked out for their validity in specific times and places with specific individuals within a given cultural region. The clues shared here are but a first step in building a personal business intelligence file about the countries in which one must function effectively.

References

Africa

Abraham, W.E., *The Mind of Africa.* Chicago: The University of Chicago Press, 1966.

Arnold, Guy, *Modern Nigeria.* London: Longman Group Limited, 1977.

Ayisi, Eric O, *An Introduction to the Study of African Culture.* Heinemann Educational Books, 1972.

Gutkind, Peter, *The Passing of Tribal Man in Africa.* Leiden: E.J. Brill Co., 1970.

Hartwig, G., *The African Sketches.* Denver, Colo.: Intercultural Associates/C.R.E., 1978.

Nwachudu, Levi A., "Nigeria's Uncertain Future." *Current History,* November, 1976.

Prospects for Business in Developing Africa. Geneva: A Business International Research Report, 1970.

Europe

Berger, Suzanne, *The French Political System.* New York: Random House, 1974.

Focus on Europe Series. Denver, Colo.: C.R.E., 1970-77.

Grosset, Serge, *Management: European and American Styles.* Belmont, California: Wadsworth Publishing Company, 1970.

Heller, Robert and Norris Willatt. *The European Revenge.* New York: Charles Schribner's Sons, 1972.

Kuhne, Robert J., "Co-Determination: A Statutory Re-Structuring of the Organization." *Columbia Journal of World Business,* Summer, 1976.

Safran, William, *The French Polity.* New York: David McKay Company, Inc., 1977.

Latin America

Davis, Stanley M. and Louis W. Goodman, *Workers and Managers in Latin America.* Lexington, Massachusetts: D.C. Heath and Company, 1972.
Glab, E. (ed.), *Latin America Culture Series.* Austin, Texas: University of Texas Press, 1977.
Gordon, Raymond L., *Living in Latin America: A Case Study in Cross-Cultural Communication.* Skokie, Illinois: National Textbook Company, 1976.
Lanier, Alison, *Your Manager Abroad: How Welcome? How Prepared?* New York: Amacom, 1975.
————, *Update Brazil.* New York: Overseas Briefing Associates, 1978.
Mayers, Marvin K., *A Look at Latin American Lifestyles.* Dallas, Texas: SIL Museum of Anthropology, 1976.
Nida, Eugene A., *Understanding Latin Americans.* South Pasadena, California: The William Carey Library, 1974.
Theberge, James D. and Roger W. Fontaine, *Latin America: Struggle for Progress.* Lexington, Massachusetts: The Third Century Corporation, Lexington Books, 1977.
Tyler, V. Lynn, *People of Brazil.* Provo, Utah: Language and Intercultural Research Center, 1977.

Middle East

Amirsadeghi, H. (ed.), *Twentieth Century Iran.* New York: Holmes and Meier, 1977.
Antoun, J., *The Arab World: Focus on Diversity.* New Jersey: Prentice-Hall, 1977.
Kilner, P. and J. Wallace, *The Gulf Handbook 1976-77.* Garrett Park, Maryland: Garrett Park Press, 1976.
Lee, E., *The American in Saudi Arabia.* Denver, Colorado: C.R.E., 1977.
Nyrop, Richard F. et al., *Area Handbook for Saudi Arabia.* Washington, D.C.: U.S. Government Printing Office, 1977.
Shilling, N., *Bakra Insha Allah! Business, Living, and Travel in the Arab World.* New York: Inter-Crescent Publishing Co., 1978.

(For those in international consulting, helpful guidance can be obtained from *Uses of Consultants by the World Bank and its Borrowers* available from the World Bank, Staff Development Office, 1818 H Street, N.W., Washington, D.C. 20433, U.S.A.)

14
American Macro- and Microcultures

The United States is, in many ways, a nation of minorities. There is tea from China, canned salsifis from Belgium, taco pastry from Mexico, Kikkoman sauce from Japan, and Polish, Italian, and German sausages. People from almost every racial origin can choose among their multifarious goods.

> "Kathy, I'm lost," I said,
> Though I knew she was sleeping.
> "I'm empty and aching and
> I don't know why."
> Counting the cars
> on the New Jersey Turnpike.
> They've all come
> To look for America.
>
> *Paul Simon*

What is America? Is there a mainstream culture shared by the "average" American? Did the melting pot theory work in practice? Is the United States a pluralistic society? Is it a multicultural society? What is America?

This chapter assumes that there is a mainstream culture (macroculture) and many minority groups (microcultures) functioning either within or on the periphery of the macroculture.

Chapter 6 discussed some of the aspects of U.S. business culture and their implications for business and international operations. The following list, taken from Stewart and others, is a summary of what can be called U.S. mainstream cultural assumptions and values. The main categories are the mode of activity, social relationships, motivation, the perception of the world, and the perception of self.

I. Definition of Activity
   1. How do people approach activity?
     • concern with "doing," progress, change external environment
     • optimistic, striving
   2. What is the desirable pace of life?
     • fast, busy
     • driving
   3. How important are goals in planning?
     • stress means, procedures, techniques
   4. What are important goals in life?
     • material goals
     • comfort and absence of pain
     • activity
   5. Where does responsibility for decisions lie?
     • responsibility lies with each individual
   6. At what level do people live?
     • operational, goals evaluated in terms of consequence
   7. On what basis do people evaluate?
     • utility (Does it work?)
   8. Who should make decisions?
     • the people affected
   9. What is the nature of problem-solving?
     • planning behavior
     • anticipates consequences
  10. What is the nature of learning?
     • learner is active (student-centered learning)

II. Definition of Social Relations
   1. How are roles defined?
     • attained
     • loosely
     • generally
   2. How do people relate to others whose status is different?
     • stress equality
     • minimize differences
     • stress informality and spontaneity
   3. How are sex roles defined?
     • similar, overlapping
     • sex equality
     • friends of both sexes
     • less legitimized
   4. What are members' rights and duties in a group?
     • assumes limited liability
     • joins group to seek own goals
     • active members can influence group

238 Managing Cultural Differences

    5. How do people judge others?
- specific abilities of interests
- task-centered
- fragmentary involvement

    6. What is the meaning of friendship?
- social friendship (short commitment, friends shared)

    7. What is the nature of social reciprocity?
- real only
- nonbinding (Dutch treat)
- equal (Dutch treat)

    8. How do people regard friendly aggression in social interaction?
- acceptable, interesting, fun

III. Motivation
    1. What is motivating force?
- achievement

    2. How is person-person competition evaluated?
- as constructive, healthy

IV. Perception of the World (World View)
    1. What is the (natural) World like?
- physical
- mechanical

    2. How does the world operate?
- in a rational, learnable, controllable manner
- chance and probability

    3. What is the nature of man?
- apart from nature or from any hierarchy
- impermanent, not fixed, changeable

    4. What are the relationships between man and nature?
- good is unlimited
- man should modify nature for his ends
- good health and material comforts expected and desired

    5. What is the nature of truth? goodness?
- tentative (working-type)
- relative to circumstances
- experience analyzed in separate components dichotomies

    6. How is time defined? Valued?
- future (anticipation)
- precise units
- limited resource
- lineal

    7. What is the nature of property?
- private ownership important as extension of self

V. Perception of the Self and the Individual
  1. In what sort of terms is self defined?
     - diffuse, changing terms
     - flexible behavior
  2. Where does a person's identity seem to be?
     - within the self (achievement)
  3. Nature of the individual
     - separate aspects (intent, thought, act, biographical background)
  4. On whom should a person place reliance?
     - self
     - impersonal organizations
  5. What kind of person is valued and respected?
       What qualities?
     - youthful (vigorous)
  6. What is the basis of social control?
     - persuasion, appeal to the individual
     - guilt

The dominant mode of activity in mainstream American society is "doing." Americans have a preoccupation with time, organization, and the utilization of resources so that everything has to have a purpose that is measurable. "Getting things done" is an American characteristic. In our social relationships we assume that everyone is equal and this removes the need for elaborate forms of social address. Our social relationships are characterized by informality and social reciprocities are much less clearly defined. Mainstream Americans are motivated by achievements and accomplishments. Our identity and, to a certain extent, our self-worth is measured by what we achieve. We also assume that the world is material rather than spiritual and man's purpose is to overcome or conquer the forces of nature. Mainstream Americans also see themselves as individual and unique. Is this an accurate description of ourselves? Like most descriptions it is probably partially accurate.

In attempting to understand ourselves, it is useful to listen to and hear what aspects of our life and culture are puzzling to other people. John Fieg and Lenore Yaffee in their book, *Adjusting to the U.S.A.*, suggest the following areas of concern for foreign visitors to the United States. They are presented to serve as a further reflection on aspects of mainstream U.S. culture.

Pace of Life. Visitors from a variety of African, Asian, and Latin American countries are amazed and often somewhat distressed at the rapid pace of American life and the accompanying emphasis on punctuality and efficiency.

Friendship. Because Americans are generally gregarious on first meeting someone, visitors often mistake this strong "come-on" for the beginning of a deep reciprocal friendship. This is because in many societies there is much more initial reserve in interpersonal relations, particularly with strangers. For many visitors, the American comes on too strong too soon and then fails to follow up with the implicitly promised friendship.

Service and Egalitarianism. The sense of egalitarianism on the part of American waiters, taxi drivers, bellboys, etc., causes them to perform their services in a brusque, businesslike manner, without the cordial (and from the American point of view, fawning) manner that many visitors are accustomed to at home. The visitor often compounds his problem by giving what the American service person perceives as an order from on high, thereby causing the service to become even more surly.

Emotional Expressiveness. Americans seem to stand near the center of an emotional spectrum that extends out to embrace the effervescent Latins at one extreme and the cooly subdued Southeast Asians at the other. While we appear unemotional and cold to the Latins, we may appear hyperbolic and impulsive to the Asians.

Individualism, Freedom, and Privacy. Some visitors are deeply impressed by the individual freedom, particularly in the political arena, that an American enjoys. Others are appalled, however, by what they sometimes call "too much freedom" in terms of excessive individualism, and cite lack of gun control laws as an example of what they mean.

Self-reliance and the Nuclear Family. Visitors have ambivalent feelings about the self-reliant American nuclear family. Some are impressed by the males' handling of household chores and the children's independent assertiveness. Others see the American pattern as abrasive, somewhat chaotic, and lacking the strong extended family supports to which they are accustomed.

Informality and Morality. Because many visitors come from societies that stress neat, formal, and (by American standards) conservative clothing styles, they are sometimes shocked by what they view as Americans' slovenly way of dressing. Often they tend to equate this informality with immorality, and they are persuaded that America is on the way to moral ruin when they observe provocative clothing styles and public displays of affection.

Crime. Reports have reached the four corners of the world about the high crime rate in American cities. Many new arrivals are thus highly concerned for their personal safety, although some are surprised and somewhat encouraged to find that the violence level is not as high as they had anticipated. We have tried to allay the fears of the visitors and at the same time to caution them about the very real danger of crime—to strike in their minds some kind of balance between incapacitating dread and complete abandon.

Tipping, Taxes, and "Sales". To many visitors, tipping appears to be giving something extra for what the waiter is already paid to do, and the failure to include the sales tax in the stated price of an article is sometimes construed as a trap for the unwary. They also want to know how they can distinguish a genuine "sale" from a phony.

Race Relations. Comments from international visitors concerning the current racial situation in the U.S. mirror the confused, conflicting views expressed by Americans. Sharp attacks on lingering racial discrimination are mingled with expressions of surprise that race relations is not as big a problem as some visitors had been led to believe.

Teacher-student Relations. Coming from cultures where the teacher is near the top of the social hierarchy, many visitors are stunned by the slouching, "disrespectful" demeanor of the students and the easy, often flippant, interchange between the teacher and students in the U.S. Many, however, come to appreciate the freedom of expression that exists in American schools.

Lack of Knowledge about Their Countries. Particularly disheartening to many visitors is the American's lack of knowledge of and interest in their countries and cultures. This attitude has developed because of our longstanding geographical isolation coupled with the immigrant experience, in which to become a full-fledged member of the "New World" one had to cast aside the customs and culture of the homeland.

Philip Slater has suggested in *The Pursuit of Loneliness* that three human desires are profoundly frustrated by the American culture:

1. The desire for *community*—the wish to live in trust and fraternal cooperation with one's fellows in a total and visible collective entity.
2. The desire for *engagement*—the wish to come directly to grips with social and interpersonal problems and to confront on equal terms an environment that is not composed of ego-extensions.
3. The desire for *dependence*—the wish to share responsibility for the control of one's impulses and the direction of one's life.

Slater also states that it is not the individual American who is struggling against society in attempting to meet these desires but that Americans participate "eagerly in producing the frustrations we endure." Slater is referring to mainstream Americans. In some microcultures in the U.S., these frustrated human desires in the mainstream culture are strongly present.

Microcultures

Walter Lippman introduced the term "stereotype" in his book on public opinion over 50 years ago. He used the word in the sense of a rigid and standardized picture that people have of others. Consider the following microcultures in the United States:

1. Appalachians
2. American Indians
3. Blacks
4. Chicanos

Now ask yourself the following questions about each of these groups:

1. What is their communication style (nonverbal as well as verbal)?
2. What clothing do they wear at work?
3. What kind of people are they?
4. What are their work habits and attitudes?
5. What is their sense of time?
6. What kinds of food do they enjoy?
7. What other customs, traditions or behaviors are you aware of?

The chances are you were able to respond to each of these questions to a certain extent. You had ideas of each of these cultures even though you may never have met anyone from that cultural group. In many ways you would probably conclude they are different from mainstream Americans.

In order to develop authentic and effective relationships with persons from these cultures, it is important to not only accept and overlook, so to speak, racial differences but to be aware of, fully accept, value, and appreciate these differences. The following brief descriptions are intended to be starting points in this challenge.

Other cultures or groups of people living in the United States such as Chinese Americans, Japanese Americans, Jews, as well as persons who are handicapped and senior citizens, to name but a few, could also be considered. Each of these groups has aspects of their lives and priorities or values that differ in part from mainstream America. To work effectively with these peoples, it is necessary to be aware of and respect differences in all areas.

The material presented for the four cultures does not follow a particular format. Rather, certain themes or aspects of their cultures are indicated in a summary fashion.

Appalachians

The Appalachian Mountains are not a high range but they are steep and rugged. The first group of people to come to Appalachia were the English who were expelled from England and came to the New World with little or no farming experience. They were stubborn, opinionated, and puritanical in their religious beliefs. They established a culture that was based not on law and authority but on equal status of all and the authority of the individual. No hierarchy or authority was allowed to form in this society. The poor Appalachians are far removed from the cultural mainstream of American life. Appalachian families grew to be self-sufficient in trying to make a living in a very difficult environment. Appalachian children were born into homes where making a living from the hard environment was the role of the father and the mother was to make the home.

Their goals for their children are not what they want for their children but what *they do not want* for their children.

Appalachians as a people are extremely conservative. They have a resistance to and suspicion of change. The future is not seen as bright. The *past*, in fact, was better in the mountains.

People from the mountains are person oriented. They want to be liked and accepted by their reference group. They view business and government, with their impersonal attitudes, as evil and threatening. Time schedules are of little concern and they do things their own way.

Once the mining companies employed many Appalachians, but many families were embittered because of lost lands and refused to work. This forced the mining companies to import labor, which resulted in camps, company stores, and made the people totally dependent on them. Then the mines ceased to be profitable. Employment opportunities rapidly declined.

The people could not fall back on agriculture as the land was largely not arable, but they did not want to leave the hills. So, even without work many remained. The people have become poorer and with the advent of strip mining, the plight of the Appalachians became almost hopeless.

The challenge for mainstream Americans is to understand the history and values of the Appalachians and imaginatively work with them in a cooperative exchange.

American Indians

There are approximately 600,000 American Indians in the U.S. of whom over half are on reservations. The average annual income is below poverty level and their unemployment rate is the highest in the country.

When America was discovered, there were probably less than one million Indians living in what is now the U.S. These Indians were scattered and their tribal organizations were unrelated. Columbus wrote of the Indians, "They are a loving people. . . . They love their neighbors as themselves, and their speech is the sweetest and gentlest in the world." Many early colonists intermarried with Indians and this was motivated largely by social and cultural factors. For example, an Indian wife was an asset to a fur trader in teaching him the language and customs of the tribe from which he bought furs. In early New England, however, Indian women had little use in the trading and farming communities and intermarriage was rare.

The U.S. government, which came into existence with the adoption of the Constitution, began its relationship with Indians by considering the various tribes as national entities and negotiated with them for land. An imperialist relationship with the Indians was thus begun. One of the early debates in the Colorado legislature was concerning bounties for the "destruction of Indians and skunks." The remark of a U.S. general in 1869, "The only good Indians I ever saw were dead," is an expression known to most Americans and conveys an implicit attitude about the conflict.

One of the negative images that many have of American Indians is that they are a savage group of hostile persons who are uncivilized. In books describing Indian and white relationships, when Indians killed settlers, it was a "massacre," but the settlers did not massacre, they only "fought" or "battled" the Indians. When Americans think of colonialism, it generally means things like the British in India but not Americans in Georgia.

Who is the Indian? An Indian is an individual whose origins can be found in the indigenous peoples of America. What are some cultural differences between Indian culture and the mainstream American culture? Faherty in the *American Indian* points out three fundamental differences, but there are many.

In the mainstream culture, time is to be "used, saved, and spent." People are paid for their time. Indians generally view time as a continuum that is related to the rising and setting of the sun and to the changes in seasons.

In the mainstream culture, decision-making is based on authority. Some people have authority to make decisions and others do not. Authority in Indian cultures is more horizontal than vertical because of the necessity of reaching unanimity on a decision before any action will be taken.

Most Americans live pretty much for the future. We ask our children what they want to be when they grow up. In contrast, Indian children are not asked the same question, because they already are—they are children and they do not have to wait to be.

Understanding the Indian way of life provides us with a challenge and an opportunity. We can learn to develop skills and to work with Indians without destroying their dignity and allow them to change at their own pace.

Black Americans

Much research has been conducted on the verbal and nonverbal communication patterns, values and many aspects of black American life and culture. It has been demonstrated that many blacks speak a dialect of English that differs from many other dialects of English. The prides or important aspects of their lives also differ in many respects from the majority white culture and from other groups in the United States. Andrea L. Rich in her book, *Interracial Communication*, portrays many of the dynamics and factors involved in interaction situations between blacks and whites. Her book presents a framework to analyze the factors that are present when black Americans and white Americans interact and communicate with one another.

In an attempt to develop authentic relationships between blacks and whites, Bertam Lee and Warren Schmidt, in *"Toward More Authentic Interpersonal Relations Between Blacks and Whites,"* *(Training Magazine,* Vol. 13, No. 4), list assumptions and behaviors that blacks and whites make about each other that hinder or facilitate authentic relations.

Assumptions that *Block* Authentic Relations

Assumptions Whites Make:

—Color is unimportant in interpersonal relations.
—Blacks will always welcome and appreciate inclusion in white society.
—Open recognition of color may embarrass blacks.
—Blacks are trying to use whites.
—Blacks can be stereotyped.
—White society is superior to black society.
—"Liberal" whites are free of racism.
—All blacks are alike in their attitudes and behavior.
—Blacks are oversensitive.
—Blacks must be controlled.

Assumptions Blacks Make:

—All whites are alike.
—There are no "soul brothers" among whites.
—Honkies have all the power.
—Whites are always trying to use blacks.
—Whites are united in their attitude toward blacks.
—All whites are racists.
—Whites are not really trying to understand the situation of the blacks.
—Whitey's got to deal on black terms.
—Silence is the sign of hostility.
—Whites cannot and will not change except by force.
—The only way to gain attention is through confrontation.
—All whites are deceptive.
—All whites will let you down in the "crunch."

Assumptions that *Facilitate* Authentic Relations

Assumptions Whites Make:

—People count as individuals.
—Blacks are human, with individual feelings, aspirations, and attitudes.
—Blacks have a heritage of which they are proud.
—Interdependence is needed between whites and blacks.
—Blacks are angry.

Assumptions Blacks Make:

—Openness is healthy.
—Interdependence is needed between blacks and whites.
—People count as individuals.
—Negotiation and collaboration are possible strategies.
—Whites are human beings and, whether they should or not, do have their own hang-ups.

Assumptions (Cont'd.) that *Facilitate* Authentic Relations

Assumptions Whites Make:

—Whites cannot fully understand what it means to be black.
—Whiteness/blackness is a real difference but not the basis on on which to determine behavior.
—Most blacks can handle whites' authentic behavior and feelings.
—Blacks want a responsible society.
—Blacks are capable of managerial maturity.
—I may be part of the problem.

Assumptions Blacks Make:

—Some whites can help and "do their own thing."
—Some whites have "soul."

Behaviors that *Block* Authentic Relations

Behaviors of Whites:

—Interruptions.
—Condescending behavior.
—Offering help where not needed or wanted.
—Avoidance of contact (eye-to-eye and physical).
—Verbal focus on black behavior rather than white behavior.
—Insisting on playing games according to white rules.
—Showing annoyance at black behavior that differs from their own.
—Expressions of too-easy acceptance and friendship.
—Talking about, rather than to, blacks who are present.

Behaviors of Blacks:

—Confrontation too early and too harshly.
—Rejection of honest expressions of acceptance and friendship.
—Pushing whites into such a defensive posture that learning and reexamination is impossible.
—Failure to keep a commitment and then offering no explanation.
—"In group" joking, laughing at whites in black culture language.
—Giving answers blacks think whites want to hear.
—Using confrontation as the primary relationship style.
—Isolationism.

Behaviors that *Facilitate* Authentic Relations

Behaviors of Whites:

—Directness and openness in expressing feelings.
—Assisting other white brothers to understand and confront feelings.
—Supporting self-initiated moves of black people.

Behaviors of Blacks:

—Showing interest in understanding white's point of view.
—Acknowledging that there are some committed whites.
—Acting as if "we have some power," and don't need to prove it.

Behaviors (Cont'd.) that *Facilitate* **Authentic Relations**

Behaviors of Whites:

—Listening without interrupting.
—Demonstration of interest in learning about black perceptions, culture, etc.
—Staying with and working through
 difficult confrontations.
—Taking a risk (e.g., being first
 to confront the differences).
—Assuming responsibility for examining one's motives.

Behaviors of Blacks:

—Allowing whites to experience
 unaware areas of racism.
—Openness.
—Expression of real feelings.
—Dealing with whites where they
 are.
—Meeting whites half-way.
—Treating whites on one-to-one basis.
—Telling it like it is.
—Realistic goal-sharing.
—Showing pride in their heritage.

It is important for us to recognize the attitudes and assumptions we make of other groups, in this case, assumptions whites and blacks make of each other. These assumptions usually are unconscious and without our awareness. The importance of our behavior—particularly nonverbal behavior that blacks and whites demonstrate to each other—is apparent in the adage: "Your actions speak so loudly, I can hardly hear what you say."

Chicanos

In Chapter 15, a case study containing many aspects and cultural characteristics of the Latin American experience is presented. The culture of the Chicano—persons with Mexican heritage yet American—is different in part and the following brief sketch is another beginning point in our search for understanding some of the peoples with whom we live and work.

The Chicano presence permeates the Southwest. In the U.S., there are approximately 7.2 million Chicanos who are concentrated in Arizona, California, Colorado, New Mexico, and Texas. In Texas, one of four persons is Chicano and in California one in five. By the year 2000, it is estimated that the Hispanic-American population will become the largest U.S. minority.

For those in business who wish to understand "La Raza"—literally "The People" of Mexican heritage living in the United States—it might be helpful to learn more about the Mexican culture. Below is a description of American and Mexican managers in contrasting positions. The Chicano manager is a mixture of both traditions. The excerpt is by Dr. Ward M. Kelly and appeared in *International Business Magazine* (reprinted in *The Bridge,* Winter 1978):

> One of the most noticeable American traits is individuality. But despite the oft-heard value he places on independence of mind and

speech, he is paradoxically oriented to the group—he is a team worker. This observation must strike a foreign observer as being incompatible; but Americans are pragmatic, at least to the extent that they place a considerable value on workability, even at the expense of individual expression. Team players are allowed to be individuals, but certainly not at the expense of the team meeting its goals.

Mexican managers, by contrast, have nothing in their cultural baggage which promotes team play. While the American tends to balance his need for individual expression against the needs of the team, the Mexican usually does not show the same balance. There is a strong need to be individualistic in the Mexican manager, a need which is not diminished by the team's needs for unanimity of action. It is prompted by his attitude toward the delegation of authority. If the Mexican manager delegates, he allows his subordinates to relegate him to a group limbo by restricting his opportunity to act as a singular entity. Hence, authority is tightly gripped, lest the boundaries to exercise his authority and thereby his individuality are circumscribed by his underlings.

The word "Chicano" is a relatively new term and is more accepted by young Mexican-Americans than by their elders who often reject the word and associate it with radicals. There is much diversity in the Mexican-American community. Many are highly educated and found in all businesses, professions and governmental posts throughout the U.S. Others work in the agricultural, assembly, food packaging and other industries along the Mexican/U.S. border. Some Chicanos are among America's lowest paid workers, and nearly 20% live below the poverty level. In 1979, the median family income for Mexican-Americans was $11,421 compared to $16,284 for non-Mexican-Americans.

The following excerpt from Richard Reeves' *Esquire* article (reprinted in *The Bridge,* Spring 1979) provides insight into these unique Americans and their thinking/problems:

Mexico has oil, and we need it; we have Chicanos, and they're tired of being pushed around. The combination is volatile. It's as if millions of angry Saudi Americans were clustered in, say, Georgia and the Carolinas, and their rich home country, Saudi Arabia, was where Florida is. "We all understand," said Ms. Martinez, "that Washington will finally have to listen to us because of Mexico."

Every Chicano I talked with felt threatened by real and imagined government drives against illegal aliens, the "wet-back," expulsions that seem to start every time the United States is in or near a recession. Félix Gutiérrez, a college professor whose family has been in California since 1812, says sometimes his mother carries her naturalization papers with her and his father-in-law carries pictures of his sons in World War II army uniforms—to prove that they are Americans.

... By any definition, they are indeed. Every one of the more than twenty Chicanos I interviewed in a week said at some point in our conversation, "Look, I'm an American"—their folks got here long before most of ours. But they did not want to be assimilated Americans—like Anglos. They wanted to keep their ways *Mexicano,* particularly their sense of family and their fierce self-destructive pride. Certainly none of us will live to see them assimilated— Chicanos almost always marry Chicanas, and their heritage, culture, and language are constantly replenished and enriched by the human flow across the border. You have to imagine what the northeastern states would be like if Italy were where Maryland is.

Because Mexico literally touches Mexican America, the bonds between the two related peoples and their countries are tangled beyond belief—perhaps, more importantly, beyond breaking. Americans will need that oil to maintain their standard of living. Mexicans need jobs: The safety valve of immigration to the north conceivably holds the country back from the brink of the governmental chaos and bloodshed that infects the rest of Latin America. Many *Norte Americanos* who have never seen a Chicano will find awareness coming with their heating oil and gasoline in a few years.

In this section we will let the chicano tell us about himself. (taken from *Voices of Aztlan,* edited by Dorothy E. Harth and Lewis M. Baldwin).

Aztec Mother

Leonardo Elias

Thank you beautiful bronze mother, for being
yourself all this time. From the conquest of Mexico,
to the present day, you are still the beautiful bronze
afterglow in my heart.
You have suffered through wars and now you are
suffering from discrimination and prejudice. I know
my beautiful bronze mother, that you will persist to
find a way to peace and happiness for your children.
The road to freedom is rough; my heart hungers with
the cries of love for all the Raza to come together
as one.
With these last words I ask you beautiful Aztec
mother, kiss my lips with death or touch my heart
with peace. . . .

when raza?

Alurista

when raza?
when . . .
            yesterday's gone

and
    mañana
mañana doesn't come*
    for he who waits
no morrow
    only for he who is now
to whom when equals now
he will see a morrow
mañana la Raza
    la gente que espera
no verá mañana
our tomorrow es hoy
    ahorita
que VIVA LA RAZA
    mi gente†
our people to freedom
    when?
now, ahorita define tu mañana hoy‡

---

*   tomorrow
     tomorrow doesn't come
†   tomorrow La Raza
     the people who wait
     will not see tomorrow
     our tomorrow is today
     right now
     long live La Raza
     my people
‡   now, right now define your tomorrow today

Chicanos now seem even more determined to enter mainstream America without losing their identity expressed in their culture and language. Theirs is an attempt to synthesize two cultures. The potential is present and there seems to be the determination.

Implications

The time has come to replace rhetoric with reality. The United States is a multicultural community. To live and work together in the social and business community, all can develop more authentic relationships if we understand and value these differences and see them as sources of mutual learning and enrichment.

In the book, *Without Bias: A Guidebook for Nondiscriminatory Communication*, the authors suggest that qualifiers in our language reinforce racial and ethnic stereotypes that in turn negatively affect our communication and relationships. The following examples were cited:

Does this sentence . . .	contain this hidden stereotype?
A well-groomed black student, John Jones, works as a part-time clerk.	Blacks are poorly groomed.
Bob Herendez, an exceptionally energetic and conscientious worker . . .	Chicanos are lazy, unmotivated.
The articulate black professor . . .	Blacks lack intelligence, verbal skills.
No retiring, quiet job for her. Betty Wong has chosen a dynamic career as supervisor of . . .	Asians are shy, docile (also female nonassertive stereotype).
Jose Rodriguez, a steady and even-tempered worker . . .	Mexicans are volatile, unpredictable.

If this identification is inappropriate . . .	is this phrasing any different?
Jerry Brown, noted white California governor . . .	Julian Bond, noted black Georgia legislator . . .
Byron White, Supreme Court justice and one of eight whites to sit on the high court . . .	Thurgood Marshall, Supreme Court justice and the only black to sit on the high court . . .

Conclusion

There are so many minority groups within the American majority that it is impossible to review them all in this chapter. Thus, four microcultures were described in limited fashion, primarily to illustrate the diversity of American culture. Although it is difficult to detail a "typical" American, the opening section provided insight into general characteristics of the macroculture.

References

Bahr, H.M., *Skid Row: An Introduction to Disaffiliation.* New York: Oxford University Press, 1973.

Bender, David L., *American Values.* Anoka, Minnesota: Greenhaven Press, 1975.

Caudill, Harry M., *Night Comes to the Cumberlands.* Atlantic: Little Brown, 1962.

Faherty, Robert L., The American Indian in L. Samovar L. and Porter R. (ed.), *Intercultural Communication: A Reader.* Belmont, CA: Wadsworth Publishing, 1976.

Fieg, John P. and Lenore C. Yaffee, *Adjusting to the U.S.A.: Orientation for International Students.* Washington, D.C.: Washington International Center of Meridian House International, 1977.

Harth, Dorothy E. and Lewis M. Baldwin, (eds.), *Voices of Aztlan.* New York, New York, New American Library, Inc. 1974.

Klassen, Frank H. and Donna M. Gollnick, (eds.), *Pluralism and the American Teacher.* American Association of Colleges for Teacher Education, 1977.

Lippman, Walter, *Public Opinion.* New York: The MacMillian Company, 1961. (Originally published in 1922.)

Pickens, Judy E., P. Rao and L. Roberts, (eds.), *Without Bias: A Guidebook for Nondiscriminatory Communication.* San Francisco, CA: International Association of Business Communications, 1977.

Rich, Andrea L., *Interracial Communication.* New York: Harper & Row, Publishers, 1974.

Rodgers, Harrell R., Jr. (ed.), *Racism and Inequality.* San Francisco: W. H. Freeman and Company, 1975.

Samovar, Larry A. and Richard E. Porter, *Intercultural Communication: A Reader.* Belmont, CA: Wadsworth Publishing Company, Inc., 1976.

Schwarzweller, H.K., et al, *Mountain Families in Transition.* Penn. State University Press, 1971.

Simmer, E., *Pain and Promise: The Chicano Today.* New York: Mentor Books, 1972.

Slater, Philip, *The Pursuit of Loneliness.* Boston, Mass.: Beacon Press, 1970.

Stewart, Edward C., Jack Danielian, and Robert Foster, *Simulating Intercultural Communication Through Role-Playing.* Alexandria, Va: Humrro, 1969.

15
Case Studies
in American Areas

Those Diverse Americans

Technically, should they even be called "Americans"? The citizens who live in the United States and its territories lay claim to this nomenclature, but citizens of Canada, and Central and South America could also call themselves after the Italian explorer, Amerigo Vespucci, who bestowed his name on the New World. The aboriginal natives who have most right to the term were mistakenly called "Indians" by Christopher Columbus when he was sidetracked in his search for a passage to India. For the sake of convenience, we will use the designation American here when considering that polyglot of peoples who live within the boundaries of the U.S. and its affiliated lands. The previous chapter provided some insight into the macro- and microcultures of this complex people.

Most of these people live in the center of the North American continent, from Pacific to Atlantic Oceans. In the colonial periods, the biggest cultural inputs came from the settlers of England, Spain, and France. Progressively, this "land of immigrants" experienced further cultural influx of future citizens who came reluctantly first as slaves from Africa, or as refugees from economic, social, religious, or political discrimination in Europe and, later, Asia. In contemporary American society, they make up such national/ethnic blocks as Black Americans, Irish Americans, German Americans, Polish Americans, Italian Americans, Chinese Americans and a legion of cultural mixes, to which there are continuously new additions. For example, in the twentieth century, there have been substantial migrations to the United States of Japanese, Vietnamese, Arabs, Iranians, and Mexicans. In this laboratory of intercultural relations, the cultural contributions come from every country on the globe.

And what of the future of this multicultural society? Some predict that in this land of many languages dominated by the American version of English, the people may be bilingual by the year 2000, because of the great influx of Spanish speaking cultures such as Mexican and Puerto Rican. The governor of the "state of the future," California, envisions that area as on the edge of the Pacific economy and culture. In a speech, Governor Jerry Brown observed:

> Just as Venice, Rome, Greece, and Egypt in centuries past have been the leaders of civilization and culture, power is shifting toward this part of the world. The Pacific basin is emerging as a center where the power and the adventure of the remainder of this century will be. It can be seen in the rapid emergence of Mexico and South America, as well as Japan and China.

The next two case studies will consider intracultural relations in terms of a special type of American, normally overlooked when analyzing this very pluralistic culture. The first will center upon two organizational microcultures, the American university and a government agency. The second will view business relations between stateside Americans and those in their commonwealth. Questions have been posed for the reader at the end of each study of "typical" American life—or should we say atypical?

Encountering Those Other Americans

Case Study 1: Mixed Americans at University International

Scenario
- The troubled dean on campus
- The disturbed customs official
- The questions to be resolved

The Troubled Dean on Campus

Dr. Joseph Polito, dean of students at University International, did not expect to open up a "can of worms" when he sponsored the special forum to facilitate the adjustment of new students to their San Diego campus. The city had become quite a cosmopolitan community since it grew beyond its border and Navy-town days. Because of the many transfers of Americans from the University's Mexico City and Hawaii campuses, he intended to foster their adjustment by this forum for "Very Special Americans." The idea had been simple—representatives of the various American subcultures would tell something about their group, and what challenges and problems they experienced since coming to California.

Thus, Lolita Lipwe from American Samoa told the audience that her homeland consisted of 7 islands, 76 square miles, and a population of 30,000. Her brother, Tali, also pointed out that their home was 2,300 miles from Hawaii, had its capital on Pago Pago, and shared its locale with 9 other islands called Western Samoa. The latter area was independent, and although they shared a common culture and language, it had a much simpler and lower living standard. Both Lipwes were fiercely loyal to the

United States and its system, and remarked, "We are U.S. nationals, carry U.S. passports, and have free movement on the U.S. mainland."

Then Tiser Guerro, another kind of American, told of his native Guam and how they had become Americanized when their island became a major staging area of the U.S. Armed Forces in WWII. A big smile rose on his flat, round, dark tan face, when he said that like all Polynesians, their ancestry included aboriginal peoples, Orientals, Spaniards, and now Americans. He liked California because of its climate and the fact that a large community of Guamanians resided in Los Angeles where he could visit them every weekend.

Manuel Ortez, a Chicano, said that he had been born in "occupied California" and that his forefathers once had a land grant in Rancho Santa Fe nearby. His hobby was Mayan art and history, and he reminded everyone that his people had a flourishing civilization before Cortez landed in 1519. He spoke with vehemence as he described the long struggle of his ancestors to throw off the Spanish and French yoke, only to lose part of their lands to the Republics of California and Texas. Although proud of his heritage and its contributions to the development of the American West, he identified himself now as an American of Mexican extraction.

Loly Gomez said that her father was born in the Philippines when it was still under American control, that he fought in the American Navy all during the occupation of their homeland by the Japanese, and finally retired from the service in San Diego. She was proud of the large Filipino-American community in the city and told how their "Association" conducted folk dances in nearby Balboa Park on Sundays.

After a parade of sharing by these unique Americans, the forum began to cause Dean Polito some trouble when there was near unanimous agreement that they generally had problems when they crossed the border south into Mexico.

The students liked to surf along the coast of Baja California, and congregate on weekends in Ensenada, Mexico. That western port city was only sixty miles south of the campus and Americans were not required a special visa or tourist cards for short visits there. The complaints centered around how they were treated by U.S. Customs officials as they came back and forth through the port of entry at San Ysidro. The Mexican-Americans complained they were treated like migrant workers and asked to show "green" work identification cards.

The Americans from the Trust Territories said the inspectors were nice but made them feel like Mexicans and always demanded a passport. A Filipino-American girl claimed that when she crossed back into the States at the Tecate entry, a male inspector made an insulting remark suggesting she was a prostitute coming over; she had reported the incident. One of the Nisei said she had gotten into trouble when she tried to bring up some relatives from Ensenada to show them the campus. The whole series of incidents prompted Dr. Polito to request an interview with the district director of the U.S. Customs.

The Disturbed Customs Official

Benjamin Fine was upset when he got the dean's telephone call. Now he sat in a large office in the downtown federal building looking out over the harbor and awaiting Dr. Polito's arrival. He had been transferred recently to Southern California after many years of service in the New York District, and he was still undergoing mild cultural shock relative to the California scene and the organization's culture. He now directed one of the busiest ports of entry into the United States. The millions of people who crossed back and forth from San Diego to Tijuana through the San Ysidro gates on the Mexican border were staggering.

His understaffed and overworked personnel were subject to enormous pressures from tourists, drug traffickers, and illegal aliens. The traffic build-up at peak hours and holidays caused monumental back-ups, and the whole inspection and processing system needed to be revised. The traveling public often projected their frustrations on his dedicated employees. He could understand why his tired workers might react negatively to some of these college students. However, to assess the dean's complaints accurately, he had invited Jose Tellez, his director of border operations, to join him. Tellez was a well-educated, widely traveled, experienced customs officer—and a Mexican-American. He should be able to provide real insight into the situation.

"O.K., Joe, you have read of these documented complaints from the University International students and checked it out, what is your opinion? The dean tells me that more than half their student body is made up of foreign students, but there are some problems between them and us because of passports. The problem seems to be with the American students who look like Mexicans."

"Well, Mr. Fine, you should know that already the Hispanic population is 8% in the United States, and growing. So apart from these Pacific Island peoples who are Americans and might be mistaken for Mexicans, there are millions of Mexican-Americans legally in this country. My point is that our staff needs some training in managing cultural differences, so they can be more effective in cross-cultural communications. This goes whether they are interacting with foreigners or with Americans who are of different cultural backgrounds. Your predecessor did a good job pushing language training, especially in Spanish, among our personnel. Now we need to follow up with training in cultural awareness."

"You may be right, Joe, because they get little input on such subjects in their basic training at the Customs Academy. I see another value internally. The workforce in this San Diego district has changed radically in the last fifteen years as I study the records. It has grown from 75 to 400 officers. It used to be white males, usually of an Anglo and military background. Now we have 21% minority and 16% women employees with new emphasis on Equal Employment Opportunity. I know there has been a very small group of hard-core opponents to our Affirmative Action efforts in the district, and they have even opposed minorities being promoted into supervision. Perhaps the time has come for some new organizational norms of behavior on this score, and the training in cultural sensitivity might help."

"Another thing, Chief, that complaint of the Nisei kid is not with our office but with the U.S. Border Patrol. She visited her Japanese-Mexican relatives in Ensenada, and tried to bring them back to visit the campus without the proper papers. That's why the guys on the "Big Green Team" (Border Patrol) stopped them. The public is always mixing us up with the people from Immigration and Naturalization, or the Border Patrol."

Ben Fine mused to himself that if that proposed Border Management Agency ever comes into being and elements of the three federal agencies converge into a new organization, then they all will need professional development in managing cultural differences. His train of thought was interrupted when his secretary buzzed to inform them that the dean had just arrived.

Questions to be Resolved

1. Do you have a stereotype of a "typical" American that excludes consideration of many special microcultures in their society?

2. What are the implications for you in this case for growing pluralism in American society?

3. Certain occupations and professions imply a role responsibility to gain intercultural skills. For example, the authors maintain that Customs officials should be "professional intercultural communicators." In your role, what responsibility do you have?

4. Consider the information obtained in this case relative to regional/ organizational culture. What are the implications of Fine's transfer from East to West? Why would the joining of three federal agencies—organizational cultures—be a challenge?

The next case involves the private sector and raises many issues. There is much specific culture information provided that would be useful to understand "stateside" Americans of Puerto Rican extraction.

Doing Business with the Puerto Ricans

Case Study 2: ¿Que Pasa? The Latin American Influence

Scenario—
- The new policy
- The briefing
- The compadres
- The issues

The New Policy

The Easting Corporation had just made a major corporate decision to give high priority in marketing to Latin America. The new strategy applied to all subsidiaries and envisioned a two-pronged focus. San Diego would become the operational center for a marketing penetration of Mexico and the western countries of South America. Puerto Rico was to become the base for the marketing in Central America and Eastern South America. This new Latino endeavor now was timely because: (1) the national administration was bound to undertake new diplomatic and economic efforts south of the U.S. borders; (2) the energy crunch would facilitate investment and development of natural resources, especially oil and gas, in the Pan American region, particularly by the U.S., United Kingdom, Germany, and Japan; (3) the ever-expanding population of consumers in such Latin countries, and the growing rise in a middle class there; (4) the gradual maturation of governments that were not adverse to enlightened, multinational operations in such nations.

Furthermore, among Easting's varied business activities, the policy indicated a major role for their learning corporation in Latin American countries. Because this subsidiary is in the business of educational service and software, the decision had been made to expand their offerings in the Spanish and Portuguese languages with emphasis on the former.

In the midst of a global knowledge and information explosion, it was reasoned that the expanding Latin managerial and entrepreneurial class would need technical, economic, and management data that would be available primarily in the Spanish language. The possibilities for sales also existed for this instructional material in Spain and in other Spanish-speaking areas of the world outside of this hemisphere. Puerto Rico was seen as a key link to the market in the Caribbean, as well as the gateway to Latin American nations. Therefore, it was to become the place for testing the new marketing plan and for launching it southward, including Cuba when that country was opened to U.S. trade.

Because the new policy was to treat the Latin American as an equal business partner, and to involve them in the company's activities, a franchise approach was being considered. It was felt that Puerto Rico would be a natural place for media production in Spanish of the learning materials, as well as provide the educated manpower from the island or mainland who understood the Spanish language and culture.

The island was considered an ideal example of cultural pluralism—a peaceful place where North and South America meet and prosper a launching pad for expanding Inter-American business. In fact, as far back as 1970, the *Wall Street Journal* had anticipated the new marketing policy when it observed: "Two million potential customers live in Puerto Rico, but hopeful industrial planners see it as the shopping center for the entire Caribbean population of 13 million." After all, America at its birth flourished on trade coming up and through the West Indies; now the time had come to reverse the flow for a new economic rebirth.

The Briefing
Sunday—San Juan, Puerto Rico

It was a balmy, sunny day . . . "Just perfect," Cy Davis mused, "like the guidebook said—travel to Puerto Rico from April through November.

Avoid Christmas, Easter, and Carnival weeks if you want to do business here." The executive vice-president of Easting Corporation was also munching his breakfast at the poolside in the Caribe Hilton, Puerto de Tierre. He had flown down from the mainland the evening before, so that he could meet today with Keith Norcutt, their assistant manager for the Caribbean area. As he drank juice and scanned the *San Juan Star,* Cy was disturbed by the lead story about a bombing in the offices of Chicago Mayor . . .

The explosion had occurred in the Cook County Building in conjunction with that city's celebration of Puerto Rican Day. Prior to the blast, Station WBBM had received a call from a man with a Spanish accent who said, "Several bombs will be going off shortly. The AFNL (Armed Forces of National Liberation) takes full responsibility. Free Puerto Rican prisoners." Cy frowned and muttered, "I thought that Puerto Rican bombing business had subsided. Some more reckless actions like that by nutty nationalists, and our new marketing policy for here could be jeopardized. No place seems safe anymore to do business—from London to Buenos Aires, or from New York to Ponce!"

He sighed, put down the newspaper, and finished his meal. He had set the morning aside to read a special report on Puerto Rico. It had been prepared for him relative to the business environment here by Norcutt whose college major had been Latin American studies. By studying it, then conversing with Keith about the contents, he hoped to be well prepared for his encounter tomorrow with Carlos Mendez. Carlos was not only from one of Puerto Rico's foremost families, but he was also Easting's general manager here. Cy expected Carlos to be the "man-on-the-spot" to spearhead their new marketing plan for central and eastern Latin America. Much depended on Carlos' enthusiasm and cooperation with the new strategy. So Cy reviewed the highlights of Keith's report. The major points provided the insight he needed into this culture and its people.

The Report in Essence

Introduction: Physical environment, technological and social change, inherited culture, and North American influences have created and altered the attitudes of Puerto Rican entrepreneurs. The principal impact on business life and economic development has been a shift from colonialism and an agricultural economy at the turn of the century to neonationalism and industrialization in the last quarter of the twentieth century. After 400 years of Spanish rule and 79 years of American affiliation, the culture is still in transition and the people still experience an identity crisis. Within the context of a Spanish-type culture, the modern Puerto Rican struggles to do business within a North American format. Ethnically unique, despite eight decades of U.S. association, the greatest catalyst for changing the Puerto Rican identity is the fact that more than one fourth of its native sons and daughters live stateside, while there is a constant in-out migration between mainland and island. Add to this the dichotomy between their feelings about "nacion" (the United States as nation) and "patria" (Puerto Rico as homeland). Of course, the minority of independence advocates see Puerto Rico as both, and they view the United States as an economic exploiter.

Demographical Factors: The Puerto Rican people are a mixture of many strains—the Spanish colonizers absorbed the native Taino Indians, but there were many other influxes of Africans, Louisiana French, Venezuelan exiles, Scotch/Irish farmers, and Canary Island laborers. Italians, Corsicans, Lebanese, Cubans, Argentinians, and finally "Americanos" have also spiced this melting pot . . .

The population is approximately 3.1 million on the island, one hundred miles long and thirty miles wide. In the continental United States, Puerto Ricans constitute our newest major ethnic group and number about 1.5 million there. The migrations from the Islands began in the 1930s, usually from among the poorest classes. Today about 19,000 Puerto Ricans on the mainland graduate annually from high school, while another 7,000 high school graduates from the island go stateside each year; about 2% may graduate from college in the United States . . . Since 1962 Puerto Rican studies have been introduced into American schools.

Puerto Rico has one of the fastest economic growth rates in the world. Its GNP (1975) was $7,446,000,000—per capita $2,127. Manufacturing income (textiles and apparel, leather and shoes, electronic companies, tuna canning, metal products, petrochemicals) is more than three times that of agriculture (sugar, tobacco, and rum). Tourism is also a major industry. Exports (1975)—$6,678 million; imports—$8,522 million. Principal trading partners—U.S.A., Venezuela, Netherlands, Spain, Canada, and Dominican Republic.

Ethnic/Culture Factors: A number of cultural factors appear to differentiate norms of Puerto Rican business behavior from those of their mainland counterparts. The older entrepreneurs are only one generation removed from a traditional, nonmobile agricultural society that had preserved the aristocratic, family-centered attitudes of an earlier age. Recognition of social distinctions based on family connections and landholdings, and reliance on family as a source of authority and security have been carried over into Puerto Rico industrial enterprise. It would appear from research that the hereditary Spanish culture has been only slightly modified after three quarters of a century relationship with the U.S. Some of the cultural differences concerning managerial enterprise, typical of large U.S. companies are:

1. Manufacturers, until recently, lacked social prestige in an aristocratic society that discourages the ablest members of middle and upper class families from a career in industry.
2. Close ties between local government and upper class control business opportunity, discouraging able persons without social and political influence.
3. Government efforts here to encourage industry are likely to benefit technological outsiders, rather than local entrepreneurs.

4. Information and ideas known in seaport cities spread slowly into the back country.
5. Tendency of wealthy islanders with capital to put it into real estate rather than industrial purposes.
6. Scarcity of indigenous administrative personnel, and the career push of the society toward the professions, rather than business.
7. Language barrier toward access to the latest and most advanced business intelligence and technology, aided by confusion of U.S. policy on the teaching of English, plus the need for strong government support of a viable bilingual education program at all levels.
8. Tendency for a downward control of information and authority because of family management control and fear of training managers who might become competitors. Patriarchial control of business was strengthened by the Spanish Code of Commerce put into effect in 1886, left in force by the U.S. and only gradually modified by later Anglo-Saxon statute or common law precedents. Thus, delegation of responsibility and authority has come slowly in those areas of business controlled by Puerto Ricans. The situation characterized by undermanagement and limited productivity is reminiscent of U.S. business in the nineteenth century. Two counter forces against the tradition were the introduction of American business practice by U.S. based companies, and the influence of business machines sales personnel who helped to improve managerial communications and procedures.
9. Unique cultural traits that add to the difficulty of modern supervision and industrial discipline. "Dignidad" can undermine working hours and foreman control when Puerto Rican workers quit their jobs after being reprimanded for lateness, absence, or poor work. The "dignidad de la persona" refers to the inner integrity or worth which every person is supposed to have and guards jealously, and has nothing to do with dignity of social position, office, or role. An allied characteristic of Spanish culture is "personalismo" or personalism— namely, the pattern that prescribes for Latin Americans trust only for those persons with whom he or she is in personal or intimate relationships. Only such persons can have a reciprocal appreciation of one's "soul," and with such individuals one can feel secure. It is at the roots of deference to and dependence upon personal authority.
10. Cultural individualism has checked mergers among competitors, and made it more difficult for entrepreneurs here to get together and pool their resources. It, along with capital limitations, contribute to little interest in technological innovations and the perpetration of inefficient methods of production.

For "Americanos" to do business successfully here or in other parts of Latin America, these cultural considerations must be understood:

1. An unusual regard for social status and prestige are more desirable than money, and can defeat operations of the "laws of the market"

as business deals are made that are based on improving family status and friendship. Concern for the arts, poetry, and abstract discussion overcome interest in technology and pragmatic action. Both realities seem contrary to the "American business creed," which prefers common sense to abstract argument, shirt sleeve economics to academic theories, and ordinary meanings of words to professional niceties of definition.

2. Greater emphasis on inner worth and justification by standards of personal feelings than the opinion of peer groups and external sources. This leads to a disinclination to sacrifice personal authority to group decisions, or to allow impersonal arrangements.

   Both factors above are a deterrent against close friendships between continentals and islanders. Often Latins consider North Americans lacking in humanistic understanding, as well as social prestige. They also make it difficult for Puerto Ricans to integrate into large U.S. corporations, and to adapt to cooperative teamwork and abstract systems of control. Naturally, the younger, educated islander and the Puerto Rican raised on the mainland might prove more amenable in this regard.

3. A concept of man stratified in a social hierarchy, coupled with the transcendental view of the world, are also part of the Latin "ethos" that is being challenged today by North American business values. The latter holds that every individual merits respect for he or she is "just as good as the next person," "has the right to equal opportunity," and upward mobility based on ability. The North American ethic is change your position in this life, rather than wait for your rewards in the next life. Such mainland attitudes challenge the islander's values placed upon secure and dignified living, a distrust of change, and a disinclination to expand enterprise.

4. Machismo or protection and defense of one's manhood, of course, is also strong among the Latin male and leads to behavior at times to prove it. This, coupled with the Spanish conviction that women's role is limited to wife, mother, and companion, runs counter to the desires of their educated females to get into business and the professions, or American government policies for equal opportunity in careers and promotions. Overprotectiveness of their wives and daughters make Puerto Rican males suspicious of Yankee business and social relations with regard to their families. These observations should also be linked to the insight that among the upper classes, both men and women, there has been in the past a lack of organized sports and competitive spirit. Traditionally, that level of society has been characterized as a "women's culture."

5. Puerto Ricans share the Latin emphasis upon the spiritual and human, rather than commercial values. One island writer noted that "Puerto Ricans are a religious people in search of a religion." Although ostensibly 99% of the population is Christian, and 80%

Roman Catholic in name, the adherence to dogma and regulations thereof are casual. The prevailing mood among many is a "womb-to-womb Catholicism" with limited practice in between—baptism, confirmation, sometimes the marriage ceremony, and, of course, the last rites. Yet, Christianity permeates the culture and the conversation with much outward display or religious symbols and enjoyment of saint's festivals.

Religion is personalistic, given to spiritism and superstition, especially among the lower classes. This is typical of what is happening elsewhere in Latin America. Fundamental and evangelical Protestantism, aided and abetted by North Americans, is a growing force. The Jewish community is small and often nonnative. The traditionalistic clergy who supported the status quo and the old values are giving way to a more activist clergy bent on promoting social justice and combating poverty and the oligarchy. Their efforts for community and social development here, as elsewhere in Latin America, within the arrabal (slums) and barrios have often been funded by American corporations and foundations, as well as the C.I.A., sometimes without the knowledge of the clergy. Within walking distance of the Caribe Hilton, you can sample the Condado which spawns social unrest, radicalism, and even communism.

In summary, Puerto Rico is a microcosm of Latin America, a culture in transformation, a hybridization, which fosters an unclear national self-image and identity. Thus, many Puerto Ricans lean too much on fantasy, hide hostility and frustration, and swing between extremes of apathy and frantic activity. If so-called advanced, technological nations are to understand the Third World, Puerto Rico is a good place to start. Understanding is the key to mutually beneficial business solutions or imposition of the North American way. Cooperation will only be achieved by respecting and appreciating their heritage.

The Conversation

It was already noon as Cy finished his final reading of the report. Just then Keith Norcutt approached for their appointment and called out, "Bienvenido, here is a santos I picked up for your kid on the way here." Cy thanked him for the gift and offered a "Piña Colada" to quench his guest's thirst. "That was quite a document you prepared for me. It was loaded with data that should prove helpful to me before we launch this marketing plan. Now you must help me make practical applications of it before I see Mendez on Monday morning."

"O.K. with me, but let's get out of this hotel and head for a more typical Puerto Rican restaurant where lunch is on me." Thus, they walked down Ponce de Leon to La Reina's. Along the way Keith urged Cy to make contact with the Institute of Puerto Rican Culture here, and, when he got back to Pittsburgh, to check out the Puerto Rican Heritage Publications. He even invited Cy to join him for a poetry reading sponsored by the

Society of Puerto Rican Writers and Poets. The highlights of his luncheon input were as follows:

● Latin America has a great need for trained technologists and information on modern business practice and techniques. Business by convention needs to be replaced by the latest data and experience from the knowledge revolution. Their learning corporation could contribute much by providing management in Central and South America with modern instructional materials, educational software, and especially aids on English as a second language.

● Keith agreed with the corporate strategy to test the new marketing plan in Puerto Rico before exporting it elsewhere and to recruit here the sales talent to promote the program southward. He pointed out that the U.S. is the main producer of the hemisphere's new technology and not only dominates its commerce, but also its language. He demonstrated how the island's Spanish vocabulary had to stretch to accommodate words that describe the new tools, processes, and products. In fact he called the tangle of tongues, "Spanglish." In particular, he thought Cy, through Carlos Mendez, should enter into dialogue with the principal manufacturing family combinations on the island—the Abarcas, the Ferres, and the Gonzalezes. These family companies brought big business to Puerto Rico, had many of its members trained and educated outside the island, had the most engineers and consulting specialists, and could provide both manpower and capital for the new project. Offer management internships to the young adults of such families and cultivate them for Easting.

● Puerto Rican salesmen are likely to succeed most with those lines that were not bought directly by the ultimate customers. Some inland firms, for example, have found it better to fly salesmen on the same day to and from San Juan to the back country. This emphasizes the key role of the salesmen, as well as personal contacts. Even key executives have to get involved in personal marketing here. Sales and management personnel must make friends with customers in Latin countries. The fact that our continentals who come to the island on assignment only stay here a few years is a deterrent to forming Latin American-type friendships. Furthermore, mergers and acquisitions can only be successfully accomplished in Latin countries if Easting builds up a network of individual relationships with tomorrow's business leaders (many of these are in the University of Puerto Rico and the Catholic University of Puerto Rico, while others may be found in mainland colleges from a variety of Latin countries.)

The Compadres
Sunday—Farjardo, Puerto Rico

A "compadre" is a deep, personal friend who is so "sympatico" as to be said to enter into one's very soul. Although casual acquaintances may use the term, in Latin cultures the relationship implies something much more meaningful—an adopted brother, in a sense, an intertwining of families. It literally means "godfather" (female equivalent is comadre or godmother). And the bond may be cemented by "compadrazgo" or coparentage when such friends do ask their compadres to literally be the godparents of their children. It is a system of improvised social security, as well as a powerful religious-mystical tie. It may occur between rich and poor, and often involves the development of a business partnership.

. Ricardo Dominquez Ortega often visited on Sunday afternoons with his compadre, Carlos Mendez. "Pepe," as he was affectionately called by his friend, was a member of MPI (Movimiento Pro-Independencia of Puerto Rico) and active in the policital effort to throw off U.S. domination. His party was small, but growing. In the last election the supporters of the Commonwealth status were obviously in the majority. He believed that North Americans had deflowered their heritage, land, and women in that order. He hoped that just as in 1797, when Puerto Ricans forced the British to withdraw from the island, that by 1997 the United States would also give up its claim here. He longed to elect the successor of Luis Munoz-Rivera, the first premier of the short-lived independent commonwealth of Puerto Rico (1898). He knew there were smaller countries in the U.N. in terms of land size and population, and that Puerto Rico possessed the natural resources to become economically viable.

However, his old "amigo," Carlos, did not quite agree with him on this, so there were endless abstract discussions on lazy Sunday afternoons at their adjoining haciendas. Mendez has been educated in an American university, did a management internship with a mainland corporation, and was now Easting's general manager for Puerto Rico. He considered his compadre a traditionalist, while he perceived himself as a modernist. In fact, he supported the political party that advocated statehood for the island. He dreamed for the day when Puerto Rico would become the 51st U.S. state and he could vote for its first state governor and legislature. He was proud to be an American citizen, and had a son who had served in Vietnam as an Army officer.

As they sipped their rum drinks, Carlos looked with satisfaction on the estate he had inherited in this northeast corner of the island, beyond El Yunque. Then his compadre, Pepe, began to joke. After many pleasantries and puffs on their Antillas cigars, Pepe remarked, "So, tomorrow you meet with the big gringo from Pittsburgh to plan how your foreign multinational can further exploit our economy and penetrate the rest of South America." Thus the debate began again and the positions of each Puerto Rican can be summarized as follows.

Pepe—There is no future for Puerto Rico except as an independent country within a Caribbean Common Market. The American occupation of Puerto Rico began with government and military men from the U.S., ruling officials who strongly reflected the plantation mentality, customs, and folkways of the Deep South, with its preoccupation with race, class, and religion. These mainlanders merely extended colonial rule to its present run of 479 years. They imposed North American citizenship like issuing a military order. Prior to the Foracker Act of 1900, Puerto Rico was already made subject to U.S. trade laws, customs systems, judicial systems and currency. The Jones Act in 1917 solidified the U.S. economic penetration and was an imperialist ploy for cultural assimilation of the islanders. He did not believe that today Puerto Rico was an Estado Libre Asociado with the U.S.A. He favored psychological and political decolonization.

Pepe maintained that the U.S. conquerors also undermined Puerto Rico's economic and social independence. He cited the ten-year tax exemptions as devices that benefitted mainland investors more than the natives. He pointed to Fomento in the 1950s as typical of the local government efforts that worked to their disadvantage. While it expanded new factories, for example, three fourths of them were owned by people from the mainland. Puerto Rico has the land and skill to feed itself, yet a quarter of the island's imports are for food and use up half of its income. When the North American supermarkets invaded our islands, they drove out of business many of the local food wholesalers and retailers. It was only the consumer cooperative and voluntary groupings of independent stores that saved some of the local merchants.

Furthermore, U.S. policy has focused on the economic development of metropolitan areas like San Juan, Ponce and Mayaquez, neglecting smaller industrial centers like Arecibo and Aquadilla. Even the vaunted "Operation Bootstrap" was a textbook example of imperialism that fed the North American sense of self-righteousness and brought enormous profits to U.S. investors. The tax shelters gave American manufacturers a 30% return on their investment because of three fourths of a million able Puerto Rican workers. Of every dollar thus produced in the island's industrial system, only 17¢ actually remained there. Only independence can reverse this trend and reverse the exploitation by foreigners of our oil, sugar, tobacco and coffee, as well as our manpower.

Pepe also blamed Operation Bootstrap as being the principal catalyst for mass migration of Puerto Ricans to the mainland. One third of our nation escaped into exile in the slums of New York and Chicago because life on our island "paradise" had become so miserable under American occupation. Yet, even stateside our people were exploited and discriminated against. In 1977, the U.S. Commission on Civil Rights admitted that the problems of second and third generation Puerto Ricans in major northern cities has worsened. So what is the value of American citizenship to us with its right to enter poverty on the continent.

But the real disaster for us, Pepe explained, was political. As a so-called free and associated commonwealth, we do not have real power to govern our lives. That is done 1500 miles away in Washington, D.C., through the U.S. House Committee on Insular Affairs and the Senate Committee on Territorial and Insular Affairs. A multitude of federal agencies and the military control our lives and lands (the Pentagon alone controls 13% of the land here for atomic and military bases). So thanks to Teddy Roosevelt, Puerto Rico has become a backward colony of the U.S.; and industrialization here has turned us into a Caribbean workshop for the

North Americans. We do not countenance violence to achieve freedom, but it is understandable how our youth can become radicalized. We have not forgotten the "Ponce Massacre" in 1937 when the American governor ordered the shooting of unarmed demonstrators. Is it any wonder that the repressions here of the '50s, especially of the Nationalist Party, lead to an attempt on the life of President Truman. We deplore but understand why the fires of the '60s damaged North American properties. After being frustrated in the drive for independence and then called to military draft in American imperialist wars, a fair person can appreciate the desperate acts of the ACL (Armed Commandos for Liberation). But it only resulted in having our island become an armed camp for the F.B.I., C.I.A., and security guards of the Wackenhut Corporation and Burns Agency. Thus Pepe reasoned, for he saw political independence as the only way to preserve Puerto Rican culture which he earnestly believed would be destroyed by statehood.

Carlos—In a post-industrial world of advance technology, there is no future for Puerto Rico but assimilation into the American union. The current commonwealth status should be replaced by the island becoming the 51st state of the U.S.A. Fortunately, the ballot indicated a trend in that direction on the part of the island's population. Carlos did not live in the past. He was a pragmatist and futurist who saw the best long-run interests of his people served with a closer alliance to the world's greatest democracy and economic power. His view of the island's history was that the U.S. had done a creditable job in fostering economic development and planning here, especially through the Puerto Rican Reconstruction Administration. It set the groundwork for the leadership and reforms of Munoz Marin and the Popular Democratic Party. Programs like Operation Bootstrap provided a major stimulant for Puerto Rican entrepreneurship and business prosperity.

Carlos often reminded his compadre of the North American contributions since Spain's rule was displaced. He pointed to Americans, like Rexford Tugwell, who as a writer, undersecretary of agriculture, governor, and chancellor of the University of Puerto Rico fought for the cause of the Puerto Rican people. Through the university, Tugwell provided the island with hard-headed, dedicated, competent political administrators. He cited the Development Bank, which provided government loans to private enterprises; the Development Company (PRIDCO) by which the Economic Development Administration expanded factories, employment, and production. He thought Fomento had spurred local business people and built up the industrial environment around San Juan. When there was not enough local capital to promote Puerto Rican business, he thought it was natural for such commonwealth agencies to attract mainland investment and firms. With such American help, income in Puerto Rico has multiplied tenfold since 1940. Carlos thought that the Puerto Ricans themselves, like their Latin American counterparts, were responsible if such income and wealth was often concentrated in the upper brackets. Many of the rich, he maintained, lacked a social conscience to seriously combat slum poverty and curtail migration. Thus, it was easy to project the blame on the North Americans. Perhaps, he mused, if we would face up to the reality of population control, Puerto Rico would not have so many impoverished who sought mainland opportunities.

Furthermore, he pointed out to his friend, we benefit from U.S. social legislation that extends to the commonwealth and ranges from the Fair Labor Standards Act to Social Security and unemployment insurance. Pepe, he countered, did not fully appreciate the development of Puerto Rico enterprises since the end of World War II. Some of them were big businesses even by mainland standards. They included foundry work, sugar and beverage production, and manufacturers of machinery, cement, and tiles. Under the American influence, our whole banking system, as well as deposits, have experienced phenomenal growth. Not just mainland branches, but Banco Popular, Banco de Ponce and Credito y Ahorro Ponceno, in which most of the personnel are Puerto Ricans. American assistance, he said, has enabled Puerto Rico to become a leading industrial state among Spanish-speaking countries.

Yes, he looked forward to his conference tomorrow with Señor Davis, for the new marketing plan meant new opportunity for Puerto Rico and its people. Many Puerto Ricans had prospered on the mainland, and those who returned usually came home with money and skills. He was proud of his U.S. citizenship and thought it gave him and his people an advantage in an increasingly complex world. Carlos concluded that he did not intend to forget or denigrate his heritage, but he saw the value of cultural pluralism and bilingualism for his offspring. He hoped his children, like their father, would become cosmopolitans and not just islanders.

The Issues

1. What is your reaction to the new Easting policy, especially as it refers to Puerto Rico?

2. What cultural and business insights did you get from Keith Norcutt's report on Puerto Rico?

3. What further perspective on the Puerto Rican scene did you obtain from the Davis-Norcutt conversation?

4. Contrast the attitudes of Pepe and Carlos and its implications for doing business in Puerto Rico.

5. What is your prognosis for the marketing plan after Cy and Carlos meet and share their thinking?

6. An anthropologist has observed that among Latin Americans, "the word is valued more highly than the thing; the manipulation of symbols (as in argument) is more cultivated than the manipulation of natural forces and objects (as in mechanics)." What is the implication of this statement for North American businessmen, especially with an engineering background, relative to their interactions with Puerto Ricans?

7. A North American scholar, William L. Schurz, wrote after a life among Latin peoples: "Above all the Latin American is an individualist. Though gregarious, he is averse to merging his personality in any group or to sacrificing its claims to mass demands . . . . He is not a good organization man, and his conferences and committees would probably be the despair of an American chairman. He does not take kindly to the restraints of teamwork and resents the discipline of the group. Among his interests, his family comes first—and the family is only a prolongation of the individual." What is the significance of that comment for U.S. corporations who employ Puerto Ricans?

8. Rexford Tugwell saw "dignidad" and "personalismo" as a formidable barrier to progress in Puerto Rico, especially in the economic sense. These unique cultural traits have been used to substitute fancy for fact, to cover up weakness and incompetence, to protect mediocrity and to avoid outside competition, as well as to perpetuate the habit of deference and dependence upon personal authority. How can your awareness of these factors benefit you in business dealings with Puerto Ricans and other Latins?

9. Among the upper-classes in Puerto Rican society, there is likely to be found attitudes and values stemming from agrarian and Spanish traditions. One professor has summarized them as "emphasis upon spiritual and human rather than commercial values; interest in poetry, literature, and philosophy rather than science and industry; and stress on interpersonal relations rather than competitive individualism." How could a North American capitalize on these supposed tendencies when dealing with Puerto Rican or Latin business leaders?

References

Cordasco, F. and E. Bucchioni, *The Puerto Rican Experience: A Sociological Sourcebook.* Totowa, N.J.: Rowan & Littlefield, 1973.

Connor, J.W., *Acculturation and Retention of an Ethnic Identity in Three Generations of Japanese Americans.* San Francisco: R & E Research Associates, 1977.

Greeley, A.M., *Why Can't They All Be Like Us? America's White Ethnic Groups.* New York: E.P. Dutton, 1975.

Hicks, G.L., *Appalachian Valley.* New York: Holt, Rinehart & Winston, 1976.

Hirsch, H. and A. Gutierrez, *Learning to Be Militant: Ethnic Identity and the Development of Political Militance in a Chicano Community.* San Francisco: R & E Research Associates, 1977.

Jackson, C.E. and M.E. Galli, *A History of the Bureau of Indian Affairs and Its Activities Among Indians.* San Francisco: R & E Associates, 1977.

Kirstein, P.N., *Anglo over Bracero: A History of the Mexican Worker in the United States.* San Francisco: R & E Research Associates, 1977.

McHenry, D.F., *Micronesia: Trust Betrayal.* New York: Carnegie Endowment for International Peace, 1976.

Madsen, W., *The Mexican-Americans of South Texas.* New York: Holt, Rinehart & Winston, 1973.

Toney, W.S., *A Descriptive Study of the Control of Illegal Mexican Migration in the Southwestern United States.* San Francisco: R & E Research Associates, 1977.

Vargus, I.D., *Revival of Ideology: The Afro-American Society Movement.* R & E Research Associates, 1977.

16
Case Studies in
Western Culture: England and Ireland

The English Cultural Impact

The language of English has almost become a universal means of communication, especially in business and international travel. It is a tribute to the world domination once engineered by a hearty race of Anglo-Saxon-Celts living on two small islands off the eastern coast of Europe. Even though the sun is setting on the British Empire, their global influence in the past, and to some extent in the present, is staggering to conceive. Not only their language, but their customs, laws, and life-styles penetrated remote corners of the planet and held sway over several continents from North America to Asia. While the United States is indebted to many nations for its cultural heritage, the English-Irish-Scotch combination provided the main thrust to its society. Through the unique format of the British Commonwealth of Nations, the United Kingdom with its royal family and social institutions impacted on most races and many cultures. The British were even the stimulant for the export of Irish immigrants, missionaries, politicians, and prisoners throughout the world. There are leaders today in Australia and Argentina, as well as Africa and the Americas, of Irish heritage whose ancestors left "Hibernia" with British encouragement. Furthermore, the British spearheaded the European effort in both World Wars I and II.

Today, the British have been forced to retreat, in many ways to the confines of their island kingdom. And they have been followed by the multicultured inhabitants of the commonwealth who used their privilege of British passport to resettle in the "mother country." Added to this influx from the "colonies," are the transfers of many affluent Middle Easterners to England seeking property, education, health services, and recreation. It would appear that the phenomenon of the Medieval Crusades has been reversed. In any event, what was once a largely white, homogeneous society is becoming quite heterogeneous. Furthermore, the United Kingdom is not so united at the moment as Scotch and Welsh separatists seek their own national parliaments, and Ulster is racked in armed struggles between Catholic and Protestant extremists. Thus, the British may someday have to give up their last foothold in the Irish isles.

Yet, as political and racial unrest abound in "Merry Olde England," economic rebirth is underway through the means of North Sea oil and the European Common Market. The United Kingdom and the Republic of Ireland are economically interdependent and share ECC membership. Perhaps the English have not yet seen "their finest hour" and both the British and Irish peoples will make their greatest future contributions in joint ventures with their European neighbors.

It is for these reasons that the two following case studies about doing business in Great Britain and Ireland were written.

Doing Business with the British

Case Study 1: American Abroad in Great Britain

Scenario—
- Background of the characters
- Briefing of the boss
- Critical incidents
- Questions

Background of the Characters

Jeff Donovan was born in Ebbensburg, Pennsylvania, U.S.A. in 1932, attended the local parochial schools and graduated with a B.B.A. in finance from St. Francis College, Loretto, Pa. His graduate studies included a Master's degree in management from Pennsylvania State University, and attendance at the Executive Institute of the Wharton School of Business, University of Pennsylvania on a corporate scholarship.

Jeff is now a transatlantic commuter and an employee of Easting, Inc. Two years ago he was appointed the corporate executive liaison officer for the British Isles, responsible for supervising the company's subsidiary there, Aquaphone, Ltd. He was quite satisfied with his rise in the new-style aristocracy of American business. He would jet four times a year to London and stay at the Claridge Hotel in some splendor. He was especially excited by the employee rallies that he addressed at Fairfield Hall, Croydon. He liked this peculiar British practice, which gave him an opportunity to provide the personnel with a pep talk so that he could counteract the cynicism in workers, a blight across so much of British industrial thinking. He hoped to instill enthusiasm, the lack of which is the biggest curse of their industry. Jeff was not only competent but highly motivated in the spirit that the "business of America is business." Up until now he seemed to have been reasonably successful on this assignment. He seemed to get along well with the man-on-the-spot in England who reported directly to him—Dudley Letts-Jones. In fact, whenever Dudley visited corporate headquarters in Pittsburgh, Jeff and his wife made a point of entertaining their guests at the Rolling Hills Country Club where they were members. Jeff was surprised that it took Dudley two years to invite him to his gentlemen's club.

Dudley Letts-Jones was born in Calcutta, India, in 1920, the son of an English colonel and a British Viscount's daughter. In early childhood, the family returned to England where he was raised in the Royal Mews—his father had become the Royal Equerry. Later he attended the public school at Eton and graduated from Cambridge with a degree in the social sciences. During World War II, he commanded a battery of antiaircraft guns in the Battle of Britain. He belongs to the Church of England and the Conservative Party, as well as to the exclusive Imperial Club in London.

After special studies in management and technology in one of the new redbrick universities, Dudley had drifted into industry with the help of some old school buddies. He was a natural leader and soon moved into executive positions. At the time Easting acquired Aquaphone, Ltd., Dudley was a managing director and the American multinational eventually confirmed him as president of their subsidiary. His wife, Dolores, was not too happy over these developments. She jokingly reminded him that his first duty was to home and family, and warned that she might be forced to act like Mrs. Terese Patten. That lady blithely accused Avon, an American-owned firm, of enticing her 33-year-old husband away from her; she had threatened to sue the corporation because her executive husband was overly influenced by a sales policy that demands all his time and attention, so that he was "married to the job."

Dudley was typically British-generous, enterprising, inventive, loyal to the Crown, and with an instinct to compromise. A perfect English gentleman, at times, he appeared to conceal character under a veneer of dandyism. On occasion, his high-pitched nasal mumblings were useful for evading precise conversation on delicate issues. However, recently Dudley was beginning to get really frustrated. He felt financially constrained by the devaluation of the pound and the taxes of a Socialist-welfare government. He had to sell his weekend country house, couldn't take the usual family vacations to the Continent or Bermuda, and was hesitant to replace his aging Bentley. His absolute assurance had been shaken. The advantages of the past for his class had eroded.

Angus McKay was born in Dundee, a bleak town on the beautiful Tayside—a city of jute, jam, and journalism. He was the son of a craftsman and attended state schools until eventually he became a mechanic's apprentice. His early employers were impressed by his self-reliance, persistence, and brains. During World War II, he served with the Royal Highlanders and rose to the rank of sergeant major with decorations. As a boy he had worked summers as a caddie at St. Andrew's, the home of golf, and met there a wealthy member of his own clan. Upon his return from the service, that gentleman advised Angus to study engineering, and loaned the funds so that he could graduate from the University of Edinburgh.

After working for a series of English firms in Scotland in minor management and technical positions, he got his first big career break when Easting took over the company with which he was employed. Now he is general manager of the Aquaphone plant in Leith and reports directly to Dudley-Letts Jones. He welcomes the periodic visits of Jeff Donovan for he says he "likes to work for Yanks—they're just like Scotsmen." Besides he has American relatives who work in the factories of New England and the coal mines of Pennsylvania.

Angus welcomes the American invasion of Scotland because he believes the London government has given exclusive advantage to English concerns, and neglected the development of Scottish industry. Before the American take-over, he complained of having to make do with obsolescent equipment in cramped conditions. He thinks Jeff has done a good job of replacing nineteenth-century ideas, pay rates, and equipment. He has urged Easting to take advantage of the favorable treatment afforded to them in Scotland, and points out that they are not restricted in locating new factories. Labor and rent are cheap and plentiful, and local authorities most accommodating. Already the Scottish Council for Development and Industry has been most helpful to Aquaphone, Ltd. With the introduction of American management know-how and advanced technology, production has soared to over 200 million pound sterling. Angus notes that as of last year Americans owned 95% of the office machine industry, 92% of the household appliances trade, and 66% of the computer output in Scotland.

And this bothers him a bit. He is still a fierce Scottish nationalist and wonders if they are exchanging one master for another. He knows that the profits he helps to earn go largely back to the U.S. and that their position is vulnerable to changes in American commercial policies, research, and development.

Briefing of the Boss

Jeff would never forget the day he got the assignment to Great Britain. His boss called him into his office and began the conversation in a unique way: "The English have a great tradition of service to the empire; they would choose their very best young men for an overseas posting to broaden their experience before returning home to a major career assignment. Jeff, I am giving you such an opportunity in the field of international business in the British Isles." Then, he described how he had served in Britain during the war when the English were at their "finest hour." He proceeded to share some remarkable insights about the British which served Jeff well in his business relations over the past two years. As he recalled the highlights of that momentous communication, Jeff had found the following points to be most significant:

Don't ever assume that the British are just like us because we *seem* to speak the same language and seem to *share* a common heritage. Centuries of civilization and empire building have given them an inner pride and composure. Yes, their current position in the world's economic and geopolitical scene has diminished, but they still have their network of commonwealth nations, and exercise considerable global influence. We have a lot to learn from the British experience in international affairs.

Furthermore, you must learn to respect the accomplishments of British technology. When they founded the thirteen colonies here, they were already pioneering the Industrial Revolution. We benefited from their technological advances from then to now, most recently from radar to atomic power. Yes, Britain is suffering today from financial reverses, but the British as a people respond best to adversity, as World War II demonstrated. North Sea Oil, tourism, and other developments may yet create a situation in which we more than welcome their friendship.

Remember, the United Kingdom is a polyglot of ancient cultural influences—Angles, Saxons, Normans, Vikings, Celts, Picts, Romans, and others. Today this so-called homogeneous isle is becoming more pluralistic with the influx of immigrants from the commonwealth nations—East and West Indians, Arabs, Africans, Orientals. Nationalism is being manifested in Scotland, Wales, and North Ireland, sometimes with bloody or devastating economic results. Even the language of these small islands range from standard English to Cockney, Scottish, Yorkshire, Norfolk, and Welsh versions. You have to be sensitive to such forces when you do business in the United Kingdom and rid yourself of the John Bull stereotype.

It is a country of paradoxes, and if you are going to be successful there, you have to understand what makes the British tick. To get inside their lifespace or mindset, you have to analyze their national character, culture, and current environment. Normally, you will find them reserved, polite, and often friendly, but don't take them for granted. For all their simulated modesty, the British can be tough and blandly ruthless when necessary. They are masters at intelligence gathering, political blackmail, and chicanery, as a reading of the book *Intrepid* will illustrate. Despite how quaint and eccentric they may appear to you at times, don't sell them short. They are a game people who built an empire with a handful of men and women. Although England and Wales are only the size of Alabama, and the population density is close to the size of France, the British once ruled 14 million square miles and more than 500 million souls.

Because their Union Jack once flew over a good portion of the globe, the people have an empire ethos which gave real meaning to those who served it.

As one of Irish ancestry, you may scowl "very noble" as you recall the other side of their colonialism and their plunder. You may decry the patronizing manner of imperial splendor and their rank consciousness, but the above quotation gets to the heart of this people's idealism. It explains their effortless superiority in world affairs, and their inward, invisible grace as a people. It produced a tradition of public service and an education and class system that was dedicated to the needs of the Empire. It also spawned a credo that natural leaders, not low-born self-made men and women, should rule among the multitude.

These are some of the underlying forces that influence the people you are about to do business with in Britain. We are a free-ranging land and people who have never experienced the feudal system. Such ancient experiences even affect modern British labor relations in a very staid society that is slow to change. There, a militant trade unionism has developed to combat the class system curtailments of the workers. It arose with the Industrial Revolution, which devalued the ancient crafts and replaced them with factory work. It even led to a radical socialism that advocates the public ownership of production, distribution, and exchanges, challenging the whole free enterprise system. Truculence and a bloody-minded reluctance to toil for the "boss class" added to the natural conservatism of British labor. It produced a class-war outlook in which profit is regarded as a dirty word and productivity is not popular currency. So tread carefully in matters of labor relations, lest you stir up deep passions. Don't think you can just translate your experience on the American labor scene to the United Kingdom.

The making of money is not an overwhelming preoccupation of the British worker, and toil is not taken as seriously there as in America. They value free time, and are content with fewer possessions (at least they were, before the advent of our mass media, consumer advertising blitz). They are careful to preserve status and convention on the work scene, even with regard to tea and the pace of work. The American view of money making and profits, efficiency and cost effectiveness, has been almost thought to be irreconcilable with the British approach.

Our whole approach to search for management talent, for example, puzzle the British who formerly waited for such candidates to apply to the company, or to surface through old school ties. It is apathy not snobbery that affects such recruitment in England, and you are going to have to introduce American management recruitment, assessment, and development into our new subsidiary, as well as a system of job evaluation.

Finally, our corporate policy is one of tactfulness and identification with a host country abroad in which we operate. We seek to adapt our company policies and ways to meet the legitimate concerns and grievances of indigenous people beyond our borders and in whose nation we operate. In the case of the United Kingdom, I do not think we can presume upon the traditional special relationship of past AngloAmerican friendship and cooperation. It springs not from formal arrangements, but from numerous personal contacts, generations of shared experiences and dangers, common traditions and perspectives. Yet, the flow of U.S. capital has caused a growing British dependency and inferiority complex. You must be alert to the reality that if American businessmen in the British Isles do not handle our relations there deftly, we could drive the English into a European economic bloc that competes with us, but permits them to regain their self-respect. Furthermore, in 1975 the problem now was the pound; in a few years our relations may reverse themselves because of a dollar devaluation!"

Critical Incidents in London and Edinburgh

As he flew British Airways back to New York, Jeff was uneasy. Those parting words of his boss some two years previously were coming back to haunt him. He thought he had the United Kingdom situation well in hand. With the changes he had introduced Aquaphone, Ltd., had increased sales and profits, better working conditions, and no significant labor strife. Yet, something had happened on his latest visits to London and Edinburgh that disturbed him and had portent for his corporation's relations with its subsidiary.

It started first with Dudley Letts-Jones. This English executive had always been most proper and gentlemanly with him. He seemed to accept and adequately implement the management changes Jeff proposed, and even came up with some worthwhile innovations of his own. Dudley did not illustrate some of the lackadaisical outlook of some of his British colleagues. The issue that surfaced his feelings was the matter of *overstaffing*. Jeff felt that Aquaphone could manage with fewer production workers, fewer researchers, and fewer maintenance personnel. In fact, he had proposed to Dudley goals for reducing personnel in each category by one fifth, one third, and forty percent, respectively. He was surprised when Dudley balked at his obvious attempts to promote improved cost effectiveness and efficiency.

The Englishman fumed, and said, "Three percent of our top management here have quit in the last few months to work for British-owned firms. They are irked by decisions like this that are made in Pittsburgh without regard or insight into our unique situation."

Jeff suspected that he did not make matters better when he pointed out that the interests of shareholders demanded such economies. In fact, he may have made the situation worse when he paraphrased Bill Keafer, vice-president of Warner Electric Clutch and Brake of Illinois, who had contrasted the performance of American and British workers: "With the same machinery the American turns out three times as much as his British counterpart. Even though we pay our workers twice as much as yours, even though we are four thousand miles from Europe and you're not two hundred years old, we each make the same product and undersell you all over the continent. Do you wonder Britain is going bust?"

Dudley had silently accepted this rebuff and the new proposals on staffing. Yet, Jeff was startled a few days later when Dudley finally invited him to be his guest for lunch at the Imperial Club. He wondered how long it would take for him to be admitted to the inner sanctuary of the English gentlemen. Dudley has greeted him graciously there and the lunch proceeds with aplomb. After a hearty meal of chops and ale, it dawned on Jeff that Dudley was still upset. In fact, it became obvious that his English partner was slightly tipsy. Jeff should have suspected the worse when Dudley suggested they retire to the rear of the gameroom for some port. Settled in comfortable leather chairs, Dudley fortified himself with quite a few glasses before this outburst ensued:

"Do you realize, Donovan, that since 1850 the U.S. has brought over 200,000 of our patents to produce products that you then sell to us. Furthermore, you hire away to America or in your companies here our best brains among our professions, scientists, and technicians. Even our most talented actors and actresses have flown away to your tax haven!

The past two bloody World Wars have put us in your debt. It drained the core of my country's strength and manpower. While we fought to preserve democracy in Western Europe and even the Pacific, as well as Africa and the Middle East, we also squandered in these bloody struggles, the patrimony that twelve generations or more of Englishmen had built. I know you Yanks came into both conflicts to help us, but our expenditure in proportion to population, in terms of lives and money, was many times that of your country. Britain may have seemed to have been a major force in defeating Germany in both wars, but America emerged as the real victor in both conflicts. We mortgaged most of our possessions in the Western Hemisphere to stop the Nazis. While the wealth of our nation declined, yours went up. While the cream of our male leaders and even our civilian population were devasted, yours were relatively untouched. While our factories deteriorated, our gold pledged for loans during World War II, your American traders prospered and your nation left rich beyond your dreams. When we were compelled in 1940 to deposit our securities with the U.S.A. for a loan to survive, other European nations got similar aid in the postwar years under the Marshall Plan for nothing."

Jeff had been startled by this line of talk from Dudley and wondered about the point of it. Yet, it was uttered with a quiet intensity and feeling that he had never before sensed in his British colleague. It could not just be written off as the effect of too much alcohol. Especially, when Dudley had continued:

"During my lifetime, England has lost a territorial empire, while America has gained a commercial empire. I have watched my country decline drastically in natural resources and productivity, while we pursued an insane internationalism. How do you think I feel when I witness Arabs and other foreigners like yourself buying up the British Isles! I almost resent having to be employed by an American-owned subsidiary!!! Many of your American business chaps over here are vulgar, noisy, and brash. Your high pressure salesmanship is causing Britons to buy what they don't need and can't afford."

The conversation was loaded with implication, and Jeff did not quite know how to deal with it, or where to begin. He tried to be empathetic and agreed that some Americans were pushy, but then got back to his favorite theme of industriousness. He suggested that the British economy was improving and people could afford more if his countrymen got over its obsession with "full employment." Americans and Germans, he countered face up to such realities as depression and overmanning. He cited the 1960 Fawley Agreement, which abolished the mate system (three watching mates to every five craftsmen), cut overtime drastically, lowered the hours of the working week to forty, increased worker pay, introduced incentive payments, and doubled productivity. This Esso-inspired management action raised the status of manual workers, diminishing the gap between white and blue collar workers. It also demonstrated his point that British workers can and do work happily in U.S.-owned plants. But Dudley ignored his input, and continued on a larger theme:

"Jolly good, I don't mind you in your country defending your way of life and doing business, but don't impose your way of life on us in Great Britain and then get upset with us if we try to preserve our way of life. You set policies in the U.S., and then expect British plants to follow instructions based on American experience and requirements. I loathe the absolute conviction of your corporate headquarters on the absolute virtuousness of their policies and the perfectness of their products. You treat us like a branch factory. There are a lot of us who feel that American executives like yourself are here mainly to watch over us. In fact, the whole form of the American take-over of business here begins to look like 'commercial apartheid.' What bugs me is that some of our own young technologists almost take the line, 'God bless the Yanks and his relations, and keep us in our proper stations.' Many of our business and government leaders have a sickening anxiety to please the Americans."

Jeff was taken back by the new direction of Dudley's responses. He has always tried hard to be fair and just in his relations with his British counterpart. Was he responsible for this ventilation of pent-up emotion? But Dudley was not finished:

"Your firms force us into a dependency relationship. The power is firmly in American corporate headquarters, so that no matter how competent or effective we may be here in Britain, we have little input into your corporation policy and finance plans that affect our business here. We often have to make parts for American products which our government then contracts to buy, such as aircraft. To make matters worse, in some of the American subsidiaries, Britons are being replaced in key positions by Americans and we are not even allowed to be shareholders. You hog all the capital! As things are now going Britain is becoming a U.S. industrial satellite. I would like to see my country next July declare a Declaration of Economic Independence from the U.S.A., or else apply to become the 51st State! With more than 1600 firms here, you have old John

Bull in a bind. Maybe with growing U.S. currency devaluation and inflation problems at home, your attitude will change."

And thus ended the tirade. Jeff thanked Dudley for his candor, said he would report back to headquarters on its implications, and get back to him to explore if anything could be done, at least by Easting, to improve their British relations.

But Jeff's troubles were not over on this United Kingdom jaunt. For when he took the Edinburgh Express up to visit the Leith plant, he hoped to relax with the genial Scot, Angus McKay, and get in a few rounds of golf. Their first few meetings went well, and by the third day when they shared a pleasant salmon dinner, Jeff thought all was in order. But then the very next morning, Angus got to the issue of expansion of research and development. He started on it quite bluntly, despite a lilting Scottish burr:

"It sticks in my gullet that because of the War, American research and development flourished, while ours declined, putting your firms in a position to follow-up and exploit many of our patents. If we are going to have a genuine business association, our people need the opportunity to develop their research capabilities. Right now most of the significant investigations and studies are being done in Pittsburgh. But you don't pick our brains enough here, so that we have an interchange of ideas and an intermixing of effort in every phase of activity, especially research and development. If we are to have a cooperative technology and relationship, there needs to be mechanisms for more cross-fertilization. I have some bright lads here who are bogged down in production, and I can offer little scope to utilize their research competencies. Now, don't get me wrong, Mr. Donovan, I am not complaining. But I think it is to Aquaphone's advantage to keep such talent here before some other American firm woos them to the States. You Americans have done much to build up the economy of Scotland, which we appreciate. Looking forward to the day when we get our own Parliament and are responsible for our own Scottish affairs, we are very grateful that twice as many American firms have invested here as in England. I am just proposing a new direction for Aquaphone's further expenditures in Leith."

Jeff thanked him for his suggestion and asked Angus to prepare a detailed memorandum on his idea for research and development expansion, along with costs and personnel to be involved. He promised to push it in Pittsburgh, but had private reservations on how receptive top management would be to this particular proposal. Then he flew home to ponder the new challenge he was facing in the British Isles.

Questions

1. Contrast the life space of the three principal characters in this critical incident and examine how their cultural values affected their perceptions and communications.

2. Review the briefing of the boss for what information it provides to you on the British character, culture, and way of doing business.
3. Review the critical incident in London with Dudley. List some of the learnings you received which help you to better understand why he reacted as he did. If you were Jeff, how would you report the situation to headquarters and what would you recommend?
4. Review the critical incident outside of Edinburgh with Angus. Is it a real issue for many American firms? If you were Jeff, how would you handle it and what would you recommend? As you reread Angus' background and the incident, what are the implications of Scottish nationalism for Americans doing business there? How would you deal with such issues, whether there or in Wales or North Ireland?
5. As you go back over this case, what applications could you make to your own situation when doing business in Britain? (Do consider the differences in British people, the social class system, the national inferiority feelings, the constraints on American executives who are not on the scene for long time periods, as well as the limitations of their own cultural backgrounds, etc.). Are there other implications from this case about doing business in Europe?

The next case study takes us into the ancient Celtic culture of Ireland and a nation that only became an independent republic in the first quarter of the twentieth century. From an occupied country that was economically and educationally deprived, it has rapidly shifted to a Common market partner in the midst of an economic and social resurgence. From an agricultural society, it is passing through its industrial stage of development in decades. With the help of foreign investment and corporate involvement, it is moving into the technological age.

Doing Business with the Irish

Case Study 2: American Business Negotiations in "Eire"

Scenario—
- The staff meeting
- The IDA data
- The Irish visit and negotiations
- Questions

The Staff Meeting

It was a gray Monday morning in Pittsburgh at the corporate headquarters of the Easting Corporation. A staff meeting was in progress with members of the International Division—C.R. Wilson, director, presiding: "You all know that we have been reviewing the possibility of expanding into Ireland. I think the time is now appropriate for moving on this matter and developing a new site for our European operations there. Any comment?"

"Yes, Chuck," interposed Henry Hanson, an international law specialist, "which Ireland are we talking of, north or south?"

"Don't get legalistic on me, Hank. You know Northern Ireland is part of Great Britain and is in Jeff Donovan's territory. We are speaking of Southern Ireland, or if you prefer the Gaelic term, Eire!"

Jeff added, "Yes, and as our corporate executive for the British Isles, I am aware that over 200 British industries have established companies within the Republic of Ireland in the past twenty years. But we have been talking about this for months. Why are you *now* ready to take action?"

"Good question!" Chuck replied. We have been studying the question of further expansion into European Common Market countries, and Ireland seems to be a prime target if I sense a consensus in this group. I am suggesting we move to a decision on the matter by fall because the political climate there had suddenly taken a turn for the better. In this June election, there was a massive antigovernment swing back to former Prime Minister Jack Lynch's Fianna Fail Party. As you may know that party is generally conservative and pro-business. It looks like they will win up to 84 seats in the 148-member Dail, the lower house of the Irish Parliament, and have a clear mandate over that Fine Gael-Labor coalition which has been in power for the previous four years. Inflation and unemployment were major election issues, not the civil disturbance up north. Lynch is from the southern city of *Cork*, the place where we are most inclined to setting up a plant."

Jim Davis, another concerned executive, piped up, "But what about the violence in Ireland; do you think it is wise for us to be there at this time until that trouble in the northern six provinces is settled?"

Chuck responded that, "That is taking place largely in the north and is the major reason for economic stagnation in that British province. Occasional flare-ups have occurred in the south but the Republic's government has taken a firm stand with the outlawed IRA, a splintered radical minority which should not be confused with the Irish Republican Army of the first quarter of this century. Lynch favors U.N. intervention into Northern Ireland and an end of eight years of sectarian bloodshed. No place on the globe today is absolutely safe to do business, and Southern Ireland is as peaceful as most places in the United States. Besides, G.E. is already there! They recognize that Republic as the fastest growing and most profitable location in Europe to invest."

"O.K., now that we have got that out of the way, when are you going over there and who is going with you?," inquired Jeff.

"We plan to leave in a month," said Chuck. "I know business vacations there are taken in July and August, but I have been assured by the Irish Industrial Development Authority that they can arrange the meetings we need with the proper people. Before we depart IDA's New York representative, Barry Ussher, will join us here at a staff meeting and provide some useful data on the phenomenal industrial and commercial development going on in Ireland. I have already met with R.D. Kahler of Minneapolis who runs a big Thermo King Corporation plant in Galway. He said that he found the Irish fantastically easy people to work with, and that the product they turn out there is as good or better than they make here in the U.S. But what I really liked about his observations was that he found the people there to be enthusiastic workers. When they finished their first 32 units for export to Germany, the employees on the line spontaneously cheered themselves. Apparently, they don't have some of the queer working habits of British laborers and none of the union problems. Now as to who is going, it will be Hanson because there are bound to be legal matters involved in any negotiation, no matter how preliminary. Although it might be logical to take someone with a name like Donovan, I am not taking you along, Jeff, on this initial trip. I need an attorney's guidance on whether we should acquire an existing company or start our own facility and subsidiary from scratch. And if and when we set up a base there, the next decision will be whether to place the operation under your jurisdiction, Jeff. In other words, do we expand your territory to include the British Isles and Ireland, or for political and cultural reasons, would it be better to have someone else in corporate headquarters serve as the liaison with the Irish. Now, Hank, suppose you give us what you see as advantages in this Irish project."

"Well, if we are looking for the best place to grow in Europe, Ireland holds promise for the following key reasons:

1. They are close to American companies already with plants in Ireland. Their feedback is positive on the experience so far, for they enjoy trade, financial and tax advantages within the European Common Market that seem to be unequalled elsewhere in Europe.
2. Manufacturers establishing plants in Ireland enjoy complete exemption from corporate taxes on exports until 1990, as well as guaranteed free transfer in dollars, dividends, profits, capital, and capital appreciation. In other words, there is complete freedom from restriction on ownership.
3. The government offers cash grants toward the cost of new fixed industrial assets for site development buildings, as well as new machinery and installation. We may purchase or rent a factory at reduced rates in a government or private industrial park. Incidentally, money for such projects can be borrowed there for 4-7%.
4. South Ireland can provide educated workers who speak English, although Gaelic is the official language. The minimum school-leaving age is 15 years. There are 600 secondary schools, 300 vocational schools, regional technical and industrial training centers that are responsible for apprenticeships, and two universities with four constituent colleges. Each year the latter turn out more engineers and scientists than the economy can currently absorb. But more important, there are nonrepayable cash grants to pay for the complete costs of *training* workers of new industrial projects in the U.S. or Irish

training centers. It also does not take a seer to see the potential market for our learning corporation's materials and services there!
5. Ireland also provides us with additional access to the EEC market with its 260 million consumers. Irish-made products enter duty free.

With a bagful of incentives like that, it is no wonder Easting anticipates an expansion there which indeed can become an "Emerald Isle" for us— all 27,137 square miles of it!"

Jeff observed philosophically, "Well, as a 'narrowback' (Irish term for an Irish-American), all I can say is that the Gaels fought 1000 years for individuality and freedom—the last 500 years with the English. I can only hope the American, German, and Japanese investment and influence there will enhance and not diminish the Irish people. When you consider that U.S. corporations have already invested about $1 billion in that small republic, and are currently announcing approximately $200 million a year, ancient Hibernia must be experiencing some trauma. In decades, it is being transformed from a sleepy, rural, agricultural society, to a bustling, urban, post-industrial nation. Anyway, Chuck, I wish you and Hank well on your journey into the land of my ancestors. I look forward to learning of your findings and recommendations. Here is a pocketbook, *Trinity* by Leon Uris, well worth your reading on the transatlantic flight! I know you will enjoy the "land of a thousand welcomes."

The IDA Data

At a subsequent meeting with the representative from the Irish Industrial Authority, the executive group confirmed the facts presented by Henry Hanson at the last staff meeting. They all received packages of information that expanded their insights. The highlights of this data were:

- Since 1922 the Republic of Ireland has functioned independently in twenty-six counties with six more still under British control. The population of "Eire" is 3.22 million with 47% employed in service occupations, 30% in industry, and 23% in agriculture.
- Stable, conservative, educated society with a positive attitude toward profit making. In the past fifteen years the GNP has grown at an annual rate of 4%, with overseas investments (1977) of 630 million Irish pounds from a diversity of nations. In the past decade, the exports increased in size and spread—the U.K. (56.4%), the E.E.C. countries (18.2%), and the U.S.A. (10.6%).
- Companies may be wholly owned by nonnationals, subject to the same regulations as native owned companies. Government grants may be negotiated up to a maximum of 60% in designated areas and 45% for the rest of the country.
- The Industrial Training Authority (AnCO) operates training centers throughout the country, in-plant courses, and mobile training centers. Training grants for both management and employees are available, as well as for hiring training consultants.
- IDA grants for research and development may be up to 50% of a project, there are research facilities available with government as-

sistance, as well as support services for research through the National Science Council, the Institute of Industrial Research, and Standards in Dublin, as well as through the country's principal institutions of higher education—University of Dublin (Trinity College, founded in 1590) and National University (Colleges in Dublin, Cork, Galway, and Maynooth).

- In addition to an effective transportation system and fine road network, factories are especially serviced by roads, parking space, heating, lighting, power, water, and sewage on planned industrial estates in which environmental considerations are respected.

- Business is generally scheduled from 10 a.m. to 5 p.m., and in some places lunch is between 12:30 and 2 p.m. The time pace is slower, for Irishmen enjoy mixing business and pleasure. But alas, that may also change.

The Irish Visit and Negotiations

Chuck and Hank flew into Shannon and launched a private survey of the Irish scene. They rented a car and literally drove 2,000 miles around Ireland and even through bits of North Ireland to get a feel for the country and its people. They avoided the "tourist trail" and headed for lovely homes with the sign in the window, "Bed and Board." Although they lacked the privacy and facilities of the big hotel, they got close to the inhabitants and their culture, often staying in quite stately houses, castles and even thatched cottages. The summer weather was pleasant and warm, and they managed to avoid too much rain. The climate is normally mild and temperate. The countryside with its lakes, hills, and mountains was incredibly beautiful—green, lush and bucolic, presumably aided by the heavy dew. The Americans got a real education in the pubs of rural and urban areas. There the Yanks were warmly welcomed and communication had not yet been replaced by television sets in most places.

Chuck and Hank were impressed by the industrial development everywhere evident. Modern, attractive factories and plants were strategically located. The trip confirmed for them their preliminary studies that the southeast coast of the republic in the vicinity of Cork City should be the place for Easting's expansion, more specifically Cobh, the port area where a number of U.S. firms have been long located. But the highlight of their journey was Dublin—a clean, sophisticated, cosmopolitan city that was attracting Europeans from throughout the Continent. There they stayed at the elegant Shelbourne hotel where they had scheduled a series of meetings with Seamus Feeney, the Industrial Development Authority representative assigned to them. While they visited the IDA offices, they felt Seamus' most significant input came over drink or dinner in the hotel's relaxed atmosphere. The most important data they wished to bring back to their colleagues in Pittsburgh was the sketch of Ireland's economic history, which he shared with them one leisurely afternoon. Seamus agreed to the following recording on cassette:

The Survey of Economic History

"It's true, the Irish are loquacious, especially with good company and liquor. But I think it important to spend some time on an aspect of our history which should interest businessmen like yourselves. From your exposure to Irish-Americans, you may have developed some stereotype thinking about us, especially with films like 'The Quiet Man' and characters like John Wayne and Barry Fitzgerald! Seriously, you know that the centuries of Irish struggle for freedom also provided the world with millions of immigrants who not only became laborers, but leaders in the United States and Canada, Australia, and New Zealand, throughout Latin America, as well as England, France, Germany and Russia. You are also aware of our poets and playrights, but are you also aware of our economic development?

For centuries, unfortunately, our biggest business partner was Britain. I say 'unfortunately' for it narrowed our economic base, usually was not of mutual benefit, and even today causes us problems with our Irish pound tied into the English pound! The English gentry have been investing heavily in Ireland since the sixteenth century. Exports then to the Empire were cattle, sheep, wool, butter and dairy products. The British promoted a gradual transition from an agricultural to an industrial economy. For example, as far back as 1670, Sir William Petty established the iron industry in Kenmare and two years later his Irish workers were producing 1000 tons a year. However, our involvement in English wars, either fighting for them or against them, caused economic deterioration except for occasional economic upswings. Thus, add to that poverty and famine, and our principal export often has been people.

But for past three hundreds years, there has been in the whole of Ireland—north and south—a slow development of light industry. Primarily, it has been in textiles, such as cotton, linens, woolens with related weaving and needle work; food processing, such as distilling, brewing, sugar refining, and flour making; glass making; paper mills; and tanneries with the accompanying bootmaking. But the age of the craftsman peaked here in the mid-nineteenth century. Perhaps you may see some analogies in the history of Anglo-Irish economic relations to that of your own American-Puerto Rican relations?

At the beginning of the twentieth century, there was a change for the better and modest prosperity. The U.S. began to become a major importer of Irish products. With the rebirth at this time of Irish nationalism, also came a revival in Irish industry and Gaelic culture. In 1905 the first all-Ireland Industrial Conference was held in Cork, and stimulated the founding of the Irish Industrial Association. The impact of British tariffs and the upsurge of the 'home rule' movement gave impetus to Irish protectionism. During the first quarter of this century, Irish foreign investments abroad had dramatic increase. The first World War brought agricultural prosperity to Ireland and the farmer's earnings rose for the first time in decades. Despite social and political 'troubles' here in this period of the 1915-21, business experienced large profits—trading and manufacturing were up.

With the founding of the Irish Free State, followed by a period of civil war, in 1922-23 economic stagnation hit us. Yet this was accompanied by a growth in investments and incomes.

With control of their own life space, the economic fortunes of the Southern Irishmen improved. National income rose and by 1929, industrial output rose by 9%. Our fledgling government pursued a cautious economic policy. Electricity was organized on a national basis with a network of power stations. The establishment of a sugar company to expand the sugar beet industry provided a new model for a semi-state organization. The latter approach became increasingly important in the next quarter of the twentieth century as the infrastructure for greater industrialization. With the coming to power of the Fianna Fail Party, the economic policies of the '20s encouraged rising exports, limited welfare, and limited taxes. The worldwide depression began to be felt in Ireland in 1931. It was followed by an economic war with England from 1932-35 which really was ended with the Anglo-Irish Trade Agreement of 1938. The '30s also brought an acceleration in industrialization with a concentration on footwear, hosiery, brick and glass making, paper manufacturing, and an increase in metals and leathers. The imports of raw materials rose while those of finished goods declined. The country was in a creditor position. At the same time laws were passed to control manufacturing in Irish hands (1932-34) and to control prices for the benefit of consumers (1937).

The second World War brought neutral Ireland a sharp drop in both imports and exports, as well as severe economic weakness. Actually both of the European wars caused a rise in foreign assets of the Irish Free State, as well as a shortage in goods. Yet, the economy expanded rapidly after 1943 in terms of industrial output and employment.

With the '50s came new government legislation (1952) that provided special grants for development of certain areas within the Republic, along with economic stagnation. On the other hand, we experienced high prices in raw materials, static industrial and agricultural situation, soaring emigration, and high tariffs throughout the decade.

The '60s witnessed economic recovery—a rise in industrial/agricultural output, trade and export of manufactured goods. Irish domestic financial policies went through more change—Financial Acts (1957-58) with a remission of taxes on business import, increased grants for plant and equipment development; the Five-Year Programme of Economic Advancement was launched in 1958, which channeled investments into more productive enterprises. As a result, there was a shift from a closed economic policy to a more open one. The age-old dependence on the primary English market was broken. The move toward European outlets lead to admittance into the Common Market in 1973.

In this decade, Ireland continues a high interest in free international trade and a high level of economic achievement. As a result, the '70s have seen Ireland in a period of phenomenal economic growth. In 1977, for instance, our former Minister of Industry and Commerce, brought back $150 million in contracts from the U.S. alone with IDA help. Currently, emigration has fallen and been reversed by immigration to our isle. That, along with a decline in the traditional late marriages, has seen both the birth rate and unemployment go up. For continued prosperity, Ireland needs more international trade and investment.

America has always been a friendly land to Ireland, and welcomed our sons and daughters—I believe your country has 25 million of Irish descent there. We here in Ireland would like to share in your prosperity. Our New York IDA office has already provided you with the latest information to facilitate your investment and presence here. Now what can I do to further Easting Corporation in this nation?"

Hank Hanson popped up after the long silence, "Seamus, you can accompany us tonight, after dinner at this fine hotel, to a production at the Abbey Theater."

Chuck chuckled and remarked, "Seriously, you can assist with a comprehensive industrial tour of the Cork area. Specifically, we would like to be linked up there with an Irish entrepreneur who is in a similar line of business as our own."

The Cork Business Leader

The most impressive businessman the Easting team met on their Irish tour was Shawn Connors, proprietor of Eireann Ltd. in Cobh. His prosperous business was in a similar product/service line, and employed 450 people. Chuck and Hank were leaning toward acquisition to facilitate a corporate base in Ireland. They felt that Connors and his son showed local management capability that could be developed into a profitable subsidiary. So, after a week of friendly meetings, the team began to move toward preliminary negotiations with Connors relative to a possible take-over of his business on the basis of 70% equity position for Easting.

Shawn was a sharp townsman, a distinctly different type from the rural folk. He had been raised in a manufacturing center where his father had been a successful merchant. A graduate of the local Christian Brothers Academy and the University of Dublin, he had studied engineering, an uncommon pursuit. His reason was to help Ireland leapfrog England in the process of industrialization by fostering modern technology. With the benefit of his mother's family wealth, he launched an electronic business that was now thriving. His timing had been perfect and he was very proud of his accomplishments. Among the professional and business class, he was considered a "big fellow"—a new type of Irishman who viewed the country as an integral part of Europe and whose future depended on cooperation with all its neighbors in the Common Market. Thanks to generous government policy, his plant was of the latest construction and equipment, and maintained a record of high productivity and reasonable costs. He had joined the ranks of the new manufacturers (tools, synthetic fibers and plastics, aluminum castings, hospital supplies, and sailboats.).

His oldest son, Liam, was one of Ireland's 20,000 university students. The lad was studying industrial engineering and training, and had spent every vacation working in the plant. When he graduated, he would take further courses at the Irish Management Institute before joining his Dad fulltime. Liam was the new breed, and belonged to the left-leaning Labor Party. He wanted to accelerate the reversal of the Irish migration, and was himself an example of the generation who could fulfill the Irish dream of simply staying at home and earning a living. His youthful radical ideology was being replaced by a pragmatic view: only heavy foreign private investment could ameliorate the country's unemployment, along with intelligent family and manpower planning. Liam wanted to do something about creating the new jobs to take care of the work needs of 30,000 youths who joined the labor market annually. He saw the current IRA as a lunatic fringe, and that the eventual reunification of Ireland would happen when economic prosperity and development in the south made it attractive for northerns to seek a political solution. Many of the young people in his family and college shared his views, especially his cousin Timothy who was now working as a chemist in the new $100 million Japanese factory of Asahi in western/Mayo County.

There were some who fretted that such youths were becoming part of a new managerial class that might stand apart from the rest of the population and eventually reject traditional Irish values. Strangely, this type of future leader also supported the government's stiff environmental controls over industrial pollution. They agreed with Pat Butler of Travenol Laboratories when he was interviewed by the *New York Times* and said, "I don't believe in selling my soul. No job or standard of living is worth ruining our environment so that the people who come after us have a few bob in their pockets and no place to enjoy it. But I think Ireland's learned from other countries, and is avoiding most of the mistakes of other countries on that score."

Eireann Ltd. was legendary for inservice training of its workers. It turned young farmers and factory workers into technicians. Shawn credited his achievement in this matter on the bright Irish lads who had a sound education from the national schools in the fundamentals, and the supervisors he brought down from Dublin's technical institutes. His company's reputation for effective management and competent employees had grown, and was even recognized on the Continent. In fact, the new foreign-sponsored factories being set up around the country were beginning to raid his workforce and offerhigher pay to get his trained and experienced personnel. Because Ireland had a lopsided workforce with more females than males, his success in training female technicians was being copied elsewhere. When Liam came on board for good, Shawn intended to make him director of human resource development, and put him in charge of a new division for the manufacturing of software to train not only their own personnel, but to sell to other commonwealth countries who spoke English.

But Shawn was finding it increasingly difficult to meet his international competition, especially in England and on the Continent. He was doing well, but he lacked sufficient capital for expansion—he had already borrowed from the government to the limit. Thus, he was interested but ambivalent about the tentative offer the big American corporation was beginning to dangle before him. His old Cork friend, Gentlemen Jack, was again back as Prime Minister with a goal of creating 20,000 jobs! The Easting investment and know-how could contribute a bit toward achieving that through his company. But those terms provided only 30 percent ownership which would not give him much control. After all, he had built the business from scratch and put much of himself into it. He could still make out without sharing with the Yanks. And what of his son, Liam, and the plans he had for the lad in the family company? Would the Americans even give him a chance if they took over. On the other hand, maybe they would and the boy would have opportunity in a multinational corporation which no local Irish firm could ever offer? "Oh, well, there is no use blathering to myself about it," he muttered loudly. "So, I am going fishing now. Tomorrow I will give them my decision to report back to Pittsburgh. Perhaps I will counteroffer for a joint venture with a 50-50 control and responsibility."

Questions

1. Review the main arguments for American corporate investment in Ireland as presented at the staff meeting and in the IDA data summary. What further reasons could you offer for such a decision? What are some of the disadvantages, especially with regard to cultural factors?
2. If an Easting operation were established in the Republic of Ireland, do you think ultimate responsibility should be placed under the corporate officer who handles the British Isles? In other words should the U.K. and Ireland be taken as one territory? Or should Ireland be included in a combined Common Market responsibility? Examine the reasons for your position, and consider the cultural factors involved.
3. What insights would you expect to get about the Irish people, culture, and situation as a result of Chuck and Hank's trip and report? Place yourself in that Pittsburgh staff meeting when the Easting Corporation team return and make their presentation of insights and findings. In other words, what would you expect to learn from them? Why are they recommending the Cork site?
4. Put yourself in Shawn's shoes. Would you sell out to Easting multinational on terms offered? What would you seek from the negotiating team if you were that Irishman? What arguments might the Easting representatives have further made to convince you to go along with the deal?

5. If you were Chuck or Hank, would you support a counteroffer for a joint venture? Or, would you suggest that they return with a proposal to start a new subsidiary in Ireland from scratch with no acquisition of a local firm? Should you take the latter position, what would your case be to the International Division to follow such a course of action?

The careful review of these previous critical incident studies points up the need for one to be well prepared before entering into business relations with peoples of another culture. Both underscore many complex factors, cultural and otherwise, which affect such international relationships. Similar analysis might be made if one moved into the European continent to study the culture and business practice of countries on either side of the Iron Curtain. For the manager who must do business with a variety of continental cultures, be aware of the complexity, and tread warily. The last four case studies offer culture specifics in doing business in the West. The next two chapters will do the same but will address the East or Oriental cultures.

References

Ball, G.W., (ed.), *Global Companies: The Political Economy of World Business.* Englewood Cliffs, N.J.: Prentice Hall, 1975.

British Central Office of Information, *Britain: 1979.* An annual volume available from HMSCO Publications, Pendragon House, 259 E. Bayshore, Palo Alto, Ca. 94303, U.S.A.

Cullen, L.M., *An Economic History of Ireland.* New York: Barnes & Noble/Harper, 1972.

Guides to Multinational Business. *Multinational Executive Travel Companion.* An annual update for business travel abroad, and packed with vital information about international transactions, including the Middle East and Eastern Europe. Also a bonus booklet on "Business Vocabulary for the Traveling Executive in English, French and German. Available from the Bridge Book Store, CRE, 2010 E. 17th Avenue, Denver, Colo. 80206.

Lanier, A.R., *Living in Europe.* New York: Charles Scribners, 1973. (Similar volume by same author and publisher on *Living in the USA*.)

O'Farrell, P., *Ireland's English Question.* New York: Barnes & Noble/Harper, 1972.

Uris, L., *Trinity* and *Ireland: A Terrible Beauty* (with Jill Uris), New York: Doubleday, 1976.

Wadia, M., *Case Studies in International Business.* Scranton: International Textbooks, 1970.

17
Working in an
Eastern Culture: Japan

Maybe the Twain Must Meet

Perhaps the old saying, "East is East, and West is West, and never the twain shall meet," needs to be revised. To those of the West, the Orient has seemed inscrutable, disconcerting, charming, and mysterious. But Asia is a polyglot of nations and cultures, so it is difficult to generalize about its diverse peoples and their mindsets. For North Americans perched on the Pacific rim, Japan is the epitome of the Far East and its seeming enigmas. Being aware of Japanese behavior will, at the the very least, raise one's sensitivities when interacting with Chinese, Vietnamese, Cambodians, Polynesians, and the multitudes of people in the East. Mutual growth in awareness of each other among orientals and occidentals contribute to the acceleration of peaceful interchanges and cooperation among both peoples.

To Americans, in particular, the Japanese may seem a paradox and source of both confusion and wonderment. They have read the history of the feudal society, which lasted until the nineteenth century when Commodore Perry's voyage helped to open Japan to the West. The typical American has a series of changing images, often distorted, about this dynamic Asian people which can be categorized into three stages. One is pre-World War II, when the Japanese were admired for their ambitious effort to catch up to European and American industrialization. At this stage and the next, many Americans viewed Japanese diplomatic endeavors as devious.

During World War II, the image shifted somewhat as Americans were abashed by the daring Japanese attack upon the citadel of Pearl Harbor, forced grudgingly to admire the fighting prowess of these "little yellow men" lampooned by the U.S. media, and puzzled by continued loyalty to their Emperor even in defeat. Finally, in the present postwar period, Americans find it hard to believe that these victims of atomic devastation and military occupation could bounce back, produce an economic miracle, and become a leading superindustrial nation. By the end of the 1970s, Americans were

further humbled to realize that Japan had regained an economic dominance
of the Far East and the globe that it failed to obtain militarily. Furthermore,
that country of high achievers is exporting more than it imports, thus contributing to grave inflation and devaluation of the American dollar. In fact,
the gross national product of "Japan, Inc.," despite a smaller population, is
beginning to surpass that of the U.S.A.

Japanese Kaleidoscope

The changing patterns of current cultural change in Japan may be appreciated somewhat in these random excerpts from the media on the contemporary Nippon scene. Specifically with regard to business, this commentary
from our public press provokes interesting images and partial truths, requiring critical reading. For example, reference to "wages keep climbing" does
not explain that wages may be relatively low in Japan, but labor costs and
benefits are high, especially with life-long employment guarantees.

San Diego Union—July 31, 1977—"View from Tokyo: Industry Merging American/Japanese Cultures"

Can the two country's organizational cultures operate together? In
Japan, for example, the emphasis is on teamwork, while U.S. managers
are trained for specific responsibilities. American companies may
motivate employees by threatening them with dismissal in the event of
failure, while in Japanese firms, the executives take the blame for mistakes and workers are guaranteed job security. Both nationals, however,
seem to be going through a successful learning process from each other.
As the scope of Japanese investment in the United States increases, the
scope for misunderstanding and even hostility may grow. But if Japanese
firms continue to act flexibly as they have until now, they and the
American consumers can benefit in a climate of cooperation.

National Geographic—March 1974—"Those Successful Japanese"

Japanese would rather do anything than sit alone and think. It is an
action-oriented culture . . . Japanese businessmen spend more than one
and a quarter trillion yen a year on tax exempt entertainment . . . After
the war, the Japanese merely shifted the focus of their loyalty from
emperor to employer . . . To understand Japanese business, you must
start with Zen Buddhism. The values of Zen—diligence, self-denial,
loyalty—shaped the knightly samurai character. These are the qualities
that make Japanese workers so productive . . .

Los Angeles Times—Tokyo report, 1978—"Decision Offers Insight into
Japanese"

"There are times when one cannot speak of law and order." With those
words, spoken in a moment of revelation about a nation's gut values,
Prime Minister Takeo Fukuda's cabinet secretary announced that Japan

would meet the demands of five radical hijackers holding a Japan Air Lines plane and more than 140 passengers ... Whereas many foreign newspapers viewed it as a "sellout" or "weak-kneed position," the Japanese viewed it as one in which the value of human life was given utmost priority ... The fact that the Japanese hold values but do not believe in principles has been a source of major misunderstanding with foreigners.

The following selected media extracts also provide unusual insights into changing, contemporary Nipponese social life.

Criminal Justice Columns Newsletter by Michael A. Schumacher, 1977

With the large population in a small land mass, one would expect that with this kind of crowding that Japan would also have an increase in crime and delinquency. This has not been the case, and, in fact, the reduction in crime over the past nine years has been startling ...

Los Angeles Times—March 19, 1978—"New Japanese Woman Slowly Emerging: Many Are Caught Between Tradition and Changing Times"

Modern Japanese females want alternate life-styles and more options than thousands of years of customs have left them. Some succeed in these aspirations, while others bow to the yoke of that tradition .... On the surface, the women's movement is well underway. They wear European and American fashions, gather in coffee shops or bars after work, and wear denims as leisure attire. Yet, they continue to learn the age-old arts of flower arranging, tea ceremony, and how to wear a kimono. Although many work, most jobs for females are menial with no chance for advancement. When women pass foreign service examinations to join the diplomatic corps or take legal steps against job discrimination, it makes newspaper headlines .... More women return to the job market after their children are grown. More girls are going to college. More are demanding equal pay for equal work .... Yet, Japan's plans for women's equality are ahead of their time because not all women are ready for it.

Los Angeles Times—April 2, 1978—"Remainder of 20th Century Worries Japan: Fundamental Change in Fabric of Society Inevitable"

Atsushi Shimokobe, author of *Third Overall National Development Program,* proposes that his country should spend $1 trillion in "social capital" for sewers, roads, housing, schools, water supplies, and the like before the end of the century. A transformation is quietly taking place in Japan, he maintains, and new frontiers, both geographical and spiritual, will have to be found to fulfill personal aspirations .... By the end of the century 40% of the high school graduates will enter college, and that group requires different challenges. By the year 2000, only 60% of the population will be under 45 years of age, demanding mammoth changes in welfare and pension systems. Also by the turn of the century, the managerial class will outnumber the working class. Shimokobe says the signs are already evident of overeducated people who are un- or underemployed. Overcrowding in cities has driven land and housing prices almost beyond the reach of the average urban dweller. Peter Drucker worries about Japan's future because countermeasures to deal with impending social change are not forthcoming!

In today's global village, business and other leaders need a more cosmopolitan perspective and approach. Not only are the earth's peoples becoming more pluralistic in these final decades of the twentieth century, but an homogenization process is underway from which may emerge a world culture for the planet's inhabitants. In his book, *World Without Borders,* Lester R. Brown reminds us:

> We live in an age when problems are increasingly worldwide—the world food problem, threat of world inflation, world environmental crisis, world monetary crisis, world drug problem and so forth. Few, if any, of mankind's more pressing problems have purely national solutions. They can be solved only through multinational or global cooperation . . . . The earth's ecosystem will continue to support life only if countries can cooperate to eventually limit the discharge of waste.

Therefore, it seems imperative that these managers develop, as Ina Corinne Brown, has noted "understanding of what culture is and what it does, and some knowledge of the variety of ways in which human behavior has been institutionalized." The following clues and cues to Japanese behavior utilize the cultural paradigm proposed in Chapter 5.

Language and Communication

1. Indirect and vague is more acceptable, than direct and specific references—ambiguous terminology preferred.
2. Sentences frequently left unfinished so the other person may conclude in his own mind.
3. Conversation transpires within ill-defined and shadowy context—never quite definite so as not to preclude personal interpretation.
4. The language is capable of delicate nuances of states of mind and relationships—while rich in imagination, it can be clumsy for science and business.
5. There are layers of soft language with various degrees of courtesy and respect. The female is especially affected by this; "plain" or "coarse" language is considered improper for her.
6. The listener makes little noises of tentative suggestion, understanding, and encouragement—"hai" may mean more than "yes" and imply, "I'm listening," or, "I understand."
7. There is a formal politeness for official negotiation and ordinary business communication, while an informal approach may be used

while socializing. Frequently, while entertaining, the real business and political deals are concluded.

Tips for Business Communications

1. Saving face and achieving harmony are more important factors in business dealings for the Japanese, than achieving higher sales and profits.
2. Third party introductions are important. They prefer this indirect approach whereby you utilize a go-between or arbitrator who may be involved until the conclusion of the negotiation.
3. Whomever you approach in the organization, do so at the highest level; the first person contacted is also involved throughout the negotiation.
4. Avoid direct communication on money; leave this to the go-between or lower echelon staff.
5. Never put a Japanese in a position where he must admit failure or impotency.
6. Don't praise your product or services; let your literature or go-between do that.
7. Use business cards with your titles, preferably in both Japanese and English.
8. The logical, cognitive or intellectual approach to them is insufficient; the emotional level of communication is considered important (e.g., as in dealing with a known business associate vs. a stranger).

Dress and Appearance

1. Neat, orderly, and conservative for managers; ordinary workers and students frequently wear a distinctive uniform and even a company pin which managers also may sport (holdover from feudal days when kimono carried a lord's symbol. Western dress is fashionable for the modern Japanese for external wear, but ancient, classical dress is frequently preferred in the privacy of the home (e.g., kimono and zoris); Western formal dress for important state occasions.
2. Traditional native dress is sexless and often neutral in color, with women sometimes tending toward flowery patterns.
3. Younger Japanese tend toward "mod" clothes and hair styles; appear to be physically larger than their parents because of dietary changes since the occupation.
4. Colors have different significance in Japanese culture (e.g., white for sorrow, black for joy).

Food and Feeding Habits

1. Eating is more ritualistic, communal, and time consuming. The interaction is considered more important than the food.
2. Tokyo is said to have a restaurant, bar, or cabaret for every 110 members of the population, fast food establishments are increasing.
3. Traditional diet emphasizes rice and fish, tempura pan and style of cooking, chop sticks.
4. The youth tend toward popular Western foods and accoutrements for eating.
5. Don't bring your wife to a business dinner, even if a Japanese host invites her out of politeness.
6. Learning to drink alcohol in public without offense is one of the important accomplishments that a young Japanese would-be executive has to learn.

Time and Age Consciousness

1. Japanese tend to resist pressure on deadline or delivery dates—supposed agreement on date may have been only to achieve harmony.
2. The are punctual yet they expect you to wait for group decisions which take time.
3. In negotiating a licensing agreement, it may take three years for a decision, but once made, the Japanese may be ready to go into production within a few weeks (unless this point of decision is followed by quick action, the Japanese may criticize the Westerner for "endless delay and procrastination").
4. Respect seniority and the elderly.
5. Young managers, recruited from the universities after stiff examinations, are expected to stay with a company until they are forty-five years of age; they then are to conform, doing what's expected of them, and showing respect and deference. Then the crucial decision is made as to whether the forty-five year-old manager is to become a company director; if he makes it, he can stay beyond the normal Western retirement age and may work into his 80s. The remainder of the managerial group not so selected become department or subsidiary directors and are expected to retire at fifty-five, though even then they can be retained in a temporary capacity.

Reward and Recognition

1. Tendency away from individual reward and recognition to the group or organization.

2. High emphasis on security needs satisfaction, as well as social need for "belonging."
3. Money, if passed to a Japanese businessman, should be in an envelope.
4. For social visiting, the guest is frequently given a present or small gift, such as a hand towel beautifully wrapped; however, on the next exchange of visit, you are expected to offer a gift in kind.
5. Personal relationships score high with them and future relationships depend on how you respond in the first encounter.
6. Cut and dry relationships with business contacts are inadequate and must be supplemented by a social relationship for maximum effect. This is usually entertaining the client for a "night on the town," but not at his home; part of the Japanese manager's reward is a generous budget for entertaining. When away from home—for example, in this country, the Japanese businessman expects to be entertained lavishly by his host (theater tickets, et al), but repays this kindness manyfold.

Relationships

1. Cohesive and crowded in a California size nation of 100,500,000 population—this accounts for rituals of bowing, politeness, etc. in crowded, urban areas.
2. Familial and group oriented, instead of individualistic.
3. Youth epitomize the culture in change—energetic, productive, yet anxious for change; gaining a new sense of "I/my/me-ness" while the pattern for other is "we-ness."
4. Group leadership regarded more than individual initiative—tendency toward clannishness based on family or group connections—know your place and be comfortable with it.
5. Drive toward agglomeration, combines, clustering of organizational relationships.
6. Sense of order, propriety, and appropriate behavior between inferiors and superiors (with women generally considered inferior to men); ancient "boss/henchmen" relationship maintained in new forms.
7. International relationships—close emotional and economic ties to U.S. but suspicious of aggressive Americans; fear China, yet emotionally allied and identify with the Chinese.
8. In business relationships, there are two Japans—officialdom and the intellectuals (e.g., politicians and businessmen). In both, decisions tend to be by group mulling for consensus, give and take inconclusiveness, and the traditional authority pyramid.
9. Symbiotic relationship between government and business—cozy but not constricting.
10. Social and self control disguise highly emotional quality of Japanese character and relationships; mesh of binding social relationships weakening and hard to comprehend.

11. Even riots, especially among the more rebellious youths, can be orderly, well-conducted public events staged within a mutually accepted framework of a dangerous game.
12. In context of social relations, Japanese tend to be clean, polite, and disciplined; but publicly with strangers, can be pushy and inconsiderate (e.g., the tourist).
13. Sensitive to what others think or expect of the individual and have a sharp sense of right and wrong; yet find it difficult to deal with the unexpected and strange (so may laugh inappropriately).
14. The general gap between the generations is very wide. In business, it is somewhat bridged for the young manager who is assigned an elder "godfather" or "guru" (to use our terminology) who is an upper middle manager, fifty-five years old or more, is rarely the young man's direct superior, is expected to know him, meet regularly and be available for advice and counsel, and to assist in transfers and discipline, when necessary. This respected elder manager is always consulted on promotions and other personnel matters concerning that young person's career. He is the human contact for the organization with the young manager, the listener and guide who provides a significant human relationship.

Attitudes and Beliefs

1. The Japanese character is diverse with a sense of poetry and of the ephemeral; there is a concern for the transitory, inconclusive qualities of life, for nature, and its observation. It is actively curious, energetic and quick, with a sense of delicacy and wistfulness.
2. These great lovers of success are extremely adaptable—basically, they do not resist change, and are open to automation and new technology.
3. Fundamentally, the Japanese have little concern for theology or philosophy, and seemingly substitute the family in this regard. Although realists, they are like their island homeland—a floating world that changes course.
4. The dominant religious thrust is the convergence of Shintoism and Buddhism (married Shinto, buried Buddhist). Christianity has made limited impact. The crusading Soka Gakkai sect is also a political party that fights inequalities of the social structure, while enshrining the idealistic, self-denial, and the espousal of the underdog.

Business Attitudes

1. Increasing concern for acquisition of second generation management skill, not simply technical, knowledge of products, or manufacturing, but sophisticated management theory and concepts transferred to the Japanese environment. This is forcing changes in the way of dealing

with foreigners. A more competitive climate is developing for foreigners that permits direct investment.
2. The following are myths to be dispelled in dealing with the Japanese business organization:

   ● Your company has more know-how and they must learn from us, not vice versa.
   ● The on-the-job training of American managers abroad can be combined with their simultaneous roles as trainers of our Japanese staff.
   ● The American "Asian expert" is the best person to handle our company relations with Japan.
   ● To overcome our lack of knowledge of the Japanese language, all we need is an interpreter to get on with building our Japanese subsidiary and developing amicable rapport with other Japanese companies and government agencies.
   ● The best place to recruit capable Japanese managers for our subsidiary in Japan is in the United States among Japanese now studying or seeking jobs.
   ● To transfer Japanese to the home office in the U.S. for management training and study tours will allow for sufficient transfer of our management practices into their situation.
   ● The Japanese need our management skills, so the best way to transplant them is by direct investment.

3. The Japanese management recruit is sent to a company training institute for orientation in spiritual awareness, consciousness, and company pride. Even laborers are sometimes sent to Buddhist temples for several days of Zen meditation, interspersed with lectures on religion and company policy.
4. The typical Japanese company attitude is for total employee involvement in return for company gymnasium facilities, free medical care, commuting allowances, subsidized lunches, cut rate groceries, bachelor quarters, and sometimes help from their marriage brokers and counselors.

Values and Standards

1. The Japanese personality generally is self-confident and flexible, demonstrating a sense of order, propriety, and appropriate behavior; there is a tendency toward diligence and thrift, balanced by a fun-loving approach which, at times, seems almost frivolous and extravagant.
2. In outlook the Japanese are cautious and given to stalling tactics, as well as insular manifested by the ingroup tendency.

3. The Japanese value social and self-control; but the rigid, ossified class system by which each man has his place as superior or inferior (women) is disappearing.

4. Today's Japanese values peace and economic progress, ensured somewhat by the fact that only 1% of the nation's gross national product is devoted to defense spending, and the country suffers from nuclear allergy.

5. This culture highly regards new ideas and technologies, swallowing them up until they are Japanized (internalized) after careful, detailed examination; there is a subtle shift of emphasis from copying to creating underway.

6. The Japanese are changing their image of themselves as a people— from being in a dark, world closet looking out to Asian leaders in the international community with the attitude, "ours is never the best, so search for improvement."

7. Japanese society values training and education, especially of the young. It also values a spirit of intensity and craftsmanship—manifest in a quality of deep penetration into work and a pride in work, no matter how humble.

8. Japanese value congenial, known surroundings and seek to create an atmosphere of well-focused energy and disciplined good cheer.

9. A basic standard of Japanese life is work and play hard—work particularly for the good of the family or company family—maintain controlled competition and cooperation in the process.

10. The yen is mightier than the sword.

11. The Japanese now fear the military man and foreign involvement.

12. The radical, revolutionary portion of Japanese youth have an entirely different set of values than the majority—they can be vicious and violent, yet espouse a spirit of self-denial, self-correction, self-dedication to what they consider a high cause.

13. Even criminal gangs (à la Mafia) will publicly apologize in press conferences to the public when they seem to cause too much violence and disruption in society.

14. Generally, the Japanese are moved to heroically inspired deeds, rather than charity or noblesse oblige.

15. The goals of Japanese society seems to be steady employment, corporate growth, product superiority, and national economic welfare, which is considered more important than profits; the goals of the individual seem to be "more" for the organization and for self, in that order.

16. Corporate social responsibility is a standard built into the Japanese system: increasingly Japanese companies are giving a percentage of profits to promote education, social welfare, and culture.

17. Another organizational standard is to provide psychological security in the job, in return for loyalty to the company; there is a concept of mutual obligation between employer and employee. Strikes are only beginning to creep into the work culture.

18. The seniority standard is slowly giving way to merit promotion.

19. The Japanese value decision by consensus. Before action is taken, much time is spent on defining the question. They decide first if there is a need for a decision and what is it all about. The focus is upon what the decision is really about, not what it should be; once agreement is reached, then the Japanese move with great speed to the action stage. Referral of the question is made to the appropriate people, in effect indicating top management's answer to the question. The system forces the Japanese to make *big decisions,* and to avoid the Western tendency toward small decisions that are easy to make (minutia). For example, instead of making a decision on a particular joint venture, the Japanese might consider the direction the business should go, and this joint venture is then only a small aspect of the larger issue. By emphasizing the importance of understanding alternative solutions, the Japanese seem to avoid becoming prisoners of their own preconceived answers.

20. The Japanese standard of lifetime employment is not as simple as it seems:

   ● Not all workers are considered permanent. A substantial body of employees (perhaps 20%) are not subject to this job security. Some positions are hired and paid for by the hour; women are generally considered in the temporary work category, and some who retire at fifty-five may be kept on in that temporary capacity: adjustments in work force can be readily made among these "temporaries."
   ● Pay as a rule is on the basis of seniority and doubles every fifteen years.
   ● Retirement is a two-year salary, severence bonus, usually at fifty-five. Western pension plans are beginning to come into companies slowly and are low in benefits.
   ● Permanent employees who leave an employer will have a very difficult time being permanent again for another employer.
   ● The whole concept of permanent employment is left over from feudal arrangements of the past, and is now being undermined by superindustrial developments.

21. Another standard of Japanese work life seems to be *continuous training:*

   ● It is performance focused in contrast to our promotion focus; in scope, it involves training not only in one's own job, but in all jobs at one's level.

- The emphasis is on productivity and the real burden of training is on the learner—"What have we learned to do the job better?"
- On the whole, they believe the older worker is more productive, and output per man hour is invariably higher in a plant with an older work population.
- The industrial engineer teaches how to improve one's own productivity and process.
- Generally, there are no craft unions or skills in Japanese industry and little mobility among blue collar workers; what mobility exists is among office workers and professionals.
- Education is seen as a preparation for life, rather than life itself; those with "graduate education" are generally too old to start in the Japanese work system, and when employed they come in as specialists.

Conclusion

The Japanese are a remarkable and unique people. Their subtle, complex culture, in particular, illustrates the differences and diversity of oriental cultures, in general. It points up why western business leaders would benefit by training in cultural awareness and area studies if they expect to succeed in their business and social relations when operating in the Far East. As Den Fujita, president of McDonald's Company of Japan, reminded us: "American exporters should study the cultural aspects of Japan more carefully. You must send first-class Americans, experts, to Japan. Before you start production, you must learn Japanese culture and what Japanese are like. Then you can export in huge quantities!" The words of this Japanese hamburger king are also valid in reverse—Asians who expect to succeed in business abroad should be equally well informed about the cultures in which they do business. Finally, remember this chapter has only touched upon the tip of the iceberg—whatever one thinks he or she knows about the Japanese, must be continuously reexamined and scrutinized for Japan has a dynamic, changing culture.

References

Adams, T. and Kobayashi, N. *The World of Japanese Business: An Authoritative Analysis.* Palo Alto, Ca.: Kodansa International Ltd., 1969.

Brown, Lester R., *World Without Borders.* New York: Vintage Books, Random House, 1973.

Brown, Ina C., *Understanding Other Cultures.* Englewood Cliffs, N.J.: Prentice Hall, 1963.

Clavell, J. *Shogun.* New York: Dell, 1976.*

Condon, J. and Kurata, K. *In Search of What's Japanese about Japan.* Tokyo: Shufunotomo, 1976.*

De Mente, B. *P's and Cues for Travelers in Japan.* Tokyo: Shufunotomo, 1977.*

Drucker, Peter F., "What We Can Learn From Japanese Management," *Harvard Business Review,* March-April, 1971, pp. 110-122.

Japan Air Lines, 655 Fifth Avenue, New York, N.Y. 10022, U.S.A. (212/758-8850). Request information about publications, films, and Japan Business Seminars.

Japan External Trade Organization, Japan Trade Center, 555 South Flower Street, 24th Floor, Los Angeles, Ca., 90071, U.S.A. (213/626-5700). Request JETRO Publications List with many complimentary offers. The Marketing Series has seventeen listings from *Japan as an Export Market* to *Changing Dietary Lifestyles in Japan.* . . . Business Information Series has eight titles ranging from *Operating a Business in Japan* to *Understanding the Japanese—If that's Possible.* . . . It also publishes an English newsletter, *Trade Times;* a monthly English magazine, *Focus Japan;* as well as special printed reports, such as, *Exporting to Japan* (March 1978) and *Living in Southern California: an Orientation Guide for Japanese; How to Succeed in Japan.*

Kahn, H. *The Emerging Japanese Superstate.* Englewood Cliffs, N.J.: Prentice Hall, 1970.

Kobayashi, S. *Creative Management.* New York: AMACOM, 1977.

Lanier, A.R. *Update Japan.* New York: Overseas Briefing Associates, 1975 (Request from same source Overseas Briefing Reports—OBR: 71-027, *Japan,* 1971; OBA Reading and Resource List for Japan, No. 038.*

Manglapus, R. *Japan in Southeast Asia: Collision Course.* New York: Carnegie Endowment for International Peace, 1976.*

McDowell, Edwin, "The Formula for Success in Japan," *Wall Street Journal,* May 9, 1974.

Mydans, Carl and Shelly, "What Manner of Men are These Japanese," *Fortune,* August 1, 1969, pp. 101-120.

Ouchi, W.G. *Type Z Management Program* (videotape or film). Chrysler Learning Inc., P.O. Box 970-A, Detroit, Michigan 48232, U.S.A. 1978.

PHP Institute, P.O. Box 4210, Grand Central Station, New York, N.Y. 10017 U.S.A. Publishes a monthly pocket-size magazine, *PHP: A Forum for a Better World* (Peace, Happiness, and Prosperity) in English with articles about contemporary Japanese life, often translations from the Japanese.

Reischauer, E.O. *United States and Japan.* Cambridge: Harvard University Press, 1968. (The author, a former American ambassador to Japan has contributed to an excellent film, *The Japanese* available on rental from the Film Marketing Division, Syracuse University, 1455 East Calvin Street, Syracuse, New York, 13210, U.S.A.)

Schwarz, E.A., and Ezawa, R. *Japanese Illustrated: Meeting Japan Through Her Language.* Tokyo: Shufunotomo, 1976.*

Seward, Jack, *The Japanese, An Essential Handbook on Their Customs and Business Practice.* New York: William Morrow & Co., 1974.

Tsurumi, Yoshi, "Myths That Mislead U.S. Managers in Japan," *Harvard Business Review,* July-August, 1971, pp. 118-127.

United States Department of Commerce, Publications Sales Branch, Room 1617, Washington, D.C. 20230, U.S.A. *Overseas Business Reports: Marketing in Japan,* April 1978, OBR# 78-16; *Foreign Economic Trends and Their Implications for the United States:* Japan, January 1978, FET # 78-010. (Such reports on Country specifics are frequently updated, so request latest edition.) *Area Handbook: Japan* No. 00520-7, 1974. (Check with regional offices of USDC about Japan Business Forums and special meetings.)

Van Zandt, Howard F., "How to Negotiate in Japan,"*Harvard Business Review,* Nov.-Dec., 1970, pp. 45-56 (Recommended reprint No. 70613).

Vision Associates, Inc., 665 Fifth Avenue, New York, N.Y. 10022, U.S.A. (213/935-1830). *Doing Business in Japan: Negotiating A Contract,* 1974. (Excellent 16 mm. color film and discussion guide produced for the Business Council for International Understanding, 420 Lexington Avenue, New York, N.Y. 10017, U.S.A.—212/490-0460.)

*Available through one central source, The Bridge Book Store, 1800 Pontiac, Denver, Colorado 80220, U.S.A.

18
Working in the
People's Republic of China

Throughout the world, especially in Asia and Taiwan, Westerners come in contact with overseas Chinese or those of Chinese heritage. However, the most exciting Sino relationships are to be established on the mainland, The People's Republic of China (PRC). This is the heart of both ancient and modern Chinese culture. It is home to a large percentage of the world's population, and over 800,000,000 Chinese. For North Americans, the barriers to communication and the forming of business and professional relationships with the PRC offer new challenges and opportunities.

Introduction

On January 1, 1979, full diplomatic relations between the People's Republic of China (PRC) and the United States of America were established. Deputy Premier Minister Teng Hsiao-ping* of the PRC came to the U.S. the last week of January. On March 1, 1979, embassies of the U.S. and the PRC opened in Peking and Washington respectively. The first U.S. ambassador to the PRC was Leonard Woodcock, former United Auto Workers' president.

The material that follows has been derived from a variety of sources including conversations with American businessmen who have been working the PRC for a number of years, as well as scholars and business people con-

---

*Pinyin—On January 1, 1979, China adopted officially the "pinyin" system of writing Chinese characters in the Latin alphabet. This is a system of romanization invented by the Chinese that has been widely used for years in China on street signs, as well as in elementary Chinese textbooks. Pinyin is now to replace the familiar Wade-Giles romanization system. The following are examples of the Wade-Giles and pinyin systems, but in this chapter, because of the reader's familiarization with Wade-Giles, it will be followed.

Wade-Giles	Pinyin
Peking	Beijing
Kwangchow/Canton	Guangzhou
Mao Tse-tung	Mao Zedong
Teng Hsiao-ping	Deng Xiaoping
Hua Kuo-feng	Hua Guofeng
Chou En-lai	Zhou Enlai

versant in the political, economic, social, and cultural considerations in that country. The materials are provided to serve as a guide for American business personnel who may be preparing for a trip to the PRC. Much of this information is of a practical nature, because there is a lack of such material.

It is expected that an exchange of business and education between the PRC and the U.S. will accelerate at a rapid pace. However, given the different political backgrounds of the two countries, it is expected the relationship will be tenuous.

A most important caution: changes between the PRC and the U.S. are occurring rapidly. The relationship is *interactive* and is subject to many forces. Reading this material and keeping in mind the ideas presented in the first two units of the book will reduce the possibility of overgeneralization.

It is expected that commerce and exchange of a business and educational nature between the PRC and the United States will accelerate at a rapid pace. However, given the different political backgrounds of the two countries, it is expected the relationship will be tenuous, interactive, and subject to many forces, especially since changes within and between the two nations are occurring rapidly. As one reads this material, do recall the ideas presented in the first two sections of this book as this will reduce the possibility of overgeneralization.

The Constitution of the People's Republic of China was adopted on March 5, 1978, by the Fifth National People's Congress of the People's Republic of China at its first session. The complete translation of this constitution is included in Appendix I in the *Encyclopedia of China Today* (pp. 321-325). Also included in another appendix of the *Encyclopedia of China Today* is the Constitution of the Communist Party of China, which was adopted by the Eleventh National Congress of the Communist Party of China on August 18, 1977. In order to have a flavor of many of the issues and prides, as well as historical background of this great people, it is suggested that prior to making any trip to the PRC these materials be read and studied.

The authors consider the following materials as essential for any person who will be traveling to the PRC either as a tourist or for business purposes: the *Encyclopedia of China Today,* published January 1979 by Frederic M. Kaplan, Julian M. Sobin, and Steven Andors; *Doing Business with The People's Republic of China,* by Bohdan O. Szuprowicz and Maria R. Szuprowicz; and the U.S. Department of Commerce publication of February 1979 entitled, *Doing Business with China.* In addition, materials provided by the National Council for U.S.-China Trade, Suite 350, 1050 Seventeenth St. N.W., Washington, D.C. 20036 are recommended reading

Background

One of China's most predominant characteristics is its tradition of isolation. It is one of the oldest advanced civilizations in this world, and over 2300 years ago China enclosed itself behind the Great Wall and forced traders and merchants to remain outside these walls in order to conduct business. This same general attitude of isolation is present today. It is also necessary to remember that in spite of the relationships with Western people and other countries, China is a communist country with the teachings of Mao, whose aim it was to cause a complete reform in the social and moral life of the people. It is very often difficult to know who is responsible for making the final decision in business transactions as a result of the emphasis on equality. All Chinese are generally dressed alike with the only distinction of upper class rank being the existence of four pockets instead of two pockets stitched on the jacket.

The Chinese have always held themselves in high esteem. The name of their country translates as "middle kingdom" for they saw themselves, their country, and culture as the center of human civilization. They expected that all other peoples and nations would pay tribute and homage to the Chinese. This situation continued until modern times, when the Chinese met head on with Europeans and Americans who did not understand this attitude and did not accept it as a condition for working and doing business with them.

The long history of western imperialism in China is one of great humiliation for the Chinese. In 1949, following the establishment of the People's Republic of China, the Chinese Communist party attempted to change basic attitudes, values, and behavior of the Chinese people. The purpose of Mao Tse-tung and his reformers was to give the country the new direction and build from a traditional feudalistic society to a modern socialistic society.

A fundamental tool in effecting these changes in basic Chinese values was the development of a people's democracy where each and every individual in the country from peasant farmer to high government official would take a part in decision making at all levels on a regular basis. To accomplish this, work crews, communities, factory organizations, and schools were organized into study teams as a part of the daily business to investigate the socialistic principles upon which the government was established. In attempting to make these changes, four major areas were identified as obstacles to overcome:

1. The reduction of the difference in economic and political development of urban and rural areas.
2. The reduction of economic and political inequality between the industrial and peasant workers.
3. The reduction of inequality between manual laborers and the elite.
4. The reduction of inequality between the sexes.

The Chinese became even more involved in the politics of the nation during two major events in their history since 1949. These are the Great Leap Forward in the late 1950s and the Cultural Revolution of the late 1960s. During these two periods, economic efficiency and social order were forsaken as the country embarked on major new programs that were designed to eliminate "revisionist" elements and to illustrate to the people the significant importance of their role.

History

China is an ancient civilization. During the Chou dynasty (1122 B.C. to 256 B.C.) the wheel, wire saw, diamond drill, and the crossbow were developed. In mathematics and astronomy, the Chinese were at times ahead of the western civilization. The pythagoram theorem of geometry was developed in China at about the same time that it developed in Greece, approximately 400 B.C. At about the same time, the Chinese mapped approximately 1500 stars, 200 years before Hipparchus mapped about one-half that number.

Philosophically there are three major influences affecting Chinese thought: the ideas of Confucius; Taoism; and the legalist.

Confucius taught that China must return to the peace and tranquility of the golden age that was supposed to have existed in the far past. Confucius was interested in the problems of the world, the problems that people experienced rather than the origin of life or the possiblility of an afterlife. Confucius also believed that the utopia, which he insisted had existed in the past, could be rediscovered and recreated in the present by an emphasis on ethics, particularly moral ethics and education, and on the ceremonies and prescriptions of social behavior.

Confucianism become the state ideology of China, and the dominant influence in the life and history of the people.

Taoism was a second major religious influence. The Taoists stressed man's relationship not to society but to nature and the environment around him. Taoism urged that man give up his worldly desires and enter a state of unity or oneness with the essence of all life, which was called Tao. With its emphasis on the individual and nature, Taoism offered more freedom of imagination than did Confucianism, and it had a deep and lasting effect on the art and literature of China.

A third major school of philosophy to come from the Chou dynasty was the legalist, which argued that man was essentially evil by nature, and therefore, he should be controlled by a totalitarian government that would rule by a system of rewards and punishment. However, this proved to be too harsh a system for the people to accept.

Of these three influences, Confucianism with its conformity and bureaucracy proved to be the most viable.

During the time of the Opium Wars between China and England, the weakness of the Manchu dynasty was demonstrated. This encouraged further European territory expansion in China. These wars were initiated by the British in about 1840 to ensure the sale of opium by the British to the Chinese in payment for the British imports from China. At that time, China was not able to halt this degeneracy of the people as a result of the opium. The French, Germans, and Japanese subsequently initiated wars with China, which China lost. As a result, China was forced to give up more and more territory. It gave up Indo-China to the French, Korea to the Japanese, Port Arthur and Darien to the Russians, as well as vast territories in Mongolia and Siberia.

The Manchu dynasty collapsed in the year 1911. Following their defeat, there was intense internal civil strife and regional landlord power grabbing, which culminated finally in the battle between the nationalists and the communists. The nationalists, led by Chiang Kai-shek, pushed the communists to the far north. The communists were led by Mao Tse-tung. At about this same time, the Japanese invaded Manchuria and forced Mao and Chiang to unite to fight against the Japanese. With the defeat of the Japanese, however, in 1945 the confrontation between the nationalists and the communists began anew. The nationalists were supported and subsidized by the United States but lost in the civil war to the communitsts led by Mao Tse-tung, who were supported and subsidized by the Soviet Union. The Soviet Union believed that the Chinese would submit to the dictates of the Soviet dominated world communist movement that was led by them. However, the Soviets and the Chinese are ideological opposites as the Soviets believe in the primacy of the industrial proletariat with little regard to the people. The Chinese on the other hand give primary importance to the peasants or the people. Therefore, it was not too long before the Chinese and the Soviet Union were in significant disagreement, which continues to the present.

During the communist renewal of mainland China, miracles have been accomplished. There is no longer starvation, disease or the lack of adequate clothing. These were for the most part accomplished by the Chinese without external help and all levels of society are proud of these accomplishments. Their social awareness is largely due to their educational system, which has a function of basically serving politics and attempting to assist with the production of goods. It is directed by the Communist party. If there is a choice between schooling and social commitment, the social commitment would take precedence. From a western perspective, there is extreme regimentation in their educational process in the sense that there is group marching, drills, and group physical exercises, all performed in great precision. Such activities are supportive of the overall theme of collective participation.

The political education of the Chinese begins in the first year of school when they are taught the values and thoughts of Mao and the goals of the socialist state. They are also taught the revolutionary process of building China into the utopian socialist state, which is their goal. Every school also has a production schedule and works to manufacture items necessary for industry and the consumption of the consumers. Students and teachers take part in the production process. This university system is designed in such a way as to anticipate future industrialization with the goal of helping to prepare the Chinese for their part in it. All the universities and technical institutes are required by law to assist in the running of the industrial plants, and in return, the industrial plants assist in the smooth running of the universities and technical institutes.

The performance of the students at the university level is not evaluated by examination alone. The student is also assessed by the combined opinion of the teachers, fellow students and the Communist party organization. As a result, there are technicians, scientists, and academics who are highly reliable and politically conscious.

From a social perspective, the individual Chinese has a new kind of relationship with his fellow man. It is called comradeship. Comradeship is a kind of new morality. It means friendliness and helpfulness between all people of the state, and has become widely accepted by most Chinese people. This new system requires that all individuals do not permit any personal relationship to interfere in any way with the collective goal of the community or of the state. To accomplish this, every person is required to participate in self-criticism, as well as the criticism of others. To the generation of younger Chinese, this is a natural condition and one which they accept without question.

The Chinese People

One out of every four or five people in the world is Chinese as it is the most populous nation in the world and one of the largest geographically.

The Chinese have a strong sense of family with a hierarchy and obligations. Before 1949, the family of China came first with the individual second, and the national a poor third. At that time, the bigger and more powerful the Chinese family, the more important was the family to the individual. The poor peasants were not able to enjoy living together with large numbers of blood relations as fathers were often serfs and brothers might be sold and contact lost.

The Chinese are fair and this sense of fairness comes from Confucianism. It teaches returning good for good, and justice for evil.

The Chinese are practical business people. The Chinese also believe that a person who pays undue attention to material things will always be anxious in his heart. The body may be clad in warm garments and rest upon a fine mat, but he will feel no comfort. This is also represented by the interaction of two opposite forces in China—the yin and yang. Yin is earth, feminine, negative, passive, dark, weak, even, and moon. The yang is heaven, male, positive, active, light, strong, odd, and sun. Yin contracts and yang expands so the universe agrees. The yin and the yang do not divide the world but unite it. There can be no good without the bad, no left without right, and no heaven without earth.

Within the PRC there is a difference between honor and face. Honor is real, and it is a matter of conscience. Face is concerned with reputation and appearance. The Chinese not only thinks of his own face, but also the face of others as he would not like to make anyone look like a fool in public.

The Chinese are hard working, industrious people, and they are concerned with the productivity and the betterment of the lives of the group of persons with which they are working. These characteristics are related to ancient tradition of pride and self-respect and to the encouragement and the indoctrination process of efficiency.

The Chinese people have a love of life and a sense of beauty that is seen in their art. They also have a high regard for the written word. Pastimes and social activities are largely under the guidance of organizations controlled by the Communist cultural center. Among the many popular games played by Chinese adults are forms of chess, and go, which is similar to the Japanese game involving black and white objects on a checkered board.

Walks and picnics that emulate the long march are a favorite diversion of the family and other groups. Community recreational activities include skits, drama, and musical performances that are approved by the government. Activities for children and youth frequently include exercising and walking, which are designed to improve physical fitness. Games that do not require a great deal of expense are also common, as there is a shortage of money for recreational activities.

Basketball and volleyball are also popular, but perhaps the most common of all games is table tennis. Sports such as boxing, which involve physical contact, have been outlawed by the government. Western movies, including American movies, are now being shown, although in general they are very old and edited. The censorship of movies has only been relaxed slightly, and movies with sexual themes, for example, are not permitted.

The Family Structure of the Chinese

The modern family structure in the PRC is very similar to that of the American family in many respects. The purpose of many social and economic measures instituted by the government in relation to the family structure appears not to have been the destruction of the nuclear family, but rather the elimination of the extended family structure. With the establishment of the communes in 1958 in conjunction with the Great Leap Forward, party theoreticians imagined a great amount of impersonalization of family relations. The communal social aspect of the program was found unworkable, and their functions reverted to the nuclear family.

The family has definitely been retained as an essential social institution. Within the family, family life is relatively intimate, and divorce is present, but the government is making every effort in such cases to assist with a reconciliation whenever possible. The general consensus among the people is that divorce is immoral and unnecessary, particularly when there are young children involved.

The Concept of Man and His Relation to Nature

The concept that the Chinese have of man and his relationship with nature has been developed over many centuries. The traditional Taoist view is that man is basically in harmony with nature, and his position is to live in harmony with nature rather than to control it. This is in conflict with the Maoist belief that man, given the right thoughts and the correct spirit of determination and time, can overcome nature.

The Role of Women

One of the most spectacular changes in the PRC has been the role of women and their traditional place of inferiority, which they held in traditional China. In times past, female infanticide was common among the poor people. The woman's inferior status was continually reinforced by such wide spread practice as concubinage, female foot binding, child marriage, the forbidding of widow remarriage, and dominance of the patrilineal kin groups. Many of these practices began losing their popularity and hold among the people, particularly western educated Chinese as early as the 1900s. However, their demise was hastened by the strong action of the PRC's Marriage Law of 1960. The equal status of men and women in the PRC applies to marriage, divorce, and inheritance, and carries with it equal obligation to become part of the national labor force. Women in the PRC are expected to put the needs of their group and its production ahead of the demands of the husband and children. In general women are encouraged to wait until they are at least 25 years old before marrying, and they are expected to have no more than two children. The wedding should be simple and should take place after the working hours so that no time is lost in production. There is some evidence that women do receive lower wages for equal work on the commune, and are given "female" jobs such as handicraft, fly swatting, and manure collecting.

Housing

In the PRC there is a critical shortage of housing, and houses are very small. A family in a new apartment generally has one or two rooms with a private bathroom and the use of public bathing facilities. The kitchen facilities are frequently shared by several families. However, the political elite and others in high income categories usually have well-furnished accommodations and adequate space.

Practical Information

Getting an Invitation

All travelers to the PRC come by invitation from either the Chinese government, a trading corporation, a friendship association, The Academy of Science, The China Travel Service, or a foreign embassy in Peking. A person will not receive a visa from the PRC's counselor office unless some organization in China will be responsible during the stay in that country. If travel outside the city where the sponsoring unit is located, the China Travel Service, on request of the sponsoring unit, may assist with travel plans. Chinese persons residing outside the PRC and members of the international press are handled separately. The length of time it takes to receive an invitation to the PRC varies as some Americans have waited several years for an invitation, whereas other persons, under special circumstances, have received an invitation within a few days. The address of the embassy of the PRC is:

> The Embassy of The People's Republic of China
> 2300 Connecticut Avenue, N.W.
> Washington, D.C. 20008

The embassy will issue a visa that is valid for a single visit of a specific number of days. Visas can also sometimes be issued at the border but this is extremely rare. One should not attempt or expect to be issued a visa at the border unless one has positive assurance that one will be issued.

Foreign Trade

China's foreign trade is controlled by a state monopoly controlled by the Ministry of Foreign Trade. Priority is given to those imports that will aid in rapidly building China into an industrialized nation. Emphasis is placed on the supply of materials and equipment from domestic sources. The concept of self-reliance is a fact of life in China that no market survey or potential exporter can afford to ignore. When a need cannot be filled domestically however, foreign sources are then acceptable.

The following is a listing of Chinese Foreign Trade Corporations (FTC), commodities handled by each, with their street, cable and telex addresses.*

China National Arts and Crafts Import and Export Corporation
    82 Dong'anmen Street
    Beijing, People's Republic of China
    Cable: ARTCHINA BEIJING
    Telex: 22165 CNART CN BEIJING

Pottery and porcelain, drawn-work and embroidered articles, ivory carvings, jade and semiprecious stone carvings, pearls and gems, jewelry, lacquer

---

*Reprinted from "Doing Business in China," U.S. Department of Commerce, February 1979.

wares, cloisonne wares, Chinese paintings and calligraphy, antiques, straw, wicker, bamboo and rattan articles, furniture, artistic handicrafts, and other handicrafts for daily use.

China National Cereals, Oils and Food-stuffs Import and Export Corporation
  82 Dong'anmen Street
  Beijing, People's Republic of China
  Cable: CEROILFOOD BEIJING
  Telex: 22111 CEROF CN or 22281 CEROF CN BEIJING

Cereals, edible vegetable and animal oils and fats, vegetable and animal oils and fats for industrial use, oilseeds, seeds, oil cakes, feedstuffs, salt, edible livestock and poultry, meat and meat products, eggs and egg products, fresh fruit and fruit products, aquatic and marine products, canned goods of various kinds, sugar and sweets, wines, liquors and spirits of various kinds, dairy products, vegetables and condiments, bean flour noodles, grain products, nuts and dried vegetables (some nuts, dried fruits, and vegetables also carried by native produce).

China National Chemicals Import and Export Corporation
  Erligou, Xijiao
  Beijing, People's Republic of China
  Cable: SINOCHEM BEIJING
  Telex: 22243 CHEMI CN BEIJING

Organic and inorganic chemicals, chemical raw materials, rubber, rubber tires, and other rubber products, crude petroleum and petroleum and petrochemical products (except aromatics), chemical fertilizers, insecticides, fungicides, antibiotics and pharmaceuticals, medical instruments, apparatus and supplies, dyestuffs, pigments, and paints.

China National Light Industrial Products Import and Export Corporation
  82 Dong'anmen Street
  Beijing, People's Republic of China
  Cable: INDUSTRY BEIJING
  Telex: 22282 LIGHT CN BEIJING

General merchandise of all kinds, paper, stationery, musical instruments, typewriters, cameras, film, radios, refrigerators, sporting goods, toys, building materials (plywood, insulation board, p.v.c. fittings and pipe, tiles, glass, sanitary ware, etc.) and electrical appliances, clocks and wristwatches, fishnets, net yarns, leather shoes, and leather products.

China National Machinery Import and Export Corporation
Erligou, Xijiao
Beijing, People's Republic of China
Cable: MACHIMPEX BEIJING
Telex: 22242 CMIEC BEIJING

Machine tools, presses, hammers, shears, forging machines, diesel engines, gasoline engines, steam turbines, boilers, industrial and institutional refrigeration and air conditioning equipment, mining machinery, metallurgical machinery, compressors and pumps, hoists, winches and cranes, transport equipment (aircraft, railroad, automotive, ships and parts thereof), power and hand tools, agricultural machinery and implements, printing machines, knitting and other textile machines, building machinery, machinery for the chemical, rubber, plastics and other industries, ball and roller bearings, tungsten carbide, electric machinery and equipment, telecommunication equipment, electric and electronic measuring instruments, and scientific instruments (except medical instruments).

China National Metals and Minerals Import and Export Corporation
Erligou, Xijiao
Beijing, People's Republic of China
Cable: MINMETALS BEIJING
Telex: 22241 MIMET CN BEIJING

Steel plates, sheets and strip, steel sections, steel pipe and tube, railway materials, cast iron products, pig iron, ferroalloys, fluorspar, limestone, nonferrous metals, precious rare metals, ferrous ores, nonferrous ores, rare earths, nonmetallic minerals, refractories, coal and coke, cement, granite, marble, bricks and other construction materials, and hardware.

China National Native Produce and Animal By-Products Import and Export Corporation
82 Dong'anmen Street
Beijing, People's Republic of China
Cable: CHINATU HSU BEIJING
Telex: 22283 TUSHU CN BEIJING

Tea, coffee, cocoa, tobacco and cigarettes, fibers (hemp, ramie, jute, sisal, flax, etc.) rosin, manioc, starches, and seeds, cotton linters and waste, timber, certain papers and forest products, waxes, spices, essential oils, aromatic chemicals, nuts, dried fruits and vegetables (see also CEROIL-FOOD), patent medicines and medicinal herbs, fireworks, nursery stock as well as other native produce, including bristles and brushes, horsetails, feathers, down and down products, feathers for decorative use, rabbit hair, goat hair, wool, cashmere, camel hair, casings, hides, leathers, fur mattresses, fur products, carpets, living animals.

China National Technical Import Corporation
Erligou, Xijiao
Beijing, People's Republic of China
Cable: TECHIMPORT BEIJING
Telex: 22244 CNTIC CN BEIJING

Importation of complete plants and technology.

China National Textiles Import and Export Corporation
82 Dong'anmen Street
Beijing, People's Republic of China
Cable: CHINATEX BEIJING
Telex: 22280 CNTEX CN BEIJING

Cotton, cotton yarns, raw silk, steam filature, wool tops, rayon fibers, synthetic and manmade fibers, cotton piecegoods, woolen piecegoods, linen, garments and wearing apparel, knitted goods, cotton and woolen manufactured goods, ready-made silk articles, drawn works.

China National Complete Plant Export Corporation
An Ding Men Wai
Beijing, People's Republic of China
Cable: COMPLANT BEIJING

Exporters only of complete factories, works and production units, usually, but not exclusively, as part of an economic aid agreement.

China National Machinery and Equipment Export Corporation
12 Fu Xing Men Wai Street
Beijing, People's Republic of China
Cable: EQUIPEX BEIJING

Exporters only of machine tools, forging and pressing equipment, woodworking machinery, measuring and cutting tools, heavy-duty machinery, mining machinery, machinery for petroleum and chemical industries, general utility machinery, agricultural machinery, power-generating machinery, electric generating sets, automobiles, roller bearings, hoisting and transport equipment, building machinery, printing machinery, electric motors, electric devices and equipment, electric instruments and meters, physical instruments, optical instruments, complete equipment for hydroelectric power stations, refrigerating works, ice-making machinery, wood screw machinery, rubber-making and plastic-making machinery.

The following questions are suggested to be considered by Overseas Business Report (1976) prior to attempting to do business in the PRC:

1. Are you prepared to invest considerable money initially without assurance of an early return?
2. Are you prepared to negotiate the first transaction for one or two years?

3. Are you prepared to assign the necessary senior talent and technical expertise to the project?
4. Are you prepared to walk away from a negotiation that does not look like it will bear fruit at any time?
5. Are you prepared to resist concessionary terms in order to penetrate the market?

If your answers to any of these questions are negative, Overseas Business Report suggests rethinking entering the PRC market.

Initial Proposals to the PRC

The question as to whether or not the proposal should be written in Chinese is raised, and if possible this would be a courteous thing to do. Also, it may facilitate the handling and processing of your proposal in the PRC. If the proposal covers products for which you are unsure that the Chinese have a need, it may be quite unnecessary to have the lengthy proposal translated into Chinese. A covering letter should also be sent as a way of demonstrating your interest. If the Chinese are interested in your proposal, they will reply. However, it very often takes considerable time, sometimes several months, for a proposal to be processed and assessed. If you do not receive a reply, it is probably an indication that there is no such requirement for your product or commodity at that particular time. Because of the delays in mail and the time that is required to process a proposal in the PRC, it is suggested that one wait at least three or four months before following up an initial proposal.

Additional literature and samples could also be sent at a subsequent time referring to the original letter and proposal. However, samples should be sent to China only after receiving permission in advance from the appropriate foreign trade corporation. Exporters should arrange to send their samples directly to the Foreign Trade Corporation (FTC) in Peking or directed to other branch offices in other parts of China. Under no circumstances should the FTC be circumvented. It may be very useful to visit the Hong Kong agents of the Chinese Foreign Trade Corporation. These agents can explain the current situation and usually report to their principals in Peking, but they are with rare exceptions allowed to conclude trade deals.

The Chinese generally prefer to deal with western companies directly, but they will not refuse to negotiate through agents of these firms if necessary.

Contacts with the Chinese Foreign Trade Corporation should be opened as soon as the company begins to pursue business in the PRC. Business negotiations with the Chinese are marked by efforts to obtain as much technical and commercial information about the company's products as possible. When foreign companies have been unwilling to discuss proprietary technical information, the Chinese generally understand and accept this situation.

Entry Requirements

All visitors must have a valid entry visa. Besides this, smallpox and cholera vaccinations must be current. Photos are required for I.D. cards, driver's licenses, and many other documents. It is suggested that all visitors bring at least one dozen small photos approximately one inch by one and one-half inches as U.S. passport size photos are not acceptable.

Geography and Climate

The PRC occupies approximately 3.7 million square miles. As such, it is the third largest country in the world, the first being the U.S.S.R. and the second being Canada. The PRC shares borders with North Korea, U.S.S.R., Afghanistan, Mongolia, India, Pakistan, Nepal, Bhutan, Burma, Laos, and Vietnam. Hong Kong and Macao are situated on the PRC's southern coast.

Only about one-tenth of the land of China is cultivated, and approximately two-thirds of China's land is mountainous or desert. Over 90% of the people live on one-sixth of the land. The country lies almost entirely in the temperate zone, and part of their southern most provinces lie within the tropics. During the summer months, warm moist air brings heavy rains to eastern China and the weather in that area is typically hot and humid. During the winter months, there is a sharp contrast when the dry cold Siberian air masses dominate and there is a fair amount of snow. In the spring, Peking is mostly dry. However, in July and August, the weather turns extremely hot and humid, and it has been likened very much to Washington, D.C Autumn is the best time of the year in the PRC with clear, warm, and pleasant days. Winter is from December to March, and it is cold and windy with occasional light snow falls in Peking.

Arriving in the PRC/Customs

Many people arrive in Peking via Tokyo. If you go via Tokyo, a person should obtain a 48-month Japanese entry visa even if it is to be used only in transit. Persons whose passports contain Taiwan/Republic of China visas should apply to the passport office for a new passport.

From Tokyo the flight takes approximately five hours. However, if one enters the PRC from Hong Kong, there are several stages. First one takes a train to the border, crosses the border on foot, has lunch, and then boards another train for a two-hour trip to Canton. At Canton, one boards a plane for Peking, which is approximately 1200 miles to the north. The whole journey takes approximately twelve hours. Returning from Peking to Hong Kong cannot be made in one day as an overnight stop is required in Canton. English speaking guides from the China Travel Service meet travelers at the railway station in Canton. One can also travel from Canton to Peking by train, which takes two nights and one day. An alternate route is to fly directly to Peking from Europe through Karachi, Tehran, or Bombay.

Briefing in the PRC

In most places that businessmen or other foreigners visit in the PRC, whether it be a commune or factory, you will be received by a person who is designated to greet and give a brief introduction of the environment to foreigners. The briefing usually takes the form of an overview of the area population, which is followed by history and a description of the conditions prior to 1949. This is followed by a talk on the improvements that have resulted since then. There will also be a description of the specific commune, crops that it grows and what their yields are, the capital equipment, and what factories or sideline occupations it runs. There will also be an opportunity for questions. Any questions that deal with the content of the materials presented are acceptable.

The Dress of the People

Chinese men and women wear trousers with a tunic, which is light and worn open-necked in the summer, and padded in the winter. The pants or trousers are generally blue, gray, or brown. The dress of the foreigners in the PRC varies, but generally reflects the current fashion of the person's home country.

Formal wear is only occasionally worn, but there are occasional black-tie dinners within the diplomatic community. Business suits and street length or long dresses and pantsuits are worn at banquets and dinners for visiting delegations where there are Chinese hosts or guests. During the winter, warm clothing including boots, are useful for dining in restaurants as they are often poorly heated and the floors are cold. Synthetic fabrics are a problem because they collect excessive electricity in the dry winter months. When entertaining in one's home, long dresses and pantsuits are acceptable and are frequently worn.

Communications

International mail service is reliable and rapid. To send an air letter from the PRC to the U.S. would cost about 19 cents if you purchase a Chinese air letter. If you use a regular air mail letter, the cost is approximately 26 cents per ounce.

The domestic telephone system in the PRC is good and phones may be obtained by the Chinese without a great deal of difficulty. All apartments have a phone and many have extensions. International calls can be made to most parts of the world. Telephone communication between the mainland and the U.S. is quite good, and telephone lines and English speaking operators are on duty 24 hours a day. Cable service is also good and reliable, internally and externally.

Peking

Peking is on the northern edge of the North China Plain. It is a large, sprawling city. During the past 25 years, a number of new, multistory buildings have been built in that city. However, Peking is mostly characterized by narrow streets with buildings of gray walls beyond which gray roofs with slightly upturned gables mark courtyards and residences. Since 1949, blocks of brick apartments for workers are characteristic of the city.

In Peking, the electrical current is 220 volts and 50 cycles. Most apartment buildings have hot and cold running water, which is provided by a central system. In the early spring, the city's hot water system is closed for a month of repairs. It is suggested that all small appliances be imported, and if they are not at least 200-volt, a transformer is required. Electric clocks, tape recorders, and other appliances of that nature will not work properly unless they are designed for or adapted to 50-cycle power. The electrical supply is generally dependable. However, wiring is inadequate, and only a limited number of appliances may be used at the same time.

Hotels and Lodging

There are few hotels and guest houses in Peking, and the quality of these varies significantly. One of the best hotels in Peking is the Peking Hotel. In Shanghai, the Chin Chiang and Peace Hotels are excellent. Many of the hotels in China are not air-conditioned. This is somewhat of a discomfort in the summer months. In the winter months, many of the smaller hotels and guest houses are not heated to a comfortable 68 degrees Fahrenheit. Besides this, the hot water is available only in the early morning and early evening.

There are extensive plans for building international hotels in china's major cities, but until such hotels are erected, the increased foreign travel will mean scarce accomodations.

Currency Banking

Local currency is called the Yuan (Y). The official title is the Renmimbi. The dollar exchange rate is set by The Bank of China and reflects the dollar's international position and is subject to fluctuation. The Yuan is a decimal currency with the fen (cents) equal to 100 cents. There are one-, two-, and five-fen coins and ten-, twenty-, and fifty-fen notes, as well as one-, two-, five- and ten-Yuan notes.

The Chinese use the metric system of weights and measures.

Traveler's checks are not available for purchase in Peking, but with the exception of American Express and First National City Bank traveler's checks, they can be cashed at The Bank of China.

Presently, credit cards and personal checks are not honored anywhere in China. One must exchange excess Yuan on leaving the PRC at the border.

It is suggested that all visitors bring enough traveler's checks for the entire trip, which would cost at least $60 a day in Peking, but considerably less in other cities. If one should run short of money during a trip to the PRC, transferring money via the telegraph is allowed and this is the quickest way of receiving funds from abroad. The Bank of China also sells Renmimbi traveler's checks in 50-Yuan and 100-Yuan denominations for foreign exchange, and these are much more convenient than cash.

Food

Many of the hotels in the PRC serving foreigners have excellent menus acceptable to all tastes. In some instances, foreign food and dishes are prepared, but is usually not of the same quality as the Chinese food. A la carte Chinese food is recommended unless one is not able to eat this.

Alcoholic Beverages

Chinese beer is very similar to German beer and is generally good. Chinese wines are generally either grape or rice wines. The grape wines are usually quite sweet, but there is also a fairly good wine that is drier. Rice wines are usually consumed hot and are quite strong. The best known of these is Shaohsing wine, which is drier and contains about 25% alcohol. The Chinese drink vodka and gin, which are comparable to the American and European brands. Chinese also have a kind of rum. Besides these, there are non-alcoholic drinks available in most places, with the consumption of Coca-Cola increasing.

Medical Problems

When traveling directly from the United States, only a valid smallpox vaccination is required. Many people recommend that a current typhoid and gamma globulin shot be received.

If you should become ill in China, you will get the best medical treatment available. All major cities have hospitals and there are sections of these hospitals that are reserved for foreigners, and someone on the staff can speak

English. If you wish, it is also possible to receive treatment by acupuncture. Payment is usually made by cash at the hospital. Chinese doctors are well skilled. However, they tend to be cautious in their diagnosis and treatment of foreigners.

Travel Within China

In all travel within China, a foreigner will be assisted by someone from the China Travel Service (CTS). These guides are full-time professionals who assist foreigners while they are in the PRC. All have some ability in English and are familiar with the area of expertise that relates to the foreigner's purpose in the PRC.

The guide usually meets the foreigners at the train or plane and helps with the travel formalities and baggage. The guide is a very useful and important part of your tour, and it is recommended that you work well with the guide.

The aircraft of the PRC's Civil Aviation Authority of China (CAAC) are usually American, British, or Soviet planes and are quite comfortable. The CAAC is rather cautious, and often flights are delayed because of poor weather.

As in the U.S., passengers are allowed 20 kilograms of luggage with overweight being charged for additional weight. Most of the domestic flights do not serve hot food on the flights. However, cold drinks and tea are served. On a plane trip, this may be the only occasion that a foreigner is able to sit next to a Chinese person whose purpose is not to work with foreigners.

Besides travel by air, there is a great deal of travel in China by train. Foreigners travel first class and may end up by sharing a compartment with other foreigners, but only rarely with a Chinese. On overnight train rides, compartments generally have four berths, which are comfortable. However, during the winter months, they may be somewhat cold and perhaps hot during the summer months. A person may be asked to share his or her compartment with another foreigner of either sex. There is usually a washroom and two toilets in each car, but it is recommended that you take soap and toilet paper with you.

For traveling within the PRC a passport or other acceptable form of identification acceptable to the Chinese, a permit to travel from the Public Security Bureau, and a letter to the China Travel Service offices along the way are necessary. If you are traveling in a group, many of these documents may be handled by the traveling guide. At each airport or train station, these documents will be checked upon arrival and departure. At the present time, there are about 30 cities in the PRC that are open to tourist travel. If you happen to be of a high ranking or a specialized technical member of a high ranking specialized technical delegation, you may be able to travel in other areas.

Personal and Prohibited Items

Personal items essential to the visitor during his stay in the PRC are allowed. Besides these, up to 4 bottles of alcohol and 600 cigarettes may be brought in or may be received by mail. Prohibited items include the currency from Taiwan; lottery or raffle tickets; and books, journals, films, or tapes that would be harmful to or cast dispersion on politics, culture, and morals. These items may be confiscated on entry.

Taxi Fare

Taxi fares generally run at 60 fen per kilometer, but can vary. There is a minimum charge of two kilometers, and it is *impossible to hail a taxi from the street*. Taxis can be arranged by the hotel.

Business Customs and Practices

Advice for Americans Doing Business in the PRC

1. The western businessman should avoid attempting to encourage the people from China to increase their productivity on the basis of "getting ahead."
2. The foreign businessman should not focus on the individual Chinese person, but rather on the group of individuals who are working for a particular goal. If a Chinese individual is singled out as possessing unique qualities, this could very well result in embarrassment to this person.
3. The visitor should also be cautious as to be perceived by the Chinese as being superior or bossy in any way. The people from the PRC have had their experience in the past of American imperialism and superiority.
4. Generally, in discussions with Chinese people, the foreigner should avoid "self centered" conversation in which the "I" is excessively utilized. The Chinese view with contempt the individual who strives to display personal attributes, as Chinese are much more oriented to the group.
5. The Chinese are somewhat more reticent, retiring, reserved, or shy when compared with North Americans. They avoid open displays of affection and the speaking distance between two people in nonintimate relationships is greater than in the West.
6. The Chinese are not a "touching" society, and in this respect, they are very similar to North Americans; nor do they appreciate loud, boisterous behavior. A foreign businessman may find himself in difficulty if he is overly aggressive and loud.
7. Another caution that foreign businessmen should be aware of is that of judging the Chinese. A single most important necessity for under-

standing and communicating with the Chinese is the necessity to avoid judgment. Presently, there are only a few Americans in China, and all Americans' behavior is closely scrutinized. If the American reveals an understanding of the social values within China or does not seek to impose his own norms on the people, he will encounter a high degree of acceptance.

8. The Chinese are also known for scrupulous honesty and high degree of morality. Any incident of rudeness or disrespect toward any person or the PRC in general will damage relations.

9. The Chinese are very relaxed when it comes to work, and they take time to gossip and talk about basic amentities and drink tea. However, they put in long hours each day and generally work six days per week, with only six national hoidays per year.

Attitude Toward Americans

Many American businessmen feel that since the death of Mao, there has been a change in the Chinese attitudes toward Americans. They take the relationship with Americans seriously, and they are very friendly. In many of the speeches made in the presence of Americans, the theme of "the Americans are a great people, the Chinese are a great people, and together many things can be accomplished" is said frequently. As in the past, they have made a distinction between the American people and the American government and policies.

Also, since the death of Mao, the industrial managers and workers are being exorted to show even more concern for production and profits. In their educational system, the Chinese have been taught to regard Americans as harmless barbarians.

Negotiating Business

The Chinese rank among the toughest negotiators in the world. In addition, China is probably one of the most difficult countries for an outsider to understand and adapt to.

The British are the most familiar with the Chinese trading business because they have been trading with the PRC since the mid-1950s. They emphasize proper preparation prior to making a trip to China. Selecting the right company representative is considered a key aspect in preparation for the trip. A typical invitation to visit China on business would have been as follows:

> We are glad to inform you that your proposed topic has been accepted.
> Please send 25 copies of your papers one month prior to your arrival.
> Please send immediately the names of your company's representatives,
> their bibliographies, their nationalities, and their passport numbers.

Technical competence is the primary criterion for the representatives according to experienced travelers to the PRC. A number of American companies that have visited China during the past few years have had to leave China midway through a visit and return later with more technically seasoned engineers.

The number of persons accepted in a negotiating team is generally from two to seven persons with three to five representatives of a foreign company being the ideal number. One person should be appointed leader and should serve as the official spokesman for the visiting team while in the PRC. The Chinese prefer to deal with senior people who are able to make decisions during the trip if these are necessary.

Besides technical competency, the next most necessary criterion is *patience*. Negotiations often run for ten days straight and these can become very tedious and tiresome. The chief negotiator of the Boeing team that in 1972 sold $125 million worth of 707's to China spent a total of 100 days in Peking. The Chinese often ask detailed questions which, to the Americans, do not seem to be important. In preparing for the presentation, the American negotiator should be well versed in making a technical presentation of their products or service.

The Chinese negotiators are always well prepared. Business negotiations usually start slowly and stiffly. As both sides begin to relax, however, the negotiations become more informal. The dress code is somewhat more informal than the West. The Chinese negotiating team will generally consist of members of the Foreign Trade Corporation and scientists. There is usually no legal representation.

During presentation and negotiation, questioning can very often become intense. The Chinese furnish the interpreters, and the foreign companies are advised *not* to bring their own interpreter unless this person is also technically competent. The quality of the Chinese translators varies. However, if the translating service seems unsatisfactory, it is suggested that the visitors speak to the leader of the Chinese delegation and request another person.

During the negotiations and in the technical presentation, it is recommended that the foreigners speak slowly and avoid jargon.

The Chinese are keen business people, and competition among western businessmen may be used by the Chinese as a lever or strategy to get the company to improve on its offer. Commercial negotiations with the Chinese often include extensive discussions on relatively, at least from the American perspective, minor aspects of the transaction. Careful preparation is a must. American and foreign businessmen should be aware of all previous correspondence as well as the details of the proposal and should expect to meet with and to negotiate with very astute bargainers.

Decisions in the PRC are usually group decisions made in coordination with a number of Chinese. Their negotiating style is to emphasize mutual understanding and the development of good, long-term relationships, both corporate and personal. If a member of the foreign company negotiating team speaks Chinese, this can facilitate the discussion and resolve potential difficulties in communicating technical and commercial information.

The Chinese prefer to make oral agreements or oral understandings beyond the written contract. Generally, they are more willing to amend their purchase contract than their export contract. However, for foreign businessmen in the final contract, it is important that these be put in writing not withstanding the oral assurance of the members of the Federal Trade Corporation, even though they may have said that their apprehensions may be unfounded. In areas of disagreement, a spirit of friendly negotiations is critical. The negotiations should avoid a formal arbitrator. The negotiations should be conducted and perpetuated by the two parties.

Business Courtesies

When you have an appointment with a Chinese official, you will generally be introduced and offered some tea and cigarettes. The offering of a cigarette in the PRC has become the single most common expression of hospitality. Prior to your entrance, your Chinese host will be briefed on who you are and why you are there. There may be initiated polite questions about your trip and the U.S., generally in the area of pleasantries, and perhaps even about your family. If your call is merely a courtesy call, it may not go beyond this. If this is more than a courtesy call, it would be appropriate to begin discussion of a business nature at this time. The Chinese host will generally indicate when it is time for a person to leave.

It is also important to reciprocate invitations if they are given by the PRC. For example, if a banquet is given in the honor of the American team, they should reciprocate by giving a banquet for the Chinese team. Small company souvenirs or American picture books often make good presents, but expensive gifts should not be given.

Some business cautions—the Chinese are very sensitive about foreigners' comments on Chinese politics. Even a joke about the PRC Chairman Mao, or any of their other political leaders, is extremely *inappropriate*. It is suggested that it is best to listen, ask questions related to your particular business for being in the PRC, and leave it at that.

Tipping is unnecessary in the PRC, and no matter how useful or how helpful your guide or interpreter has been, *do not try to tip these persons*.

The Chinese are punctual, and you should arrive promptly on time for each meeting.

The Chinese do not like to be touched or slapped on the back or even to shake hands. A slight bow and a brief shake of the hands is more appropriate.

In the PRC, pre-marital sex is frowned upon and is not encouraged or discussed. Other "no-nos" include questioning about the fallen leaders, or the so called "Gang of Four," and discussion of the Taiwan issue. Americans generally feel that they are greeted with a spirit of camaraderie. However, some Americans feel that the people they meet are programmed and they are given canned propaganda speeches. The Chinese have for a long time been noted for a concern for not losing face. The self-critical attitude that now prevails seems to indicate that this concern is no longer as pervasive.

In China, the family name is always mentioned first. For example, Teng Hsiao-ping should be addressed as Mr. Teng. During one's stay in the PRC, a visitor could be invited to a dinner in a restaurant by the organization that is sponsoring the visit. The guest should arrive on time or even perhaps a little early. The host would normally toast the guest at an early stage of the meal with the guest reciprocating after a short interval. During the meal, alcoholic beverages should not be consumed until a toast has been made. It is a custom to toast other persons at the table throughout the meal. At the end of the dinner, the guest of honor makes the first move to depart. The usual procedure is to leave shortly after the meal is finished. Most dinner parties usually end by 8:30 or 9:00 in the evening.

Although tipping is forbidden in the PRC, it is appropriate to thank the hotel staff, and other persons for efforts made on your behalf.

It is customary to use business cards in the PRC, and it is recommended that one side be printed in Chinese. However, business cards from the Chinese to Americans may not be given in return. Americans or foreign businessmen traveling to Peking via Hong Kong can easily have these cards printed in a matter of hours in that city.

The Chinese do not appreciate or like to do business on the telephone or with telex machines. The personal touch is required, and letters and telephones should be avoided if a personal contact is possible.

Another topic to be avoided is the discussion of the Taiwan issue by foreign visitors.

The Chinese generally believe that foreign businessmen will be highly qualified technically in their specific areas of expertise. The Chinese businessmen do not have a need to show their intellectual expertise or to make an impression on the foreign guest. The foreigner or foreign businessman who is worthy and a true professional will have discreet but lavish attention showered on him while he is in China.

The Chinese businessman traditionally places a great deal of emphasis on proper etiquette. It is recommended that the qualities that foreign businessmen possess going to the PRC have are *dignity, reserve, patience, persistence,* and a *sensitivity to* and *respect for Chinese customs and temperament.*

The Chinese generally give preference to companies with long standing relationships with state trading companies. Newcomers and new business organizations have to adjust to the Chinese style of making contracts, negotiating, and arranging for contracts.

One should also attempt to be a good guest and listen politely to talks on Mao and the great progress China has made during the last several years. The

Chinese are known as tough bargainers but they are also known as being reputable and honorable.

Very often, several visits to the PRC are necessary to consummate any business transaction. The foreign businessman should realize this. It has been found by many American businessmen that three, four, and five business negotiating sessions are often required in order to finalize the negotiations.

Traders coming to sell products in China must be prepared to spend a much longer time than *buyers,* and may find themselves waiting for appointments day after day. This requires a great deal of patience, time, and perseverance, as well as a sensitivity to Chinese customs and way of doing business.

When a foreign businessman has made a good impression on the Chinese, the courtesy conversation may be extended beyond the allocated time. Another indication that a good impression has been made is when the Chinese may suggest that the discussion be continued. Most flattering of all, however, is a phone call from the Chinese delegation asking the visitor to be their guest for lunch or dinner. If, at this time, the Chinese brings his wife, it could be assumed that you have made "a big hit."

References

Books

Andors, Stephen, *China's Industrial Revolution: Policy, Planning and Management 1949 to the Present.* New York: Pantheon Books, 1977.

Barnett, A. Doak, *China and the Major Powers in East Asia.* Washington, D.C.: Brookings, 1977.

Boarman, Patrick M. and Jayson Mugar, *Trade with China.* Los Angeles: Center for International Business, 1973.

Brandt, Conrad, Benjamin Schwartz, and John K. Fairbank, *A Documentary History of Chinese Communism.* New York: Atheneum, 1971.

Cheng, Chu-yuan, *China's Petroleum Industry: Output Growth and Export Potential.* New York: Praeger, 1976.

Eckstein, Alexander, *China's Economic Revolution.* Cambridge: Cambridge University Press, 1977.

Fairbank, John K., *China Perceived: Images and Policies in Chinese-American Relations.* New York: Knopf, 1974.

Fairbank, John K., *The United States and China,* (rev. ed.) Cambridge: Harvard University Press, 1971.

Felber, John E., *The American's Tourist Manual for the People's Republic of China.* Newark, N.J.: International Trade Index, 1975.

Harding, Harry, Jr., *China and the U.S.: Normalization and Beyond.* The China Council of the Asia Society and the Foreign Policy Association, 1979.

Hsiao, Gene T., *The Foreign Trade of China: Policy, Law and Practice.* Berkeley: University of California Press, 1977.

Hsu, Francis L.K., *Americans and Chinese.* Garden City, N.Y.: Doubleday, Natural History Press, 1972.

Isaacs, Harold R., *Images of Asia: American Views of China and India.* New York: Harper & Row, Publishers, 1972.

Kaplan, Frederick, et al, *Encyclopedia of China Today.* Fair Lawn, N.J.: Eurasian Press, 1979.

Karnow, Stanley, *Mao and China.* New York: Viking, 1972.

Leng, Shao-chuan (ed.), *Post-Mao China and U.S.-China Trade.* Charlottesville, Va.: University Press of Virginia, 1977.

Metcalf, John E. and Vember K. Ranganathan, *China Trade Guide.* First National City Bank, September, 1972.

Neilan, Edward and Charles R. Smith, *The Future of the China Market: Prospects for Sino-American Trade.* Washington, D.C.: American Enterprise Institute for Public Policy Research, 1974.

Salisbury, Harrison E., *To Peking and Beyond.* New York: Berkley Publishing Corp., 1973.

Szuprowicz, Bohdan and Maria, *Doing Business with the People's Republic of China: Industries and Markets.* New York: John Wiley & Sons, 1978. Sons, 1978.

———, *The People's Republic of China: Foreign Trade in Machinery and Equipment Since 1952.* Special Report No. 11, The National Council for US-China Trade, February 1975.

Articles

Jackson, Howell, "Giving Technical Seminars in China," *China Business Review.* Volume 5, Number 1, January-February, 1978.

National Foreign Assessment Center, "China: In Pursuit of Economic Modernization." Washingon, D.C.: Central Intelligence Agency, December 1978.

National Foreign Assessment Center, "China: International Trade 1977-78." Washington, D.C.: Central Intelligence Agency, December 1978.

U.S. Department of Commerce, Industry and Trade Administration, "Doing Business with China." Washington, D.C., February 1979.

———, "China Apparently Ready for Revolutionary Step: Foreign Equity Welcomed." *Business China,* January 10, 1979.

———, "China Industry Profile: Diesel Engines—2." *Business China,* December 27, 1978.

———, "China Industry Profile: Diesel Engines—3." *Business China,* January 24, 1979.

———, "China Moves to Grant Protection for Patents of Foreign Companies." *Business China,* January 24, 1979

———, "China's New Leaders Start Looking Outward." *Business Week,* September 5, 1977.

———, "Chinese Pacts with France, Sweden." *Business China,* January 10, 1979.

———, "Coca-Cola in China." *Business China,* December 27, 1978.

———, "Countertrade Agreements Signed or Pending." *Business China,* January 24, 1979.

———, "Doing Business with China." Overseas Business Reports, U.S. Department of Commerce, November 1976.

———, "Dramatic Development in China Portend Vast Opportunities in 1979." *Business China,* December 27, 1978.

———, "Firms' Reaction to US-China Normalization." *Business China,* December 27, 1978.

———, "First Clues Point to China's View of Coming Joint Venture." *Business China,* January 24, 1979.

———, "Foreign Investment in China: The Likely Shape of Things to Come." *Business China,* January 10, 1979.

———, "Industry Monitor. . .What's New In." *Business China,* January 10, 1979.

———, "Peking's Attempt to Clarify Countertrade is Brief but Unrevealing." *Business China,* January 10, 1979.

———, "Recent Countertrade Agreements." *Business China,* December 27, 1978.

———, "Representative Offices in Peking: Operating Conditions." *Business China,* January 10, 1979.

———, "South Korea Expects Mutual Benefits from Open Trade with China." *Business China,* January 24, 1979.

———, "Tourism Facilities Going Up in China Across From Macao." *Business China,* January 24, 1979.

———, "The China Breakthrough." *Newsweek,* December 25, 1978.

———, "The New China." *Newsweek,* February 5, 1979.

———, "The PRC to 1985." *Business China,* January 10, 1979.

———, "UK Banks' Overture to China May Be Major Boost to Sales." *Business China,* January 10, 1979.

———, "UK Importers' Mission to China Will Submit Product Buy-Back Bids." *Business China.* January 10, 1979.

———, "World Trade Outlook for Eastern Europe, Union of Soviet Socialist Republics and People's Republic of China." Overseas Business Reports, U.S. Department of Commerce, 1978.

19
Working
in the Middle East

During the latter part of 1978 and early 1979, events in the Middle East, and in particular Iran, changed very rapidly. The number of U.S. nationals in Iran decreased from over 50,000 to a handful, and even their safety was not secure at all times. The number of foreign nationals from other countries also decreased, and Ayatollah Khomeini's rule and the return of Iran to an Islam Republic had serious implications for the United States and many other countries. Billions of dollars in contracts were lost.

It is not the purpose of this volume to interpret or predict political events in any country. In Iran, there are many forces influencing the direction and changes in their society and its relationship to the rest of the world. At least two things can be said from the perspective of this volume. One, almost all political and written commentaries on the events in Iran during that time were *interpretations based on Western terms.* Many officials were shocked and surprised at what happened. Our *cultural blinders* did not allow us to see what was happening from an Iranian perspective. The second theme, which became clearer as Khomeini consolidated his power, was that Americans and foreign nationals in general were not welcome in Iran because they did not adjust to Iranian customs and way of life.

The following material is presented illustrating a number of cultural differences between the United States, Iran, and Saudi Arabia.

West Meets the Middle East

A midwestern banker is invited by an Arab sheik to meet him at the Dorchester Hotel in London. The banker arrives in London and waits to meet the sheik. After two days he is told to fly to Riyadh in Saudi Arabia, which he does. He waits. After three days in Riyadh, he meets the sheik and the beginning of what was to become a very beneficial business relationship between the two persons and their organizations began. The American's experience may have been unique but he demonstrated one of the fundamental qualities for doing business in Saudi Arabia—patience.

"There is no god but Allah and Mohammed is his Messenger." This is written on the Saudi Arabian national flag in stylized Arabic script. Saudi Arabians of all professions and at all social levels reaffirm this statement and all its implications. In spite of a rapid introduction into Saudi Arabia of technology and machinery, there will not be a rapid departure from traditional religious values. The purpose of this chapter is to consider some of the important cultural aspects of Iran and Saudi Arabia.

The themes presented constitute some basic concepts that illustrate potential communication problems and misunderstandings between Saudi Arabians or Iranians and Americans. As in previous chapters, *critical incidents* will illustrate the themes, which represent a broad perspective and are not meant to be comprehensive. Some are modified from V. Lynn Tyler's *Reading Between the Lines* and the Arab and Iran cultural assimilators originally developed and produced by the University of Illinois for the Defense Language Institute. Others are taken from personal experience and those of selected Iranian, Saudi, and U.S. scholars.

The critical incident learning method presents a brief situation involving persons from the two cultures. Following this, the reader is asked to select an alternative among three or four possibilities that would best indicate an understanding of the culture. After a choice is made, the reader continues and reads the explanation of each choice. In this way, selected themes can be studied and a problem solving strategy developed.

The purpose in presenting the material in this form is twofold. One is to present more culture specific information and cultural contrasts between the Americans and Saudi Arabians or Iranians. The other purpose is to suggest and provide opportunities for utilizing an effective cross-cultural problem solving strategy. This strategy requires knowing the respective cultures in which a person is working or living and using this knowledge.

Critical Incidents in Saudi Arabia

An American businessman, while in Saudi Arabia, was invited to a formal meal. Initially things seemed to be going along fairly well, but during the course of the meal he noticed he was beginning to be ignored by his hosts. Following the dinner he thanked his hosts for the spectacular food. What happened?

1. The host did not like him.
2. He should have brought his wife to the meal.
3. He should have thanked them for the entire evening rather than just for the meal.

4. He is left-handed and ate with his left hand, which is not considered good manners in Saudi Arabia.

Alternative One: This is unlikely, as the host probably would not have invited him if he did not like the American.

Alternative Two: His wife was not invited to come so he made the right decision not to bring her.

Alternative Three: This is true. However, this is not why he was ignored during the meal. He should have thanked them for the entire evening and not just the meal.

Alternative Four: This is correct. The left hand is not used for eating from a communal serving platter. He insulted the host by using this hand during dinner and as a result they ignored him. He would have been better to handle the food ineptly with his right hand than to use his left hand for eating.

After making many trips to Saudi Arabia and working successfully with a Saudi businessman and others in his family for some time, an American businessman and his wife were invited by the Saudi's for dinner. The couple arrived and were served by the Saudi's wife, yet she never joined them in conversation or eating. The Americans, afraid of offending the host, didn't ask why. What explains the behavior of the Saudi's wife?

1. Arab women are fabulous cooks and it is proper etiquette to serve your guest.
2. Arab women generally do not meet with businessmen.
3. Women in Saudi Arabia are not allowed to join in social affairs.
4. The Arab woman was intimidated by her Western guests and felt uncomfortable joining them.

Alternative One: This is not entirely correct, although it is expected that Arab women are to serve guests.

Alternative Two: This is the correct response. Arab women generally do not participate in these activities.

Alternative Three: Arab women generally do not participate completely in the social and business relationships of their husbands.

Alternative Four: This is incorrect. Although she may have been intimidated by foreigners, this was not the case.

A French Canadian visiting Saudi Arabia bought an expensive opal ring for his wife. He wanted to buy her a nice gift because she was unable to accompany him on the trip because of an extended illness and he wanted to send the ring home to her by mail. He wanted to buy insurance for the ring but was unable to find anyone who would insure the package. The man became frustrated because he felt the Arabs were being unfriendly and uncooperative in not telling him where and how he could buy insurance. The man ended up taking the ring with him but was unhappy with the entire situation. He left Saudi Arabia with a bitter opinion of Arab hospitality. Which alternative is correct?

1. In Saudi Arabia foreigners cannot be given insurance on articles bought within the country.
2. Saudi Arabians are not materialistic and view luxuries as unnecessary, and thus, could not be insured.
3. There is no such thing as insurance in Saudi Arabia. Saudi Arabians do not believe in insurance.
4. Saudi Arabians do not like foreigners and will not cooperate or help foreigners who are traveling within their country.

Alternative One: This is not entirely correct. It is true that foreigners cannot get insurance in Saudi Arabia but they are not the only people unable to get insurance. The fact of the matter is, there is no insurance. No one can get insurance. This alternative is not the best because it is not entirely comprehensive. This alternative leads one to think that only foreigners are unable to get insurance.

Alternative Two: This is not correct. Saudi Arabians are not materialistic but this has nothing to do with obtaining insurance. Insurance is not used in Saudi Arabia as in many other countries. The statement or implication that "luxuries are noninsurable" is misleading and not pertinent to the real issue.

Alternative Three: This is the most complete and direct answer. The reason the foreigner was unable to get insurance is because there isn't any! Saudi Arabians believe in "the will of God." What will be will be.

Alternative Four: This is completely wrong and a hasty generalization. Whether a Saudi Arabian likes foreigners or not is an individual preference and has nothing to do with not being able to buy insurance in Saudi Arabia.

An American couple who are guests in a Saudi Arabian couple's home mentions how finely articulate the wood carving on the table is. She turns to her husband and tells him that they must find one like it. Following their visit, the Saudi couple insists that the Americans take the wood carving home as a gift from them. What could the American couple do in the situation, or should they have done, in admiring the carving?

1. The American couple could have asked about the wood carving without actually expressing a desire to have one like it.

2. The Americans could have refused to accept the carving.
3. The Americans could have offered to pay the Saudis for the carving.

Alternative One: This action is the most diplomatic way to talk about an object in their home. This method would communicate a general interest in wood carvings as opposed to a specific interest in the one belonging to the Saudi couple. It is also important to state how perfect the object looks in its present place.

Alternative Two: This would have been difficult as it would have strained the relationship between the people.

Alternative Three: This is inappropriate.

An Arab asked his two Western friends if they would go to lunch with him. The Arab insists on paying. The American insisted on paying publically. The Arab became cool. Which alternative explains his coolness?

1. The Arab must have got an upset stomach.
2. The Arab had wanted to pay for their lunches and he was hurt that they wouldn't let him.
3. The Arab felt the Americans thought it was their turn to pay, but he still wanted to be the host.

Alternative One: A stomach upset can come on suddenly, but this was not the reason.

Alternative Two: The Arab wanted to pay for their lunches and he was hurt that they wouldn't let him. Many Americans would not interpret the Arab's invitation as implying that he intended to pay for their lunches. In Arab culture, a suggestion that others join you in eating is an indication that you are inviting them to be your guest; it is a gesture of hospitality and generosity.

Alternative Three: This is highly unlikely from the Arab perspective.

Mr. Johnson has been working in Saudi Arabia for approximately 18 months on a complicated technology transfer project. His position requires him to interact daily with Saudi Arabians who have been trained in various aspects of the project. His candid opinion of their expertise is varied in that some of them are well-trained and others are not proficient. One person, Mohammed X, has been delinquent and has made several serious errors during the past several months in his areas of responsibility. Johnson finally blew his cool and criticized Mohammed in the presence of his coworkers. After this Mohammed was very distant to Mr. Johnson.

1. Arabs do not like to be criticized in public and this caused Mohammed to lose face in front of his colleagues.

2. Mohammed did not like Mr. Johnson anyway, and this simply reinforced his feelings towards him.
3. Mohammed had a personal matter that affected him and this carried over into his work relationships.

Alternative One: Arabs do not like to be criticized in public and have a saying, "God loveth not the speaking ill of anyone in public." When Mr. Johnson criticized Mohammed publically he did severe damage to their relationship, which would be difficult to restore.

Alternative Two: Up to this time, Mohammed had a good relationship with Mr. Johnson and the criticism was the determining factor in changing the situation.

Alternative Three: Something personal may have been affecting Mohammed. However, Arabs tend to keep these to themselves or with close friends, and would not let it affect the work situation.

The marketing manager for a large U.S. multinational corporation has been invited to Riyadh, Saudi Arabia, and has noticed that appointments that he schedules with the various Saudi officials in government and private enterprise never take place on time. Why?

1. Arabs are very busy and other things come up.
2. It is a matter of keeping face with the less important people being kept waiting for a longer period of time.
3. Arab time sense is different than the Western time sense and they lose track of it.

Alternative One: It is true the Arab businessman is generally very busy, but this is not completely true in this situation. Other matters may have come up such as meeting with other members of his family or other Arab businessmen, and this takes precedence over meeting with foreigners. The loyalties of Arab businessmen are important and his family and fellow countrymen come before anyone else.

Alternative Two: This is not entirely true, though persons of lower rank may be kept waiting for a longer period than persons of higher rank.

Alternative Three: The Arab sense is different. However, appointments are generally maintained when possible. The American businessman should remember that patience is a prerequisite for doing business in Saudi Arabia.

During important business discussions with Arab officials concerning the price of a product and its engineering considerations, an American observes that his competitors are present in the same room during these discussions.

This is disturbing to the foreigner, and he wonders why such important matters cannot be discussed in private. Which situation explains this?

1. The Arabs use this as a negotiating strategy to reduce the bargaining position of the foreign negotiators.
2. The Arabs do business in public—even important business.
3. There is a lack of space in many buildings in Saudi Arabia, and it is simply a matter of convenience.

Alternative One: It is true that the Arabs sometimes use this to their advantage. However, this is not the main reason.
Alternative Two: The Arabs traditionally do much of their business in public and this was what was experienced by the American. In government negotiating, as opposed to private negotiations, this is especially true.
Alternative Three: There is a shortage of office space in many Saudi cities. However, this is not the reason for doing business in public.

John Geer has worked in Saudi Arabia for a considerable length of time and has become friendly with Abdul, the son of his Saudi partner. While drinking one evening, he called Abdul a "son of a bitch" in jest. He noticed the relationship immediately cooled. What response explains this sudden coolness?

1. Abdul was insulted by his expression.
2. Abdul took the meaning of the words literally.
3. Something else happened and it had nothing to do with his use of the expression.

Alternative One: Abdul was insulted by Mr. Geer's use of the expression and these kinds of words, although understood by Americans in their context, are to be avoided in working with Saudi Arabians.
Alternative Two: Abdul was fluent in English and therefore he knew the expression was not to be taken literally.
Alternative Three: This is not true.

In Saudi Arabia there is a social hierarchy and on occasion it is very difficult to determine who is the most important Saudi Arabian and how much respect should be given to the individuals entering a room. The opinion of one American who is not familiar with Saudi Arabia, to a great extent, is that there is no order. Which of the following alternatives would be a clue to the rank of the various persons entering a room?

1. There is no rank or social hierarchy.
2. The last person to enter the room is the most important.
3. The first person to enter a room is the most important.

Alternative One: This is not correct and the Saudi's, although before God are equal, are very conscious of rank and hierarchy.

Alternative Two: The last person in is probably the least important.

Alternative Three: The first person to enter the room is usually the most important individual, but this is not always true. Sometimes it is very difficult to determine the rank of the Arab persons.

The preceding critical incidents provide additional information on the Saudi culture, but more importantly, suggest a problem solving strategy. As a foreigner in another country, it is suggested that one interpret events and situations from the perspective of that culture. In this way, misunderstandings and cultural faux pas will be reduced.

Foreigners in Iran

As stated earlier, the number of foreigners in Iran has decreased significantly. The following suggestions are made so that foreigners who go to Iran in the future have a better knowledge of some customs and courtesies.

Iranian Culture—Some Do's and Don't's

Greetings and Introductions

1. Don't discuss politics. Iranians like to discuss politics but are careful of speaking for or against a viewpoint unless they know a person well.
2. Be positive about the country and culture.
3. Women are respected and treated as special.
4. Use last names (at first meeting) not first names until later in the relationship.
5. Use good eye contact in the beginning of a relationship but don't stare.
6. A guest extends his hand first (whether man or woman). That is, an American extends his hand to an Iranian host.
7. A man stands closer to a man than a woman.
8. A man may shake hands with both hands, or hold the other person's arm, especially if the person is a friend and well liked.
9. A man stands sideways to a woman, not face on. Also, do not directly face head on with an Iranian man.
10. The husband introduces his wife to the Iranian host.

11. An older person initiates the conversation with a younger person (whether male or female). Again, use last name, not first name alone.
12. It is much better to use a few phrases in Farsi. Iranians will really appreciate it and encourage you to speak more.

When Visiting—

1. Visiting Iranian families is very important; it is the way that you really become friends.
2. Iranians will usually arrive late for a meal or party.
3. You, as an American, should arrive close to the agreed upon time—especially if the Iranian host has been around Americans.
4. Iranians will expect you to bring your spouse or friend (the tradition is that "your friend is my friend").
5. Iranians always cook more than is needed. (The saying is "we'll just add a little water to the soup," or "we're just having bread and cheese.")
6. You should bring flowers. They are most appropriate to bring when invited to the home of an Iranian.

What You Shouldn't Do

1. Don't turn your back on an Iranian. It is impolite.
2. Never show the soles of your feet to a friend or guest. It is an extreme insult. Thus, don't put your feet up on the desk or coffee table—as Americans often do.
3. Don't continue making the same cultural mistake over and over again. Iranians will forgive you the first time because you are a foreigner. If you repeat the mistake over and over, they may become angry and will probably not forgive you.
4. Don't take pictures in shrines.
5. Don't take pictures of a woman in rural areas without asking permission.
6. Iranians are more formal than Americans.
7. Adults don't wear shorts. Shorts are O.K. for children only.
8. Don't wear dresses that show a large portion of one's body.

Compliments and Gifts

1. If you admire an Iranian's possession one time, it is a compliment.
2. If you continually admire an Iranian's possession, he might feel an obligation to give it to you.
3. If an Iranian offers you a gift, you should accept it. It is an insult to refuse it. Therefore, be careful when giving compliments, or compli-

ment in context. For example, "Your vase is beautiful in your home. It goes well with your entire decor."

4. Don't make compliments to an Iranian man about his wife or sister.

Islam. Respect their religion. They believe you have the right to believe what you want, and they have the right to believe what they want.

Bachelors. Girls are not allowed to date in the manner that is customary in the U.S. Unmarried male-female relationships in Iran are serious, not casual.

Women in Rural Areas. Men shouldn't talk directly to women in rural areas. American women can speak directly to Iranian women, however.

Critical Incidents in Iran

An American construction engineer is working in Northern Iran where there is a high probability of earthquakes. In the design of several buildings he has made suggestions for changes that would make them safer, but he has had difficulty in having his recommendations accepted. Why is this so?

1. The Iranian workers with whom he is working do not like to accept advice from foreign engineers.
2. The Iranians do not believe that it is necessary to make any changes as the building will collapse if it is meant to collapse.
3. The Iranians know that the suggestions the American engineer has made are not feasible.

Alternative One: Iranians will accept advice from foreign experts and that is why they are invited to participate in special projects in Iran. Sometimes the communication between Americans and Iranians is not completely understood and the Iranian might be reluctant to tell the American. In this particular situation, this was not true.

Alternative Two: The concept of "enshaallah" is strong in Iran and sometimes explains the resistance of Iranians to make changes. Literally the expression means "may it please God that" or "God willing," and it is part of their religious faith. God has determined everything from the beginning and what happens is seen as part of the divine plan. Whatever a person does, is influenced by the will of God and this is often interpreted by foreigners as a resistance to change.

Alternative Three: The suggestion may not be feasible but the Iranian would be reluctant to state this directly to the American as it may cause the American to "lose face."

A Canadian has an appointment with an Iranian. The Canadian is somewhat frustrated with the Iranian because most previous meetings have not taken place on time. Why is this so?

1. The Iranian sense of time is different than the Canadian sense of time.
2. A friend may have come by to see the Iranian and the Iranian is talking with him.
3. The Iranian is simply tardy and this is not typical.

Alternative One: This is true. Appointments in Iran, according to Canadian norms, often begin later than the designated time. They are generally far less exacting about time than Canadians, who usually have strict schedules that they try to adhere to.

Alternative Two: For an Iranian, time is not wasted if it is spent chatting and talking to friends. Friends are treasured and often business appointments may have to take a second priority.

Alternative Three: This may be true, but it is also a cultural trait.

An Iranian businessman, during the course of a discussion with foreigners present, is given some information by a subordinate that is not correct. How will the Iranian businessman respond to this situation?

1. He will reprimand his subordinate at the time and request that he make whatever changes are necessary.
2. He will not display any awareness to the others present that he has noticed the errors.
3. He will explain to his subordinate that there are mistakes and ask him to make the changes later.

Alternative One: The Iranian is not likely to show an external expression of anger in the presence of other persons. The maintenance of dignity or face are important to Iranians and is respected. Confronting others in public and causing them to lose face is not done usually and when it happens, it affects the relationship between the persons involved.

Alternative Two: The businessman probably will not display any awareness of the errors to others who may be present but he will not overlook the mistakes. They will be discussed with the person involved at a later time.

Alternative Three: This is the correct alternative and the Iranian businessman would explain to his subordinate the errors but in such a way that he would not be caused to lose face. He would also ask him to correct the mistakes.

Mr. Williams has noticed that Iranians are always courteous and friendly. However, this is somewhat frustrating as he wants them to express their opinions and critique his ideas more freely. Mr. Williams once read an Iranian poem that had the following line: "A suitable lie is better than a disturbing truth." How can Mr. Williams know the opinions of the Iranians?

1. He will never learn what they think because it is very unlikely they will tell him.
2. If an Iranian hesitates then agrees and continues to agree, it is a good clue that this is his opinion.
3. An Iranian will tell a "white lie" in order to avoid a confrontation or lose face.

Alternative One: It is true that the Iranians are courteous, and an Iranian does not tell another his opinion as directly as an American might.

Alternative Two: The best way to tell whether an Iranian agrees or disagrees with you is to watch and see what happens. Another way is to watch Iranians very carefully and see how they express negative feelings or disagreements.

Alternative Three: This is also true. However, one can learn to read the cues that are being given to determine the reaction of Iranians to an idea or opinion.

Mr. Cohen is working in Iran as a helicopter instructor and has the responsibility of working with five Iranian pilots. Shortly after arriving at the air base he met the men and found out each of them was married. He asked about their children and wives. He sensed he had done something wrong. What was it?

1. Mr. Cohen should have asked about the families and wives earlier as they would be very important to the men.
2. Mr. Cohen should not have asked personal questions about the men's wives.
3. Mr. Cohen should not have asked about the family at all.

Alternative One: Families are very important to Iranians, but one must be careful how to ask about the member of an Iranian family.

Alternative Two: This is correct. Iranian women generally take a secondary role and asking about an Iranian's wife in the early stages of a friendship or relationship is considered by the Iranians as presumptuous and rude.

Alternative Three: This is not correct as it is perfectly acceptable to ask about one's family and children in a general sense.

After the time of Norooz, the Iranian New Year, an American finds that some of his employees do not seem to be working as hard as they had in the past. What could be a possible explanation?

1. The employees did not receive a Norooz bonus.
2. The employees had looked forward to a vacation after Norooz but did not receive it.
3. Norooz is a sad time and the employees were merely reflecting this mood.

Alternative One: Employees in Iran receive a bonus at Norooz that is approximately one month's salary. This depends on the length of employment, but it is a custom that should be respected by American employers.

Alternative Two: In the villages there is a vacation period at Norooz, but most government offices and businesses remain open except for a three-day vacation period.

Alternative Three: Norooz is a happy time.

A California purchaser ordered a number of parts for a machine and received a letter from his Iranian supplier that the parts would be ready by a certain date. When the time came, the parts were not ready and the American called the Iranian for an explanation. Why weren't the parts ready as promised?

1. The parts were not ready and the Iranian didn't feel obligated to inform the American.
2. The supplier did not feel obligated to deliver the parts on the agreed upon day even though there was a written agreement.
3. There was no intention on the part of the Iranian to deliver the material on time from the beginning.

Alternative One: The Iranian would probably not have called the American to inform him of the delay as this would have caused him to look inefficient and therefore lose face in the eyes of the American.

Alternative Two: Iranians do not have a strong sense of meeting deadlines as long as they eventually fulfill the agreements even though they are late.

Alternative Three: This is not true because the Iranian would have put the American off with a variety of excuses if he didn't have any intention of fulfilling the obligation from the beginning. In Iran the most binding agreements are those that are personally negotiated as personal contacts—and connections are of utmost importance.

Mr. Howell decides that his Iranian colleague should point out to some of their Iranian subordinates areas that need improvement in their operations. The Iranian says that this is necessary and that he will do it immediately. Mr. Howell is somewhat fluent in Farsi, and in attempting to read the nonverbal cues of his colleague didn't feel that he was being firm enough. He asked the Iranian why he wasn't firmer. How was the matter handled by the Iranian supervisor?

1. He couched his criticism in such a way that it was not offensive to the Iranians.
2. He didn't make any critical comments to his subordinates as he was afraid of offending them.
3. The American may have thought he was proficient in Farsi but he just didn't understand enough to catch the subtleties.

Alternative One: It is acceptable to criticize in Iran but it is not as direct or blunt as in the United States. When criticism is necessary, it is said in such a way that the person being criticized does not lose dignity or pride.

Alternative Two: This is not true as the Iranian would tell his subordinates about their errors, but he would tell them in such a way that they would not be overly offended.

Alternative Three: The American may have been proficient in Farsi, but understanding the subtle nuances and the nonverbal cues of another language is difficult and many of these may have been missed.

A top-level executive of a large British multinational corporation has requested a meeting with a high government official of Iran. He has attempted to set up this meeting in a variety of ways and when he calls the office of the official his secretary tells him that the meeting will be scheduled as soon as it is possible. After a number of days, the meeting still has not been scheduled. Why can't he get an appointment?

1. Perhaps the Iranian government official has been out of town and therefore is not available.
2. The Iranian government official does not want to meet with the visitor and he is stalling.
3. The Iranian is willing to meet with the Englishman but he has been too busy to set a time for the meeting.

Alternative One: If the government official had been out of town, even out of the country, for a few days, the secretary may not have told this to the Englishman.

Alternative Two: Supposing the Iranian government official did not want to meet with the Englishman, the repeated delays and the lack of scheduled meeting may be a clue to the Englishman that this is the case.

Alternative Three: The Englishman will have to determine if this is the case by repeatedly requesting a meeting. Patience is important and reading all the cues that are provided by all the persons involved in the situation.

Conclusion

In the preceding pages, we have identified a number of themes or cultural contrasts between two countries in the Middle East and the United States. Reading these situations will provide one with some specific cues that are important for a person to know in order to effectively work in that part of the world. However, they are just the beginning point. More importantly, the way the situations were presented will give the reader practice in problem solving using the critical incident method of learning. This has been demonstrated to be effective. In stressful and ambiguous situations, it has been found that we do not use all available clues or information and therefore our problem-solving strategies are ineffective and our conclusions are not correct.

The ideas represent a broad spectrum as some are from a social context and others are more directly business related. The choices or alternatives to the situations presented are based on a different set of cultural values. The reader is asked to make a judgment and the important consideration is also to ask "why"?

There will be variations of responses according to context and the personality of the individuals involved. J. Bronowski in the *Ascent of Man*, said, "There is no absolute knowledge and those who claim it, whether they are scientists or dogmatists, open the door to tragedy."

References

Saudi Arabia

Alireza, M., *At the Drop of a Veil.* Boston: Houghton Mifflin, Co., 1971.

Hopewood, D. (ed.), *The Arabian Peninsula: Society and Politics.* Totowa, N.J.: Rowman and Littlefield, 1970.

Kilner, P. and J. Wallace, *The Gulf Handbook.* Garrett Park, Md.: Garrett Park Press, 1978.

Knauerhase, R., *The Saudi Arabian Economy.* New York: Praeger Publications, 1975.

Laffin, J., *The Arab Mind Considered: A Need for Understanding.* New York: Taplinger Publishing, 1975.

Mansfield, P., *The Arabs.* London: Allen Lane, 1977.

Nycop, R., et al, *Area Handbook for Saudi Arabia.* Washington, D.C.: U.S. Government Printing Office, 1977.

Patai, R., *The Arab Mind.* New York: Charles Scribners and Sons, 1976.

Sarhan, M., *Who's Who in Saudi Arabia, 1976-77.* Jeddah and London: Tihama and Europa Publications, 1977.
Schilling, N.A., *Doing Business in Saudi Arabia and the Arab Gulf States.* New York: Intercresent Publishing and Information Company, 1975.
Schuon, F., *Understanding Islam.* (translated by D. Matheson). Baltimore, Maryland: Penguin Books, 1972.

Iran

Arastch, A., *Man and Society In Iran.* Leiden, Netherlands: E.J. Brill, 1970.
Hoyt, E., *The Still Glittering Story of Iran and Its People.* New York: Erickson, 1976.
Hureau, J., *Iran Today.* Paris: Arthaud Jeune Afrique, 1977.
Sutton-Elwell, L., *Modern Iran.* New York: Gordon, 1976.
The Study of the Middle East. New York: John Willey, 1976.
Tyler, V.L. and J.S. Taylor, *Reading Between the Lines.* Provo, Utah, 1978.
Wilber, D., *Iran Past and Present.* Princeton, NJ: Princeton, 1975.

Finally, the reader should realize that Saudi Arabia and Iran are but two very different manifestations of Moslem culture. There is a wide variety of beliefs and sects with Islam, and there is a major revival underway in that religion to Mindanao, as well as in the Middle East. The cosmopolitan should be alert to such religious and nationalistic sensibilities and avoid simplistic generalizations. For example, some Arabs are Christians, not all Moslems are Arabs.

20
Effectiveness With
Cultural Differences

The End or the Beginning

Now the time has come to draw this book to a close, to pull together the threads of thought into a meaningful whole. The three words in the title of this concluding chapter are part of the theme that has been continually emphasized throughout this text. Perhaps, it would be appropriate to define these terms again, but with the assistance of the *Random House Dictionary:*

> *Effectiveness*—able to produce an intended result; skillful use of energy for a desired purpose.
>
> *Cultural*—from a sociological viewpoint, having to do with the sum total of the ways for living built up by a human group, that is transmitted from one generation to another.
>
> *Differences*—significant changes or variations, a distinctive quality or feature, dissimilarity or diversity.

The authors expect that this volume will enable its readers to use their energies in intercultural relations, or international business, for the purpose of improving communication and cooperation between and among people.

In the U.S., there has been a rise in the "new ethnicity." Social philosopher, Michael Novak, explains this as a movement of *self-knowledge* on the part of members of third and fourth generation of southern and eastern European immigrants here. Novak contends that in a broader sense, the new ethnicity includes a renewed self-consciousness on the part of many other American ethnic groups, be they Irish, Norwegian, Swede, German, Chinese, Japanese, or Italian. With 17 million Hispanic-Americans now constituting a major segment of the U.S. population, it is understandable why those Americans with Mexican, Cuban, Puerto Rican, or some other Latin origin, are not only seeking new expression of identity, but also political-social power in the society. The conciousness-raising pride in heritage and accomplishment has been especially evident among the native Indians and Black-Americans in the U.S. during the last half of this century.

Writing in *The Center Magazine* (July/August 1974), Novak observes:

> The new ethnicity entails, first, a growing sense of discomfort with the sense of identity one is supposed to have—universalist, "melted," "like everyone else"; then a growing appreciation for . . . their historical roots; a growing self-confidence and social power; a sense of being discriminated against, condescended to, or carelessly misapprehended; a growing disaffection regarding those to whom one has always been taught to defer; and a sense of injustice regarding the response of liberal spokesmen to conflicts among various ethnic groups . . . . There is, in a word, an inner conflict between one's felt personal power: a sense of outraged truth, justice, and equity.

This quotation captures the essence of what the authors tried to convey in Chapter 7's discussion of identity crisis and culture shock. It also expresses what a modern woman, or for that matter a "gay" person, often experiences in trying to liberate self from culturally-conditioned, prescribed roles. As society becomes more pluralistic, and cultures become more "open," people become more aware of both dissimilarities and similarities between themselves and others. They also demand the freedom to be themselves, regardless of cultural context. Minorities of all types seek acceptance and tolerance, rather than discrimination and prejudice. Becoming more culturally sensitive fosters a living environment in which internal dignity, as well as equity of treatment, can coexist. A sense of one's separateness, one's uniqueness, one's ethnic or racial background, need not hamper an individual from becoming a multicultural cosmopolitan. Rather, it may enhance the contribution of a new infusion of diversity toward a *common culture*. Michael Novak explains that this world culture "struggling to be born is a creature of multicultural beauty, dazzling, free, a higher and richer form of life. It was fashioned in the painful darkness of the melting pot and now, at the appointed time, it awakens."

Canadians are a special example of a people in search of a common culture. Their experiment in confederation seeks to bring together two majorities, French and English in a coalition of national unity. Within a single political enterprise, the inhabitants of its many provinces painfully evolve a country in which two distinct peoples, and their cultures, respect one another and work together. Canada is a microcosm of what is happening in many lands throughout the world as different peoples struggle to overcome their dissymmetries, while creating a new synergy. It requires a sharing of the other—a sharing of power, language, customs, perspectives, stages of development. This is true whether one speaks of Canada, Scotland, North Ireland, the Palestinian West Bank and Gaza, Cambodia, or Rhodesia/Zimbabwe, and South Africa. In the process of managing cultural differences, people can learn a solidarity that is beyond nationalism, an interdependence that will someday characterize the whole human family as it probes the universe.

Futurist, Herman Kahn, reminds us that the historical reaction to culture contact may be constructive or pathological; with reactions to the intruding culture that are either nonviolent or violent, rational or apocalyptic. Cultural exchange requires, as Octavio Paz observes, " . . . the experience of the other, the essence of change!" The paradox seems to be that for every loss a culture may experience through breakdown or interchange, there is also possible a gain in the development of new cultural patterns. Like biological evolution, cultural evolution requires adaptation for survival and development. Cultural change is, of course, multicausal. Yet, while moderns today create change at an ever rapid pace, they can regulate progress and have the skill to plan change. It is important to remind ourselves that culture is indeed a human product, subject to alteration and improvement.

Emerging Role of the Multinational Manager

The first unit in this book explored the egress of organizational leaders as intercultural communicators, change agents, and cultural transmitters. Specifically, we examined the role of the multinational manager in changing world culture. Stanford Research Institute's Center for Social Policy has done a forecasting study of international societal problems. Among the forty-one issues identified, all of them have implications for this changing world culture (*The Futurist*, October 1977). Although we cannot explain each, they are listed in the following section. An asterisk indicates those that have special meaning within the framework of this volume. Then, we will provide some related commentary by that Center's director, which will help put the message of our opening unit in a broader context.

Future Problems of World Culture

Based on the predictions of the SRI staff in the Center for Social Policy, Palo Alto, California, U.S.A., these forty-one "crises of tomorrow" were identified in 1976. Peter Schratz was project leader for the social researchers.

1. Malnutrition-induced mental deficiencies leading to social instability.
* 2. The cultural exclusion of the aged, especially in developed countries.
3. Global firewood shortage when one third of world population still depend on such fuel.
* 4. Critical advances in biomedical technology, including life extension, genetic engineering, and euthanasia.
5. The growing conflict between central control and individual freedom.
6. The conflict between low growth limitations and rising expectations.

7. Police alienation from the general population.
* 8. Loss of cultural diversity with the emergence of an interdependent world.
9. Potential for urban violence in deteriorating older cities with depressed population.
10. The "invisible" famine with slight variations in world climate.
11. Persistent malnutrition in the midst of affluence because of dietary inadequacies.
12. Teenage alcoholism, especially in "advanced countries," contributing to juvenile crime.
*13. Lack of functional life skills in adults for a complex, superindustrial society.
*14. Growing subculture of the *information-poor* in a knowledge society.
15. Increasing barriers to large-scale technologies because of failures, discouragements.
*16. Social impact of changing role of women, especially in the work force.
*17. Sociocultural impact of mass media, causing withdrawal from direct social and political involvement, as well as distortions of social reality.
*18. Social implications of changing family forms.
*19. Effect of stress on individuals and society (a symptom of future shock?).
20. Potential use/misuse of "consciousness technologies" and alternative medicine.
21. Decreasing capital productivity of new technology (small return on investment).
22. Regulatory restraints on healthy economic growth.
23. Conflict between developments in weapons technology and right to bear arms.
24. Cumulative negative effects of pollution.
*25. Limits to management of large, complex systems.
*26. Apparent conflict between world peace and justice, and preservation of inequities.
27. Catastrophic experiments with emerging technologies, and lack of control mechanisms.
28. Vulnerability of water supplies.
29. Dangers of computer dependency, and risks due to accidental or intentional disruptions.
30. Decreasing utility or relevance of higher education.
31. Effects of technology on individual psyche (e.g., television).
*32. Loss of political and social cohesion—the sense of shared purpose.
*33. Institutional boundaries as impediments to societal problem-solving.
*34. Need for better socioeconomic models for effective human systems.

35. Advanced microcomputers and the rights to privacy.
*36. Chronic unemployment, even in advanced countries with increase in cybernation.
37. Negative social response to energy development/use disappointments.
38. Growing need for "appropriate" technology—an intermediate technology.
39. Societal changes required for adaptation to new energy sources.
40. Emerging/developed nations' depletion of oil reserves.
*41. Social effects in redefining legal liability for decisions, making entrepreneurial and professional risk-taking more hazardous.

The director for the Center, which issued that report, is Willis Harman. In his book, *An Incomplete Guide to the Future* (San Francisco: The Portable Stanford/San Francisco Book Company, 1976), Harman is generally optimistic about the future of world culture, but points out the need for the citizenry to be involved and informed about "microdecisions" in their organizations that will help to transform us into a transindustrial society; these add up to "macrodecisions" that can be of global benefit or detriment. As a result of the studies at SRI's Center for Social Policy, his hope is that "when society's future seems to be beleaguered, that it is most likely to achieve a metamorphosis in growth toward maturity, toward more truly enhancing and fulfilling the human spirit than even before." Harman is aware that societal transformation may experience a period of chaos and disruption, yet he expects a quantum leap in human maturity.

While problems may seem almost staggering in complexity, and individuals seemingly become more alienated, he envisions an evolutionary jump into what some have called "cyberculture." Harman is realistic about the challenges of long-term multifold modernization, and sees them as a fresh vision of a society in formation. Chapters 1 and 3 discussed such issues, as well as the need to form new images of the human person. Researcher Harman says some of the characteristics of this emergent image are already clear for those who can see, based on these propositions:

1. The potentiality of the individual person far exceeds typical levels of actualization and beliefs about what is possible.
2. World and self-perceptions are strongly conditioned by the cultural matrix; as a result, individuals and entire societies can have belief systems that appear to be validated by their experience, but are in fact quite dysfunctional.
3. A major portion of significant human experience (perceiving, learning, thinking, creative activity) centrally involves unconscious processes.
4. Basic expectations and beliefs, conscious and unconscious, tend to be self-fulfilling; belief systems create reality.

All of this points to a potential system for change in human cultures higher than our present experience.

To balance this optimistic perspective on emerging world culture, Margaret Mead offered some sobering, pragmatic counterpoints. After spending more than a half century observing cultures around the world, the renowned anthropologist stated:

> Survival is at stake. Threats to the environment increase faster than the efforts we make to preserve it. We are making the world more and more vulnerable every minute. . . .The world is an interdependent community, and we need somehow to think in terms of this whole.

In a speech at Northwestern University (*Northwestern Alumni News,* January 1978), Dr. Mead observed that society is in a runaway growth process based on the theory that the world must become industrialized. But the energy crisis confronted the myth of "the more production, the more growth, the more affluence." She believed we need a more balanced, rational society that does not keep people alive as a burden, and does not waste human energy and talent. "We kill men off with retirement; we kill women off with uselessness!" She had a hope for the future of world culture in which "individuals have a sense of responsibility for the world. Human beings share the same problems on this 'interconnected' planet. . . .We have this situation in which we really are our brother's keepers in a way we have never been before!"

Thus, the modern multinational manager must be sensitive to the broader implication of his or her actions and decisions upon organizational and world cultures. Furthermore, such leaders need both a sense of history and of the future, so that they may share their visions, as well as their sense of responsibility, with their fellow employees, regardless of what country or community in which they may be located.

Cultural Impact on International Management

The second unit of this text focused attention upon cultural factors that influence behavior and decision-making both for the multinational manager and the persons with whom he or she interacts. Chapters 5 and 6 provided insights into ways of analyzing and understanding a foreign culture. Information was shared to indicate how culturally-conditioned assumptions, values, attitudes, and practices of key personnel, such as sales representatives, buyers, and overseas managers, can influence the success or failure of intercultural business relations.

Specifically, Chapter 7 was devoted to the phenomenon of culture shock, which can restrict or enhance the international experience, depending on how the individual responds to its challenge. The concept was linked to the more fundamental issue of identity crises, heightened in a cross-cultural exchange, and this was related to other life traumas that challenge people to change (e.g., role crises, reentry shock).

Finally, Chapter 8 utilized the anthropological perspective to *organizational* culture and shock, especially significant when an enterprise moves beyond its home culture into the world marketplace. It underscored how rapid alterations in society demands changes in organizational models and environment, particularly with a more pluralistic, international work force.

When a corporation, association, or agency goes outside its parent culture into that of another "foreign" country, a two-way action takes place. First, the other culture impacts upon the organization and its representatives. There is a broadening of perspective, attitude about the foreign people change, adaptations are made to the way they do business. This influence can be both positive and negative. On the plus side the transnational organization may learn new managerial or technical practices, as well as different values and goals. For example, Americans who do business in Japan can benefit if they will take the time to study in depth Japanese business operations—the Japanese economic system is possibly the most successful in the world. Foreign business persons would do well to discover, for instance, some of the factors contributing to

1. 10% yearly GNP growth rate.
2. The successful application of technology for high production, often twice the volume of other leading nations (e.g., steel and television manufacturing.
3. An inordinately favorable balance-of-payments, despite a quadrupling of fuel prices since 1973.
4. The transfer of Japanese management methods successfully abroad to foreign acquisitions (e.g., the corporation's first duty is to the employees).
5. The accent on harmony, not conflict in business enterprises between labor and management, between competing companies in the same industry.
6. The corporate philosophy that emphasizes social responsibility, equality among all employees in contrast to executive elitism.

The point is that the transnational enterprise can gain many constructive inputs from the host culture and people, if expatriate management will take the time to listen and to learn. On the minus side, the multinational corporation, for example, may find itself pressured to conform to local unwritten norms of questionable behavior that can range from bribery and corruption on the one hand, to racism and class distinction on the other.

The transnational actor also has an impact upon the indigeneous culture, the effects of which can be healthy or adverse upon the native society or economy. The issue is sensitive in terms of developed and less developed countries, or information-rich versus information-poor peoples. There are naïve multinational executives who think what is good for their corporation, is automatically good for the nation in which they operate. Like the missionary "do-gooders" of the past, they point to what they are doing for these less fortunate peoples of underdeveloped lands—they bring jobs, technical know-how, training, and capital. Some scholars, such as futurist Herman Kahn, will point with pride to the gradual affluence and industrialization that advanced, technological societies bring by their presence in Third and Fourth World nations. Kahn maintains that while the rate of growth in these areas will not be as spectacular as in the First and Second Worlds, it will be significant in raising the inhabitants above existing poverty levels, and will help to close the gap between the rich and poor nations.

When one considers the impact of these transnational enterprises (TNE), it is wise to remember that they are not limited to the West or capitalistic organizations. It has been estimated that the Soviet Union and Eastern European socialist nations have over 700 trading and manufacturing concerns abroad—about two thirds were located in developed countries (DCs), while the remaining were in less developed countries (LDCs).

Perhaps two quotations may provide some focus on the negative influence a supranational corporation can have in another culture, especially one that has not experienced fully the industrial stage of development:

> The plows of the rich can do as much harm as their swords. . . .Once the Third World has become a mass market for the goods, products, and processes which are designed by the rich for themselves, the discrepancy between demand for these Western artifacts and the supply will increase indefinitely. . . .(Ivan Illich, "Outwitting the More Developed Countries," *New York Review of Books,* December 1969, p. 20.)

To illustrate the unsuitability of some TNE consumer products in the socioeconomic context of some consuming nations, consider the issue of soft drinks in Mexico and Brazil:

> In Mexico soft drinks have successfully penetrated the market from abroad, and now account for 75 percent of the output with a per capital consumption of soft drinks up to 220 bottles a year. Thus, a person drinks about four bottles of such drinks every week in a country where there is a shortage of protein and vitamins in the general diet. Father Crisoforo Florencie mentions that in very remote villages, the great majority of the poor people are convinced that soft drinks must be consumed every day. Families sell their natural products—fruits, cereal, and poultry—for buying them. Others spend disproportionate portions of their meager incomes for cola drinks which contain little except calories. . . .In the case of Brazil, a survey taken in 1973 by Anne Dias of the Instituto de Nutrico, has shown that soft drinks have become a regular part of the diet of children coming from rich and upper middle classes, despite the fact that they suffer from vitamin deficiencies and show signs of

> malnutrition. Obviously, even affluent children may prefer soft drinks to milk and juices. (Robert J. Ledogar, *Hungry for Profits: U. S. Food and Drug Multinationals in Latin America,* 1975, pp. 111-126.

Obviously, the reader may respond to these quotes by saying that the same effects may be found in the countries of origin for the multinational enterprise. The point is simply to consider that not every endeavor of advanced countries and their representatives is a benefit to the consuming nation. Colonialism in some less developed areas of the world has been replaced by corporate imperialism or economic exploitation.

To help leaders become more aware of their influence in international operations, the Center for Cultural and Technical Interchange Between East and West has a project underway that is pregnant with meaning for our readers: Transnational Organizations and Networks: Policy Options for Interdependence. (This East-West Center was established in Hawaii by an act of the U.S. Congress.) The project leader, Krishna Kumar, has issued a preliminary report in August 1978, *On The Social and Cultural Impacts of Transnational Enterprises.* An example of one such impact is the promotion by the TNE of a consumption-oriented value-system through effective advertising and marketing strategies in host LDCs. In the process, the TNE may raise the level of knowledge and skills among the locals, but the training imparted is utilized primarily by the TNE's themselves, not widely diffused in the country, and may not profit indigeneous sectors of the economy. Perhaps this extract from Kumar's working paper (pages 128-132) will contribute something to reader enlightenment on the issue of interventions in other cultures, and their side effects. The investigators sought to answer the questions: (a) What are the ways in which TNEs can affect societies and cultures? (b) What are the major elements of social structures and processes that are likely to be affected by them? (c) What are their consequences for the cultural systems of the LDCs? The researchers identified three modes of TNEs' impact:

> First, it has been suggested that TNEs directly produce and diffuse certain elements of cultural systems. In this connection, consider the role of communication by TNEs, especially those involved in television, book publishing, news dissemination and advertising deserve special mention. They do not only disseminate news, information and the arts, but also a set of beliefs and values. . . .they affect the structures and functioning of local organizations. . . .often influence life styles and values. . . .
>
> Second, TNEs transfer social and mechanical technologies to host nations. . . .that these effects are likely to be significant in most cases. Technological innovations can influence family, community, social classes, ethnic relationships, economic disparities, knowledge and beliefs of the people. Moreover, the products and services made available by the TNEs can affect consumption patterns, social interactions, symbolic

systems and the like. Finally, TNEs can exert pressure on host governments for following certain social and cultural policies.

Having sketched this broad role of the supranational organization in host cultures, the East-West Center investigators also pointed out these realities:

> TNEs give higher wages which can sometimes create cleavages and social differentiations among workers....TNEs operations can have both functional and dysfunctional consequences for the local entrepreneurial class....TNEs can contribute to the emergence of a small stratum, comprised of senior technical and management executives, which by virtue of position, play transnational roles....(and may) widen the gulf between different groups.

> TNEs undertake very limited research and development in LDCs, and their contribution to the building up of an infrastructure for scientific research is negligible in most LDCs....We are not very clear about the nature of TNEs impact on cultural identities. It has been suggested that by diffusing the cultural elements of the DCs, TNEs can undermine people's faith in their indigenous culture and generate a feeling of dependence.

Kumar emphasizes that their ideas are only working hypotheses needing empirical testing on the basis of cross-national, multidisciplinary involvement. However, he welcomes feedback from anyone on the project insights (East West Culture Learning Institute, 1777 East-West Road, Honolulu, Hawaii 96848). Regardless of whether one agrees with their tentative findings, they do stimulate thinking of multinational managers on the effects of their decisions and actions upon the host culture and its people. Certainly, it confirms the point of Chapter 3 regarding their role as agents of change.

Organizational Responsibilities and Cultural Differences

Our third unit examined what transnational enterprises should do in the preparation of their representatives and dependents for foreign deployment. It all begins with some form of *cultural awareness training,* which is also valid for managers of minorities within the home culture; in fact, our premise is that such general culture training should become an integral part of all management development. Having reviewed in Chapter 9 the scope and content of such human resource development, Chapter 10 provided some additional information on methods and techniques for such a learning experience, while Chapter 11 examined the special needs of family members for cross-cultural assignments. For multinational organizations involved in the world marketplace, constantly exchanging personnel from one nation to another, a foreign deployment policy and system was recommended. This cosmopolitan approach would include four major phases:

1. Recruitment, assessment, and selection of candidates for overseas' service.

2. Orientation in culture general and specifics for the assignment.
3. On-site applied research, monitoring, and support services for the expatriate family.
4. Reentry assistance, counseling, and studies.

In other words, the organization has a responsibility to help its people cope with cultural differences. This makes good sense from the viewpoint of economic and social policy, as well as public relations. Without such information and insight, productivity, job effectiveness, sales, and community relations are undermined. Perhaps our rationale can be emphasized again in these true, critical incidents which made the public press. Each one highlights the value of cultural sensitivity and awareness on the part of personnel:

● Many advertisers and and marketing specialists do not understand the Latin mindset, and barely tap this buyer group effectively for their client's products and services. For example, they do not comprehend the intricacies of dealing with the Hispanic market in Southern California. The Mexican-Americans in two counties alone—Los Angeles and Orange—are 2.7 million people without inclusion of illegal aliens; their spendable income in this area is $3 billion ($50 billion nationally). Yet, when Spanish language radio stations tried to give away two tickets to movie previews or Disneyland, there were few takers; they had forgotten that these Hispanics tend to go as a family group or two couples—when they offered four tickets, they were deluged by their listeners. . . .The advertising industry has yet to learn that Hispanic families are heavy purchasers of consumer goods, especially food; that they wish to be invited in their language to buy, but in such a way that they are treated with dignity and stereotyping is avoided; that Latins are brand conscious—if they see it on television, for instance, they have faith in it, for they tend to buy visually; that when the marketing message is translated into Spanish by someone who is not fully bilingual, it can lose its meaning, or worse. The head of Cervera International, an advertising and production service in Los Angeles, cites the classic incident of L'eggs pantyhose as one product that can cause trouble in translation: "There is a Spanish word for eggs, of course, but it also means testicles. It's a perfectly good word, but if you use it in Spanish, you're in trouble."

● Cultural bias in tests—are standard examinations fair to minorities? Twenty-five black applicants to the District of Columbia bar exam took a case to the Supreme Court on this issue. They charged the exam was culturally biased against blacks as a group, and echoed one of the persistent debates among psychologists and educators. Many minorities claim that white, middle-class values, thinking, and terminology dominate entrance tests and constitute yet another barrier to full social and economic equality for the "have-nots" in America. The real issue is cultural bias as a deterrent to self-realization and individual advancement in the U.S. Cultural bias is an apprehension we feel in the presence of the unknown and socially unfamiliar. It is the burden to be faced in adapting to a situation in which others know the rules, and you do not. If it is present in the avenues to economic, political, social success, then minorities are prevented from traveling those roads on which, according to American tradition, the only tools necessary are ambition, ability, and tireless work—the means to negotiating in the mainstream culture. If the U.S. is to have truly a shared culture, then cultural bias in entrance examinations, textbooks, job requirements, and the public media must be counteracted, or opportunity for growth is denied those citizens who do not possess the perspectives and skills of the dominant majority. Then poverty or racial chauvinism discourage acculturation, and foster a psychological barrier in the self-image of minorities that continues to exclude them from the majority cultural mileau. Competency, not cultural distortions, should be the only criterion, for admission to any segment of society.

Many governments, nonprofit organizations, and corporations send their people abroad supposedly to help others in less developed countries. Often this is done under the umbrella of foreign aid. The third item for consideration is from an interview reported in *World Issues* between two political science professors, Gerald L. Bender and Otis L. Graham (Oct./Nov.'78), on the subject of superpowers involvement in Africa:

Graham: If Americans want to know how best to be effective at helping Africans, what kind of people should we be sending, with what sort of outlook and techniques?. . . .

Bender: The Chinese and Cubans are effective there for different reasons. The Chinese stay away from the Africans when their work is done for the day. The Cubans mix with the people without any of the cultural and racial arrogance that one often sees in the representatives from developed societies, like the U.S., the Soviet Union, Hungary, Czechoslovakia, Bulgaria, and others. For example, Cuban engineers on a project do not say, "Go do this, go do that." Instead, they will take somebody actually by the hand—the Cuban is not afraid to hold a black hand—and he will walk with the African, explaining in a very patient, nonarrogant way what has to be done and how to do it. . . .I don't think socialism explains that Cuban attitude. I think it is because Cuba is not a highly developed, or racist, society. Americans tend to be much more sensitive to African feelings than Eastern Europe or Russian technicians are. . . .Bascially, the Peace Corps has been successful because—and this is what I observed in Cubans—there is motivation. Call it ideological motivation, call it altruism, call it internationalism. But it is there.

Common sense, good will, or good business in each of the above statements point up the value to the organization to select representatives who are culturally aware, to train personnel to be culturally sensitive, and to be culturally egalitarian in both employee and customer practices.

Furthermore, any endeavors to apply the insights and methodology of cultural anthropology to the organizational environment will pay off in future dividends. The work culture is changing, and management needs all the assistance it can get to understand these developments, and to cope more effectively with them. Writing on "Work in the Year 2001" (*The Futurist,* February 1977), William Abbot cited these trends and forecasts to challenge organizations in their modernization of the work space:

1. Skilled workers will have to be totally retrained and attend school several times on company time: lifelong learning will be accepted.
2. Autonomous work teams, making their own production decisions, will be common in factories and plants that are organized horizontally.
3. The European innovation of codeterminism will spread beyond that continent (i.e, workers represented on corporate boards, and increased joint labor-management decision-making).
4. Workers will spend less time on the jobs, share jobs on a half-time basis, and even schedule their own hours under flexitime.
5. Labor relations will become a battle of intellects and more cooperative, while unions will become more a way of life and care for the whole personality needs of members (i.e., sabbatical leaves, family education centers, utilization of retired workers).
6. Workers of all ages, classes, and occupations will demand and obtain more educational and training opportunities, as an occupational revolution takes place to the activities of the knowledge worker (i.e., information processers, researchers, interpreters, writers, technicians).
7. Middle-class work values of the past will gradually be replaced by personal growth, nonmaterial values, as employees seek to "raise their consciousness" while improving the quality of work life.

Obviously, these developments are most evident in the so-called "advanced nations," but they are part of a world-wide phenomenon of rising human expectations, stimulated partially by innovations in mass communications. Multinational management, therefore, has a responsibility to examine the organizational culture with a view to providing a more creative corporate environment that will motivate personnel into the twenty-first century.

Culture Specifics for Management Effectiveness

Our final unit got into cultural details, and its seven chapters composed the largest segment of this book. It attempted to take the theory and put it all into practical context within the framework of international business. Chapter 14 began by examining the concept of macro/microcultures within a single society, and used the U.S. as an example. The next four chapters are in a case-study format for in-depth analysis by the reader, and possibly group discussion. Target countries were selected from key global regions— America, Europe, Asia, and the Middle East—in the hope that the reader would take the insights and information gained from these culture specifics, and extrapolate for better understanding of other nationals in these areas.

The authors regret that space limitations prevent consideration of every cultural group.

Armed with knowledge about specific peculiarities of a culture, transnational management can avoid costly blunders. Consider if you were an expatriate manager in each of the following countries, how this data might be useful to you in the matter of personnel policies and practices:

Japan—Vacations—Scarcely anyone takes an extended vacation, and few take all of the annual vacation time to which they are entitled; most vacations are taken in short spurts of two or three days. And when the Japanese do take leave to celebrate, they do it with a vengence and usually in groups. For religious or national holidays, three major vacation breaks occur—late April, early May, and late August, as well as four days at New Year's.

England—Religious Holidays—London has replaced Beirut as the capital of the Arab world. It has the largest Moslem population outside the Middle East with one estimate set at 2 million people. Some British cities have constituencies almost entirely Moslem on the voting register, and many churches have been converted to mosques.

Saudi Arabia—Business Travel—One may fly or go by automobile to Taif, the cool summer capital on the cliffs inland from Jidda, a Red Sea port. Recently, a meeting of the oil ministers for the Organization of Petroleum Exporting Countries was held there. An American reporter was ordered by his editor back in the U.S. to "grab a cab over there and get that story!" The journalist took a "shertax" with three other passengers for the hundred-mile trip from Jidda to Taif. The taxi was forced to take the road around Mecca. The driver explained, "We don't call it Infidel Road, but only infidels use it. Because you are the only infidel here, the price of this trip will go up because of this detour." Road signs along the way reflect the cultural mix of the larger Saudi cities—they are written in Arabic, English, French, Italian, German, Korean, and Japanese. Sometimes the taxi stops to cope with "green snow," locusts in masses. The roadside is marked by shelters for moneychangers who service the Mecca pilgrims, and by dynamite blasts for a large irrigation tunnel being built through an escarpment. Four hours out of Jidda, the driver asks for directions to the Intercontinental Hotel where the ministers are meeting. No one seems to know where it is. After much time is lost, the reporter got to the hotel and completed his assignment. He decided, on his own, to fly back. When he arrived in the airport in Jidda, he discovers that it is being swept by Filipinos, and that outside the electric cable ditches in front of Citibank are being dug by Koreans. The mayor of Jidda says less than one-third of the million persons in the city are Saudis.

When an organization assigns a representative to a foreign culture, it has a responsibility to provide that person with as much useful information about that country and its people as possible—it can save time, energy, money, and gain goodwill everywhere. So too, when an employee receives such an overseas' assignment, self-preservation dictates that the individual seek out as much culture specific data as feasible to facilitate one's own and family's adjustment to the strange circumstances. Furthermore, it will contribute to the successful accomplishment of one's mission.

If fact, the same approach should be used when a company or agency reassigns personnel from one part of their own country to another. As this is being written a big conglomerate is about to shift a large number of its employees from the Midwest to San Diego, California. Smart management would insist that as part of the relocation service it contracts for, information and orientation be provided to those who must move to the California subculture, as well as the adjoining Mexican culture, which dominates Southwest living. One Hispanic American executive referred to their new homeland as "Occupied California," which indicates a whole new perspective. The relocated employees will not only have to adjust to the whole new California life style and mindset, but they will be living in a border community. Thus, they had better know something about the Mexican heritage, and the paradox of their neighbors to the south. First, that it supplies the largest contingent of some eight million illegal aliens in the U.S., who take jobs here at the bottom of the wage structure that are unattractive to Americans, yet contribute to the economy, and who will be in demand within a decade when the available U.S. labor force experiences a sudden decline. Second, Mexico with its growing middle class, growth in tourism, and new discoveries in oil and gas is about to take off economically and is a mighty useful neighbor, friend, and customer to cultivate.

General culture and specific culture knowledge are vital not only inside or outside one's country, but for understanding contemporary and future world culture. Alvin Toffler writing on popular culture reminds us that over the past two hundred years mass media has standardized the culture of the world's industrialized societies to a great degree. Those who engineer the media stamp out sets of images that cause a homogenization of ideas, values, and lifestyles, creating what sociologists call the "mass society." Toffler already sees a break-up of the "old" mass society, and the formation of new social, political, and cultural diversity through the birth of revolutionary new information systems. With the help of copiers, tape/video recorders, inexpensive film and cameras, and cable television, the post-industrial civilization offers the individual the opportunity to become his or her own publisher, television or media producer, and broadcaster of special messages and customized programs. Futurist Toffler believes that the evidence of this shift away from mass-machined and mass-distributed popular culture is seen in the rise of ethnic consciousness, the rise of secessionism, the growing sectionalism (even in the U.S.), as well as the development of nationally oriented marxist movements in contrast to monolithic communism. The emerging technological age offers opportunities for new individuality, for increasingly designing and creating our own culture.

Conclusion

Novelist James Michener observed in a television special that "we are on the eve of man's supreme achievement in which our ancestors will die on other planets." The disintegration of the earth's cultures may be in preparation for the creation of a world culture that we transfer out into the universe. Perhaps our greatest human accomplishment may come in the way we manage the cultural differences met in "encounters of the third kind" in outer space?

Anthropologist Ruth Benedict was dissatisfied with the concept of cultural relativity, and tried a way of comparing societies in terms of a unitary whole or system. Finally, she decided that the basic differences were in *why* a people behaved as they did, rather than in *how* they behaved. Thus, in some societies suicide is considered an act of honor, not despair. Benedict contrasted cultures with reference to *low synergy* and *high synergy*. The latter society would seem to be preferable at this point in time—a culture with high synergy is characterized by people who cooperate for mutual advantage and the customs of the society make it worthwhile, where the individual seeks to serve one's own advantage and that of the group, where nonaggression is conspicuous, and social institutions encourage people to develop their potential for achievement, growth, collaboration, and love.

It is hoped the accelerating process of human emergence will lead to a more global synergistic society in which new relationships are forged as a result of cultural convergences. Of all living creatures, only the human species has learned to mold its environment to its own benefit, and to pass on the learned techniques by cultural, rather than just genetic, means. This infinitely faster and more efficient biological dimension of culture has enabled *Homo Sapiens* to occupy a far wider range of environmental control over the planet earth than any other creature on it. Although it is possible to pollute and corrupt our environment to the detriment of all life, the authors are optimistic that mankind will use the group-problem-solving tool of culture to enhance the quality of life, to transcend to a new stage of human evolution, and to create our own destiny.

Culture teaches us what to value and what to fear, which behavioral signals to watch for in others and which to send, which words to use and which to avoid. It guides everything from our method of reasoning and our choice of mates, to our style of clothes and life. It is the act, says Webster, of "developing by education, discipline, and social experience, the training and refining of moral and intellectual faculties." It is a body of customary beliefs, social forms, and material traits which constitute a distinct complex for a group's social, racial, and religious traditions. It is a standardization of typical behavior or characteristics peculiar to a specific group, occupations, sex, age, grade, or social class. *Culture is, in fact, the very web of our lives.*

If the message of this book motivates the reader to seek further information on this fascinating subject, Appendix D provides a listing of additional resources helpful for cross-cultural education and international business.

Appendix A
So You're Going Abroad—
A Checklist

The following is a list of questions that could be used to determine your preparedness for an overseas living or working experience. These questions are not meant to cover every situation. Many more could be suggested and it is expected that persons reading these questions will think of many of their own.

Some General Considerations

1. Do you have a clear idea of the purpose of your trip or assignment?
   - From a professional perspective?
   - From a personal perspective?
2. Do you know know the names and responsibilities of the persons you will be meeting? Do you know their responsibilities?
3. Will these persons be able to make the decisions related to your assignment?
4. What do you know of their background?
5. There are many contemporary and historical persons of whom the country is proud. Can you name one of each?

	Contemporary	Historical
Politician		
Poet		
Philosopher		
Musician		
Writer		
Actor		
Actress		
Photographer		
Inventor		
Artist		
Sports figure		

Politics

6. Can you name current political leaders and their current titles?
7. Do you know the names of the political parties?
8. Do you know the function of the political institution?
9. How would you describe the political process?
10. Do you know the name of the parliament or legislature?
11. What is the form of the executive? Or is there one?
12. Is power delegated?
13. What are the interest groups and how do they express their concerns?
14. What kind of citizen is valued?
15. What are the political myths of the country?
16. What penalties exist for disobeying the law?
17. Is corruption a part of the government? Does this affect business? If so, in what ways?
18. Do women vote and hold public office?
19. Is politics an appropriate topic of conversation?

The Country

20. Are there states, provinces, counties or other? How many? Can you name them? What are examples of different climates in each?
21. What are the main cities? The population? The main industries? The kinds of problems?
22. Do you know the basic history? Date of independence? Relationship to other countries?

Nonverbal Communication (65% of meaning is communicated nonverbally)

23. Will they understand our nonverbal communication?
24. Are there any nonverbal behavior patterns you use which might be offensive?
25. What about their nonverbal behavior? Do you understand it?
26. When is it appropriate to cry? To express other emotions?
27. What is the appropriate speaking distance between persons, who are getting to know each other in a social context? In a business context?

Daily Life

28. What are some courtesies you should observe?
29. How do people greet each other? foreigners?

30. How do people say goodbye?
31. Is gift-giving a custom? What kind of gift for what kind of occasion?
32. Do colors have a certain meaning? What about flowers? Do any numbers have a particular significance?
33. How many days a week do people work? each day? from when to when? Are business and social conversations mixed?
34. Is alcohol permitted? What about nonalcoholic beverages and their place in the business and social environment?
35. How do people spend their free time? Upper, middle, and lower classes?
36. Is T.V. available? Movies? What kinds of each?
37. Do people employ servants? What is their place?

Religion

38. Is there a state religion? How many religions are there?
39. How does religion influence the people?
40. What are the religious holidays?
41. What are five dominant religious values?
42. What are some differences between your religious beliefs and the beliefs of this religion?

Social Structure

43. What are the class divisions?
44. The ethnic divisions?
45. Is there a kind of discrimination? against whom?
46. Does dress reflect social or economic status?
47. What is the nature of social mobility?
48. Has the experience of colonialism or foreign domination affected class structure? The attitudes toward foreigners? How?
49. Is there intergroup friction?
50. What are the occupations of various people?
51. What is the size of the average family?
52. Is there family planning?
53. What qualities make a good husband? Wife? Daughter? Son? Business person?
54. Is there an extended family? What are the roles of the various members?

55. Is the group more important than any individual member of the group?
56. Who do people go to for advice with different problems?

Education

57. Is education free? Compulsory? To what age/grade level?
58. How does the education system compare to yours? Advantages/Disadvantages from your perspective?
59. How are children disciplined at school? At home? By whom? What implications does this have for adult behavior

Roles of Men and Women

60. Are female and male children equally desired?
61. Do they share equally? Have similar responsibilities?
62. Are there differences between male and female roles in business? Do women have positions in all areas?

Business Customs and Social Customs

63. What are the most important elements needed to succeed?
64. Is there a strong task orientation?
65. What are some dominant business values?
66. What determines whether you succeed or fail?
67. Should you invite your business colleagues to you home? Will you probably be invited to their home?
68. Should you be on time or late for a meeting?
69. How do you tell a colleague he/she has made an error? In public? In private?
70. How do you reward? With increase in pay? Benefits?
71. How are people motivated?

Food

72. What kinds of food are eaten?
73. Are you expected to eat all foods?
74. Will you be expected to drink the local beverage? What is it?
75. Is cooking an art? What are the methods?
76. What rules govern eating away from home? Who pays?

Newpapers and Media

77. Which newspapers are most popular? Is censorship a practice?
78. Are all subject matters of books available? In what languages?
79. What is the government's attitude toward the media?

Health

80. What medical facilities are available?
81. What preventive measures are necessary to maintain good health?

Humor

82. What kinds of humor are understood and appreciated?
83. What are the elements of a good story?
84. Is odd behavior considered amusing? What is considered odd behavior?

Their Attitude Toward You

85. What is the relationship between this country and the U.S.? Presently, in the past 10 years, and before that time? What is the projection of their future attitude?
86. Are Americans liked, disliked, and for what reasons?
87. Is there a large U.S. expatriate community? Do they live in a ghetto?
88. What concerns you most about this assignment?
89. How will you cope with these concerns?
90. What concerns you least about this assignment?
91. What do you expect will be their attitudes toward you?
92. When you return home will you have changed?
93. If you experienced culture shock do you know the symptoms?
94. What about "culture fatigue"?
95. Can you anticipate some possible miscommunication problems?
96. What is *your* attitude toward the people? Do you feel superior? Inferior?
97. Do you know any effective ways to persuade?
98. Will you be formal or informal? In what situation?
99. Will you be able to find the intellectual/social/recreational stimulation you need?
100. What else do you think you should know about this culture in which you will be a "foreigner"?

Appendix B
Questionnaire on Cross-Cultural Management Perspectives*

In the statements that follow, please circle the number that accurately represents the extent to which you agree with either the statement on the left or the statement on the right:

Circle 1—if you *agree strongly* with the statement on the left
      2—if you *agree* with the statement on the left
      3—if you are somewhat indifferent, but tend to agree more with the statement on the left
      4—if you are somewhat indifferent, but tend to agree more with the statement on the right
      5—if you *agree* with the statement on the right
      6—if you *agree strongly* with the statement on the right

Circle only *one* number for each question.

---

*Designed by George W. Renwick and Stephen H. Rhinesmith as *An Exercise in Cultural Analysis for Managers* (Intercultural Network, Inc., 906 North Spring Avenue, La Grange Park, Illinois 60525). Reprinted with permission.

Planning, Evaluating, Innovating

Harmony. When planning, evaluating and innovating there should be an attempt to take into consideration the way things are and to initiate change only within the context of the social order and the order which nature has established in the universe.

1 2 3 4 5 6 **Control.** Individuals and organizations should constantly set goals, plan actions to accomplish goals, develop means to evaluate progress toward these goals, and initiate changes when old ways cannot meet new demands.

Past. Plans should be based upon, and evaluated in terms of, the customs and traditions of the organization and society. Innovation and change are justified only to the degree that precedent can be found in the past for the new action.

1 2 3 4 5 6 **Future.** Plans should be based upon, and evaluated in terms of, the projected future benefit to be gained from a specific activity. Innovation and change are justified in terms of future payoffs with little regard for customs and traditions.

Abstract. Plans should be made and evaluated in terms of general, abstract, social, and moral values that are used as the yardstick for measuring man's activities in his personal life and in organizations. Innovation and change must be justified in terms of these social and moral values.

1 2 3 4 5 6 **Concrete.** Plans should be made and evaluated in terms of concrete, quantifiable results that can be measured and compared against other individual and organizational performance to determine competitiveness and effectiveness.

Limited Good. Plans should be based upon the recognition that the resources necessary for, as well as the benefits to be gained from, individual or organizational activity are *limited*; i.e., these resources and benefits exist in finite quantity and cannot be obtained without "taking an equal amount of good" from others.

1 2 3 4 5 6 **Unlimited Good.** Plans should be based upon the recognition that the resource necessary for, as well as the benefits to be gained from, individual and organizational activity are *unlimited*; i.e., these resources and benefits exist in infinite quantity and can be obtained by everyone to the extent that they are willing to seek, develop and utilize them.

Wisdom. The older personnel in the organization should be given as much or more respect than the younger ones. The older personnel, because of their experience and perspective, should be trusted and relied upon for advice, sound planning and direction.

1 2 3 4 5 6

Energy. More attention should be paid to the younger personnel in an organization than to the older personnel. Because they know more about current problems and modern techniques of dealing with them, the younger personnel should be relied upon for dynamic planning and direction.

Organizing and Controlling

Collectivity. Organizational structure and controls should emphasize group and organizational needs with little concern for the individual. A high degree of organizational control should be maintained in order to maximize organizational solidarity against any potentially disruptive individuals. Emphasis should be upon organizational loyalty and years of service.

1 2 3 4 5 6

Individualism. Organizational structure and controls should emphasize individual growth and development within the organization. There should be high concern for job satisfaction. If necessary, organizational structures and controls may be altered to meet individual need preferences and interests. Emphasis should be upon individual freedom.

Dependence. Authority and responsibility should be centralized. Organizational structure should be tightly organized and controlled, and should require high conformity and adherence to a strict set of rules and regulations in order to ensure individual conformity.

1 2 3 4 5 6

Independence. Authority and responsibility should be decentralized. Organizational structure should be loose, and should require little control over individual performance. Emphasis should be upon self-reliance and upon individual accountability for decision and results.

Recruiting, Selecting, Rewarding

Affiliation. Strong emphasis should be placed on recruiting and selecting persons who are compatible with persons already in the organization. Rewards should be given in the form of personal praise and support with emphasis upon loyalty and personal leadership.

1 2 3 4 5 6 **Achievement.** Emphasis should be placed on recruiting and selecting persons who have unique accomplishments and are highly skilled in areas of organizational need. Persons should be rewarded with more challenging and complex tasks and greater responsibility which motivates them to work against inner standards of excellence.

Ascription. Social and family background should be stressed in recruiting and selecting personnel. Rewards should be given to those related to family, caste or social connections.

1 2 3 4 5 6 **Achievement.** Unusual competence, accomplishments, and highly developed skills necessary to the organization should be sought in recruiting and selecting personnel. Rewards should be given to those who perform best under competitive conditions.

Leadership

External. Because of man's dislike for work, he must be coerced, controlled, directed or threatened with punishment to get him to put forth adequate effort toward achieving organizational objectives.

1 2 3 4 5 6 **Internal.** The threat of punishment and external control are not the only means of getting people to work toward organizational objectives. Men will exercise self-direction and self-control toward achieving objectives to which they are committed.

Communication

One-Way. Information should flow down through the hierarchy of the organization in the form of orders and directives which are not questioned by subordinates.

1 2 3 4 5 6

Two-Way. Information should flow both up and down through the organization with subordinates suggesting alternatives to their superiors and testing alternatives in order to arrive at the best decision.

Indirect. When one has opinions and complaints to express, it is best to join with others and let representatives present the views.

1 2 3 4 5 6

Direct. Opinions and demands should be presented to one's superiors in person. An individual should be known to hold the views he does and should accept responsibility for them.

Interpersonal Relations

Hierarchical. Protocol and codes to regulate interpersonal relations are extremely important; persons must observe a strict separation between different levels in the hierarchy.

1 2 3 4 5 6

Egalitarian. While a pattern of relating to one another across authority levels and different functions exists, it should be flexible; persons should be encouraged to alter formal relationships when necessary to meet the needs of the situation.

Relationship Between Work and Social Life

Integrated. Little distinction should be made between social relationships and work relationships. Friendships should easily cross the line between work and social life.

1 2 3 4 5 6

Separated. There should be much concern for separation of work and social relations. Care should be taken to avoid "conflicts of interests" and to avoid personal obligations that might affect job performance.

Problem-solving

1 2 3 4 5 6

Abstract. Problem-solving should be approached from the perspective of a system of theories and principles. As problems arise, they should be classified under well-known principles and the solution is automatically indicated. The Managerial challenge lies in the proper classification of problems as they arise.

Concrete. Problem-solving should be approached from a concrete perspective with emphasis upon a cost-benefit analysis of alternative solutions. The managerial challenge lies in formulating the alternative solution and choosing among them based upon their future operational consequences.

Decision-making

1 2 3 4 5 6

Being. The primary concern should be expression. Criteria for decision-making should be based upon the degree to which the results will allow the manager to express his or her personality.

Doing. The primary concern should be achievement. Criteria for decision-making should be based upon the degree to which the results will allow the manager to achieve goals that are measurable and valued by society.

Negotiating

1 2 3 4 5 6

Autocratic. Negotiating strategies should be based upon management's assumption that subordinates have little to contribute to organizational decisions and no right to make demands on management or the organization.

Collaborative. Negotiating strategies should be based upon management's assumption that subordinates share equal interests, organizational goals and success; they should be consulted on major organizational decisions in order to reach a total organizational consensus.

Managing Conflict

Smoothing. Organizational and interpersonal conflict may be recognized, but there should be 1 2 3 4 5 6 little attempt to carry through an analysis of the conflict for management or resolution. Conflicts, if concentrated upon and dealt with directly, are seldom resolved to anyone's satisfaction.

Confrontation. Organizational and interpersonal conflicts should be identified and dealt with directly. Their causes should be diagnosed and plans should be made for their management or disolution. All problems can be overcome with concerted effort on the part of the individuals involved.

Training

Cognitive. Training should take place in highly structured situations in which the supervisor or 1 2 3 4 5 6 instructor explains facts and theories which the trainee should know; the trainee should listen and attempt to remember what he is taught.

Experiential. Training should involve actual experience. One learns from experience through reflection, generalization and further testing in order to determine what lesson or principles are are transferable to other cases or situations. The trainee takes much responsibility for his own learning, depending upon his particular needs and interests.

Note: Analyze the profile which emerges on your managerial perspectives based upon the above data, and ascertain the significance of cultural influences upon your leadership philosophy.

Appendix C
Organizational Culture
Survey Instrument

Instructions

This questionnaire should be as complete and authentic as possible. It provides you with an opportunity for: (a) giving feedback *anonymously* to foster your organization's development, (b) for evaluating its key management, including yourself; and (c) for understanding better your organizational environment, whether at home or abroad.

There are 6 major sections to this inquiry, and a total of 99 items seeking your opinion. A maximum of 50 minutes should be allowed for thoughtful completion of this inventory. Please consider your answers carefully for each point. Your first effort at responding should reflect your spontaneous reactions and thoughts on how you view your organizations culture from your position. If time permits, review your replies, and make changes if necessary.

Please check the appropriate categories that best depict your response to the inquiry. Where necessary, *fill in* the information requested.

This analysis will be for the total organization ( )

or for the subsystem of which you are a part ( )
(e.g. division, department, subsidiary)

The majority of questions are to be answered by checking one column in a 7-point scale with the lowest evaluations on the left or low side of the continuum, average in the middle area, and higher assessments on the right side. The exceptions are questions #23, 68, 69-81, which require a checking of the appropriate category provided.

Organizational Diagnosis

On this scale of *lowest* (1) to *highest* (7), circle your rating of your organization's effectiveness or ineffectiveness on the following items. On question 23, simply mark the appropriate category for your response.

Over-all Analysis   **Effectiveness**

1. The goals/objectives of this organization
   are clearly defined and regularly reviewed.   1 2 3 4 5 6 7

2. Managers and supervisors at all levels have the
   opportunity to participate in this process of set-
   ting goals/objectives.   1 2 3 4 5 6 7

3. The organization has mechanisms for periodic
   evaluation of its achievement of goals/objectives. 1 2 3 4 5 6 7

4. Key management devotes adequate time to
   advanced, dynamic planning, and involves sub-
   ordinates in the process as appropriate.   1 2 3 4 5 6 7

5. Key management in this organization supports
   high achievers among employees.   1 2 3 4 5 6 7

6. Management regularly reviews the assignment of
   roles and responsibilities, as well as the dele-
   gation of authority for performance.   1 2 3 4 5 6 7

7. Key managers ensure that adequate personnel
   development and training is available for em-
   ployees to carry out assigned tasks.   1 2 3 4 5 6 7

8. Management has an adequate system for regular
   and meaningful performance evaluation of
   employees.   1 2 3 4 5 6 7

9. The organization emphasizes cooperation as an
   operational norm.   1 2 3 4 5 6 7

10. The organization demonstrates commitment to
    providing satisfactory service to its clients/
    customers.   1 2 3 4 5 6 7

11. The organization utilizes well, the human
    energies of its work force.   1 2 3 4 5 6 7

12. The organization rewards personnel on the basis
    of merit and performance, encouraging com-
    petence.   1 2 3 4 5 6 7

13. The work climate encourages employees to do
    their best and perform well.   1 2 3 4 5 6 7

14. The atmosphere in the organization encourages
    people to be open and candid with management.   1 2 3 4 5 6 7

15. The organization treats employees equally,
    regardless of their sex or race.   1 2 3 4 5 6 7

Organization Communication

16. Are you satisfied with the present state of organizational communications? 1 2 3 4 5 6 7

17. Do you think the communication between management and yourself is adequate? 1 2 3 4 5 6 7

18. Do you believe that organizational communications between the central headquarter's staff and field personnel are satisfactory? 1 2 3 4 5 6 7

19. Do you believe that in your area of responsibility, communication is satisfactory between you and your subordinates? 1 2 3 4 5 6 7

20. Do you think there is adequate written communication in the organization? 1 2 3 4 5 6 7

21. Do you think there is adequate oral and group communication? 1 2 3 4 5 6 7

22. Are you satisfied that adequate communication is provided about organizational changes? 1 2 3 4 5 6 7

23. Is your communication with various levels of management around you *largely*

downward ( )
upward ( )
circular ( )

Management Team Evaluation

In terms of upper level management, the emphasis as I evaluate it is:

24. Clear organizational objectives and targets. 1 2 3 4 5 6 7
25. Competency in themselves and their subordinates. 1 2 3 4 5 6 7
26. Providing a leadership model for subordinates. 1 2 3 4 5 6 7
27. Continuous, planned organizational renewal. 1 2 3 4 5 6 7
28. High productivity standards. 1 2 3 4 5 6 7
29. High service standards. 1 2 3 4 5 6 7
30. Experimenting with new ideas and approaches. 1 2 3 4 5 6 7
31. Encouragement of human resource development. 1 2 3 4 5 6 7
32. Coordination and cooperation in and among the organizational work units. 1 2 3 4 5 6 7

33. Conducting meaningful and productive meetings. 1 2 3 4 5 6 7

34. Confronting conflict directly and settling disagreements rather than avoiding or ignoring it. 1 2 3 4 5 6 7

35. Promoting creative thinkers and innovative performers. 1 2 3 4 5 6 7

36. Always *trying* to do things better. 1 2 3 4 5 6 7

37. Equal employment opportunity and affirmative action. 1 2 3 4 5 6 7

38. Creating a motivating environment for employees. 1 2 3 4 5 6 7

39. Open, authentic communications with each other, and their subordinates. 1 2 3 4 5 6 7

40. Seeking suggestions and ideas from employees and the public (feedback). 1 2 3 4 5 6 7

41. Clarifying organizational roles and responsibilities so there is no confusion or overlap. 1 2 3 4 5 6 7

42. Team work and collaboration within and among upper level management. 1 2 3 4 5 6 7

43. Effective concern for training subordinates to perform competently. 1 2 3 4 5 6 7

44. Willingness to consider innovations proposed to increase organizational effectiveness. 1 2 3 4 5 6 7

45. Sharing of power, authority, and decision-making with lower level management. 1 2 3 4 5 6 7

46. Policies and procedures which counteract absenteeism, slackness, and uproductivity. 1 2 3 4 5 6 7

47. Management of responsibility on the part of employees they supervise. 1 2 3 4 5 6 7

48. Problem-solving and confronting issues. 1 2 3 4 5 6 7

49. Constantly improving working conditions, both physical and psychological. 1 2 3 4 5 6 7

50. Consistency in organizational policies and procedures. 1 2 3 4 5 6 7

Work Group Assessment

Please answer this section in terms of the work group you manage. That is, respond in terms of personnel who report to you or for whom you are responsible.

51. The atmosphere and interpersonal relations in my group are friendly and cooperative. 1 2 3 4 5 6 7

52. The members encourage one another's best efforts, reinforcing successful behavior.   1 2 3 4 5 6 7

53. The group organizes and problem solves effectively.   1 2 3 4 5 6 7

54. The members maintain adequate standards of performance.   1 2 3 4 5 6 7

55. The group is open to and ready for organizational changes.   1 2 3 4 5 6 7

56. The members work effectively as a team.   1 2 3 4 5 6 7

57. The group communicates well within our work unit.   1 2 3 4 5 6 7

58. The group communicates satisfactorily with other work units.   1 2 3 4 5 6 7

59. The members provide group input and may participate in the management process as appropriate.   1 2 3 4 5 6 7

60. The group makes effective use of available equipment and resources (both material and human.)   1 2 3 4 5 6 7

61. The members generally demonstrate pride in themselves and in their work.   1 2 3 4 5 6 7

62. The group actively seeks to utilize the skills and abilities of its members.   1 2 3 4 5 6 7

63. The members do not feel constrained by rules, regulations, and red tape in accomplishing their work.   1 2 3 4 5 6 7

64. The group is dynamic in its approaches and activities, that is, the work environment "turns people on."   1 2 3 4 5 6 7

65. The members of this group are not characterized by conformity and dependency.   1 2 3 4 5 6 7

66. The group has a record of consistent accomplishment in the organization.   1 2 3 4 5 6 7

67. The members in my work group generally exercise responsibility and achievement.   1 2 3 4 5 6 7

Managerial Self-Perception

68. As a leader in this organization, check the words or word combinations that best describe your management approach:

( ) idealistic   ( ) realistic

( ) innovative   ( ) pragmatic

(continued)

( ) cooperative	( ) individualistic
( ) task oriented	( ) sensitive
( ) change maker	( ) change reactor
( ) hard-nosed	( ) imaginative
( ) inspiring	( ) participative
( ) traditional	( ) futuristic

Managerial Self-Perception (check appropriate category)

Rarely | Sometimes | Usually

69. Do you seek out and use improved work methods?

70. Does your managerial performance demonstrate sufficient skill in
● administration
● human relations
● obtaining results?

71. Do you reinforce and support positive behavior and performance in your subordinates?

72. Do you actively encourage your subordinates to make the most of their potential?

73. Are you willing to take reasonable risks in the management of your work units?

74. Do you take responsibility to ensure that the employees you manage make their best contribution toward achieving organizational goals and production targets?

75. Do your key subordinates really know where you stand on controversial organizational issues?

76. Do you demonstrate by example personal standards of competency and productivity?

77. Are you generally objective, friendly but business-like in dealing with employees?

78. Are you doing something specific for your own personal and professional development?

79. Do you take responsibility to seek change in organizational norms, values, and standards when these are not relevant and in need of updating?

80. Please read back to yourself the above twelve statements. In light of the demands of modern management and employee expectations, how would you rate the above evaluations of your leadership role?
Please check one: Inadequate ( ) Adequate ( ).

81. A study by Michael Maccoby describes the new post-industrial organizational leader in this way: A gamesman, "in contrast to the jungle-fighter industrialist of the past, is driven not to build or to preside over empires, but to organize winning teams. Unlike the security-seeking organization man, he is excited by the chance to cut deals and to gamble." The author also states that such new leaders in top management are more cooperative and less hardened than the classical autocrats, as well as less dependent than the typical bureaucrats. This sociologist suggests that the new leader is more detached and emotionally inaccessable than his predecessors, yet troubled that his work develops his head but not his heart.
How does this description of the emerging executive fit you? (check one)
This is comparable to the way I am/feel ( ).
I do not identify with this new type of manager ( ).

Organizational Relations

Please check the category that best describes the present situation for you.

82. Employees generally trust top management.   1 2 3 4 5 6 7

83. Employees usually "level" in their communications with management, providing authentic feedback.   1 2 3 4 5 6 7

84. Employees usually are open and authentic in their work relations.   1 2 3 4 5 6 7

85. If employees have a conflict or disagreement with management, they usually work it out directly, or seek mediation.   1 2 3 4 5 6 7

86. When employees receive administrative directives or decisions with which they do not agree they usually conform without dissent.   1 2 3 4 5 6 7

87. Older managers are threatened by younger, competent staff members or subordinates who may have more knowledge, information, or education.   1 2 3 4 5 6 7

88. Managers are able to interact effectively with minority and female peers or subordinates.   1 2 3 4 5 6 7

89. Managers really try to be fair and just with employees, using competency only as their evaluative criteria of performance.   1 2 3 4 5 6 7

90. Many managers have generally "retired" on the job, and are indifferent to needs for organizational renewal.   1 2 3 4 5 6 7

91. Employees have opportunities to clarify changing
roles and relationships. 1 2 3 4 5 6 7

92. Is organization concerned about the needs of
people as well as getting the task done? 1 2 3 4 5 6 7

93. Organization encourages and assists employees
in the development of community relations. 1 2 3 4 5 6 7

Organizational Changes

94. The organization is able to adapt as to the
dramatic shifts and changes underway in society
and the larger culture. 1 2 3 4 5 6 7

95. The organization is able to handle the new
demands made upon it as a result of the changes
in top administration and management emphasis. 1 2 3 4 5 6 7

96. The organization does seek adequate input from
employees on those changes that affect them,
or they are to implement. 1 2 3 4 5 6 7

97. The organization is able to deal effectively with
the new kind of person coming into your workforce and management. 1 2 3 4 5 6 7

98. The organization has changed its management
priorities and approaches with regard to scarce
resources, as well as environmental and ecological concerns. 1 2 3 4 5 6 7

99. The organization is innovative in finding ways
to improve the institutional environment. 1 2 3 4 5 6 7

Note: Please recognize that cultural factors influenced the way the above
questions were constructed, and the way in which you responded. However, this evaluation can provide insight into your organizational culture
in terms of Western perspective and future trend criteria.

Appendix D
Resources for
Intercultural Effectiveness

For those in international management or working with minority groups, there is a growing variety of resources available to improve intercultural effectiveness. This emerging body of learning materials ranges in scope from print and electronic technology to live programs and specialized consultants.

In the first section of this appendix is included a list of organizations that provide cross-cultural briefing and training programs for managers and their families. We have also included a list of learning aids for intercultural education and a list of periodicals where the reader can find references to the subjects about which we have written. Because this book will be of use to undergraduate and graduate students in business and other areas, we have included articles and books in the field of cross-cultural education and management. These are in addition to those references provided at the end of each chapter.

Organizations Providing Cross-Cultural Briefing, Training Programs, and Seminars

In 1968, there were approximately 200 organizations (business, government, private consulting, religious, academic) that were involved in the design and conduct of intercultural education and training programs. At this time, there are over 500 organizations located in 42 states in the United States and in more than 23 countries.

In the spring of 1979, through the Society of Intercultural Education, Training and Research (SIETAR) and Intercultural Network, Inc., there was published a directory containing information on 472 of these organizations. In this volume we have included a number of these organizations that are providing the training for businessmen and women in the international and intercultural area.

Besides providing the names and addresses of these organizations, a brief description of their services will be given. Most of these engage in intercultural training and teaching. Many also conduct research and assist with the development of audio-visual materials. In some cases, a contact person is indicated.

American Graduate School of International Management

Thunderbird Campus
Glendale, Arizona 85306

This school, founded in 1946, offers a residential graduate studies program leading to a Master of International Management, MIM, degree. Also offered is a Certificate of Advanced Study. Stress on language competence is strong, especially in French, Spanish, Portuguese, German, Japanese, Chinese, Arabic, and English as a second language.

The American Graduate School of International Management recently established a training and research department called INTERCOM. This department assists international companies and their personnel to develop both the personal and technical skills necessary to succeed in the highly complex, competitive world of international business. The objectives of INTERCOM are to provide special training for managers to equip them to carry out international assignments, language training, cross-cultural communications training, area briefings, and functional business subjects are covered.

For information on INTERCOM, contact Professor R. Duane Hall, Executive Director; The Key Managers Program of Language, Professor Lawrence Finney; and The Cross-Cultural Management and Training Program, Robert T. Moran.

American Management Association

135 West 50th Street
New York, New York 10020

The AMA offers short courses and seminars which are held in various parts of the country dealing with area studies and many aspects of foreign business. The main centers are New York, Chicago and San Francisco. For information on their international programs, contact Jack Cunningham.

American Society for Training and Development

Post Office Box 5307
Madison, Wisconsin 53705
Washington, D.C. Office: One DuPont Circle
Washington, D.C. 20036

This professional organization has recently organized an International Division and is addressing the training and development issues from an international perspective. For information on the International Division, contact Vincent A. Miller.

The Business Council for International Understanding

The American University
Washington, D.C. 20016

This institute was established in 1958 and offers residential courses and a variety of programs of various lengths, covering area and country studies, and behavioral approaches. It also offers "High Intensity" instruction in more than 47 languages.

BCIU conducts training programs for managers and their families that provide knowledge of how people in other cultures think, insights into the U.S. cultural perspectives, skills for coping, country and area specific information, understanding of how to do business, training in languages, and specific functional information. For information, contact Gary E. Lloyd.

Brigham Young University, Language and Intercultural Research Center

240, B-34
Provo, Utah 84502

The Language and Intercultural Research Center engages in research, training, and dissemination of information in many areas: orientation, communication indicators, evaluation aids, resource lists, etc. for all fields of intercultural communication and language concerns, including translation and intercultural writing. For information, contact V. Lynn Tyler.

Canadian International Development Agency, Briefing Centre

122 Bank Street
Ottawa, Ontario, Canada

The monthly Briefing programs include a basic content of country-specific information, health and travel briefing, intercultural communication and an introduction to aspects of international development. In addition to a core program, participants are offered a variety of optional teaching modules, e.g., nonverbal communication, culture shock, time management, community involvement, women overseas, and Canadian identity. For information, contact Daniel Kealey.

Center for Research and Education

1800 Pontiac
Denver, Colorado 80220

A variety of programs and training materials are offered by this organization. The Center for Research and Education (CRE) has also done a significant amount of work for the U.S. Navy and the Peace Corps. CRE publishes *The Bridge* four times a year.

Experiment in International Living

Kipling Road
Brattleboro, Vermont 05301

The purpose of this organization is to improve mutual interaction and understanding between individuals from all cultures. Cultural orientation programs for students and businessmen from the United States and many other countries have been conducted. For information contact Donald Batchelder.

Harris International

P.O. Box 2321
La Jolla, California 92038

This is a management consulting firm engaged in organizational development services, action research on human factors problems, custom designed cross-cultural training programs, and foreign deployment systems. For information, contact Philip R. Harris.

Human Resources Research Organization

300 North Washington Street
Alexandria, Virginia 22314

The Human Resources Research Organization (HumRRO) primarily conducts research, but training in intercultural communication for Americans going aboard, for Americans in the U.S. who work with foreign visitors, and for trainers who conduct programs for those going abroad or working with foreign visitors. For information, contact Alfred J. Kraemer.

Intercultural Communication, Inc.

P.O. Box 14358
University Station
Minneapolis, Minnesota 55414

Intercultural Communication, Inc. offers training in communication skills useful in situations where cultural, language, and value differences exist. The goal of their individualized programs is to help people who are successful in their own culture become successful in other cultures. Services include: general intercultural training, specific cultural orientation, language training, assessment, cross-cultural counseling and reentry training. For information, contact Helen L. McNulty.

Intercultural Network, Inc.

906 North Spring Ave.
La Grange Park, Illinois 60525

Intercultural Network is a consulting, training and research organization committed to the development of the field of intercultural education and management training through a variety of services to individuals and organizations. The Network assists international and multi-cultural organizations in analyzing the intercultural aspects of their operations. For information contact David S. Hoopes.

Overseas Briefing Associates

201 East 36th Street
New York, New York 10016

Overseas Briefing Associates (OBA) offer training materials and briefings for corporate managers and families. They also have programs for foreign nationals coming to the United States. OBA has a series of updates for 22 countries. These materials contain most of the necessary information for a family expatriating to one of these countries. For information, contact Alison R. Lanier or Claudia B. Isaac.

Society for Intercultural Education, Training and Research

Georgetown University
Washington, D.C. 20057

The Society for Intercultural Education, Training and Research (SIETAR) is a professional association designed to serve the needs and interests of persons working in intercultural education, training, and research. SIETAR is interdisciplinary and cross-professional and gives attention to all phases of the intercultural field.

SIETAR holds an annual conference normally in February and publishes the *International Journal of Intercultural Relations* and the newsletter *Communique*. In cooperation with the Intercultural Network, Inc., the society also publishes books and monographs of value to the field. Other activities include sponsoring or cosponsoring seminars, symposia, and institutes, as well as serving as a clearinghouse on an individual basis with student and regular memberships and on an institutional basis with regular institutional memberships and sustaining memberships. For information, contact Diane L. Zeller.

Stanford Institute for Applied Intercultural Communication

P.O. Box AD
Stanford, California 94350

The institute is sponsored jointly by the Stanford School of Education and the Experiment in International Living. It conducts a multidisciplinary, multicultured program for one to two weeks each summer. For information, contact Clifford Clarke.

Systran

70 West Hubbard St.
Chicago, Illinois 60610

Systran (Systems for International Training) is an international company that specializes in technical, vocational, and cross-cultural training. Systran has also designed training and curriculum development programs in pre-technical English. For information contact Serge Ogranovitch.

The World Trade Institute

One World Trade Center
55th Floor
New York, New York 10048

The World Trade Institute is the educational arm of the World Trade Center in New York. The institute is charged with the task of disseminating information and providing needed training in the international area. Their seminars range from one to five days on all matters of practical international subjects, including cross-cultural matters. There is also a language school offering a unique approach to the learning of a wide range of languages. For information, contact Peter C. Goldmark, Jr.

In addition to all the organizations described above, the following also provide intercultural training information and services:

Business International, One Dag Hammarskjold Plaza, New York, N.Y. 10017 (212/750-6300).
CTM Associates for International Business, 1704 Ivy Oak Square, Reston, Va. 22090 (703/437-0260 or 202/483-7869).
Inter-American Cultural and Scientific Center, University of Florida, Gainesville, Fla. 32601 (904/392-3261).
International Training Institute, 1346 Connecticut Ave., Washington, D.C. 20036 (202/466-2655).
International Cultural Consultants, 5237 North Central Expressway, Dallas, Tex. 75205.
International Consultants Foundation, 5605 Lamar Road, Washington, D.C. 20016 (301/320-4409) or 11 The Green, London, W5, UK (01-567-4745).

Language and Area Center for Latin America, Ortega Hall, The University of New Mexico, Albuquerque, N.M. 87131 (505/277-2636).

Telemedia, Inc., 500 North Michigan Ave., Chicago, Ill. 60611 (312/644-4100).

University of Rochester Management Research Center, College of Business Administration/ INSTAD and IRGOM, P.O. Box 9650, Midtown Plaza Station, Rochester, N.Y. 14604 (716/275-3396).

Learning Aids for Intercultural Education

American Management Associations, 135 W. 50th St. New York, New York 10020. Audio-cassettes on "How to Do Business in the PRC, Japan, Malaysia and other countries. Contact John C. Cunningham.

Berlitz, Charles, Self-Teaching Language Courses. Audio-cassettes in French, Spanish, German and Italian, and many other languages. Berlitz Publications Inc., Ridgefield, N.J.

BFA Educational Media, *Land and People,* 16 mm film, 2211 Michigan Avenue, P.O. Box 1795, Santa Monica, CA 90406.

Bostain, James, *How to Read a Foreigner.* Video-tape. Naval Amphibious School. Coronado, California.

Harris, Philip R., "Effective Management of Change." Audio-cassettes and program study manual. This program is designed to help modern administrators and leaders better plan and control change and to lessen the impact of modern organization shock.

Harris, Philip R. and Dorothy L., "Improving Management Communication Skills." Audio-cassettes and program study manual. This audiotutorial course teaches today's manager all the steps involved in the vital process of communication. Both learning systems cited above by Harris are available from Edu Pac, Inc., 231 Norfolk St., Walpole, Mass. 02081.

Harris, Philip R. and Dorothy L., "Leadership Effectiveness with People." Cassette album, 1979. General Cassette Corp., Box 6940, Phoenix, Az. 85005.

International Operations Simulation (INTOP), Professors Hans B. Thoerelli (University of Indiana), and Professor Robert Graves (University of Chicago). INTOP is a computer-simulation, through which there is trainee involvement. It increases involvement as decisions are made and their effects calculated. This management game simulated international business operations. Results of computer choices can be evaluated in the context of simulated organizations and their environments. INTOP provides participants with greater awareness of the problems encountered when products and decisions cross national boundaries, particularly with reference to international business. Interpersonal dimensions and culture issues are not covered so such a technique in cross-cultural training should be used in connection with intercultural role play.

International Training Programs, *Anglo-Latin American Perspectives Cross-Cultural Communication,* Developed and produced by Richard Hancock, Ralph Cooley and Don Singleton. The University of Oklahoma. Audio-visual tapes.

Kraemer, Alfred, *Contrast American Videotapes.* Human Resources Research Organization, 300 N. Washington St., Alexandria, Virginia 22314.

Language House, 430 N. Michigan Avenue, Suite 618, Chicago, Illinois 60611. "The Aural/Oral way to learn a new language which utilizes books, study guide and up to 60 prerecorded lessons."

Non-Verbal Communication. Video-tape. Ithaca, New York: Department of Communications, School of Agriculture and Life Sciences, Cornell University, 1974.

Orientation/Media International, Box 424, Pacific Grove, CA 93950. Two provocative sound slide films that prepare staff and families for life in a second culture.

Redden, W.J., *Culture Shock Inventory—Manual,* Fredericton, New Brunswick, Canada: Organization Tests Ltd., 1975.

Shirts, Garry, *BAFA, BAFA, RAFA RAFA, RELOCATION CRISIS, HUMANUS, ACCESS*—six simulation games with cross-cultural implications. Simile 11, Box 910 Del Mar, CA 92014

Smith, Gary, and George Otero, *Teaching About Cultural Awareness,* Center for Teaching International Relations, CTIR Denver University, 1977.

The Center for Human Resources Planning and Development, Inc. *The Americans: Boricuas,* training package including 16 mm film or videotape cassette, two audio cassettes and manual. *The Americans* series is designed to provide an understanding of the cultural dynamics of our different racial and ethnic groups.

Selected English Language Periodicals
Addressing Intercultural Communication and Management Concerns

American Management Association Publications
AMACOM
135 West 50th Street
New York, New York 10020

American Journal of Sociology
University of Chicago Press

5801 Ellis Avenue
Chicago, Illinois 60637

Annals of the American Academy of Political and Social Science
3937 Chestnut
Philadelphia, Pennsylvania 19104

Asia
P.O. Box 379
Fort Lee, New Jersey 07024

The Bridge
Center for Research and Education
1800 Pontiac, Box 104
Denver, Colorado 80220

Business Abroad
Circulation: P.O. Box 3088
Grand Central Station
New York, New York 10017

Business Horizons
Graduate School of Business
Indiana University
Bloomington, Indiana 47401

California Management Review
Graduate School of Business Administration
350 Barrows Hall
University of California
Berkeley, California 94720

Columbia Journal of World Business
Columbia University
408 Uris
New York, New York 10027

Exchange
International Communication Agency
Washington, D.C. 20547

International Business Magazine
14842 1st Avenue South
Seattle, Washington 98169

International Journal of Intercultural Relations
Rutgers—The State University
New Brunswick, New Jersey 08903

International Management
McGraw-Hill House
Maidenhead, Berkshire,
England SL62QL

International Studies Quarterly
Sage Publications, Inc.
P.O. Box 776
Beverly Hills, California 90213

Journal of Black Studies
Sage Publications, Inc.
P.O. Box 776
Beverly Hills, California 90213

Journal of Cross-Cultural Psychology
275 South Beverly Drive
Beverly Hills, California 90212

Journal of International Business Studies
Rutgers University, GSBA
92 New Street
Newark, New Jersey 07102

Journal of Social Issues
P.O. Box 1248
Ann Arbor, Michigan 48106

The International and Intercultural Communication Annual
Speech Communication Association
5205 Leesburg Pike
Falls Church, Virginia 22041

Training and Development Journal
American Society for Training and Development
P.O. Box 5307
Madison, Wisconsin 53705

Articles from Periodicals

Adler, P., "The Translational Experience: An Alternative View of Culture Shock," *Journal of Humanistic Psychology* 1975, 15 (3).

Alexander, W., Jr., "Mobil's four-hour Environmental Interview," *Worldwide P & I Planning,* Jan.-Feb., 1970, *18*. (TIE, Summer, 1970, p. 21).

Allen, H.T., "U.S.-Chinese Dialogue, 1969-1972," *Journal of Communication,* Vol. 26, No. 1. Winter, 1976, pp. 81-86.

Almaney, Adan, "Intercultural Communication and the MNC Executive," *Columbia Journal of World Business,* Winter 1974.

Alpander, G., "Drift to Authoritarianism: The Changing Managerial Styles of the U.S. Executive Overseas," *Journal of International Business Studies,* Fall, 1973.

Baker, J.C. and J.M. Ivancevich, "Multinational Management Staffing with American Expatriates. *Economic and Business Bulletin,* Fall, 1970, Vol. 23, No. 1, p. 55.

Baker, J.C. and J.M. Ivancevich, "The Assignment of American Executives Abroad: Systematic, Haphazard or Chaotic?" *California Management Review,* Vol. XIII. (1971) No. 3, pp. 39-44.

Bass, B.M., The American Advisor Abroad," *Journal of Applied Behavioral Science,* 1971, 7(3), 285-307.

Beeth, G., "How to Build an Excellent International Staff," *International Management Practice; AMACOM,* 1973, pp. 66-81.

Benson, P., "Measuring Cross-Cultural Adjustment: The Problem of Criteria, *International Journal of Intercultural Relations,* in press.

Benson, T. and K. Franklin, "An Orientation to Nonverbal Communication," Science Research Associates, Inc., 1976.

Bochner, S., The Mediating Man: Cultural Interchange and Transnational Education. Honolulu, Hawaii: East-West Center, 1973.

Brislin, R., "Interaction Among Members of Nine Ethnic Groups and the Belief-Similarity Hypothesis," *Journal of Social Psychology.* 1971, 85, 171-179.

Burk, J.L., "The Effects of Theocentrism Upon Intercultural Communication: Functional and Dysfunctional," in Fred L. Casmir, ed., *International and Intercultural Communication Annual,* Vol. III, Falls Church, Virginia: Speech Communication Association 1976, pp. 20-34.

Bystrom, J., "Increasing Intercultural Communication: The PEACESAT Experiment, A Study in The Social Benefits of International Interactive Exchange by Communication Satellite," in Fred L. Casmir, ed., *International and Intercultural Communication Annual,* Vol. I, Falls Church, Virginia: Speech Communication Association, 1974, pp. 39-43.

Campbell, C.K., "Cross-Cultural and Cross-Functional Development of Personnel in IBM World Trade Corporation," mimeographed (New York: National Foreign Trade Council, Feb. 1970) NFTC.

Clarke, C., "Personal Counseling Across Cultural Boundaries," from *Readings In Intercultural Communication,* Vol. IV, Paul Pedersen, ed.,

The Society for International Training, Education, and Research, Pittsburgh. 1975.

David, K., "Intercultural Adjustment and Applications of Reinforcement Theory to Problems of Culture Shock, *Trends,* 1972 4 (3), 1-64.

David, K., "Effect of Intercultural Contact and International Stance in Attitude Change toward Host Nationals." *International Journal of Psychology,* 1972.

de Bettignies, H.C. and D.B. Louis, "Men at the Crossroads: Europe's Personnel Managers." *European Business,* Summer, 1973.

de Bettignies, H.C. "Management Development: The International Perspective." In Chapter 1 of Taylor & Lippi, (eds.), *Management Development and Training Handbook.* New York: McGraw-Hill, 1975.

Downs, J., Training Government Employees and Military Personnel for Overseas Assignments. Paper presented at the meeting of the SIETAR, Chicago, February 25-27, 1977.

Drucker, P.A., "What We Can Learn from Japanese Management," *The McKinsey Quarterly;* Winter, 1973.

Eldin, H.K. and S. Sadig, "Suggested Criteria for Selecting Management Consultants in Developing Countries," *International Management Review,* 1971/4-5, pp. 123-132.

Flack, M.J., "Cultural Diplomacy: Blindspot in International Affairs Textbooks," *International Educational and Cultural Exchange,* Vol. 8, no. 3, Winter, 1972-1973., pp. 11-18.

Goodyear, F.H., and Alan West, "An Organizational Framework for Cross-Cultural Communication," *The Southern Speech Communication Journal,* 42 (Winter 1977), pp. 178-190.

Graves, D., "Cultural Determinism and Management Behavior," *Organizational Dynamics:* Autum 1972, 14 pp.

Gudykunst, W.B., "A Model of Group Development for Intercultural Communication Workshop," in Fred L. Casmir, (ed.), *International and Intercultural Communication Annual,* Vol. III, Falls Church, Virginia: Speech Communication Association, 1976, pp. 86-93.

Hall, E.T., "How Cultures Collide," (as interviewed by Elizabeth Hall) *Psychology Today,* Vol. 10, No. 2, July 1976.

Harris, J.G., Jr., "A Science of the South Pacific: Analysis of the Character Structure of the Peace Corps Volunteer," *American Psychologist,* 1973, 28, 3, pp. 232-247.

Harris, P.R. and D.L. Harris, "Intercultural Education for Multinational Managers," *International and Intercultural Communication Annual.* Speech Communication Association, Vol. 3, December 1976, pp. 70-85.

Hays, R.D., "Ascribed Behavioral Determinants of Success-Failure Among U.S. Expatriate Managers," *Journal of International Business Studies,* Spring 1971, 2(1), pp. 40-46.

Heenan, D., "The Corporate Expatriate: Assignment to Ambiguity," *Columbia Journal of World Business,* May-June 1970, pp. 49-54.

Hildebrandt, H.W., "Communication Barriers Between German Subsidiaries and Parent American Companies," *Michigan Business Review;* July, 1973.

Hindrichs, J.R., "A Cross-National Analysis of Work Attitudes," presented at meeting of the American Psychological Association, Chicago, September 3, 1975.

Hinrichs, J.R., S. Haanpera, and L. Sonkin, "Validity of a Bio-graphical Information Blank Across National Boundaries," *Personnel Psychology,* 1976, 29, pp. 417-421.

Hinrichs, J.R. and S. Haanpera, "Reliability of Measurement in Situational Exercise: An Assessment of the Assessment Center Method," *Personnel Psychology,* 1976, 29, pp. 31-40.

Hitti, P.K., *Islam: A Way of Life.* South Bend, Ind.: Gateway Editions, Ltd., 1971.

Hoopes, D.S. (ed.), *Readings in Intercultural Communication.* Vol. I-III. Pittsburgh: Regional Council for International Education, University of Pittsburgh, 1971-1973.

Hoopes, D.S. (ed.), *Readings in Intercultural Communication: Intercultural Programming.* Vol. V. Pittsburgh, Pennsylvania: The Intercultural Communications Network, 1976.

"How Firms Prepare Executives for Foreign Posts," *Business International,* August 14, 1970, pp. 262.

"How Grumman Manages Expatriate Staffing for Major Iranian Project," *Business International,* December 3, 1976, pp. 387-388.

Howard, C.G., "Model for the Design of a Selection Program for Multinational Executives," *Public Personnel Management,* March-April 1974, pp. 138-145.

Hsu, F.L.K., *Americans and Chinese.* La Jolla, California: Natural History Publications Company, 1972.

Hull, F., "Changes in World Mindedness After a Cross-Cultural Sensitivity Group Experience." *Journal of Applied Behavioral Science,* 1972, 8 (1), 115-121.

Ivancevich, J.M. and J.C. Baker, "A Comparative Study of the Satisfaction of Domestic United States Managers and Overseas United States Managers," *Academy of Management Journal,* March 1970, pp. 69-77.

Johnson, Dixon C., "Ourselves and Others: Comparative Stereotypes," from

International Educational and Cultural Exchange, Vol. IX, Nos. 2-3, Fall 1973-Winter 1974.

Johnson, M.B. and G.L. Carter, Jr., "Training Needs of Americans Working Abroad," *Social Change,* 1972, 2(1), pp. 1-3.

Johnson, R.T. and W.G. Ouchi, "Made in America (under Japanese Management)," *Harvard Business Review;* September-October, 1974, pp. 61-69.

Kraemer, A.J., "Cultural Self-Awareness and Communication," International Education and Cultural Exchanges, Vol., 10, No. 3, Winter 1975, pp. 13-16.

Leich, D.N., Transnational Executive Development in the Royal Dutch Shell Group of Companies, mimeographed (New York: National Foreign Trade Council, February, 1970) NFTC ref. no. M-9293.

Lipsett, L. and M. Gebhardt, "Identifying Managers," in D.P. Schultz, *Psychology and Industry,* Chapter 8. London: The MacMillan Co., 1970.

Maddox, R.C., "Problems and Trends in Assigning Managers Overseas." *Personnel,* Jan.-Feb. 1971, pp. 53-56.

Merritt, R.L., "Transmission of Values Across National Boundaries," Richard Merritt, (ed.), *Communication in International Politics,* University of Illinois Press: Chicago, 1972, pp. 3-32.

Miller, E.L., "The International Selection Decision: A Study of Some of the Dimensions of Managerial Behavior in the Selection Process," *Academy of Management Journal,* Vol. 16, 1973, pp. 239-252.

Miller, E.L., "The Selection Decision for an International Assignment: A Study of the Decision Maker's Behavior," *Journal of International Business Studies,* Fall 1972, 3(2), 49-65.

Miller, E.L., "The Overseas Assignment: How Managers Determine Who is Selected," *Michigan Business Review,* May 1972, 12, (TIE, Fall, 1972, p. 9).

Miller, E.L., "The Overseas Decision for an International Assignment: A Study of the Decision Maker's Behavior. *Journal of International Business Studies,* Fall 1972.

Miller, M.M., et al, "The Cross-Cultural Student: Lessons in Human Nature," from *Bulletin of the Menninger Clinic,* Vol. 35, No. 2, March 1971, pp. 128-131.

Moran, R.T., J.A. Mestenhauser, and P.B. Pedersen, "Dress Rehersal for a Cross-Cultural Experience," *International Educational and Cultural Exchange,* Vol. 10, No. 1, Summer 1974, pp. 23-27.

Nath, R., "Training International Business and Management Personnel (an overview)." Paper presented at the meeting of the SIETAR, Chicago, February 25-27, 1977.

Oates, D., "What it Takes to Work Abroad," *International Management,* October 1970, pp. 24-27.

"Preparation for Assignment Abroad—A Checklist on What to Take—and What to Expect," *Business International,* May 29, 1970, pp. 172-173.

Renwick, G.W., "Australian and American Cultures: Similarities, Differences, Difficulties," *Intercultural Management Series,* No. 1; Intercultural Network, Inc., Scottsdale, Arizona, 1976, p. 26.

Reynolds, C., "Career Paths and Compensation in the MNC's," *Columbia Journal of World Business,* Nov.-Dec. 1972, pp. 77-87.

Rhinesmith, S., "Training for Cross-Cultural Operations," *Training and Development Journal,* 1970, 24, pp. 20-23.

Rock, M. and C. Ian Sym-Smith, "Incentives for Foreign Nationals," *Harvard Business Review,* March-April 1973, pp. 33-42.

Ruben, B.D., "Assessing Communication Competency for Intercultural Adaptation." *Group and Organization Studies,* September 1976, 1(3), pp. 334-354.

Ruben, B.D., L.R. Askling, and D. Kealey, "A Descriptive Profile of the Canadian Technical Advisor and Spouse After One Year in Kenya: Psychological, Social and Vocational Dimensions," prepared for the Briefing Center, Canadian International Development Agency, Ottawa, Ontario, April 1977.

Ruben, B.D. and D.J. Kealey, "Behavioral Assessment and the Prediction of Cross-Cultural Shock, Adjustment, and Effectiveness," paper presented at the meeting of the SIETAR, Chicago, February 25-27, 1977.

Rubin, J., "How to Tell When Someone is Saying 'NO'," in Richard W. Brislin (ed.), *Topics in Culture Learning,* Volume IV, Honolulu, Hawaii: East-West Center, 1976, pp. 61-65.

Ruhly, S., "Orientations to Intercultural Communication," from *Modcom,* Science Research Associates, Inc., 1976.

Ryan, M.G., "The Influence of Speaker Dialect and Sex on Stereotypic Attribution," in Fred L. Casmir (ed.), *International and Intercultural Communication Annual.* Vol. I, Falls Church, Virginia: Speech Communication Association, 1974, pp. 87-101.

Sale, R.T., "The Shah's Americans," *The Bridge,* Fall 1977, pp. 11-13.

Shearer, J.C., "The External and Internal Manpower Resources of MNC's," *Columbia Journal of World Business,* Summer 1974, pp. 9-17.

Shetty, Y.R., "International Manager—A Role Profile," *Management International Review,* 1971, 11(4-5), pp. 19-25.

Simonetti, S.H. and J. Weitz, "Job Satisfaction: Some Cross-Cultural Effects," *Personnel Psychology,* Vol. 25, 1972, pp. 107-118.

Sirota, D. and J.M. Greenwood, "Understand Your Overseas Workforce," *Harvard Business Review,* January-February 1971, pp. 53-60.

Slocum, J.W. Jr., and P.M. Topichak, "Do Cultural Differences Affect Job Satisfaction?", *Journal of Applied Psychology;* Vol. 55, 1971, pp. 177-178.

Slocum, J.W. Jr., P.M. Topichak and D.G. Kyhn, "A Cross-Cultural Study of Need Satisfaction and Need Importance for Operative Employees," *Personnel Psychology,* Vol. 24, pp. 435-445.

Smutkupt, S. and L.R.M. Barna, "Impact of Non-Verbal Communication in an Intercultural Setting: Thailand," in Fred L. Casmir (ed.), *International and Intercultural Communication Annual,* Vol. III, Falls Church, Virginia: Speech Communication Association, 1976, pp. 130-138.

Spradley, J.P. and M. Philips, "Culture and Stress: A Quantitative Analysis." *American Anthropologist,* 1972, 74, pp. 518-529.

Stessin, Lawrence, "Culture Shock and the American Businessman Overseas," *International Educational and Cultural Exchange,* Vol. 9, No. 1, Summer 1973. pp. 23-35.

St. Martin, Gail M., "Intercultural Differential Decoding of Non-verbal Affective Communication," in Fred L. Casmir (ed.), *International and Intercultural Communication Annual,* Vol. III, Falls Church, Virginia: Speech Communication Association, 1976, pp. 44-57.

Stoner, J.A., J.D. Aram, and I.M. Rubin, "Factors Associated with Effective Performance in Overseas Work Assignments." *Personnel Psychology,* 1972, 25, pp. 303-318.

Teague, B., "Selecting and Orienting Staff for Service Overseas," The Conference Board, Inc., New York, 1976.

Teague, F.A., "International Management Selection and Development." *California Management Review,* Spring 1970, pp. 1-6.

Trifonovitch, G., "On Cross-Cultural Orientation Techniques," *Topics in Culture Learning,* 1973, 1, pp. 38-47.

Tucker, M.F., "Screening and Selection for Overseas Assignments: Assessment and Recommendations to the U.S. Navy." Center for Research and Education, July 1974.

Tucker, M., H. Raik, D. Rossiter, and M. Uhes, "Improving Cross-Cultural Training and Measurement of Cross-Cultural Learning," *Center for Research and Education,* Vol. 1, June 4, 1973.

Tyler, V.L., "Dimensions, Perspectives, and Resources of Intercultural Communication," in Fred L. Casmir (ed.), *International and Intercultural Communication Annual,* Vol. 1, Falls Church, Virginia: Speech Communication Association, 1974, pp. 65-74.

Vicker, R., "Understanding the Arab Psyche," *Wall Street Journal,* October 19, 1973.

Wallin, T.O., "The International Executive's Baggage: Cultural Values of the American Frontier," *M.S.U. Business Topics,* Spring 1976, pp. 49-58.

Wigand, R.T., and G.A. Barnett, "Multidimensional Scaling of Cultural Processes: The Case of Mexico, South Africa, and the United States," in Fred L. Casmir (ed.), *International and Intercultural Communication Annual,* Vol. III, Falls Church, Virginia: Speech Communication Association, 1976, pp. 139-172.

Wight, A.R., M.A. Hammons, and W.L. Wight, Guidelines for Peace Corps Cross-Cultural Training: Part III, Supplementary readings. Office of Training Support, Peace Corps, Washington, D.C. Published by Center for Research and Education, March 1970.

Wight, W.L., Guidelines for Peace Corps Cross-Cultural Training: Part IV, Annotated Bibliography. Office of Training Support, Peace Corps, Washington, D.C. Published by Center for Research and Education, March 1970.

Wilce, H., "How to Ease the Culture Shock," *International Management,* June 1971, pp. 18-22.

Wilsted, W., R. Hendrick, and R. Stewart, "A Judgment Policy Capture of Bank Loan Decisions: An Approach to Developing Objective Functions for Foal Programming Models," paper presented to American Institute of Decision Sciences, Western Division meeting, San Diego, March 1973.

Yousef, F.S. and N.E. Briggs, "The Multinational Business Organization: A Scheme for the Training of Overseas Personnel in Communication," *International and Intercultural Communication Annual.* Speech And Communication Association, Vol. II, Dec. 1975, pp. 74-85.

Youssef, S.M., "The Integration of Local Nationals into the Managerial Hierarchy of American Overseas Subsidiaries: An Exploratory Study," *Academy of Management Journal,* Vol. 16, 1973, No. 1, pp. 25-35.

Yun, C.K., "Role Conflicts of Expatriate Managers: A Construct," *Management International Review;* Vol. 13, No. 6, 1973.

Zeira, Y., "Overlooked Personnel Problems of Multinational Corporations," *Columbia Journal of World Business,* Summer 1975, pp. 96-103.

Additional Books on International Intercultural Themes

Al-Issa, I. and W. Dennis, (eds.), *Cross-Cultural Studies of Behavior.* New York: Holt, Rinehart and Winston, 1970.

Barnlund, D., *Public and Private Self in Japan and the United States: Communicative Styles of Two Cultures.* Forest Grove, Oregon: International Scholarly Book Services, Inc., 1975.

Bergsma, L.C., *A Cross-Cultural Study of Conformity in Americans and Chinese*. San Francisco: R & E Research Associates, 1977.

Blubaugh, J.A. and D. Pennington, *Communicating Across Difference*. Columbus, Ohio: Charles E. Merrill Publishing, 1976.

Brislin, R.W., (ed.), *Topics in Cultural Learnings*, Vol. I-IV. Honolulu, Hawaii: East-West Center, 1973-1976.

Brislin, R.W., *Translation: Applications & Research*. New York: Gardner Press, 1976.

Brislin, R., W. Lonner, and R. Thorndike, *Cross-Cultural Research Methods*. New York: Wiley-Interscience 1973.

Buchanan, W., *How Nations See Each Other: A Study in Public Opinion*. Westport, Conn.: Greenwood Press, Inc., 1972.

Bureau of Naval Personnel, *Overseas Diplomacy: Guidelines for United States Navy: Trainer*. Washington, D.C.: U.S. Government Printing Office, 1973.

Burling, R., *Man's Many Voices: Language in its Cultural Context*. New York: Holt, Rinehart and Winston, Inc., 1970.

Burmeister, I. (ed.), *Meeting German Business: A Practical Guide for American and Other English Speaking Businessmen in Germany*. Hamburg: Atlantik-Brucke, 1973.

Canadian International Development Agency (CIDA), *Going Abroad with CIDA*. Unpublished handbooks. (LIPC #2261, #2261a, #2261, PB).

Carpenter, J. and G. Plaza, *Intercultural Imperative*. New York: Council for Intercultural Studies and Programs, 1973.

Carrillo-Beron, C., *Changing Adolescent Sex-Role Ideology Through Short Term Bicultural Group Process*. San Francisco: R & E Research Associates, 1977.

Carroll, J.B. (ed.), *Language, Thought and Reality*. San Francisco: International Society for General Semantics.

Casmir, F.L. (ed.), *International and Intercultural Communication Annual*. Vol. I-III. Published by the Speech Communication Association.

Cole, M., et. al., *The Cultural Context of Learning and Thinking: An Exploration in Experimental Psychology*. New York: Basic Books, 1971.

Cole, M. and S. Scribner, *Culture and Thought: A Psychological Introduction*. New York: John Wiley and Sons, 1974.

Coles, R., *Eskimos, Chicanos, Indians*. Boston: Little, Brown & Co., 1978.

Condon, J., *The Simple Pleasures of Japan*. Elmsford, New York: Japan Publications Trading Center, 1975.

Condon, J. and M. Saito, *Communicating Across Cultures for What?* Tokyo: The Simul Press, 1976.

Condon, J. and M. Saito, *Intercultural Encounters with Japan*, Communication, Contact and Conflict, Tokyo: The Simul Press, 1974.

Coplin, W.D., *Interdisciplinary Approaches to Cross-Cultural Social Science Education for Undergraduates.* Pittsburgh, Penn., International Studies Association, 1977.

Davis, S.M., *Comparative Management: Organizational and Cultural Perspectives.* Englewood Cliffs, N.J.: Prentice Hall, 1971.

DeBeauvoir, S., *The Ethics of Ambiguity.* Secaucus, N.J.: Citadel Press, 1975.

Defense Language Institute, *Intercultural Communication Training Manual.* Vol. 1 and 2. Monterey, Calif.: Defense Language Institute, 1973.

DeMenth, B., *P's and Cues for Travelers in Japan.* Elmsford, N.Y.: Japan Publications Trading Center, 1974.

Dodd, C.H., *Perspectives on Cross-Cultural Communication.* Dubuque, Iowa: Kendall-Hunt, 1977.

Downs, J.F., *Cultures in Crisis.* (2nd ed.). Beverly Hills, Calif.: Glencoe Press, 1975.

Eisenberg, A. and R.R. Smith, *Nonverbal Communication.* Indianapolis, Ind.: Bobbs-Merrill, 1971.

Farb, P., *Word Play.* New York: Alfred A. Knoph, Inc., 1973.

Feidler, F., *Cultural Assimilators—Programmed Text.* Seattle: University of Washington Press, 1971.

Feig, J.P., *Adjusting to the U.S.A.* Washington, D.C.: Meridian House International, 1977.

Feig, J.P. and J.G. Blair, *There is a Difference: Twelve Intercultural Perspectives.* Washington, D.C.: Meridian House International, 1975.

Financial Times-London, *Japan: A Businessman's Guide.* New York: American Heritage Press, 1970.

Foerstel, L.S., *Cultural Influence on Perception.* Washington, D.C.: American Association for the Advancement of Science, 1976.

Fritsch, A.J. and B.I. Castleman, *Lifestyle Index.* Washington, D.C.: Center for Science in the Public Interest, 1974.

Gavaki, E., *The Integration of Greeks in Canada.* San Francisco: R & E Research Associates, 1977.

Geertz, C., *The Interpretation of Cultures.* New York: Basic Books, 1973.

Greenberg, S., *Management: American and European Styles.* Belmont, Calif.: Wadsworth Publishing Company, Inc., 1970.

Hall, E.T., *The Silent Language.* Garden City, New York: Anchor-Doubleday, 1973.

Hansen, G.C., *The Chinese in California: A Brief Bibliographic History.* Portland, Oregon: Richard Abel & Company, Inc., 1970.

Harms, L.S., *Intercultural Communication.* New York: Harper and Row, 1973.

Harms, L.S., et. al., *Right to Communicate: Collected Papers.* Science and Linguistics Institute of the University of Hawaii. Honolulu: University Press of Hawaii, 1977.

Hays, R.D., C.M. Korth, and M. Roudiani, *International Business: An Introduction to the World of the Multinational Firm.* Englewood Cliffs, N.J.: Prentice-Hall, Inc., 1972.

Heenan, D.A. and H.V Perlmutter, *Multinational Organization Development.* Reading, Mass.: Addison-Wesley, 1979

Heinz-Dietrich, F. and J.C. Merrill (eds.), *International Communications.* New York: Hastings House, 1970.

Henle, P. (ed.), *Language, Thought and Culture.* San Francisco: International Society for General Semantics.

Hoopes, D.S. (ed.), *Readings in Intercultural Communication,* Vol. III. Pittsburgh: Regional Council for International Education, 1973.

Hoopes, D.S. and P. Ventura (eds.) *Intercultural Source Book: Cross-Cultural Training Methodologies.* Washington, D.C.: SIETAR, Georgetown University, 1979

Hurh, W.M., *Comparative Study of Korean Immigrants in the United States: A Typological Approach.* San Francisco: R & E Research Associates, 1977.

Issacs, H.R., *Images of Asia: American Views of China and India.* New York: Harper and Row, 1972.

Kelman, H.C. (ed.), *International Behavior: A Social-Psychological Analysis.* New York: Irvington Press, 1977.

Key, M.R., *Nonverbal Communication: A Research Guide & Bibliography.* Metuchen, N.J.: Scarecrow Press, 1977.

Kiev, A., *Transcultural Psychiatry.* New York: The Free Press, Macmillian Publishing Co., 1972.

Kirkland, F.R., LTC, U.S. Army (ret.), and P.L. McGrew, *A Cultural Assimilator: For Interaction with Persons of Different Cultural Backgrounds.* 8 Volumes. Philadelphia, Penn.: Center for Social Development.

Kitano, H.N.L., *Japanese Americans: The Evolution of a Subculture.* Englewood Cliffs, N.J.: Prentice-Hall, Inc., 1976.

Kolde, E.J., *The Multinational Company.* Lexington, Mass.: Lexington Books, 1974, see Chapter 11 pp. 155-174.

Kotter, J.P. *Organizational Dynamics: Diagnosis and Intervention.* Reading, Mass.: Addison-Wesley 1978.

Language Research Center, *So You Speak English Too.* Provo, Utah: Brigham Young University, 1975.

Lanier, Alison. *Living in the U.S.A.* New York: Charles Scribner's Sons, 1973.

Larson, D.H. and W.A. Smalley, *Becoming Bilingual: A Guide to Language Learning.* South Pasadena, Calif.: William Carey Library, 1974.

Leavitt, R.R., *Women Cross-Culturally: Change and Challenge.* Chicago, Ill.: Aldine Publishing Company, 1975.

Legra, W.P. (ed.), *Culture-Bound Syndrome, Ethnopsychiatry and Alternate Therapies.* Honolulu: University Press of Hawaii, 1977.

Levine, A.J., *Alienation in the Metropolis.* San Francisco: R & E Research Associates, 1977.

LeVine, R.A. and D.T. Campbell, *Ethnocentricism: Theories of Conflict, Ethnic Attitudes, and Group Behavior.* New York: John Wiley and Sons, 1972.

Levine, L.W. and R. Middlekauff, *The National Temper: Readings in American History.* (2nd ed.). New York: Harcourt, Brace, Jovanovich, 1972.

Lewald, H.E., *Latino-America: Sus Culturas y Sociedades.* New York: McGraw-Hill, Inc., 1973.

Liebman, S.B., *Exploring the Latin American Mind.* Chicago: Nelson-Hall, 1976.

Lindborg, K. and C.J. Ovando, *Five Mexican-American Women in Transition: A Case Study of Migrants in the Midwest.* San Francisco, R & E Research Associates, 1977.

Lines, K., *British and Canadian Immigration to the United States Since 1920.* San Francisco: R & E Research Associates, 1978.

Managing the Multinationals. Business International Staff. Santa Fe Springs, Calif.: Davlin Publications, Inc., 1972.

Mapp, E., *Puerto Rican Perspectives.* Metuchen, N.J.: Scarecros Press, Inc., 1974.

Marsh, H.L., *Re-Entry Transition Seminars: Report of the Wingspread Collequin.* Washington, D.C.: NAFSA, 1975.

Marshall, R.A., *Can Man Transcend His Culture? The Next Challenge in Education for Global Understanding.* Washington, D.C.: American Association of State Colleges and Universities, 1973.

Maslow, A.H., *The Farther Reaches of Human Nature.* New York: Viking Press, 1971.

McLuhan, M., *Culture is Our Business.* New York: McGraw Hill, 1970.

Mehrabian, A., *Silent Messages.* Belmont, Calif.: Wadsworth Publishing Company, 1971.

Miller, V.A., *The Guidebook for International Trainers in Business and Industry.* Madison, Wis.: American Society for Training and Development, 1979.

Minami, H., *Psychology of the Japanese People.* Ontario: University of Toronto Press, 1972.

Morawska, E.T., *The Maintenance of Ethnicity: Case Study of the Polish-American Community in Greater Boston.* San Francisco: R & E Research Associates, 1977.

Morris, C., *Signs, Language and Behavior.* San Francisco: International Society for General Semantics.

Multinational Executive Travel Companion. Guides to Multinational Business, No. 047.

Munroe, R. and R., *Cross-Cultural Human Development.* Monterey, Calif.: Brooks/Cole, 1975.

Myrdal, G., *Asian Drama: An Inquiry Into the Poverty of Nations.* New York: Pantheon, 1972.

Okimoto, D. *American in Disguise.* New York: John Weatherhill, 1971.

Olien, M.D., *Latin American: Contemporary Peoples and their Cultural Traditions.* New York: Holt, Rinehart & Winston, Inc., 1973.

Osgood, C.E., et al, *Cross-Cultural Universals of Affective Meaning.* Urbana, Ill.: University of Illinois Press, 1975.

Otero, G.G., *Teaching About Perception: The Arabs.* CTIR. Denver, Colorado: University of Denver, 1977.

Palmquist, B. and K. Darrow, (eds.), *Transcultural Study Guide.* Stanford, Calif.: Volunteers in Asia, Inc., 1975.

Paddock, W. and E., *We Don't Know How: An Independent Audit of What They Call Success in Foreign Assistance.* Ames, Iowa: Iowa State University Press, 1973.

Patai, R., *The Arab Mind.* New York: Charles Scribner's Sons, 1976.

Pearson, R.P., *Through Middle Eastern Eyes.* New York: Frederick A. Praeger Publisher, 1975.

Pedersen, P. and W. Lonner (eds.), *Counseling Across Cultures.* Honolulu, Hawaii: University Press of Hawaii, 1976.

Pederson, P. (ed.), *Readings in Intercultural Communication.* Vol. IV. Pittsburgh, Penn.: The Intercultural Communication Network, 1974.

Pineda, H. (author) and G.W. Renwick (ed.), *Americans in Chile: A Practical Approach to Cultural Interaction:* Intercultural Management Series, No. 3; Intercultural Network, Inc., Scottsdale, Arizona, 1978, p. 28.

Prasad, S.B. and Y.K. Shetly, *An Introduction to Multinational Management.* Englewood Cliffs, N.J.: Prentice-Hall, 1976.

Price-Williams, D.R., *Cross-Cultural Studies Readings: Explorations in Cross-Cultural Psychology.* San Francisco, Calif., Chandler & Sharp, 1975.

Prosser, M.H., *Intercommunication Among Nations and Peoples.* New York: Harper and Row, 1973.

Prosser, M.H., *USIA Intercultural Communication Course: 1977 Proceedings*. Washington, D.C.: Foreign Service Training Office, 1977.

Prosser, M.H., *The Cultural Dialogue*. Boston, Mass.: Houghton Mifflin Co., 1978.

Ramirez III, M. and A. Castaneda, *Cultural Democracy, Bicognitive Development and Education*. New York: Academic Press, 1974.

Rapoport, A., *Fights, Games and Debates*. Ann Arbor, Mich.: University of Michigan Press, 1974.

Renwick, George W., *Australian and American Cultures: Similarities, Differences, Difficulties;* Intercultural Management Series, No. 1; Intercultural Network, Inc., Scottsdale, Arizona, 1976, p. 26.

Renwick, G.W., *Malays and Americans: Definite Differences, Unique Opportunities;* Intercultural Management Series, No. 2; Intercultural Network, Inc., Scottsdale, Ariz., 1977, p. 61.

Reischauer, E., *The Japanese*. Cambridge, Mass.: Harvard University Press, 1977.

Rich, A.L., *Interracial Communication*. New York: Harper and Row, 1974.

Ricks, D., et al, *International Business Blunders*. Columbus, Ohio: Grid, Inc., 1974.

Rivera, J., *Latin America: A Sociocultural Interpretation,* (2nd ed.). New York: Irvington, dist. by Halsted Press, 1978.

Ross, S.R. (ed.), *Views Across the Border: The U.S. and Mexico*. University of New Mexico Press, 1978.

Ruben, B.D. and R.W. Budd, *Human Communication Handbook: Simulations and Games,* Vol. 1. Rochelle Park, N.J., Hayden Book Company, Inc., 1978.

Ruben, B.D. and R.W. Budd, *Interdisciplinary Approaches to Human Communication*. Rochelle Park, N.J., Hayden Book Company, Inc., 1978

Ruben, B.D., *Human Communication Handbook: Simulations and Games,* Vol. 2. Rochelle Park, N.J., Hayden Book Company, Inc., 1978.

Rubin, R.H., *Family Structure and Peer Group Affiliation as Related to Attitudes About Male-Female Relations Among Black Youth*. San Francisco: R & E Research Associates, 1977.

Rudhyar, D., *Culture, Crisis & Creativity*. Wheaton, Ill.: Theosophical Publishing House, 1977.

Scarbaugh, L.E., *Intercultural Communication*. Rochelle Park, N.J., Hayden Book Company, Inc., 1978.

Scheflen, A.E., *How Behavior Means*. Garden City, N.J.: Anchor Press, 1974.

Schwartz, F., F. Fluckiger, and I. Weisman, *A Cross Cultural Encounter: A Non-Traditional Approach to Social Work Education*. San Francisco: R & E Research Associates, 1977.

Schwarz, E.A. and R. Ezawa, *Japanese Illustrated*. Elmsford, N.Y.: Japanese Publications Trading Center, 1974.

Screening and Selection for Overseas Assignment: An Assessment and Recommendation to the U.S. Navy, 1974.

Sethi, S.P., *Advanced Cases in Multinational Business Operations*. Pacific Palisades, Calif.: Goodyear Publishing Company, 1972.

Sexton, V.S. and H. Misiak, *Psychology Around the World*. Monterey, Calif.: Brooks/Cole Publishing Company, 1976.

Sitaram, K.S., and R.T. Cogdell, *Foundations of Intercultural Communications*. Columbus, Ohio: Charles E. Merrill, 1976.

Smith, A.L., *Transracial Communication*. New Jersey: Prentice Hall, 1973.

Smith, Bruce L. and M. Chitra, (eds.), *International Communication and Political Opinion*. Westport, Conn.: Greenwood Press, Inc., 1972.

Smith, E.C. and L.F. Luce, *Toward Internationalism: Readings in Cross-Cultural Communications*. Rowley, Mass.: Newbury House, 1979.

Smith, H., *The Russians*. New York: Ballantine, 1976.

Smith, Karen H. (author) and George W. Renwick (ed.), *Americans and Malaysian Chinese: Common Work Habits and Contrasting Values;* Intercultural Management Series, No. 4; Intercultural Network, Inc., Scottsdale, Arizona, 1978.

Snyder, B., *Encuentros Culturales: Cross-Cultural Mini-Dramas*. Skokie, Ill.: National Textbook Co., 1975.

Spielberger, C.D. and R.D. Guerrero, (eds.). *Cross-Cultural Anxiety*. New York: Wiley and Sons, 1976.

Tacgujum, A., et al (eds.), *Roots: An Asian-American Experience*. A Project of the UCLA Asian American Studies Center. Los Angeles, Calif.: Continental Graphics, 1971.

Taylor, L., *Management Development and Training Handbook*. New York: McGraw-Hill, 1975.

Toffler, A., *Future Shock*. New York: Bantam, 1970.

Triandis, H.C., *The Analysis of Subjective Culture*. New York: Wiley-Interscience, 1972.

Tucker, M., H. Raik, D. Rossiter, and M. Uhes, *Improving Cross-cultural Training and Measurement of Cross-cultural Learning*. Center for Research and Education, Vol. 1, June 4, 1973.

Tucker, M., H. Raik, D. Rossiter, and M. Uhes, *Improving the Evaluation of Peace Corps Training Activities*. Center for Research and Education, Vol. III, June 4, 1973.

UNESCO: Handbook of International Exchanges. Paris, France: UNESCO. Various years.

United States Department of State. *Diplomatic Social Usage: A Guide for United States Representatives and their Families Abroad*. Washington,

D.C.: Department of State (Superintendent of Documents, U.S. Government Printing Office, Washington, D.C. 20402), 1971.

United States-Japan Trade Council. *Communication: The Key to U.S. Japan Understanding.* Washington, D.C., 1973.

Vantine, L.L., *Teaching American Indian History: An Interdisciplinary Approach.* Palo Alto: R & E Research Associates, 1978.

Wallace, A.F., *Culture and Personality,* (2nd ed.). New York: Random House, 1970.

Watson, O., *Proxemic Behavior: A Cross-Cultural Study.* The Hague: Mouton, 1970.

Watts, A.W., *The Book: On the Taboo Against Knowing Who You Are.* New York: Vintage, 1972.

Weeks, W.H., P.B. Pedersen, and R.W. Brislin, *A Manual of Structured Experiences for Cross-Cultural Learning.* Pittsburgh, Penn.: Society for Intercultural Education, Training and Research, 1977.

Weitz, S., *Nonverbal Communication Readings with Commentary,* (2nd ed.). New York: Oxford University Press, 1978.

Wells, E.E., *The Mythical Negative Black Self Concept.* Palo Alto: R & E Research Associates, 1978.

White, L. and B. Delingham, *Concepts of Culture.* Minn.: Burgess, 1973.

Wiggins, J.S., *Personality and Prediction: Principles of Personality Assessment.* Reading, Mass.: Addison-Wesley Publishing Co., 1973.

Wolforth, S., *The Portuguese in America.* San Francisco: R & E Research Associates, 1978.

Wong, J.L., *Aspirations and Frustrations of the Chinese Youth in the San Francisco Bay Area: Aspersions Upon the Societal Scheme.* San Francisco: R & E Research Associates, 1977.

Yousef, F.S., *Cross-Cultural Social Communicative Behavior: Egyptians in the U.S.* University Microfilm. Ann Arbor, Mich.: University of Michigan, 1972.

Note: The authors regret that they have been unable to cite in this appendix every relevant organization and publication related to the fields of comparative management, cross-cultural communications, and international training. They have included those valuable resources of which they were aware for the decade of the 1970's. They welcome readers' feedback on new entries for the next decade and subsequent editions. They recommend the IFTDO *International Resource Directory* published periodically through the American Society for Training and Development, P.O. Box 5307, Madison, Wisconsin 53705

Index